Towards the end of the 1980s it looked as if television had displaced cinema as the photographic medium for bringing Shakespeare to the modern audience. In recent years there has been a renaissance of Shakespearian cinema, including Kenneth Branagh's *Henry V* and *Much Ado About Nothing*, Franco Zeffirelli's *Hamlet*, Peter Greenaway's *Prospero's Books* and Christine Edzard's *As You Like It*.

In this volume a range of writers study the best known and most entertaining film, television and video versions of Shakespeare's plays. Particular attention is given to the work of Olivier, Zeffirelli and Kurosawa, and to the BBC Television series.

In addition the volume includes a survey of previous scholarship and criticism and an invaluable filmography.

SHAKESPEARE AND
THE MOVING IMAGE

SHAKESPEARE AND THE MOVING IMAGE

THE PLAYS ON FILM AND TELEVISION

Edited by

ANTHONY DAVIES

Director of Drama, Brentwood School, Essex

and

STANLEY WELLS

Director of the Shakespeare Institute, University of Birmingham

CAMBRIDGE
UNIVERSITY PRESS

PUBLISHED BY THE PRESS SYNDICATE OF THE UNIVERSITY OF CAMBRIDGE
The Pitt Building, Trumpington Street, Cambridge, United Kingdom

CAMBRIDGE UNIVERSITY PRESS
The Edinburgh Building, Cambridge CB2 2RU, UK
40 West 20th Street, New York, NY 10011-4211, USA
477 Williamstown Road, Port Melbourne, VIC 3207, Australia
Ruiz de Alarcón 13, 28014 Madrid, Spain
Dock House, The Waterfront, Cape Town 8001, South Africa

http://www.cambridge.org

First published 1994
Reprinted 1995, 1997, 1999, 2002

Printed in the United Kingdom at the University Press, Cambridge

A catalogue record for this book is available from the British Library

Library of Congress Cataloguing in Publication data
Shakespeare and the moving image / edited by Anthony Davies and
Stanley Wells
p.   cm.
Filmography
Includes bibliographical references and index.
ISBN 0 521 43424 6 (hardback) – ISBN 0 521 43573 0 (paperback)
1. Shakespeare, William, 1564–1616 – Film and video adaptations.
2. English drama – Film and video adaptations.   3. Television
adaptations.   4. Film adaptations. I. Davies, Anthony, 1936–
II. Wells, Stanley W., 1930–
PR3093.S53   1994   791.43′75–dc20   93-42524 CIP

ISBN 0 521 43424 6 hardback
ISBN 0 521 43573 0 paperback

CONTENTS

ILLUSTRATIONS

Numbers 1–13 were provided by the BFI Stills, Posters and Designs

CONTRIBUTORS

SAMUEL CROWL, *Ohio University*
ANTHONY DAVIES, *Brentwood School, Essex*
ROBERT HAPGOOD, *University of New Hampshire*
GRAHAM HOLDERNESS, *University of Hertfordshire*
PETER HOLLAND, *Trinity Hall, Cambridge*
RUSSELL JACKSON, *The Shakespeare Institute, University of Birmingham*
MICHAEL MANHEIM, *University of Toledo, Ohio*
CHRISTOPHER McCULLOUGH, *University of Exeter*
E. PEARLMAN, *University of Colorado*
ACE G. PILKINGTON, *Dixie College, Utah*
KENNETH S. ROTHWELL, *University of Vermont*
NEIL TAYLOR, *Roehampton Institute*
STANLEY WELLS, *The Shakespeare Institute, University of Birmingham*
MICHÈLE WILLEMS, *Faculté des Lettres et Sciences Humaines, University of Rouen*

PREFACE

In 1987, when *Shakespeare Survey 39: Shakespeare on Film and Television* appeared, it looked as if television had displaced cinema as the photographic medium for bringing Shakespeare to the modern audience. The trend seemed logical. Raising money for a television production presents far fewer difficulties than finding financial backing for a film: television could be assumed to reach sectors of the public who were neither cinema nor theatre devotees, but who were nevertheless – it was further assumed – eager to receive performed Shakespeare plays on the small screen in their living rooms. And there was another development which made the argument especially plausible. Cinema had arrived at an artistic self-consciousness. In responding to the rival attractions of domestic television, cinema strove to cultivate or to target more limited audiences, and Shakespearian film was no exception. A comparison of the cinematic and interpretative priorities in the Reinhardt/Dieterle *A Midsummer Night's Dream* (1935) with those in Derek Jarman's *The Tempest* (1980) will readily illustrate this point.

If these perceived trends and obvious economic arguments were not enough, the BBC Shakespeare series and the memorable *King Lear* made by Granada Television in 1984 with Laurence Olivier as Lear seemed to give a stamp of creative acknowledgement to television.

Not everyone, however, saw this as the new Shakespearian dawn. Some saw the attempt to reach a domestic audience as 'a more urgent contemporary challenge . . . more in line with the social habits and economic thrust of the 1980's'.[1] Jack Jorgens, reviewing the first six BBC productions in *Shakespeare Quarterly* in 1979, was distinctly disillusioned, complaining that

as a culture, we have apparently decided to invest in the convenience and cheapness of TV . . . [and] to settle for mindless zooming and dollying, sloppy editing and compositions, crude music and sound effects.[2]

More recently, the cinema has taken us by surprise. We have seen Kenneth Branagh's *Henry V* (1989) and *Much Ado About Nothing* (1993), Franco Zeffirelli's *Hamlet* (1990), Peter Greenaway's *Prospero's Books* (1991) and Christine Edzard's *As You Like It* (1992), as well as a newly restored version of Orson Welles's *Othello* (1952, 1992). If indeed we are witnessing a renaissance of Shakespearian cinema, then the tilt of emphasis in this volume towards film is justified. Among the essays reprinted from *Shakespeare Survey 39* are two dealing exclusively with televised Shakespeare, and several television versions of the plays are discussed in other essays. But it is difficult not to draw the conclusion, from the available evidence, that the rhetorical and dramatic range within a Shakespeare play can be accommodated with more versatility on the big screen with sharply defined images.

As well as including essays reprinted from *Survey 39*, appropriately updated and revised, we have commissioned important new contributions, and our aim here has been to cover particular areas of the field of screened Shakespeare – individual plays of which several cinema or TV films are currently available, like *Othello* and *Hamlet*, or play categories like the histories, the comedies and the Roman plays, or the work of individual directors like Kurosawa and Zeffirelli – rather than solicit essays exclusively devoted to single films. At the same time, we have encouraged our contributors to select films for more detailed discussion rather than to aim at a fully comprehensive approach. A few films such as Zeffirelli's *Hamlet* are discussed in more than one essay, and we hope the overlaps may be justified by the differing angles of approach.

We are sensitive to the danger of Shakespeare's becoming increasingly confined to academic study rather than being made accessible to wider general response and we have, therefore, striven to provide a range of views and reactions which will be stimulating to both the student of Shakespeare and the general reader whose interests embrace the interplay of theatre, film and television.

Notes

1 Anthony Davies, *Filming Shakespeare's Plays* (Cambridge, 1988), p. 187.
2 Jack J. Jorgens, 'The BBC-TV Shakespeare', *Shakespeare Quarterly*, 30 (1979) 411–15, p. 415.

SHAKESPEARE ON FILM AND TELEVISION: A RETROSPECT

ANTHONY DAVIES

I

When in 1916 Hugo Münsterberg claimed that the photoplay overcomes 'the forms of the outer world . . . by adjusting events to the forms of the inner world', he perceived the major shift from the theatre stage to the cinema screen as being psychological rather than technological.[1] Any survey of available criticism in the field of Shakespeare and film tends not only to confirm that perception but to suggest that it persists not merely as an aesthetic issue but as an issue affecting the collective critical mind. While theatre remains the legitimate expressive medium for authentic Shakespeare, kept alive by a scattering of theatrical companies playing to audiences for whom theatre is both accessible and familiar, only comparatively recently has it become respectable to concentrate serious discussion on the media of cinema, radio and more especially television. These media have become the most practical means of making Shakespeare's plays in performance a world heritage rather than a national one passed on through educational systems.

The widely scattered and often tentative nature of critical writing on Shakespearian film is the result of three distinctly psychological legacies. Firstly, the motives behind the production of all films were seen to be brashly commercial, so that Richard Watts could write in his response to the Reinhardt-Dieterle film of *A Midsummer Night's Dream* (1936) that 'almost every film company makes what it calls "prestige" pictures [which are] planned by magnates . . . as proofs that they are artists as well as businessmen'.[2] Secondly, the historical moment of cinema's meeting with theatre was especially traumatic. As Nicholas Vardac makes clear, just when the spectacular extravagance of the late nineteenth-century theatre was breaking down, the cinema arrived as a new and effective rival, forcing theatre back upon itself in order to compete commercially in the production of massive visual effects.[3]

Cinema was seen, therefore, as the betrayer of a movement that would otherwise have redirected theatre towards its original essentials. Finally, cinema was quickly perceived as posing a threat to traditional aesthetic distinctions. Not only did it dissolve the demarcations between the actor and the inanimate spatial detail within the cinema frame, but it also manipulated the relationship of the perceiver with the fictional world of the film.[4] Furthermore, as Suzanne Langer suggests, cinema's omnivorous capacity 'to assimilate the most diverse materials and turn them into elements of its own' appeared to threaten with extinction what had formerly seemed clearly separate artistic disciplines.[5]

II

The middle 1930s were significant years both for Shakespearian film and for the development of critical writing in the field. Not only were three films (Reinhardt's *A Midsummer Night's Dream*, Cukor's *Romeo and Juliet*, and Paul Czinner's *As You Like It*) released, but Allardyce Nicoll's perceptive book, *Film and Theatre*, was published. Early in the book, Nicoll argues that the social and economic forces governing the production of films in the 1930s were not so very different from those which promoted the theatrical fare of Shakespeare's day. 'The theatrical managers', he maintains, 'exploited freely whatever came uppermost at the moment, heaping ghosts upon the stage when the going of ghosts was good and mad ladies in white linen when ghosts began to pall.'[6] Nicoll asserts himself as no enemy to the cinema. Recognizing that literacy had changed the ear's alertness to the complexities of the spoken word since Shakespeare's plays were first produced, he suggests that the expressive potential of cinema 'may merely be supplying something that will bring us nearer to the conditions of the original spectators for whom Shakespeare wrote'. Nicoll further rightly discerns one difficulty in adapting theatrical material for film when he distinguishes the cinematic – as opposed to the theatrical – development of character. While the theatre stage can accommodate and effectively present characters who bear 'the lineaments of universal humanity', the realism of the cinema tends to deal with characters as individuals without exceptional stature.[7]

In 1936, there also emerged a vigorous debate between Harley Granville-Barker and Alfred Hitchcock. Granville-Barker is prompted, in his reactions to the films of Reinhardt and Cukor, to draw attention to the visual images in Shakespeare's dialogue and to castigate Reinhardt and Cukor for unnecessary pictorial indulgence. He reaches the conclusion that cinema and theatre 'are in their nature and their methods . . . radically and fatally opposed'. He does,

2

however, see cinema's potential as a narrative art and suggests that cinema should exploit Shakespeare stories 'to suit its pictorial purpose, without respect to him. . . . Shakespeare in the cinema will do – with Shakespeare left out'.[8] Alfred Hitchcock's vehement reply is at once an attack on what he sees as a purist and pedantic attitude to Shakespeare as well as an assertion of cinema's right to afford Shakespeare's dramatic action realistic locations.[9]

The exchange between Granville-Barker and Hitchcock is chiefly interesting in its revelation that up until the Second World War the most lively debate about Shakespearian film centred upon issues that were in essence extensions of that conflict which had erupted within the realm of theatre some fifty years before.

III

The critical response to Shakespearian film began to take on a more impressive stature as cinematic technology improved and the adaptive endeavour could become more versatile. The year 1944 was a major turning point in both the creation and the public acceptance of Shakespearian film. Laurence Olivier's *Henry V* was released in that year, and for the first time critics and reviewers were faced with a cinematic adaptation which operates on too many levels to be patronizingly dismissed or glibly celebrated. James Agee's ebullient eulogy, while it does not attempt to be analytical, shows an awareness of cinematic complexity when he considers the film 'essentially less visual than musical', and he recurrently refers to the powerful impact throughout the film of Shakespeare's language.[10]

Olivier's *Hamlet*, released in 1948, has attracted a greater volume of critical literature than any other Shakespearian film. Bosley Crowther not only wrote a carefully considered review for the *New York Times*, but promoted critical dialogue by inviting comment and discussion in the paper's columns, from readers.[11] Simultaneous with the release of the film, a book, *'Hamlet', the Film and the Play*, was published. Together with the screenplay dialogue, a foreword by Olivier, and an essay on editing the text by Alan Dent, there is an illuminating essay by Roger Furse, which discusses the relation between the film's set design and its dramatic action. The priorities of the film designer are made unambiguously clear when Furse asserts that 'the essence of the film is that it is *not* still. It is in motion, and . . . the designer's business is to do everything he can to assist the mobility and flow; not to freeze it into a series of orderly compositions.'[12] Not only does this essay suggest some of the spatial intentions within this particular film, but it opens the way to intelligent criticism of other Shakespearian films.

Orson Welles's *Macbeth*, also released in 1948, attracted a different strand of critical response. Whereas Olivier's films had been considered by most reviewers as extensions of theatre, Welles's first Shakespearian film rightly attracted interest as cinema rather than as Shakespeare. The French critics quickly pursued a specifically cinematic line. André Bazin wrote that 'those strange settings trickling with water, shrouded in mists which obscure a sky in which the existence of stars is inconceivable, literally form a prehistoric universe . . . a prehistory of the conscience'.[13] And Claude Beylie describes the décor as 'veritably "telluric", almost sublunar, a décor that is essentially the pathetic reflection of the conscious, or rather the unconscious, of the hero'.[14]

The essay by Furse and the critical reviews by Bazin and Beylie point to spatial strategy as being more important than authenticity of location, and cinematically more crucial than the actor's performance.

IV

With the release of Welles's *Othello* in 1952 there emerged the first complete volume devoted to the making of a Shakespearian film by a single author. The diary account written by Micheál MacLiammóir, who played Iago, covers the shooting of the film from January 1949 until March 1950. Despite the occasionally indulgent subjectivity of the account and its eschewing of technical details, it is an intelligent and essential contribution to the body of writing in this field. The entries are written from the point of view of a stage actor feeling his way before the film director and the camera. 'One's first job', writes MacLiammóir, 'is to forget every single lesson one ever learned on the stage: all projection of the personality, build-up of a speech, and sustaining for more than a few seconds of an emotion are not only unnecessary but superfluous.'[15]

In 1968 appeared the first volume to essay a survey of Shakespearian film. Robert Hamilton Ball's *Shakespeare on Silent Film* is at once a meticulously documented and scholarly history of the development of silent cinematic adaptations as well as an amusing and stimulating account with a lively sense of personal interest. It covers the period from 1899 (the year in which the first recorded Shakespearian film, Herbert Beerbohm Tree's *King John* scene, was made) to 1929 when the first synchronized-sound adaptation, Sam Taylor's notorious *The Taming of the Shrew*, was released. Tree, the first established stage actor to be filmed in a Shakespearian role, is quoted as finding film acting something of an adventure. 'One throws oneself into the thing as one goes into a submarine. You take a dive – a plunge as it were – into the unknown, and calmly await the result.' Also quoted at some length is the report of a Chicago police lieutenant on the Vitagraph film of *Macbeth* (1908). It is perhaps unfortunate that the report was offered in the interests of censorship because it might otherwise stand unabashed as the first piece of intelligent criticism in the field of Shakespearian film. In selecting for special mention the film's visualizing of Duncan's murder, in which 'you see the dagger enter and come out and see the blood flow and the wound that's left', the censor was reacting as many reputable critics have since reacted to Polanski's film of 1969. Ball's historical survey is interesting, not least for its suggestion that cinema's search for respectability was a major impulse towards the endeavour to adapt Shakespeare's plays for the screen.[16]

In 1971 the first survey of sound-film adaptations, Roger Manvell's *Shakespeare and the Film*, was published. It is a most useful volume, which gives interesting background information on some twenty-five films made between 1929 and 1970, when Brook's film of *King Lear* was released. The text is accompanied by well-produced stills, and includes extensive verbatim interviews with Akira Kurosawa on his Japanese adaptation of *Macbeth*, *Throne of Blood* (1957), and with Laurence Olivier who, unlike MacLiammóir, believes 'there is much less difference between film acting and stage acting than people think – much less'.[97]

The complex cinematic achievement of Olivier's *Henry V* was first given just treatment in the slim, compact volume written by Harry Geduld and published in 1973. Among other issues, the analysis of the film contained in the book examines the major spatial transitions, the deliberate mixture of cinematic styles, the relation of the film to its source, its generic affinities, and the nature of Olivier's specific directorial intrusion.[18] This short but penetrating volume stands apart from others devoted to individual films in being an objective analysis by a writer not involved in the making of the film.

In 1977 two very different volumes on Shakespearian film were published, Jack Jorgens's *Shakespeare on Film* and the English translation of Grigori Kozintsev's *King Lear: The Space of Tragedy*. Jorgens attempts, with more academic and analytical emphasis, to do what Manvell had first done in 1971, though he limits his field to seventeen Shakespearian films, each considered in more detail than in Manvell's survey. In his introductory chapter, Jorgens notes a distinction in filming Shakespearian material which John Russell Taylor had emphasized in 1960 when he maintained that it is 'the film-maker's job' either 'to record Shakespeare' or 'to put the requirements for the film medium first'.[19] Jorgens advances the distinction into three essential cinematic modes: the 'theatrical mode', which 'uses film as a transparent medium' to encapsulate theatrical space and performance, the 'realistic mode', which 'shifts the emphasis from the actors to actors-in-a-setting', and the 'filmic mode', which 'is the mode of the film poet whose works bear the same relationship to the surfaces of reality that poems do to ordinary conversation'.[20] Where Manvell's text concentrates on background information on the selected films, Jorgens illuminates, with considerable success, the capturing of each play's essence on film. A surprising omission is any extended discussion of Yutkevich's *Othello* (1955).

The volume of diary entries on the making of his *King Lear* (1970) by Grigori Kozintsev is perhaps the most engaging of all written works in the field of Shakespearian film, revealing, as it so clearly does, the creative mind of its author, his love and reverence for Shakespeare the dramatist, and the intelligence with which he strove to transpose *King Lear* to the medium of cinema. The book's material remains in its rough-hewn diary-note form, and of the twenty-four chapters five have titles which give interesting if cryptic indications of the creative processes of the author's mind. The theatrical influence on Kozintsev comes through very strongly, and his grasp of the theories of Meyerhold and Gordon Craig clearly enables him to relate the dramatic language of the theatre stage to that of the cinema screen. Kozintsev's perception of the devising of a spatial strategy as the essence of cinematic adaptation emerges clearly in his notes on the making of his own *Hamlet* (1964), when he writes that 'the time strata must seem to be laid bare in the visual development of Elsinore . . . like the rings on a huge cross section of a tree' and suggests that the medieval, Renaissance and modern layers in the play, associated respectively with old King Hamlet, the prince and Claudius, should be visually articulated.[21]

As its title suggests, the central chapters in the *King Lear* diary are those which deal with the cinematic dramatization of the Lear universe. 'In choosing the location for a film', writes Kozintsev, 'you have to consider every possibility. You go on fantastic journeys . . . We have begun by fighting the theatrical, trying to find means of showing reality on the screen – not copies of historical ornaments but the everyday life of history – we had cleared the décor, leaving only genuine material . . . This was not a case of overcoming the conventionalities of the studio, but of uncovering nature's hidden significance.'[22]

More esoteric, partly because of its somewhat singular approach and partly because of its extended comparisons with particular paintings (reproductions of which are not given with the text), is Dale Silviria's book, *Laurence Olivier and the Art of Film Making*.[23] Though this volume tends to analyse moments in Olivier's Shakespeare films in theatrical terms, it eschews any sustained discussion of the relationship of film to theatre. It is divided into four lengthy chapters, the last three (dealing with the Shakespeare films) being the most rewarding, with close observation of moments like Gertrude's drinking of the poisoned wine, and detailed comparisons, like that of the Agincourt battle in *Henry V*, with other memorable battles on film.

Perhaps the major disappointment of the book is its attempt to give to Olivier's Shakespeare films a hermeticism incompatible with the forces which have made the films endure as classic adaptations. Neither its style nor its underlying assumptions make it a particularly accessible volume for the reader whose interest in Shakespeare is essentially either theatrical or literary. The attempt to pay tribute to Olivier purely as a film director and to view the films as autonomous works of art is not entirely successful, but it does place the volume in a category different from its forerunners.

V

The growth of interest in Shakespearian film evidenced in the emergence of whole volumes devoted to the subject was matched by an increasing versatility in the critical material which began to appear in a widening variety of journals between the late 1950s and the early 1980s.

In 1965, John Blumenthal argued that Kurosawa's *Throne of Blood* (1957) 'is the only work, to my knowledge, that has ever completely succeeded in transforming a play of Shakespeare's into a film', and also drew attention to Kurosawa's use of the forest as a visual expression of the Macbeth mind.[24] Eight years later, John Gerlach, in a deliberate response to Blumenthal, maintained that in disrupting Shakespeare's balance between action and reflection, and in trapping Washizu (Kurosawa's Macbeth figure) within an ordained prophetic framework, Kurosawa 'betrayed the power of the play'.[25] The question of a film's fidelity to the play was taken up again in 1978 when Gorman Beauchamp revealed in convincing detail the extent to which Olivier's *Henry V* is a distortion of the play's view of war. While the play's only direct reflection of the battle is the inglorious encounter between Pistol and M. le Fer, Olivier depicts the battle as 'bloodless, beautiful and in technicolour'.[26]

For the most part, penetrating critical essays on Shakespearian film remain widely scattered. In 1972 Charles Eckert edited a volume which includes judiciously selected essays on important Shakespearian films made between 1935 and 1966.[27] A much more general volume on cinema published in 1974 includes a section on Shakespearian film, and reprints material by Peter Brook, who maintains that so far cinema has not found a language 'so as to reflect the mobility of thought that blank verse demands',[28] and by Frank Kermode who, in a reference to Brook's *King Lear* (1970), sees cinema as a medium ensuring that the greatness of the Shakespeare plays can only be retained if their dramatic potential is 'reborn in the imagination of another'.[29]

// to Translation

7

Two questions remain to be answered. Has the gradual accumulation of writing on Shakespearian film thrown up any clear statement about the difficulties of moving Shakespeare from the stage to the cinema screen? And can methods of enquiry employed in the relatively new specialism of film studies be brought fruitfully to bear upon cinematic adaptations of the plays?

J. L. Styan has written of the theatre audience's special situation, which allows it to make 'simultaneous perceptions' which are 'the basis for interpretation by an audience . . . To relate and synthesise what is perceived from moment to moment is to make drama meaningful.' The camera's selection, he continues, is really the director's controlling of our perception and our thinking. The loss of simultaneity is the loss of 'the very basis of tension felt in the audience'. Styan's essay, illustrated with judicious reference to the 'play' scene in *Hamlet*, is the most lucid identification of an essentially theatrical experience which is inevitably lost in the cinema.[30] Paul Acker's 1980 article on Brook's *King Lear* (1970) is the clearest evidence that much can be learned about a director's treatment of a play on the screen simply by examining the use of rudimentary cinematic conventions. Acker maintains that in stretching conventions of dialogue and framing beyond their customary application, Brook deliberately creates a tension which enforces upon the cinema audience a new and disturbing encounter with Shakespeare's tragedy.[31] But it is perhaps well to remember that Brook's *King Lear* is unique among Shakespearian films in the expressions of disenchantment as well as the profound admiration it has elicited.

VI

Unlike cinema, television adaptations had to await those technological developments which made it possible not only to capture performance but also to broadcast it to a domestic audience.

In December 1932, Filson Young suggested that the BBC prepare to broadcast the entire cycle of Shakespeare plays as an attempt to provide 'the highest kind of entertainment combined with high educative and cultural value'.[32] The project was not undertaken on radio, but the now famous BBC television cycle which commenced in 1978 and was completed in 1985 has constituted a dramatic achievement of the greatest significance. While it has been generally agreed that the individual productions in the series vary in their effectiveness, the project has promoted the most intelligent critical debate about the accessibility of classical drama in our time and about the problems inherent in transposing Shakespeare from the theatre to the domestic television screen. The natural dynamic development of such a debate has been given added impetus by two other impulses. One is the policy of *The Times Literary Supplement* in approaching academics for reviews of the television productions. The other is the growth of interest, manifested in numerous academic journals, in the study of plays in performance.

Until the mid-1980s the predominant thrust in critical writing about televised Shakespeare was directed at performance, and television's achievement was measured by the extent to which it managed or failed to promote the sense of a *theatrical* experience. It has been during the last six years that there has emerged sustained, probing, and vigorous discussion about such issues as the nature of the television audience, the nature of the television idiom, and the relation of artistic to realistic presentation in that medium.

Film Quarterly gives prominence to 1953 as an important year for televised Shakespeare in the United States and, in drawing conclusions in his review of four television adaptations broadcast during that year, Marvin Rosenberg focuses necessary, though brief, attention to two aesthetic problems which beset the respective directors. He recognizes first the compulsively selective nature of television, suggesting that 'in the close relationship TV establishes, a brilliant clarity can often be given to the music of the verse as well as to its meaning', but complaining that where a character's action requires wide visual context, such as Lear's entrance with the dead Cordelia, the small screen can have the effect of making a moment 'ludicrous'. Secondly he discerns the danger of 'background clutter' as 'poison to complex drama'.[33] He also discusses the vexed problem of trying to contain a play's dramatic substance within a slotted playing time ordained by a television network, though he does not rail against the necessary dramatic truncation in such despondent tones as Flora Rheta Schreiber does.[34] Nor does he protest with such vehemence as Frank Wadsworth, who concludes his review of Peter Brook's 'Omnibus' *King Lear* (1953) with an assertion that the director's 'cuts and revision of material' resulted in a production that 'was not only an abridgement of Shakespeare's great tragedy, but a perversion as well'.[35]

John Russell Taylor gives a useful chronological outline of the major adaptations screened by the BBC from 1938, the year of 'the first full-scale Shakespeare production on television . . . the BBC's modern-dress *Julius Caesar*', until 1963, and he highlights two composite projects which treated groups of plays as 'coherent sequences, with a continuity of theme'. The first, *An Age of Kings* (1960), combined the English history plays; the second was a unified arrangement of 'the classical history plays . . . under the title, *The Spread of the Eagle*' (1963). Concluding that *An Age of Kings* 'probably offers the fairest ground to date for judging television's potential in adapting Shakespeare', he maintains that 'even if the effect of Shakespeare on the television screen is, even

9

at its very best, considerably less than in a passable stage performance, television production still has a number of advantages', these being the increased audience size 'and the durability' of a taped production as a record.[36]

VII

Despite fleeting judgements on television's particular strengths and weaknesses as a medium for Shakespeare in scattered critical response in the 1950s and 1960s, the overall tendency was to write about adaptations as second-division theatre, and to consider the likely viewers as people who, in all probability, would go to see Shakespeare in a theatre if they could. It is only in the early 1980s that there begins to surface a wholly new approach in the critical discussion of television as a potential medium for Shakespeare, not the least significant aspect of which is the fact that the discussion engaged the minds and pens of academics and directors whose opinions had not been prominent in this field before. Apart from the series of volumes published concurrently with the broadcasts by the BBC, which contain introductions by John Wilders and production comments by individual directors, there was published in 1981 an absorbing interview with Jonathan Miller.[37] With characteristic precision and insight, Jonathan Miller gave the long awaited answer to those who in the early days of cinema had clashed over the issue of authentic locations. Of the setting for *Antony and Cleopatra* he says, 'What details you do introduce must remind the audience of the sixteenth-century imagination, not of the archaeologically accurate Egypt and Rome to which the play nominally, and only nominally refers.' And, in considering the question of television's realistic idiom, he concedes that 'as soon as you put Shakespeare on that box where . . . people are accustomed to seeing naturalistic events presented, you are more or less obliged to present the thing as naturally as you can'. The limits to realism have to be established, however, because the language of Shakespeare's dialogue 'comes from the past' and 'it doesn't come from the naturalistic past. It comes from the artistic past, with a style and an idiom of its own which can't be violated.'[38]

Also in 1981 appeared Sheldon Zitner's article, which deals with 'some consequent differences between the situations of the theatre and the television audiences'. In the shift from that 'ceremony, generating expectations, attitudes, behaviour' which Zitner calls 'the stage play ritual', to the relatively casual group before the television set which 'transforms all drama to closet drama, to plays for ones, if not for one', significant factors modify the relationship of the audience to the dramatic presentation. The inevitable 'de–ritualization' which television effects upon the viewing situation must in significant ways alter the nature of a Shakespeare play, though it will not necessarily reduce 'the depth of feeling one can expect from televised versions'. The alteration is rather one produced by the absence 'of the flywheel effect of live audience reaction'.[39] This point is stressed, too, by Stanley Wells in his comprehensive and carefully considered discussion of the BBC Shakespeare project.[40] When Wells originally delivered his lecture, in April 1982, the series was little more than half complete, but one of the conclusions which emerges (and which is endorsed in Wells's later comments in 1985),[41] is that 'a general problem . . . is the difficulty of achieving a really comic effect on television with Shakespeare's comic episodes . . . Concerted comic scenes seem far less likely to work well, and I suspect that this is because one important participant is invariably missing: the reacting audience.'[42]

VIII

Perhaps the most penetrating questions which Wells raises concern the 'degree of permanence' which the productions can be expected to enjoy as a consequence of each being a part of 'a grand, perhaps grandiose scheme . . . Has there ever, in the whole history of television (such as it is), been a production of Shakespeare which has borne repetition more than a few years after it was made?' It is a question which must be asked, particularly in view of the enthusiasm with which the sale of the videotapes has been envisaged for educational purposes, and it can probably only be answered as Wells suggests. In time, the productions will, like cinematic adaptations, retain a value 'as period pieces, of interest as documents' of television history, 'or as records of performances' by particular actors or perhaps of productions by particular directors.[43]

Both Wells and John Wilders (the literary consultant on the BBC series) discuss important areas of understandable conflict, such as text cutting and dramatic location. Both agree that despite the series' attempt to provide authoritative Shakespeare, some cutting, in the interests both of the medium and of its particular audience, is justified, Wilders maintaining that some dialogue could, to a modern domestic audience, be so mystifying that it might prompt 'the very people in whom we hoped to arouse enthusiasm for Shakespeare . . . to switch off'. Of the various styles and locations used for setting the action of the plays, Wilders regards the attempt 'to make the productions look like paintings . . . as the most satisfactory answer the directors have yet found',[44] though such a tendency, as Wells clearly perceives, carries with it the danger of inhibiting action and freezing camera movement.[45]

The question as to whether some plays are more suited to the medium than others is perhaps not so insistent in the light of a major project which sets out to televise the whole canon. However, H. R. Coursen in a review of the BBC-TV *Measure for Measure* writes that 'it seems almost to have been written for television. Not only is it melodramatic and episodic, but, as episodic narratives often are, it is a series of vivid one-on-one confrontations. Such scenes work very well within the limited space of (a) studio, and (b) a picture tube.'[46]

Jack Jorgens concluded his review of the first six plays of the BBC series with a sombre verdict:

As a culture we have apparently decided to invest in the convenience and cheapness of TV as compared to the relative expense of the theatrical film. In place of the clarity, subtle colours, and carefully controlled light values of the motion picture, we have decided to accept nervous, ill-defined images, comic-book colours, and blurred night scenes. In place of the fine image- and sound-making and meaningful technique of good films, we have decided to settle for mindless zooming and dollying, sloppy editing and compositions, crude music and sound effects.[47]

He is to some extent right. Cinema is beyond doubt a more versatile medium, affording a wider range of creative resources than television in the adaptation of drama which operates on so many and such complex levels as Shakespeare. And Wells, too, is largely right when he concludes, of the BBC series, that 'few of these productions would grip a reluctant viewer by the throat, nor do they comprehensively tackle – let alone solve – the problems of adapting Shakespeare to the television medium'.[48] But no one can regret the attempt to bring Shakespeare to vastly increased audiences, and no one can discount the value of the critical debate which televised Shakespeare has promoted.

IX

From the dominant thrust of critical discussion of screened Shakespeare, so enlivened in the mid-1980s by the completion of the BBC/Time-Life project, there emerged in the late 1980s and early 1990s a number of separate stems, each flourishing with its own vigour. Two trends become clear. One is the emergence of a number of volumes which pursue particular lines of enquiry into the filming of Shakespeare's plays. The other is the shift of emphasis from cinematic to televisual adaptations of the plays. However, eleven years were to elapse after the publication of Jack Jorgens's *Shakespeare on Film* in 1977, before another single-author volume which dealt with Shakespearian film as a genre was published. In these years, critical discussion continued to thrive in journals. *Shakespeare Survey* devoted its volume 39 to a coverage of Shakespeare on film and television[49] and the *Shakespeare on Film Newsletter* deserves special mention for its combination of a broad coverage of the fields of both cinema and television Shakespeare together with its delivery of clearly committed and pithy reviews. Edited by Kenneth Rothwell and Bernice Kliman, its publication as a quarterly newsletter devoted exclusively to film and television Shakespeare became especially appreciated in the 1980s with the rapid growth in the availability of video-cassettes and the rise of interest in performance studies.[50]

In 1988 Anthony Davies's volume, *Filming Shakespeare's Plays*, appeared.[51] It broke with the pattern set by its predecessors, the volumes by Manvell and Jorgens, in not being a survey, but in attempting a study of the aesthetic issues which arise in the transposition of Shakespeare's plays from theatrical to cinematic drama. The author suggests that in view of the reduced impact of dialogue in cinematic drama, it is necessary to devise for Shakespearian film an effective visual compensation. Since the dominant element in transposition is that of space, the book goes on to explore spatial strategies in the Shakespeare films directed by Olivier and by Welles, and to consider the very distinct strategies in Brook's *King Lear* and Kurosawa's *Throne of Blood*. The volume concludes with a comparison of the nature of the actor's work in the theatre and in film.

A volume which approaches Shakespearian cinema along similarly aesthetic lines is Lorne Buchman's distinguished *Still in Movement: Shakespeare on Screen*, published in 1991. Its line of study 'is, for the most part, concerned not so much with individual films, or with comparisons of different cinematic treatments . . . as much as with central issues that illuminate how the plays are operating as products of cinematic technique'.[52] Like Davies, Buchman restricts his coverage to selected films made primarily for the cinema screen, dealing especially with those directed by Welles, Olivier, Kozintsev and Polanski.

Two other volumes directed essentially towards Shakespearian cinema are Peter Donaldson's *Shakespearean Film: Shakespearean Directors*, and Samuel Crowl's *Shakespeare Observed*. Donaldson's volume examines a selection of films in order to connect their thematic predilections with the particular casts of mind of their respective directors. The psycho-analytic approaches in this study distinguish it as controversial. Not every reader will find an intellectual affinity with a view of Olivier's *Hamlet* as 'the artistic reprise of a childhood sexual trauma suffered by the director'.[53] Crowl's volume incorporates essays on Polanski's *Macbeth*, Welles's *Chimes At Midnight* and *Othello*, and Branagh's *Henry V*. The stated aim of the volume is to 'attempt to articulate ways of recovering those pleasures we have shared in several modern film and stage productions of Shakespeare'.[54]

The growing interest in televised Shakespeare during the late 1970s and the 1980s nudged the study of screened Shakespeare away from cinema as an exclusive domain, and one result was the publication of volumes which incorporated studies of adaptations for both media. The first such volume was Bernice Kliman's 'Hamlet': Film, Television and Audio Performance, published in 1988. Its appeal is both to 'people who not only go to every stage performance they can find' and who will 'stay up until 4.00 a.m. to see even a cut version of Olivier's Hamlet', and to 'Shakespeareans who feel standoffish toward moving images'.[55] It contains penetrating discussion of the Olivier and Kozintsev Hamlet films and covers television productions from 1953 to 1984, including the Maximilian Schell Hamlet (1960) and the BBC production with Derek Jacobi.

While Kliman's volume covers various adaptations of one play and devotes separate chapters to film and television productions, Ace Pilkington's Screening Shakespeare from Richard II to Henry V published in 1991 would seem to suggest that we are dealing with a single aesthetic in its covering both BBC television adaptations of Richard II, Henry IV Parts 1 and 2 and Henry V as well as Olivier's Henry V and Welles's Chimes At Midnight. Pilkington's essential thrust is towards opening the receptiveness of the new audience to screened Shakespeare, and he concludes that 'the worst danger to the future of filmed Shakespeare is not insufficient funds but inefficient imaginations'.[56]

A volume with a vigorously different approach to the field, and which incorporates both television and cinema adaptations, is John Collick's Shakespeare, Cinema and Society, published in 1989. As a volume, it breaks new ground in concerning itself with how the treatment of Shakespeare's drama has been determined by social, economic, political and cultural interests. Collick condemns the traditional critical approach to Shakespearian film in England for being intolerant of 'intervention in the way the text is reproduced', and he sees the internationally financed BBC television series as evidence of the 'attempts within Anglo-American culture to create a world-wide cultural hegemony based on the orthodoxy of the New Criticism'.[57]

The first of three volumes which devote their coverage exclusively to televised Shakespeare is Michèle Willems's Shakespeare à la Télévision, published in 1987.[58] It contains engaging and illuminating interviews with, among others, Shaun Sutton, Jane Howell and Patrick Stewart. There are also analytical essays by six different authors, covering particular BBC adaptations. The essential impulse behind the compilation of the volume was the BBC Shakespeare series. Shakespeare on Television is a collection of thirty essays compiled by J. C. Bulman and H. R. Coursen covering politico-cultural issues as well as analyses of individual productions. It announces clearly in its introduction that the authors have chosen not to deal with video versions of cinema since 'they remain films, more visual, less verbal, less intimate than television productions, products of . . . a "hotter medium" than television'.[59]

Susan Willis's *The BBC Shakespeare Plays: Making the Televised Canon* published in 1991 is most engaging in its exploration of the particular potential of the medium under the directorship of Jonathan Miller, Elijah Moshinsky and Jane Howell. The volume is a history of process rather than an attempt to assess the educational or aesthetic value of the BBC project.[60]

In conclusion, high praise must be given to the volume compiled and edited by Kenneth Rothwell and Annabelle Henkin Melzer. Their work in *Shakespeare on Screen*, published in 1990, makes it the most comprehensive, thorough and authoritative listing of film and television adaptations extant.[61] It lists both cinema and television adaptations under sections devoted to each play title. The information on each production is meticulously detailed, and presented with 'reader-friendly' accessibility. It must clearly rank as one of the most significant scholarly achievements in the field.

Despite the many new directions which critical writing has taken in the last seven years, we have not come appreciably nearer to an understanding of just how palatable and engaging a Shakespeare play might be to the small domestic audience sitting around a television screen. The extent to which film and television have the potential to re-establish Shakespeare as a popular dramatist and the degree to which cultural authorities will continue to attempt the imposition of a traditional Shakespeare orthodoxy is the subject of an absorbing essay published by Graham Holderness in 1985[62] and it is more extensively explored (as we have seen) in John Collick's 1989 study.[63] But these questions together with more general discussion of screened Shakespeare would seem to have become lodged in volumes and institutions of higher learning. In his foreword to *New Prefaces to Shakespeare*, John Wilders makes clear that the essays 'were designed primarily to be read by television viewers, an audience as varied as the one for which Shakespeare wrote, and far more numerous'.[64] It seems fair to conclude, however, that while the videos have become a part of Shakespeare teaching programmes in school classrooms, the most obvious consequence of the BBC TV Shakespeare series has been the publication of much writing by academics for academics.

Notes

1 Hugo Münsterberg, 'The Means of the Photoplay', in *Film Theory and Criticism* (1st edn), edited by Gerald Mast and Marshal Cohen, pp. 239–48; p. 240.
2 Richard Watts, 'Films of a Moonstruck World', in *Focus on Shakespearean Film*, edited by Charles W. Eckert (Englewood Cliffs, NJ, 1972), pp. 47–52; p. 48.
3 Nicholas Vardac, *Stage to Screen* (New York, 1968), p. xxvi.
4 Béla Balázs, *Theory of Film: Character and Growth of a New Art* (London, 1953), p. 412.
5 Suzanne Langer, *Feeling and Form: A Theory of Art* (London, 1953), p. 412.
6 Allardyce Nicoll, *Film and Theatre* (London, 1936), p. 20.

7 Allardyce Nicoll, 'Film Reality: The Cinema and the Theatre', in *Focus on Film and Theatre*, edited by James Hurt (Englewood Cliffs, 1974), pp. 29–50; p. 48.

8 Harley Granville-Barker, 'Alas Poor Will!', *The Listener* (3 March 1936), 387–9, 425–6; p. 425.

9 Alfred Hitchcock, 'Much Ado About Nothing? I', *The Listener* (10 March 1936), 448–50; p. 448.

10 James Agee, '*Henry V*', in *Film Theory and Criticism*, pp. 333–6; p. 334.

11 Bosley Crowther, *New York Times* (3 and 7 October 1948), Section 2, p. x.

12 Roger Furse, 'Designing the Film *Hamlet*', in *'Hamlet', the Film and the Play* (London, 1948), unpaged.

13 André Bazin, *Orson Welles: A Critical Review* (London, 1978), p. 101.

14 Claude Beylie, '*Macbeth* or the Magical Depths', in *Focus on Shakespearean Film*, edited by Charles W. Eckert (Englewood Cliffs, NJ, 1972), pp. 72–5; p. 72.

15 Micheál MacLiammóir, *Put Money in Thy Purse: The Filming of Orson Welles's 'Othello'* (London, 1952), pp. 96–100.

16 Robert Hamilton Ball, *Shakespeare on Silent Film* (London, 1968), pp. 42 and 82.

17 Roger Manvell, *Shakespeare and the Film* (London, 1971), pp. 37–8.

18 Harry Geduld, *Film Guide to 'Henry V'* (Bloomington, 1973).

19 John Russell Taylor, 'Shakespeare in Film, Radio and Television', in *Shakespeare: A Celebration*, edited by T. J. B. Spencer (Harmondsworth, 1964), pp. 97–113; p. 104.

20 Jack J. Jorgens, *Shakespeare on Film* (Bloomington, 1977), p. 10.

21 Grigori Kozintsev, *Shakespeare, Time and Conscience* (London, 1967), p. 265.

22 Grigori Kozintsev, *King Lear: The Space of Tragedy* (London, 1977), p. 132.

23 Dale Silviria, *Laurence Olivier and the Art of Film Making* (Rutherford, 1985).

24 John Blumenthal, '*Macbeth* into *Throne of Blood*', in *Film Theory and Criticism*, pp. 340–51; p. 340.

25 John Gerlach, 'Shakespeare, Kurosawa and *Macbeth*: A Response to J. Blumenthal', *Literature/Film Quarterly*, 1 (1973), 352–9; p. 352.

26 Gorman Beauchamp, 'Henry V: Myth, Movie, Play', *College Literature*, 5 (1978), 228–38; p. 232.

27 Charles W. Eckert, ed., *Focus on Shakespearean Film* (Englewood Cliffs, NJ, 1972).

28 Geoffrey Reeves, 'Finding Shakespeare on Film: From an Interview with Peter Brook', in *Film Theory and Criticism*, pp. 316–21; p. 321.

29 Frank Kermode, 'Shakespeare in the Movies', in *Film Theory and Criticism*, pp. 322–32; p. 332.

30 J. L. Styan, 'Sight and Space: The Perception of Shakespeare on Stage and Screen', in *Shakespeare, Pattern of Excelling Nature*, edited by D. Bevington and J. L. Halio (Newark, 1978), pp. 198–209; pp. 205–6.

31 Paul Acker, 'Conventions for Dialogue in Peter Brook's *King Lear*', *Literature/Film Quarterly*, 8 (1980), 219–24.

32 John Drakakis, 'The Essence That's Not Seen', in *Radio Drama*, edited by Peter Lewis (London, 1981), pp. 111–33, p. 116.

33 Marvin Rosenberg, 'Shakespeare on TV: An Optimistic Survey', *Film Quarterly*, 9 (1953), 116–74; esp. pp. 166, 169 and 172.

34 Flora Rheta Schreiber, 'Television's *Hamlet*', *Film Quarterly*, 8 (1953), 150–6; p. 156.

35 Frank W. Wadsworth, ' "Sound and Fury" – *King Lear* on Television', *Film Quarterly*, 8

(1953), 254–68; p. 267. 'Omnibus', the title of the television series by CBS has, it seems, no connection with the commercial framing of this programme. See Kenneth Rothwell's 'Representing *King Lear* on the Screen' in this volume.

36 Russell Taylor, 'Shakespeare in Film, Radio and Television', pp. 101–3.

37 Tim Hallinan, 'Interview: Jonathan Miller on the Shakespeare Plays', *Shakespeare Quarterly*, 32 (1981), 134–45.

38 Hallinan, 'Interview', pp. 136 and 134.

39 Sheldon P. Zitner, 'Wooden O's in Plastic Boxes: Shakespeare and Television', *University of Toronto Quarterly*, 51, no. 1 (1981), 1–12; pp. 1–3.

40 Stanley Wells, 'Television Shakespeare', *Shakespeare Quarterly*, 33 (1982), 261–77.

41 Stanley Wells, 'The Canon in the Can', *Times Literary Supplement* (10 May 1985), p. 522.

42 Wells, 'Television Shakespeare', p. 272.

43 Wells, 'Television Shakespeare', p. 264.

44 John Wilders, 'Shakespeare on the Small Screen', *Deutsche Shakespeare-Gesellschaft West Jahrbuch* (1982), 56–62; pp. 57 and 59.

45 Wells, 'Television Shakespeare', p. 268.

46 H. R. Coursen, 'Why *Measure for Measure?*', *Literature/Film Quarterly*, 12 (1984), 65–9; p. 67.

47 Jack J. Jorgens, 'The BBC–TV Shakespeare', *Shakespeare Quarterly*, 30 (1979), 411–15; p. 415.

48 Wells, 'The Canon in the Can', p. 522.

49 *Shakespeare Survey 39*, edited by Stanley Wells (Cambridge, 1987).

50 *Shakespeare on Film Newsletter*, edited by Kenneth Rothwell and Bernice Kliman. In 1992, this quarterly newsletter merged with *The Shakespeare Bulletin*.

51 Anthony Davies, *Filming Shakespeare's Plays* (Cambridge, 1988).

52 Lorne M. Buchman, *Still in Movement: Shakespeare on Screen* (New York, 1991), p. 5.

53 Peter Donaldson, *Shakespearean Film: Shakespearean Directors* (Boston, 1990), p. xiii.

54 Samuel Crowl, *Shakespeare Observed* (Athens, Ohio, 1992), p. 18.

55 Bernice Kliman, *'Hamlet': Film, Television and Audio Performance* (Cranbury, 1988), p. 13.

56 Ace G. Pilkington, *Screening Shakespeare from 'Richard II' to 'Henry V'* (Cranbury, 1991), p. 163.

57 John Collick, *Shakespeare, Cinema and Society* (Manchester, 1989), pp. 188–9, 194–5.

58 Michèle Willems, *Shakespeare à la télévision* (Rouen, 1987).

59 J. C. Bulman and H. R. Coursen, eds., *Shakespeare on Television* (Hanover and London, 1988), p. x.

60 Susan Willis, *The BBC Shakespeare Plays: Making the Televised Canon* (Chapel Hill, 1991).

61 Kenneth S. Rothwell and Annabelle Henkin Melzer, eds., *Shakespeare on Screen* (London, 1990).

62 Graham Holderness, 'Radical Potentiality and Institutional Closure: Shakespeare in Film and Television', in *Political Shakespeare*, edited by Jonathan Dollimore and Alan Sinfield (Manchester, 1985), pp. 182–201.

63 Collick, *Shakespeare, Cinema and Society*.

64 John Wilders, *New Prefaces to Shakespeare* (Oxford, 1988), p. v.

SHAKESPEARE ON THE SCREEN: A SELECTIVE FILMOGRAPHY

compiled by GRAHAM HOLDERNESS *and*
CHRISTOPHER McCULLOUGH

This filmography is a reference list of 'complete', straightforward versions of Shakespeare's plays in film, television and videotape form.[1] It specifically *excludes* free adaptations;[2] film and television programmes containing insets of recorded performance;[3] educational films based on pedagogic manipulations of Shakespeare's texts;[4] material recording rehearsals, workshops, conversations with actors and directors;[5] and all operatic and balletic adaptations. There is much material in all these categories of great potential interest to researchers; this modest compilation should be regarded as the provision of basic information rather than the establishing of a comprehensive reference source.

We have listed international film, and English-language television versions, providing in each case title, date, format and medium;[6] production company (where known); producer (where applicable); director; designer (where known); and a selective cast list. Where the film is currently available for purchase or rental we have supplied the name and address of the distributor, and indicated its whereabouts if stored in an archive. It should be emphasized that specific enquiries to any distributor or archive should be undertaken to establish availability or accessibility of any individual item.

We wish to thank the following people and institutions for assistance in gathering information: the British Film Institute, the National Film Archive, the British Universities Film and Video Council, the BBC Data Enquiry Service, Thames Television, Granada Television; Russell Jackson, Kenneth Richards, Kenneth Rothwell, Carol Evans. We gratefully acknowledge the receipt of a research grant from University College, Swansea.

Abbreviations used

ARC	archive		NFA	National Film Archive
AVP	Audio-Visual Productions		NT	National Theatre
BD	Blue Dolphin		NYT	National Youth Theatre
BFI	British Film Institute		p.c.	production company
b/w	black and white		PD	Peter Darville Associates
CEMIW	Columbia-EMI-Warner		pro.	producer
col.	colour		RFL	Rank Film Library
Cont.	Contemporary Films		RSC	Royal Shakespeare Company
des.	designer		sil.	silent
DHS	distribution, hire or sale		SMT	Shakespeare Memorial
dir.	director			Theatre
FL	foreign language		SUM	Sony-U-Matic
FSL	Folger Shakespeare Library		TTV	Thames Television
GTV	Granada Television		v.c.	videocassette
HF	Harris Films		v.t.	videotape

Index of distributors and Archives

Audio-Visual Productions
Hocker Hill House
Chepstow, Gwent

Blue Dolphin
15–17 Old Compton Street
London W1

Columbia-EMI-Warner *see* Harris Films

Contemporary Films *see* Harris Films

Peter Darville Associates
280 Chartbridge Lane
Chesham, Bucks

Folger Shakespeare Library
Washington DC 20003, USA

Granada Television Ltd
Manchester 3

Harris Films Ltd
Glenbuck House
Glenbuck Road
Surbiton, Surrey

National Film Archive
81 Dean Street
London W1

Rank Film Library *see* Harris Films

Shakespeare Centre
Henley Street
Stratford-upon-Avon, Warwickshire

Thames Television Ltd
306 Euston Road
London NW1

Notes

1 'Complete' may in itself be misleading if it is taken to mean an *uncut* version of the received texts. Many screenplays are cut drastically – Olivier's *Henry V* by approximately one-half. Early silent versions were usually 'condensed'. We interpret 'complete' as a full though possibly abridged version of the play's action.

2 Except where, as in the case of Kurosawa's *Throne of Blood*, the film has been placed at the centre of critical debate on the screening of Shakespeare.

3 E.g. a programme made for the Open University's Arts Foundation course contains filmed extracts from Peter Brook's production of *A Midsummer Night's Dream*: 'Interpret-

ing a Dream' presented by Arnold Kettle, produced by Paul Kafno, BBC/Open University (1978).

4 Many such programmes are made by the Open University. Those still extant are listed by the British Universities Film and Video Council.

5 E.g. series of televised workshops such as John Barton's *Playing Shakespeare* (1984) and Michael Bogdanov's *Shakespeare Lives!* (1983).

6 Modern conditions of production are rendering the distinction between 'film' and 'television programme' ambiguous: as their respective techniques become more akin, independent film and national television companies enter into closer relationship and films made for television (e.g. by Channel 4) are initially released in cinemas. We have attempted to preserve a distinction between a film made specifically for theatrical distribution and one made for television transmission.

ALL'S WELL THAT ENDS WELL

All's Well that Ends Well
(GB, 1968): TV, b/w
p.c.: RSC/BBC
pro.: Ronald Travers
dir: Claude Watham (BBC), John Barton (RSC)
des.: Timothy O'Brien
Bertram, Ian Richardson; Helena, Lynn Farleigh; Countess, Catherine Lacey; King of France, Sebastian Shaw
ARC: BBC, v.t.

All's Well that Ends Well
(USA, 1978): TV, col.
p.c.: New York Shakespeare Festival
pro: Joseph Papp
dir: Wilford Leach
Bertram, Marc Linn; Helena, Pamela Reed; Countess, Elizabeth Wilson; Parolles, Larry Pines; Diana, Frances Conroy; Widow, Barbara Williams; Lavache, John Ferraro
DHS: New York Shakespeare Festival

All's Well that Ends Well
(GB/USA, 1981): TV, col.
p.c.: BBC/Time-Life TV
pro.: Jonathan Miller
dir.: Elijah Moshinsky
des.: David Myerscough-Jones
Countess, Celia Johnson; Bertram, Ian Charleson; Helena, Angela Down; King of France, Donald Sinden
DHS: BBC, 16mm, v.c.
ARC: BBC, v.t.

ANTONY AND CLEOPATRA

Antony and Cleopatra
(USA, 1908): Film, b/w, sil.
pro./dir.: J. Stuart Blackton
Maurice Costello, Florence Lawrence, Paul Panzer, William V. Ranous, Earle Williams

Antony and Cleopatra
(USA, 1908): Film, b/w, sil.
p.c.: Vitagraph
dir.: Charles Kent
Cleopatra, Betty Kent; Antony, Charles Chapman

Antony and Cleopatra
(France, 1910): Film, b/w, sil.
p.c.: Pathe
pro./dir.: Henry Andreani
Cleopatra, Madeleine Roche; Le Messager, Stacia de Napierkowska

Antony and Cleopatra
(GB, 1951): Film, b/w
p.c.: Parthian Productions
Cleopatra, Pauline Letts; Antony, Robert Speaight

The Spread of the Eagle: Part 7, 'The Serpent', Part 8, 'The Alliance', Part 9 'The Monument'
(GB, 1963): TV, b/w
p.c.: BBC
pro./dir.: Peter Dews
des.: Clifford Hatts
Antony, Keith Michell; Cleopatra, Mary Morris; George Selway, David William
ARC: BBC, 35mm

Antony and Cleopatra
(Switzerland/Spain/GB, 1972): Film/col.
p.c.: Transac (Zurich)/Izaro (Madrid)/Folio
Films (London)
pro.: Peter Snell
dir.: Charlton Heston
des.: Maurice Pelling
Antony, Charlton Heston; Cleopatra, Hildegard Neil; Enobarbus, Eric Porter; Octavius, John Castle
DHS: VU, v.c.
ARC: FSL (USA), 35mm

Antony and Cleopatra
(GB, 1972): v.t./col.
p.c.: RSC/Audio-Visual Productions
pro.: Jon Scofield (AVP)
dir.: Trevor Nunn, Buzz Goodbody, Euan
Smith (RSC)
des.: Christopher Morley, *et al.*
Antony, Richard Johnson; Cleopatra, Janet
Suzman; Enobarbus, Patrick Stewart; Octavius, Corin Redgrave
DHS: AVP, v.c.

Antony and Cleopatra
(USA, 1981): TV, col.
p.c.: Berkeley Shakespeare Festival
DHS: Berkeley Shakespeare Festival, v.c.

Antony and Cleopatra
(GB/USA, 1981): TV/col.
p.c.: BBC/Time-Life TV
pro./dir.: Jonathan Miller
des.: Colin Lowrey
Antony, Colin Blakely; Cleopatra, Jane
Lapotaire; Octavius, Ian Charleson; Enobarbus, Emrys James
DHS: BBC, 16mm, v.c.

AS YOU LIKE IT

As You Like It
(USA, 1908): Film, b/w, sil.
p.c.: Kalem Co. (George Klein, Samuel
Long and Frank Marion)
pro./dir.: Kenean Buel

As You Like It
(USA, 1912): Film, b/w, sil.
pro.: J. Stuart Blackton
dir.: James Young

Orlando, Maurice Costello; Rosalind, Rose
Coghlan; Celia, Rosemary Theby

As You Like It
(USA, 1912): Film, b/w, sil.
p.c.: Vitagraph
pro./dir.: Charles Kent
Rosalind, Rose Coghlan; Orlando, Maurice
Costello

As You Like It
(GB, 1936): Film, b/w
p.c.: Inter-Allied
pro./dir.: Paul Czinner
des.: Lazare Meerson
Duke, Henry Ainley; Orlando, Laurence
Olivier; Jaques, Leon Quartermaine; Rosalind, Elisabeth Bergner; Celia, Sophie
Stewart
ARC: FSL (USA), 35mm; NFA, 16mm

As You Like It
(GB, 1946): TV, b/w
p.c.: BBC
pro.: Robert Atkins
dir.: Ian Atkins
Bankside Players

As You Like It
(GB, 1953): TV, b/w
p.c.: BBC
pro.: Campbell Logan
dir.: Peter Ebert
des.: Stephen Bundy
Duke, Walter Hudd; Rosalind, Margaret
Leighton; Orlando, Laurence Harvey;
Celia, Isabel Dean

As You Like It
(GB, 1963): TV, b/w
p.c.: RSC/BBC
pro.: Richard Eyre (BBC)
dir.: Michael Elliott (RSC)
des.: Richard Negri (RSC), Andrée Welstead (BBC)
Rosalind, Vanessa Redgrave; Orlando,
David Buck; Duke, Patrick Allen; Patrick
Wymark
ARC: BBC, 35mm

As You Like It
(GB/USA, 1978): TV, col.
p.c.: BBC/Time-Life TV

pro.: Cedric Messina
dir.: Basil Coleman
des.: Don Taylor
Duke, Tony Church; Orlando, Brian Stirner; Rosalind, Helen Mirren; Celia, Angharad Rees
DHS: BBC, 16mm, v.c.

THE COMEDY OF ERRORS

The Comedy of Errors
(GB, 1954): TV, b/w
p.c.: BBC
pro./dir.: Lionel Harris
des.: James Bould
Solinus, Gerald Cross; Antipholus of Ephesus, David Peel; Antipholus of Syracuse, Paul Hansard; Adriana, Joan Plowright; Luciana, Jane Wenham

The Comedy of Errors
(GB, 1964): TV, b/w
p.c.: BBC
pro.: Peter Luke
dir.: Clifford Williams (RSC), Peter Duguid (BBC) Antipholus of Ephesus, Ian Richardson; Antipholus of Syracuse, Alec McCowen; Solinus, Donald Sinden; Aegeon, John Welsh; Adriana, Susan Engel; Luciana, Tina Packer
ARC: BBC, 35mm

The Comedy of Errors
(FDR, 1964): Film, b/w, FL
p.c.: Bavaria Atelier GmbH
pro.: Alexander May
dir.: Hans Dieter Schwarze
des.: Walter Blokesch
Erik Schumann, Clauss Biederstaedt, Ruth Kahler, Irene Marhold, Klaus Schwarzkopf, Manfred Lichtenfeld
DHS: Bavaria Atelier GmbH

The Comedy of Errors
(GB, 1976): v.t., col.
p.c.: RSC/Audio-Visual Productions
pro.: Philip Casson (AVP)
dir.: Trevor Nunn (RSC)
des.: John Napier
Adriana, Judi Dench; Luciana, Francesca Annis; Solinus, Brian Coburn; Antipholus

of Syracuse, Roger Rees; Antipholus of Ephesus, Mike Gwilym
DHS: AVP, v.c.

The Comedy of Errors
(GB/USA, 1984): TV, col.
p.c.: BBC/Time-Life TV
pro.: Shaun Sutton
dir.: James Cellan Jones
des.: Don Homfray
Aegeon, Cyril Cusack; Solinus, Charles Gray; Antipholus, Michael Kitchen; Dromio, Roger Daltrey; Adriana, Suzanne Bertish; Luciana, Joanne Pearce
DHS: BBC, 16mm, v.c.

The Comedy of Errors
(USA, 1986): Video, col.
p.c.: Company Commedia Ltd
dir.: Robert Shampain
DHS: Company Commedia Ltd

The Comedy of Errors
(USA, 1987): Video, col.
p.c.: PBS at Lincoln Center, New York
pro.: Bernard Gersten
dir.: Gregory Mosher, Robert Woodruff
des.: David Gropman
Antipholus of Syracuse, Paul Magid; Antipholus of Ephesus, Howard Jay Patterson; Dromio of Syracuse, Sam Williams; Dromio of Ephesus, Randy Nelson; Luciana, Gina Leishman; Adriana, Sophie Haydn; Luce and Duke, Karla Burns; Egeon, Daniel Mankin
DHS: Lincoln Center (Vivian Beaumont Theater)/PBS, v.c.

CORIOLANUS

Coriolanus
(USA, 1951): Video, b/w
pro.: Worthington Miner
dir.: Paul Nickell
Coriolanus, Richard Greene; Volumnia, Judith Evelyn; Richard Purdie, Frederic Worlock, Sally Chamberlin, Tom Peston
DHS: Facets Multimedia Inc., Chicago

The Spread of the Eagle: Part 1, 'The Hero', Part 2, 'The Voices', Part 3, 'The Outcast'

(GB, 1963): TV, b/w
p.c.: BBC
pro./dir.: Peter Dews
des.: Clifford Hatts
Coriolanus, Robert Hardy; Volumnia, Beatrix Lehmann; Menenius, Roland Culver
ARC: BBC, 35mm

Coriolanus
(GB, 1965): TV, b/w
p.c.: NYT/BBC
pro.: Bernard Hepton
dir.: Roger Jenkins
des.: Christopher Lawrence
Coriolanus, John Nightingale; Volumnia, Mary Grimes; Cominius, Timothy Block; Menenius, David Stockton

Coriolanus
(USA, 1979): Video, col.
p.c.: New York Shakespeare Festival
pro.: Joseph Papp
dir.: Wilford Leach
des.: Patricia McCourtney
Coriolanus, Morgan Freeman; Volumnia, Gloria Footer; Agrippa, Maurice Woods; Cominius, Earle Hyman
DHS: New York Shakespeare Festival

Coriolanus
(GB/USA, 1984): TV, col.
p.c.: BBC/Time-Life TV
pro.: Shaun Sutton
dir.: Elijah Moshinsky
des.: Dick Coles
Coriolanus, Alan Howard; Volumnia, Irene Worth; Menenius, Joss Ackland
DHS: BBC, v.c.

CYMBELINE

Cymbeline
(USA, 1913): Film, b/w, sil.
p.c.: Thanhouser
pro./dir.: Frederic Sullivan
Imogen, Florence La Badie; Leonatus, James Cruze; William Russell, William Garwood, Jean Darnell

Cymbeline
(Germany, 1925): Film, b/w, sil.
dir.: Ludwig Berger

Cymbeline
(USA, 1981): Video, col.
p.c.: Berkeley Shakespeare Festival
dir.: Patrick Tucker
des.: Warren Travis
Arviragus, Michael Sicilia; Belarius, Steve Henry; Cloten/Posthumus, Julian Lopez-Morillas; Cymbeline, Gail Chugg; Guiderius, David Parr; Iachimo, Robert Sicular; Imogen, Rebecca Engle; Philario, Phillip Henriques; Pisanio, Luiz Orozep
DHS: Berkeley Shakespeare Festival, v.c.

Cymbeline
(GB/USA, 1984): TV, col.
p.c.: BBC/Time-Life TV
pro.: Shaun Sutton
dir.: Elijah Moshinsky
des.: Barbara Gosnold
Cymbeline, Richard Johnson; Queen, Claire Bloom; Imogen, Helen Mirren; Posthumus, Michael Pennington; Iachimo, Robert Lindsay
DHS: BBC, 16mm, v.c.

HAMLET

Hamlet
(France, 1900): Film, b/w, sil.
pro./dir.: Clement Maurice
Hamlet, Sarah Bernhardt; Laertes, Pierre Magnier

Amleto
(Italy, 1908): Film, b/w, sil.
p.c.: Cines
pro.: Guiseppe de Liguoro

Amleto
(Italy, 1908): Film, b/w, sil.
p.c.: Milano
dir.: Luca Comerio
ARC: NFA, 35mm (incomplete; German titles)

Hamlet
(France, 1909): Film, b/w, sil.
p.c.: Lux
Hamlet, Mounet-Sully

Amleto
(Italy, 1910): Film, b/w, sil.
p.c.: Cines

pro./dir.: Mario Caserini
Hamlet, Dante Capelli; Maria Gasperini

Hamlet
(Denmark, 1910): Film, b/w, sil.
p.c.: Nordisk
pro./dir.: August Blom
Hamlet, Alwin Neusz; Ophelia, Emilie San-
nom; Claudius, Aage Hertel; Gertrude, Ella
La Cour

Hamlet
(GB, 1910): Film, b/w, sil.
pro./dir.: William G. Barker
Hamlet, Charles Raymond

Hamlet
(France, 1910): Film, b/w, sil.
p.c.: Eclipse Film
pro./dir.: Henri Desfontaines
Hamlet, Jaques Gretillat; Gertrude, Colanna
Romano

Hamlet
(GB, 1913): Film, b/w, sil.
p.c.: Hepworth Mfg. Co. (for British
Gaumont)
pro./dir.: E. Hay Plumb
Hamlet, Sir Johnston Forbes-Robertson;
Ophelia, Gertrude Elliott; Claudius, Ade-
line Bourne; Horatio, S. A. Cookson
ARC: NFA, 35mm

Hamlet
(Italy, 1914): Film, b/w, sil.
pro./dir.: Arturo Ambrosio
Hamlet, A. Hamilton Revelle

Hamlet
(Italy, 1917): Film, b/w, sil.
p.c.: Cines
pro./dir.: Eleuterio Rodolfi
Hamlet, Ruggoro Ruggeri; Ophelia,
Helena Makowska; Claudius, Martelli; Gertrude, Mercedes Brignone

Hamlet
(Germany, 1920): Film, b/w, sil.
p.c.: Art Film
dir.: Sven Gade
Hamlet, Asta Nielsen; Ophelia, Lilly
Jacobsson; Claudius, Eduard von Winter-
stem; Gertrude, Mathilde Brandt
ARC: NFA, 35mm

Khoon Ka Khoon
(India, 1935): Film, b/w, FL
p.c.: Minerva Movietone
pro./dir.: Sohrab Modi
Hamlet, Sohrab Modi

Hamlet
(GB, 1947): TV, b/w
pro.: George More O'Ferrall
dir.: Basil Adams
des.: Peter Bax
Hamlet, John Byron; Ophelia, Muriel Pav-
low; Claudius, Sebastian Shaw; Gertrude,
Margaret Rawlings; Horatio, Patrick
Troughton

Hamlet
(GB, 1948): Film, b/w
p.c.: Two Cities Film/Olivier/Rank
pro./dir.: Laurence Olivier
Hamlet, Laurence Olivier; Claudius, Basil
Sydney; Gertrude, Eileen Herlie; Ophelia,
Jean Simmons; Horatio, Norman Wooland
DHS: RFL, 16mm, v.c.
ARC: NFA, 35mm

Hamlet
(India, 1954): Film, b/w, FL
p.c.: Hindustan Chitra
pro./dir.: Kishore Sahu
Kishore Sahu; Mala Sinha; Venus Banerji

Moi, Hamlet
(Italy, 1952): Film, FL
pro./dir.: Giorgio C. Simonelli
Erminio Macario, Rossana Podesta, Franca
Marzi, Luigi Parese, Adriano Rimoldi,
Elena Giusti

Hamlet
(GB/USA, 1959): TV, b/w
p.c.: Old Vic/CBS
pro.: Ralph Nelson/Paul Orr
dir.: Ralph Nelson/Michael Benthall
des.: Ken Kransgill
Hamlet, John Neville; Ophelia, Barbara
Jefford; Claudius, Oliver Neville; Gertrude,
Margaret Courtney; Polonius, Joseph
O'Connor
ARC/DHS: Museum of Broadcasting,
New York

Hamlet
(FDR, 1960): Film, b/w, FL, dubbed
p.c.: Bavaria Atelier GmbH
pro.: Hans Gottschalk
dir.: Franz Peter Wirth
Hamlet, Maximilian Schell; Claudius, Hans
Caninenberg; Gertrude, Wanda Rotha;
Ophelia, Dunja Movar

Hamlet
(USSR, 1964): Film, b/w, FL
p.c.: Lenfilm
dir.: Grigori Kozintsev
des.: Evgeni Enei, G. Kroplachev
Hamlet, Innokenti Smoktounovski; Ophelia, Anastasia Vertinskaia; Claudius, Mikhail
Nazvanov; Gertrude, Elza Radzin-Szolkonis; Polonius, Iouri Tolubeyev
DHS: HF, 16mm
ARC: NFA, 35mm (English subtitles)

Hamlet at Elsinore
(GB, 1964): TV, b/w
p.c.: BBC/Danmarks Radio
pro.: Peter Luke
dir.: Philip Saville
des.: Paul Arnt Thomsen
Hamlet, Christopher Plummer; Claudius,
Robert Shaw; Ophelia, Jo Maxwell Muller;
Horatio, Michael Caine
ARC: BBC, 35mm

Hamlet
(USA, 1964): Video/col.
p.c.: New York Shakespeare Festival
pro/dir.: Joseph Papp
Hamlet, Alfred Ryder; Ophelia, Julie Har-
ris; Claudius, Howard da Silva; Gertrude,
Nan Martin
DHS: New York Shakespeare Festival

Hamile
(Ghana, 1964): Film
p.c.: Ghana Film Industry Co.
dir.: Terry Bishop
Joe Akonor, Kofi Middetan-Mends, Ernest
Abbequaye, Frances Sey, Mary Yirenkyi

Hamlet
(USA, 1964): Film, b/w
p.c.: Electronovision
pro.: William Sargent Jr, Alfred W. Crown,

John Heyman
dir.: John Gielgud (Stage), Bill Colleran
(Electronovision)
des.: Ben Edwards
Hamlet, Richard Burton; Ophelia, Linda
March; Claudius, Alfred Drake; Gertrude,
Eileen Herlie
ARC: NFA, 35mm

Hamlet
(GB, 1969): Film, col.
p.c.: Woodfall Production Co.
pro.: Neil Hartley
dir.: Tony Richardson
des.: Jocelyn Herbert
Hamlet, Nicol Williamson; Claudius,
Anthony Hopkins; Gertrude, Judy Parfitt;
Ophelia, Marianne Faithfull
DHS: HF
ARC: FSL (USA), 35mm; NFA, 35mm

Hamlet
(USA, 1970): TV, col.
p.c.: Hallmark Hall of Fame, NBC
pro.: George La Maire
dir.: Peter Wood
des.: Peter Roden
Hamlet, Richard Chamberlain; Ophelia,
Ciaran Madden; Gertrude, Margaret Leighton: Claudius, Richard Johnson; Polonius,
Michael Redgrave; Ghost, John Gielgud
DSH: Films Inc., Chicago, 16mm

Heranca
(Brazil, 1970): Film, FL
p.c.: Longfilm Produtora Cinematografica
David Cardoso, Barbara Fazio, Rosalva
Cacador, America Taricano, Deoclides
Gouveia

Hamlet
(GB/USA, 1972): TV, col.
p.c.: Prospect Theatre Co./BBC
pro.: Eddie Kulukundis
dir.: David Giles
Hamlet, Ian McKellen; Faith Brook, John
Woodvine, Susan Fleetwood
ARC: BBC, v.t.

Hamlet
(Canada, 1973): Film, col.
p.c.: Toronto Theatre Co./Crawley Films

pro.: F. R. Crawley
dir.: René Bonnière/Stephen Bush
DHS: Crawley Films, Ottowa

Hamlet
(GB, 1976): Film, col.
p.c.: Essential Cinema
dir.: Celestino Coronada
Hamlet and Laertes, Anthony and David
Meyer; Ophelia and Gertrude, Helen Mirren; Polonius, Quentin Crisp

Hamlet
(Netherlands, 1980): Video, col.
p.c.: Footsbarn Co./CBR
pro.: Footsbarn Collective
ARC/DHS: Nederlandes Theater Instituut,
Amsterdam

Hamlet
(GB/USA, 1980): TV, col.
p.c.: BBC/Time-Life TV
pro.: Cedric Messina
dir.: Rodney Bennett
des.: Don Homfray
Hamlet, Derek Jacobi; Gertrude, Claire
Bloom; Claudius, Patrick Stewart; Ophelia,
Lalla Ward; Polonius, Eric Porter
DHS: BBC, 16mm, v.c.
ARC: BBC, v.c.

*Den Tragiska Historien om Hamlet, Priz ar
Danmark*
(Sweden, 1984): Film, video, col.
p.c.: Swedish Television
dir.: Ragnar Lyth
Hamlet, Stellan Skarsgaard; Gertrude,
Mona Malm; Claudius, Frej Lindquist;
Ophelia, Pernella Wallgren; Polonius, Sven
Lindberg
DHS: WNET/Thirteen Television, New
York, 16mm, v.c.

Hamlet
(GB, 1987): Video, col.
p.c.: Cambridge Experimental Theatre/
Cambridgeshire College of Art and
Technology
dir.: Roland Kenyon, Rod MacDonald
Ophelia, Tricia Hitchcock; Gertrude, Melanie Revell; Claudius, Richard Spaull;
Hamlet, all cast
DHS: Anglia Polytechnic University, v.c.

HENRY IV, PART ONE

An Age of Kings: Part 3, 'Rebellion from the
North', Part 4, 'The Road to Shrewsbury'
(GB, 1960): TV, b/w
p.c.: BBC
pro.: Peter Dews
dir.: Michael Hayes
des.: Stanley Morris
Henry IV, Tom Fleming; Prince, Robert
Hardy; Hotspur, Sean Connery; Falstaff,
Frank Pettingell
ARC: BBC, 16mm (two parts)

Falstaff (Chimes at Midnight)
(Spain/Switzerland, 1965): Film, b/w
p.c.: International Films Espagnol Alpine
pro.: Emiliano Piedra, Angel Escoloano
dir.: Orson Welles
des.: Jose Antonio de la Guerra, Mariana
Erdorza
Falstaff, Orson Welles; Hal, Keith Baxter;
Henry IV, John Gielgud; Mistress Quickly,
Margaret Rutherford; Doll Tearsheet,
Jeanne Moreau
DHS: HF
ARC: FSL (USA), 35mm

Henry IV, Part One
(GB/USA, 1979): TV, col.
p.c.: BBC/Time-Life TV
pro.: Cedric Messina
dir.: David Giles
des.: Don Homfray
Henry IV, Jon Finch; Prince, David Gwillim; Falstaff, Anthony Quayle
DHS: BBC, 16mm, v.c.
ARC: BBC, v.c.

HENRY IV, PART TWO

An Age of Kings: Part 5, 'The New Conspiracy', Part 6, 'Uneasy Lies the Head'
(GB, 1960): TV, b/w
p.c.: BBC
pro.: Peter Dews
dir.: Michael Hayes
des.: Stanley Morris
Henry IV, Tom Fleming; Prince, Robert
Hardy; Falstaff, Frank Pettingell; Hotspur,
Sean Connery
ARC: BBC, 16mm (two parts)

Henry IV, Part Two
(GB/USA, 1979): TV, col.
p.c.: BBC/Time-Life TV
pro.: Cedric Messina
dir.: David Giles
des.: Don Homfray
Henry IV, Jon Finch; Prince, David Gwillim; Falstaff, Anthony Quayle
DHS: BBC, 16mm, v.c.

HENRY V

Henry V
(GB, 1944): Film, col.
p.c.: Two Cities Films
pro./dir.: Laurence Olivier
des.: Paul Sheriff, Roger Furse
Henry V, Laurence Olivier; Chorus, Leslie Banks; Princess Katherine, Renée Asherson; Pistol, Robert Newton
DHS: RFL, 16mm, v.c.

Henry V
(GB, 1951): TV, b/w
p.c.: BBC
pro./dir.: Royston Morley, Leonard Brett
des.: Barry Learoyd
Henry V, Clement McCallin; French King, Norman Claridge; Pistol, Willoughby Gray; Princess Katherine, Varvara Pitoëff

Henry V
(GB, 1953): TV, b/w
p.c.: BBC
pro./dir.: Peter Watts
Henry V, John Clements; Princess Katherine, Kay Hammond; French King, John Garside; Pistol, John Laurie

The Life of Henry V
(GB, 1957): TV, b/w
p.c.: BBC
pro./dir.: Peter Dews
des.: Guy Sheppard
Henry V, John Neville; Fluellen, Dudley Jones; Pistol, Geoffrey Bayldon; Bardolph, Michael Bates
ARC: BBC, 35mm

An Age of Kings: Part 7, 'Signs of War', Part 8, 'The Band of Brothers'
(GB, 1960): TV, b/w

p.c.: BBC
pro.: Peter Dews
dir.: Michael Hayes
des.: Stanley Morris
Henry V, Robert Hardy; Chorus, William Squire; Bardolph, Gordon Gostelow; Princess Katherine, Judi Dench
ARC: BBC, 16mm (two parts)

Henry V
(Canada, 1966): TV, col.
p.c.: CFTO/TV, Toronto (for CTV)
dir.: Michael Langham (stage), Lorne Freed (TV)
des.: Desmond Heeley
Henry V, Douglas Rain; William Hutt, Bernard Behrens, Tony Van Bridge, Jean Gascon

Henry V
(GB/USA, 1979): TV, col.
p.c.: BBC/Time-Life TV
pro.: Cedric Messina
dir.: David Giles
des.: Don Homfray
Henry V, David Gwillim; Pistol, Bryan Pringle; Katherine, Jocelyne Boisseau; Chorus, Alec McCowen
DHS: BBC, 16mm, v.c.

Henry V
(GB, 1989): Film, col.
p.c.: Renaissance Films plc.
pro.: Stephen Evans/Bruce Sharman/David Parfitt
dir.: Kenneth Branagh
des.: Hugh Cruttwell/Norman Dorme/Tim Harvey
Henry V, Kenneth Branagh; Chorus, Derek Jacobi; Bardolph, Richard Briers; Pistol, Robert Stephens; Falstaff, Robbie Coltrane; Catherine, Emma Thompson
DHS: Samuel Goldwyn Co.

HENRY VI, PART ONE

An Age of Kings: Part 9, 'The Red Rose and the White'
(GB, 1960): TV, b/w
p.c.: BBC
pro.: Peter Dews

dir.: Michael Hayes
des.: Stanley Morris
Henry VI, Terry Scully; Margaret, Mary
Morris; Bedford, Patrick Garland; Glouces-
ter, John Ringham; Joan la Pucelle, Eileen
Atkins; Charles the Dauphin, Jerome Willis
ARC: BBC, 16mm

The Wars of the Roses: Part 1, 'Henry VI'
(GB, 1965): TV, b/w
p.c.: RSC/BBC
pro.: Michael Barry (BBC)
dir.: Peter Hall, John Barton (RSC), Robin
Midgley, Michael Hayes (BBC)
des.: John Bury
Henry VI, David Warner; Margaret, Peggy
Ashcroft; Joan, Janet Suzman; Talbot, Clive
Morton; Winchester, Nicholas Selby
ARC: BBC, 35mm

Henry VI, Part One
(GB/USA, 1983): TV, col.
p.c.: BBC/Time-Life TV
pro.: Jonathan Miller
dir.: Jane Howell
des.: Oliver Bayldon
Henry VI, Peter Benson; Talbot, Trevor
Peacock; Joan, Brenda Blethyn; Margaret,
Julia Foster; Gloucester, David Burke
DHS: BBC, 16mm, v.c.

HENRY VI, PART TWO

An Age of Kings: Part 10 'The Fall of a
Protector', Part 11, 'The Rabble from Kent'
(GB, 1960): TV, b/w
p.c.: BBC
pro.: Peter Dews
dir.: Michael Hayes
des.: Stanley Morris
Henry VI, Terry Scully; Margaret, Mary
Morris; Gloucester, John Ringham; York,
Jack May; Eleanor, Duchess of Gloucester,
Nancie Jackson; Cade, Esmond Knight
ARC: BBC, 16mm

The Wars of the Roses: Part 1, 'Henry VI',
Part 2, 'Edward IV'
(GB, 1964): TV, b/w
p.c.: RSC/BBC
pro.: Michael Barry (BBC)

dir.: Peter Hall, John Barton (RSC), Robin
Midgley, Michael Hayes (BBC)
des.: John Bury
Henry VI, David Warner; Margaret, Peggy
Ashcroft; York, Donald Sinden; Glouces-
ter, Ian Holm; Cade, Roy Dotrice
ARC: BBC, 35mm

Henry VI, Part Two
(GB/USA, 1983): TV, col.
p.c.: BBC/Time-Life TV
pro.: Jonathan Miller
dir.: Jane Howell
des.: Oliver Bayldon
Henry VI, Peter Benson; Gloucester, David
Burke; York, Bernard Hill; Cade, Trevor
Peacock
DHS: BBC, 16mm, v.c.

HENRY VI, PART THREE

An Age of Kings: Part 12, 'The Morning's
War', Part 13, 'The Sun in Splendour'
(GB, 1960): TV, b/w
p.c.: BBC
pro.: Peter Dews
dir.: Michael Hayes
des.: Stanley Morris
Henry VI, Terry Scully; York, Jack May;
Clifford, Jerome Willis; Edward, Julian
Glover; Clarence, Patrick Garland; Glou-
cester, Paul Daneman
ARC: BBC, 16mm

The Wars of the Roses: Part 2, 'Edward IV',
Part 3, 'Richard III'
(GB, 1964): TV, b/w
p.c.: RSC/BBC
pro.: Michael Barry (BBC)
dir.: Peter Hall, John Barton (RSC), Robin
Midgley, Michael Hayes (BBC)
des.: John Bury
Henry VI, David Warner; Margaret, Peggy
Ashcroft; Clifford, John Corvin; York,
Donald Sinden; Edward IV, Roy Dotrice;
Clarence, Charles Kay; Gloucester, Ian
Holm
ARC: BBC, 16mm

Henry VI, Part Three
(GB/USA, 1983): TV, col.

p.c.: BBC/Time-Life TV
pro.: Shaun Sutton
dir.: Jane Howell
des.: Oliver Bayldon
Henry VI, Peter Benson; Edward IV, Brian Protheroe; Margaret, Julia Foster; York, Bernard Hill
DHS: BBC, 16mm, v.c.

HENRY VIII

Henry VIII
(GB, 1911): Film, b/w, sil.
p.c.: Barker Motion Photography
dir.: William G. B. Barker
Henry VIII, Arthur Bourchier; Wolsey, Herbert Beerbohm Tree; Katherine, Violet Vanbrugh; Buckingham, Henry Ainley

Henry VIII
(GB/USA, 1979): TV, col.
p.c.: Cedric Messina
dir.: Kevin Billington
des.: Alun Hughes
Henry VIII, John Stride; Wolsey, Timothy West; Katharine, Claire Bloom
DHS: BBC, 16mm, v.c.
ARC: BBC, v.t.

JULIUS CAESAR

Julius Caesar
(USA, 1908): Film, b/w, sil.
p.c.: Vitagraph
pro./dir.: William V. Ranous
Julius Caesar, William V. Ranous

Julius Caesar
(USA, 1908): Film, b/w (tinted), sil.
p.c.: Vitagraph
pro./dir.: J. Stuart Blackton
Julius Caesar, Charles Kent; Mark Antony, William V. Ranous; Florence Lawrence, Paul Panzer, Earle Williams

Julius Caesar
(GB, 1911): Film, b/w, sil.
p.c.: Co-operative Cinematograph
dir.: F. R. Benson
Julius Caesar, Guy Rathbone; Mark Antony, F. R. Benson; Brutus, Murray Carrington; Portia, Mrs Benson; Cassius, Eric Maxim

Giulio Cesare
(Italy, 1914): Film, b/w, sil.
p.c.: Cines
pro./dir.: Enrico Guazzoni
Amleto Novelli, Gianna Terribili-Gonzales, Ignazio Lupi, Lea Orlandini, Bruto Castellini

Julius Caesar
(GB, 1938): TV, b/w
p.c.: BBC
pro./dir.: Dallas Bower
des.: Malcolm Baker-Smith
Julius Caesar, Ernest Milton; Mark Antony, D. A. Clarke-Smith; Brutus, Sebastian Shaw; Cassius, Anthony Ireland

Julius Caesar
(GB, 1945): Film, b/w
p.c.: Theatrecraft
dir.: Henry Cass
ARC: NFA, 35mm

Julius Caesar
(USA, 1949): Film, b/w
p.c.: Avon Productions
pro.: Robert Keigher, David Bradley
dir.: David Bradley
Julius Caesar, Harold Tasker; Brutus, David Bradley; Cassius, Grosvenor Glenn; Mark Antony, Charlton Heston; Portia, Molly Darr
ARC: FSL (USA), 16mm

Julius Caesar
(USA, 1949): Video, b/w
p.c.: NBC-TV
pro.: Owen Davis
dir.: Garry Simpson
Caesar, George Bliss; Brutus, Arch Taylor; Cassius, Donald Roberts; Antony, Raymond McDonell
ARC/DHS: NBC/FSL

Julius Caesar
(GB, 1951): Film, b/w
p.c.: Parthian Productions
Robert Speaight, Cecil Trouncer

Julius Caesar
(GB, 1951): TV, b/w
p.c.: BBC
pro.: Stephen Harrison
dir.: Leonard Brett
des.: Barry Learoyd
Julius Caesar, Walter Hudd; Octavius, Richard Bebb; Mark Antony, Anthony Hawtrey; Brutus, Patrick Barr; Portia, Margaret Diamond

Julius Caesar
(USA, 1953): Film, b/w
p.c.: MGM
pro.: John Houseman
dir.: Joseph Mankiewicz
des.: Cedric Gibbons, Edward Carfagno
Julius Caesar, Louis Calhern; Mark Antony, Marlon Brando; Brutus, James Mason; Cassius, John Gielgud
DHS: HF, 16mm
ARC: FSL (USA), 35mm

Julius Caesar
(GB, 1959): TV, b/w
p.c.: BBC
pro./dir.: Stuart Burge
des.: Barry Learoyd
Caesar, Robert Perceval; Brutus, Eric Porter; Antony, William Sylvester; Cassius, Michael Gough
ARC: BBC, 35mm

Julius Caesar
(GB, 1960): TV, b/w
p.c.: BBC
pro./dir.: Richard Eyre
des.: Austen Spriggs
Ralph Michael, James Maxwell, Michael Goodliffe, Ellen McIntosh, John Laurie, Tim Seely
ARC: BBC, 16mm (Parts 1–3), 35mm (Part 4)

The Spread of the Eagle: Part 4, 'The Colossus', Part 5, 'The Fifteenth', Part 6, 'The Revenge'
(GB, 1963): TV, b/w
p.c.: BBC
pro./dir.: Peter Dews
des.: Clifford Hatts
Caesar, Barry Jones; Mark Antony, Keith Michell; Cassius, Peter Cushing; Paul Eddington, David William
ARC: BBC, 35mm

Julius Caesar
(GB, 1964): TV, b/w
p.c.: BBC
pro.: John Vernon (BBC)
dir.: Michael Croft (NYT)
des.: Christopher Lawrence
National Youth Theatre
ARC: BBC, 16mm

Julius Caesar
(GB, 1969): TV, b/w
p.c.: BBC
pro.: Cedric Messina
dir.: Alan Bridges
des.: Spencer Chapman
Robert Stephens, Frank Finlay, Maurice Denham, Edward Woodward
ARC: BBC, 16mm, v.c.

Julius Caesar
(GB, 1969): Film, col.
p.c.: Commonwealth United
pro.: Peter Snell
dir.: Stuart Burge
des.: Julia Trevelyan Oman
Mark Antony, Charlton Heston; Brutus, Jason Robards; Julius Caesar, John Gielgud
DHS: HF, 16mm
ARC: FSL (USA), 35mm

Julius Caesar
(GB/USA, 1979): TV, col.
p.c.: BBC/Time-Life TV
pro.: Cedric Messina
dir.: Herbert Wise
des.: Tony Abbott
Caesar, Charles Gray; Brutus, Richard Pasco; Calphurnia, Elizabeth Spriggs; Antony, Keith Michell
DHS: BBC, 16mm, v.c.

Julius Caesar
(USA, 1979): Video, col.
p.c.: New York Shakespeare Festival
pro.: Joseph Papp
dir.: Michael Langham
Cicero, Earle Hyman; Mark Antony, Jaime Sanchez; Casca, Morgan Freeman; Caesar, Sonny Jim Gaines

ARC: Lincoln Center Library of Performing Arts, New York, v.c.

Julius Caesar
(Belgium, 1985): Video, col.
p.c.: Audio-visuele Dienst, Katholiecke Universiteit Leuuen
dir.: P. Peyskens
ARC: Katholiecke Universiteit Leuuen

Giulio Cesare
(Italy, 19?): Video, b/w
dir.: Maurizo Scaparro
Caesar, Riezo Gionampietro; Mark Antony, Pino Micol
DHS: Italian Institute A/V Service, Belgrave Square, London

KING JOHN

King John
(GB, 1899): Film, b/w, sil.
p.c.: His Majesty's Theatre, London
dir.: Herbert Beerbohm Tree
King John, Herbert Beerbohm Tree

King John
(GB, 1951): TV, b/w
p.c.: BBC
pro./dir.: Stephen Harrison
des.: Barry Learoyd
King John, Donald Wolfit; Queen Elinor, Una Venning; Prince Arthur, Michael Croudson; Faulconbridge, John Southworth

King John
(GB/USA, 1984): TV, col.
p.c.: BBC/Time-Life TV
pro.: Shaun Sutton
dir.: David Giles
des.: Chris Pemsel
King John, Leonard Rossiter; Constance, Claire Bloom; Hubert, John Thaw; Blanche, Janet Maw
DHS: BBC, 16mm, v.c. VHS
ARC: BBC, v.c.

KING LEAR

King Lear
(USA, 1909): Film, b/w, sil.
p.c.: Vitagraph

pro./dir.: William V. Ranous
King Lear, William V. Ranous; Thomas H. Ince

King Lear
(USA, 1909): Film, b/w, sil.
pro./dir.: J. Stuart Blackton
King Lear, Maurice Costello; Julia Arthur, Edith Storey, Mary Fuller

Re Lear
(Italy, 1910): Film, b/w, sil.
p.c.: Milano
pro./dir.: Guiseppe De Liguoro
King Lear, Guiseppe De Liguoro; Arturo Padovani

Re Lear
(Italy, 1910): Film, b/w, sil.
p.c.: Film d'Arte Italiana
dir.: Gerolamo Lo Savio
King Lear, Ermete Novelli; Cordelia, Francesca Bertini; Giannina Chiantoni

King Lear
(USA, 1916): Film, b/w, sil.
p.c.: Thanhouser/Pathe
dir.: Ernest Warde
King Lear, Frederick Warde; Cordelia, Lorraine Huling; King of France, Boyd Marshall; Edgar, Ernest Warde

King Lear
(GB, 1948): TV, b/w
p.c.: BBC
pro./dir.: Royston Morley
des.: Barry Learoyd
Kent, Robert Sansom; Edmund, Patrick Troughton; King Lear, William Devlin; Goneril, Rosalie Crutchley; Cordelia, Ursula Howells; Regan, Nicolette Bernard; Fool, Alan Wheatley; Gloucester, Henry Oscar; Edgar, Robert Harris

King Lear
(USA, 1953): TV, b/w
p.c.: CBS/Omnibus
pro.: Fred Rickey
dir.: Andrew McCullough/Peter Brook
des.: Georges Wakhevitch
King Lear, Orson Welles; Cordelia, Natasha Parry; Albany, Arnold Moss; Goneril, Beatrice Straight
ARC: FSL (USA)

King Lear
(GB/Denmark, 1969): Film, b/w
p.c.: Filmways (London), Athena/Laterna Films (Copenhagen)
pro.: Michael Birkett
dir.: Peter Brook
des.: Georges Wakhevitch
King Lear, Paul Scofield; Goneril, Irene Worth; Regan, Susan Engel; Cordelia, Anelise Gabold; Gloucester, Alan Webb
DHS: HF, 16mm
ARC: FSL (USA), 35mm

Korol Lir
(USSR, 1970): Film, b/w, FL
p.c.: Lenfilm
dir.: Grigori Kozintsev
des.: Evgeni Enei
King Lear, Yuri Yarvet; Goneril, Elza Radzins; Regan, Galina Volchek; Cordelia, Valentina Shendrikova; Edmund, Regimanias Adamaitis; Fool, Ofar Dal
DHS: Cont. 16/35mm
ARC: FSL (USA), 35mm

King Lear
(GB, 1975): TV, col.
p.c.: BBC
pro./dir.: Jonathan Miller
des.: Vic Symonds
King Lear, Michael Hordern; Cordelia, Angela Down; Fool, Frank Middlemass; Goneril, Sarah Badel; Regan, Penelope Wilton; Edgar, Ronald Pickup; Edmund, Michael Jayston
ARC: BBC, v.t.

King Lear
(GB, 1976): Film, col.
p.c.: Triple Action Theatre/BFI
dir.: Steve Rumbelow
Chris Aurache, Genzig Saner, Monica Buford, Helena Paul
ARC: NFA

King Lear
(USA, 1977): Video, col.
p.c.: New York Shakespeare Festival
pro.: Joseph Papp
dir.: Edward Sherin
des.: Loquasto Santo
King Lear, James Earl Jones; Kent, Douglas Watson; Gloucester, Paul Sorvino; Edmund, Raul Julia; Edgar, Rene Anberjonois; Goneril, Rosalind Cush; Regan, Ellen Holley; Cordelia, Lee Chamberlain; Fool, Tom Aldredge
DHS: New York Shakespeare Festival

Re Lear
(Italy, 1979): Video, col.
p.c.: RAI Productions
pro.: Carlo Battistoni
dir.: Giorgio Strehler
Tino Carrarro, Renato de Carmine
ARC: Archivo Storino, Venice
DHS: Videtaca Radiotelevisione Italiano

King Lear
(GB/USA, 1982): TV, col.
p.c.: BBC/Time-Life TV
pro.: Shaun Sutton
dir.: Jonathan Miller
des.: Colin Lowrey
King Lear, Michael Hordern; Goneril, Gillian Barge; Regan, Penelope Wilton; Cordelia, Brenda Blethyn; Fool, Frank Middlemass
DHS: BBC, v.c.

King Lear
(GB, 1984): TV, col.
p.c.: Granada TV
pro.: David Plowright
dir.: Michael Elliott
King Lear, Laurence Olivier; Fool, John Hurt; Regan, Diana Rigg; Goneril, Dorothy Tutin
DHS: GTV, v.c.

Ran
(Japan, 1984): Film, col.
pro.: Serge Silberman/Masato Hara
dir.: Akira Kurosawa
des.: Yoshiro Muraki
Lear, Tatsuya Nakadai
DHS: Insight Media, New York, 35mm

LOVE'S LABOUR'S LOST

Love's Labour's Lost
(GB, 1965): TV, b/w
p.c.: BBC

pro.: George R. Foa
dir.: Roger Jenkins
Berowne, Richard Pasco; Rosaline, Barbara Leigh-Hunt; Princess of France, Eithne Dunn; Costard, Russell Hunter

Love's Labour's Lost
(GB/USA, 1985): TV, col.
p.c.: BBC/Time-Life TV
pro.: Shaun Sutton
dir.: Elijah Moshinsky
des.: Barbara Gosnold
King, Jonathan Kent; Longaville, Christopher Blake; Dumain, Geoffrey Burridge; Berowne, Mike Gwilym; Princess of France, Maureen Lipman; Maria, Katy Behean; Katharine, Petra Markham; Rosaline, Jenny Agutter

MACBETH

Macbeth
(USA, 1908): Film, b/w, sil.
p.c.: Vitagraph
dir.: William V. Ranous
Macbeth, William V. Ranous; Lady Macbeth, Miss Carver; Macduff, Paul Panzer

Macbeth
(Italy, 1909): Film, b/w, sil.
p.c.: Cines
dir.: Mario Caserini
Macbeth, Dante Capelli; Lady Macbeth, Maria Gasperini; Amleto Palormi

Macbeth
(France, 1910): Film, b/w, sil.
p.c.: Film d'Art
dir.: Andre Calmettes
Macbeth, Paul Mounet; Lady Macbeth, Joanne Delvair

Macbeth
(GB, 1911): Film, b/w, sil.
p.c.: Co-operative Cinematograph
dir.: Frank R. Benson
Macbeth, Frank R. Benson; Lady Macbeth, Mrs Benson; Guy Rathbone; Murray Carrington

Macbeth
(Germany, 1913): Film, b/w, sil.

p.c.: Filmindustrie Gesellschaft Heidelberg
dir.: Arthur Bourchier
Macbeth, Arthur Bourchier; Lady Macbeth, Violet Vanbrugh

Macbeth
(France, 1916): Film, b/w, sil.
p.c.: Eclair
Lady Macbeth, Georgette Leblanc-Maeterlink; Severin Mars

Macbeth
(USA, 1916): Film, b/w, sil.
p.c.: Triangle Reliance
dir.: John Emerson, D. W. Griffith
Macbeth, Herbert Beerbohm Tree; Lady Macbeth, Constance Collier; Macduff, Wilfred Lucas; Banquo, Ralph Lewis

Macbeth
(Germany, 1922): Film, b/w, sil.
p.c.: Elel Film/Filmindustrie, Heidelberg
dir.: Heinz Schall

Macbeth
(GB, 1945): Film, b/w
p.c.: Theatrecraft
dir.: Henry Cass
ARC: NFA, 35mm

Macbeth
(USA, 1946): Film, b/w
p.c.: Willow
pro.: David Bradley
dir.: Thomas A. Blair
des.: Charlton Heston
Macbeth, David Bradley; Jain Wilimorsky, William Bartholmay, Louis Northrop
ARC: FSL (USA), 16mm; NFA, 16mm

Macbeth
(USA, 1946): Film, b/w
p.c.: Mercury Films and Republic Pictures
pro./dir.: Orson Welles
des.: John McCarthy Jr, James Redd
Macbeth, Orson Welles; Lady Macbeth, Jeanette Nolan; Duncan, Erskine Sanford; Macduff, Dan O'Herlihy; the Three Witches, Lurene Tuttle, Brainerd Duffield, Peggy Webber; Malcolm, Roddy McDowall
DHS: HF, 16mm; IPC, v.c.
ARC: FSL (USA), 35mm; NFA, 35mm

Macbeth
(GB, 1949): TV, b/w
p.c.: BBC
pro./dir.: George More O'Ferrall
des.: Peter Bax
Macbeth, Stephen Murray; Lady Macbeth, Bernadette O'Farrell; Duncan, Arthur Wontner; Banquo, Esmond Knight; Malcolm, Patrick McNee

Macbeth
(USA, 1951): Film, col.
p.c.: Unusual Films, Bob Jones University
dir.: Katherine Stenholm
Members of the university faculty
ARC: FSL (USA), 16mm

Macbeth
(USA, 1954): Film, b/w
p.c.: Hallmark Hall of Fame NBC
dir.: Maurice Evans
Macbeth, Maurice Evans; Lady Macbeth, Judith Anderson
ARC/DHS: FLS, v.c.

Kumonosu-Djo (Throne of Blood)
(Japan, 1957): Film, b/w, FL
p.c.: Toho
dir.: Akira Kurosawa
des.: Yoshiro Murai
Macbeth/Taketoki Washizu, Toshiro Mifune; Lady Macbeth/Asaji, Isuzu Yamada; Duncan/Kunihara Tsuzuki, Takamaru Sasaki
DHS: HF, 16mm
ARC: FSL (USA), 35mm

Macbeth
(GB/USA, 1960): Film, col.
p.c.: Grand Prize Films
pro.: Phil C. Samuel
dir.: George Schaefer
des.: Edward Carrick
Macbeth, Maurice Evans; Lady Macbeth, Judith Anderson; Macduff, Ian Bannen; Duncan, Malcolm Keen
ARC: FSL (USA), 35mm

Macbeth
(GB, 1966): TV, b/w
p.c.: BBC
pro.: Michael Simpson
des.: Charles Lawrence

Macbeth, Andrew Keir; Lady Macbeth, Ruth Meyer; Duncan, Donald Eccles; Macduff, Anthony Bate
ARC: BBC, 35mm

Macbeth
(GB, 1970): TV, col.
p.c.: BBC
pro.: Cedric Messina
dir.: John Gorrie
des.: Natasha Kroll
Macbeth, Eric Porter; Lady Macbeth, Janet Suzman; John Alderton
ARC: BBC, 16mm, v.c.

Macbeth
(GB, 1971): Film, col.
p.c.: Playboy Productions/Caliban Films
pro.: Andrew Braunsberg
dir.: Roman Polanski
des.: Wilfrid Shingleton
Macbeth, Jon Finch; Lady Macbeth, Francesca Annis; Banquo, Martin Shaw; Macduff, Terence Bayler
DHS: HF, 16mm
ARC: FSL (USA), 35mm

Macbeth
(GB, 1979): TV, col.
p.c.: RSC/Thames TV
pro.: Philip Casson
dir.: Trevor Nunn
des.: John Napier (RSC)
Macbeth, Ian McKellen; Lady Macbeth, Judi Dench; Duncan, Griffith Jones; Malcolm, Roger Rees; Macduff, Bob Peck
DHS: TTV, v.c.
ARC: NFA

Macbeth
(USA, 1981): v.c, col.
p.c.: Bard Productions Ltd
pro.: Jack Nakano
dir.: Arthur Allan Seidelman
des.: John Retsek
Macbeth, Jeremy Brett; Lady Macbeth, Piper Laurie; Macduff, Simon MacCorkindale; Banquo, Barrie Primus
DHS: University of Illinois, v.c.

Macbeth
(USA, 1982): Video, col.
p.c.: Lincoln Center for the Performing

Arts
pro.: Richmond Crinkley
dir.: Sarah Caldwell/Kirk Browning
des.: Herbert Senn
Macbeth, Philip Anglim; Lady Macbeth, Maureen Anderman; Macduff, Kenneth J. Campbell; Banquo, Fritz Sperberg; Malcolm, John Vickery; Witches, Michael Dash, Ellen Gould, Heard Cordis, Dana Ivey
DHS: Films for the Humanities, Princeton USA, v.c.

Macbeth
(GB/USA, 1983): TV, col.
p.c.: BBC/Time-Life TV
pro.: Shaun Sutton
dir.: Jack Gold
des.: Gerry Scott
Macbeth, Nicol Williamson; Duncan, Mark Dignam; Lady Macbeth, Jane Lapotaire
DHS: BBC, v.c.

MEASURE FOR MEASURE

Dente per Dente
(Italy, 1942): Film, b/w, FL
p.c.: Atlas (Artisti Associati)
dir.: Marco Elter
Carlo Tamberlani, Caterina Boratto, Oswaldo Genazzani, Memo Bennassi, Lamberto Picasso, Amelia Chellini

Zweierlei Mass
(FDR, 1963): Film, b/w, FL
p.c.: Bavaria Atelier GmbH
dir.: Paul Verhoeven
des.: Walter Blokesch
Hans Caninenberg, Lothar Blumhagen, Martin Berliner, Erik Schumann

Measure for Measure
(GB/USA, 1979): TV, col.
p.c.: BBC/Time-Life TV
pro.: Cedric Messina
dir.: Desmond Davis
des.: Odette Barrow
Duke, Kenneth Colley; Isabella, Kate Nelligan; Angelo, Tim Piggot-Smith
DHS: BBC, 16mm, v.c.

THE MERCHANT OF VENICE

The Merchant of Venice
(USA, 1908): Film, b/w, sil.
p.c.: Vitagraph
dir.: William V. Ranous
Shylock, William V. Ranous; Portia, Julia Swayne-Gordon; Jessica, Florence Turner

Il Mercante di Venezia
(Italy, 1910): Film, b/w, sil.
p.c.: Film d'Arte Italiana
dir.: Gerolamo Lo Savio
Shylock, Ermete Novelli; Portia, Francesca Bertini; Olga Giannini Novelli
ARC: NFA, 35mm

The Merchant of Venice
(USA, 1912): Film, b/w, sil.
p.c.: Thanhouser
dir.: Barry O'Neil
Shylock, William J. Bowman; Portia, Florence La Badie; Bassanio, Harry Benham; Antonio, William Russell; Jessica, Mignon Anderson

The Merchant of Venice
(USA, 1914): Film b/w, sil.
p.c.: Universal Pictures
dir.: Phillips Smalley, Lois Weber
Shylock, Phillips Smalley; Portia, Lois Weber; Bassanio, Douglas Gerrard; Antonio, Rupert Julian; Jessica, Edna Maison

The Merchant of Venice
(GB, 1916): Film, b/w, sil.
p.c.: Broadwest Film Co.
dir.: Walter West
Shylock, Matheson Lang; Portia, Hutin Britton; Bassanio, J. R. Tozer; Antonio, George Skillan; Jessica, Kathleen Hazel Jones

Der Kaufmann von Venedig
(Germany, 1923): Film, b/w, sil.
dir.: Peter Paul Felner
ARC: NFA, 35mm

The Merchant of Venice
(GB, 1947): TV, b/w
p.c.: BBC
pro./dir.: George More O'Ferrall
des.: Barry Learoyd
Antonio, Austin Trevor; Shylock, Abra-

ham Sofaer; Bassanio, Andre Morell; Portia, Margaretta Scott; Jessica, Jill Balcon

Le Marchand de Venise/Il Mercante di Venezia
(France/Italy, 1952): Film, b/w, FL
p.c.: Venturini Films/Elysées Films
dir.: Pierre Billon
des.: G. C. Bartolini-Salimbeni
Shylock, Michel Simon; Portia, Andrée Debar; Antonio, Massimo Serato

The Merchant of Venice
(GB, 1955): TV, b/w
p.c.: BBC
pro./dir.: Hal Burton
des.: Hal Burton
Antonio, Raymond Westwell; Shylock, Michael Hordern; Bassanio, Denis Quilley; Portia, Rachel Gurney; Jessica, Veronica Wells

The Merchant of Venice
(GB, 1969): VT, col.
p.c.: Audio-Visual Productions
dir.: Jonathan Miller
Shylock, Laurence Olivier; Portia, Joan Plowright
DHS: AVP, v.c.

The Merchant of Venice
(GB, 1972): TV, col.
p.c.: BBC
pro.: Gerald Savory
dir.: Cedric Messina
des.: Tony Abbott
Shylock, Frank Finlay; Antonio, Charles Gray; Portia, Maggie Smith; Bassanio, Christopher Gable
ARC: BBC, 16mm, v.t.

The Merchant of Venice
(GB/USA, 1980): TV, col.
p.c.: BBC/Time-Life TV
pro.: Jonathan Miller
dir.: Jack Gold
Shylock, Warren Mitchell; Portia, Gemma Jones; Antonio, John Franklyn-Robbins; Bassanio, John Nettles
DHS: BBC, 16mm, v.c.

THE MERRY WIVES OF WINDSOR

The Merry Wives of Windsor
(USA, 1910): Film, b/w, sil.
p.c.: Selig Polyscope Co.

Die Lustigen Weiber von Windsor
(Germany, 1917): Film, b/w, sil.
p.c.: Beck-Film
dir.: William Waner

The Merry Wives of Windsor
(GB, 1952): TV, b/w
p.c.: BBC
pro.: Ian Atkins
dir.: Julian Amyes
des.: James Bould
Falstaff, Robert Atkins; Page, Rupert Davies; Ford, Anthony Sharp; Mistress Ford, Betty Huntley-Wright; Mistress Page, Mary Kerridge

The Merry Wives of Windsor
(GB, 1955): TV, b/w
p.c.: BBC
pro.: Stephen Harrison
dir.: Glen Byam Shaw (SMT), Barrie Edgar (BBC)
des.: Motley
Falstaff, Anthony Quayle; Mistress Page, Angela Baddeley; Mistress Ford, Joyce Redman
ARC: NFA

The Merry Wives of Windsor
(USA, 1980): video, col.
p.c.: Berkeley Shakespeare Festival
dir.: Richard E. T. White
Bardolph, Steven Jonsen; Dr Caius, John Vickery; Falstaff, Gail Chugg; Ford, Robert Sicular; Mistress Ford, Beth Sweeney; Nym, J. P. Phillips; Pistol, Kevin Carr; Mistress Page, Linda Hoy; Shallow, Charles Dean; Quickly, Jean Afterman
ARC: Lincoln Center Library of the Performing Arts, v.c.

The Merry Wives of Windsor
(GB/USA, 1982): TV, col.
p.c.: BBC/Time-Life TV
pro.: Shaun Sutton
dir.: David Jones

des.: Don Homfray
Falstaff, Richard Griffiths; Mistress Page, Prunella Scales; Mistress Ford, Judy Davis; Ford, Ben Kingsley
DHS: BBC, 16mm, v.c.

A MIDSUMMER NIGHT'S DREAM

A Midsummer Night's Dream
(USA, 1909): Film b/w, sil.
p.c.: Vitagraph
dir.: J. Stuart Blackton
Lysander, Maurice Costello; Puck, Gladys Hulette; Bottom, William V. Ranous
ARC: NFA, 35mm (incomplete)

Le Songe d'une Nuit d'Été
(France, 1909): Film, b/w, sil.
p.c.: Le Lion
Stacia de Napierkowska

Ein Sommernachtstraum in unserer Zeit
(Germany, 1913): Film, b/w, sil.
p.c.: Deutsche Bioscop GmbH
dir.: Stellan Rye
Puck, Grete Berger; Carl Clewing, Jean Ducret, Anni Mewes

A Midsummer Night's Dream
(Italy, 1913): Film, b/w, sil.
p.c.: Gloria Films
Socrate Tommasi, Bianca Hubner

Ein Sommernachtstraum
(Germany, 1925): Film, b/w, sil.
p.c.: Neumann-Prod. GmbH
dir.: Hans Neumann
Bottom, Werner Krauss; Puck, Valeska Gert; Oberon, Tamara

A Midsummer Night's Dream
(USA, 1935): Film, b/w
p.c.: Warner Brothers
pro.: Max Reinhardt
dir.: Max Reinhardt, William Dieterle
des.: Anton Grot
Bottom, James Cagney; Titania, Anita Louise; Puck, Mickey Rooney; Oberon, Victor Jory; Hermia, Olivia de Havilland; Helena, Jean Muir; Demetrius, Ross Alexander; Lysander, Dick Powell

DHS: RFL, 16mm
ARC: FSL (USA), 35mm; NFA, 35mm

A Midsummer Night's Dream
(GB, 1946): TV, b/w
p.c.: BBC
pro./dir.: Robert Atkins
Bankside Players
Theseus, Desmond Llewelyn; Hippolyta, Angela Shafto, Oberon, John Byron; Titania, Vivienne Bennett; Bottom, Robert Atkins

A Midsummer Night's Dream
(GB, 1947): TV, b/w
p.c.: BBC
pro.: Robert Atkins
dir.: I. Orr-Ewing
From the Open Air Theatre, Regent's Park
Theseus, Desmond Llewelyn; Lysander, Andrew Faulds; Demetrius, Peter Bell; Bottom, Hugh Marning; Hippolyta, Angela Shafto; Helena, Iris Baker; Hermia, Patricia Hicks; Oberon, John Byron; Titania, Vivienne Bennett; Puck, Mary Honer

A Midsummer Night's Dream
(GB, 1958): Film, TV, b/w
p.c.: BBC
dir.: Rudolph Cartier
des.: Clifford Hatts
Bottom, Paul Rogers; Puck, Gillian Lynne; Titania, Natasha Parry; Oberon, John Justin; Flute, Ronald Fraser; Quince, Peter Sallis

A Midsummer Night's Dream
(GB, 1968): Film, col.
p.c.: RSC/Filmways
pro.: Michael Birkett
dir.: Peter Hall
des.: John Bury, Ann Curtis
Oberon, Ian Richardson; Titania, Judi Dench; Puck, Ian Holm; Bottom, Paul Rogers; Lysander, David Warner; Demetrius, Michael Jayston; Helena, Diana Rigg; Hermia, Helen Mirren
DHS: FD, 16mm
ARC: FSL (USA), 35mm

A Midsummer Night's Dream
(GB, 1968): Film, TV, b/w

p.c.: Rediffusion TV
dir.: Joan Kemp-Welch
des.: Michael Yates
Bottom, Benny Hill; Puck, Tony Tanner;
Peter Wyngarde, Alfie Bass, Jill Bennett,
Anna Massey, Bernard Bresslaw

A Midsummer Night's Dream
(GB, 1971): TV, col.
p.c.: BBC
pro.: Cedric Messina
dir.: James Cellan Jones
des.: Roger Andrew
Titania, Eileen Atkins; Bottom, Ronnie
Barker; Helena, Lynn Redgrave; Oberon,
Robert Stephens
ARC: BBC, v.t.

A Midsummer Night's Dream
(GB/USA, 1981): TV, col.
p.c.: BBC/Time-Life TV
pro.: Jonathan Miller
dir.: Elijah Moshinsky
des.: David Myerscough-Jones
Hippolyta, Estelle Kohler; Theseus, Nigel
Davenport; Titania, Helen Mirren;
Oberon, Peter McEnery
DHS: BBC, 16mm

A Midsummer Night's Dream
(USA, 1982): TV, col.
p.c.: ABC Video Enterprises
pro.: Joseph Papp
dir.: James Lapine/Emile Ardolino
des.: Heidi Landesman/Randy Barcelo
Hippolyta, Diane Venora; Theseus, James
Hurdle; Titania, Michele Shay; Oberon,
William Hurt; Bottom, Jeffrey DeMunn;
Puck, Marcel Rosenblatt
ARC: FLS

A Midsummer Night's Dream
(GB/Spain, 1984): TV, Film, col.
p.c.: Cabochan/Channel 4
pro.: Celestino Coronado, David Meyer
dir.: Celestino Coronado
des.: Lindsay Kemp, Mark Baldwin
The Incredible Orlando, Lindsay Kemp,
Manuela Vargas, Michael Matou, François
Testorg, David Meyer, David Haughton,
Annie Huckle
DHS: HF, 16mm

MUCH ADO ABOUT NOTHING

Much Ado About Nothing
(USA, 1926): Film b/w, sil.
dir.: Arthur Rosson
Raymond Griffith, Helene Costello, Bryant
Washburn

Much Ado About Nothing
(GB, 1937): TV, b/w
p.c.: BBC
dir.: George More O'Ferrall
Beatrice, Margaretta Scott; Benedick,
Henry Oscar

Mnogo Shuma Iz Nichego
(USSR, 1956): Film, b/w, FL
p.c.: Moscow Studio
dir.: L. Samkovoi
des.: Ia Rapaport
Don Pedro, N. Bubnov; Don John, A.
Katsynski; Claudio, N. Malishevski; Benedick, Iu Liubimov; Beatrice, L.
Tselikorskaia

Much Ado About Nothing
(USA, 1958): TV, col.
p.c.: Matinee Theatre
Beatrice, Nina Foch; Benedick, Robert
Norton

Viel Larm um Nichts
(DDR, 1963): Film, col., FL
p.c.: DEFA-Studio (for Spielfilme)
dir.: Martin Hellberg
des.: Hans Jorg Mirr
Christel Bodenstein, Rolf Ludwig, Wilfrid
Ortmann

Much Ado About Nothing
(GB, 1967): TV, b/w
p.c.: National Theatre/BBC
pro.: Cedric Messina, Robert Stephens
(BBC)
dir.: Alan Cooke (BBC), Franco Zeffirelli
(NT)
Don Pedro, Derek Jacobi; Don John,
Ronald Pickup; Benedick, Robert Stephens;
Beatrice, Maggie Smith

Beaucoup de Bruit pour Rien
(USSR, 1973): Film, col., FL
dir.: Samson Samsonov

Beatrice, Galina Loguinova; Benedick, Konstantin Raikine

Much Ado About Nothing
(USA, 1974): TV, col.
p.c.: NY Shakespeare Festival Production, BBC
pro.: Joseph Papp
dir.: A. J. Antoon
des.: Donald Sadler
Benedick, Sam Waterston; Beatrice, Katherine Widdows; Don Pedro, Douglas Watson; Dogberry, Barnard Hughes; Hero, April Shawnham; Don John, Jerry Mayo
ARC: NFA
DHS: New York Shakespeare Festival, 16mm

Much Ado About Nothing
(GB/USA, 1978): TV, col.
p.c.: BBC/Time-Life TV
pro.: Cedric Messina
dir.: Donald McWhinnie
des.: Don Taylor
Don Pedro, Nigel Davenport; Don John, Ian Richardson; Claudio, Anthony Andrews; Hero, Ciaran Madden; Benedick, Michael York; Beatrice, Penelope Keith
DHS: BBC, 16mm, v.c.

Much Ado About Nothing
(GB/USA, 1984): TV, col.
p.c.: BBC/Time-Life TV
pro.: Shaun Sutton
dir.: Stuart Burge
des.: Jan Spoczynski
Don Pedro, Jon Finch; Don John, Vernon Dobtcheff; Hero, Katharine Levy; Benedick, Robert Lindsay; Beatrice, Cherie Lunghi
DHS: BBC, 16mm, v.c.

OTHELLO

Othello
(Germany, 1907): Film, b/w, sil.
pro.: Oskar Meszter
dir.: Franz Porten
Othello, Franz Porten; Desdemona, Henny Porten; Emilia, Rosa Porten

Otello
(Italy, 1907): Film, b/w, sil.
p.c.: Cines
dir.: Mario Caserini
Mario Caserini, Maria Gasperini, Ubaldo del Colle

Othello
(USA, 1908): Film, b/w, sil.
p.c.: Vitagraph
dir.: William V. Ranous
Othello, William V. Ranous; Desdemona, Julia Swayne-Gordon; Iago, Hector Dion; Cassio, Paul Panzer

Otello
(Italy, 1909): Film, b/w, sil.
p.c.: Film d'Arte/Italiana-Pathe
dir.: Gerolamo Lo Savio
Othello, Ferrucio Garavaglia; Desdemona, Vittoria Lepanto; Iago, Cesare Dondine

Otello
(Italy, 1914): Film, b/w, sil.
pro.: Arturo Ambrosio
dir.: Arrigo Frusta
Othello, Paslo Colaci; Desdemona, Lena Lenard; Iago, Ricardo Tolentino; Cassio, Ubaldo Stefani

Othello
(Germany, 1918): Film, b/w, sil.
p.c.: Max Mack-Film
dir.: Max Mack
Othello, Beni Montano; Desdemona, Ellen Korth; Rosa Valetti

Othello
(Germany, 1922): Film, b/w, sil.
p.c.: Worner Film
dir.: Dimitri Boukhoyietski
Othello, Emil Jannings; Desdemona, Ica de Lenkoffi; Iago, Werner Krauss
DHS: BFI, 16mm
ARC: NFA, 16mm

Othello
(GB, 1946): Film, b/w
p.c.: Marylebone Productions
dir.: David McKane
Othello, John Slater; Desdemona, Luanna Shaw; Iago, Sebastian Cabot; Emilia, Sheila Raynor

Othello
(GB, 1950): TV, b/w
p.c.: BBC
pro.: George More O'Ferrall
dir.: Kevin Sheldon
Othello, André Morell; Emilia, Margaretta Scott; Iago, Stephen Murray; Desdemona, Joan Hopkins; Cassio, Laurence Harvey; Roderigo, Alan Wheatley; Brabantio, Frank Birch

Othello
(Morocco/USA, 1952): Film, b/w
p.c.: Mogador-Films (Mercury)
pro./dir.: Orson Welles
des.: Alexander Trainer, Luigi Schiaccianoce, Maria de Matteis
Othello, Orson Welles; Iago, Micheál MacLiammóir; Desdemona, Suzanne Cloutier; Cassio, Michael Lawrence
DHS: BFI, 16mm
ARC: FSL (USA), 35mm; NFA, 35mm

Othello
(Canada, 1953): TV, b/w
p.c.: CBC
dir.: David Green
des.: Nicolai Soloviov
Othello, Lorne Greene; Desdemona, Peggi Loder; Iago, Joseph Furst; Cassio, Patrick McNee; Emilia, Katherine Black; Roderigo, Richard Easton
ARC: Canadian Broadcasting Company

Othello
(GB, 1955): TV, b/w
p.c.: BBC
pro./dir.: Tony Richardson
des.: Reece Pemberton
Othello, Gordon Heath; Iago, Paul Rogers; Desdemona, Rosemary Harris; Emilia, Daphne Anderson
ARC: BBC, 35mm

Otello
(USSR, 1955): Film, col., FL, dubbed
p.c.: Mosfilm
dir.: Sergei Yutkevitch
des.: A. Vaisfeld, V. Dorrer, M. Karyakin, O. Kroutchinia, N. Tchikirev
Othello, Sergei Bondarchuk; Iago, Andrei Popov; Desdemona, Irina Skobtseva; Cas-sio, Vladimir Soshalsky. English voices: Othello, Howard Marion Crawford; Iago, Arnold Diamond; Desdemona, Katherine Byron; Cassio, Patrick Westwood
ARC: FSL (USA), 35mm

Othello
(France, 1962): Video, b/w
dir.: Claude Barma
des.: Maurice Jarre
Desdemona, Francine Berge; Othello, Daniel Sorano; Iago, Jean Topart
ARC: La Videotèque 'Arts du Spectacle', Avignon

Othello
(GB, 1965): Film, col.
p.c.: National Theatre/ABHE
pro.: Anthony Havelock-Allen, John Brabourne
dir.: Stuart Burge
Othello, Laurence Olivier; Iago, Frank Finlay; Desdemona, Maggie Smith; Cassio, Derek Jacobi
DHS: HF, 16mm; IPC, v.c.
ARC: FSL (USA), 35mm

Othello
(USA, 1979): Video, col.
p.c.: New York Shakespeare Festival
dir.: Joseph Papp
Iago, Richard Dreyfuss; Othello, Raul Julia; Desdemona, Frances Conroy
ARC: Lincoln Center Library of the Performing Arts

Othello
(USA, 1980): Film, col.
pro.: Liz White
dir.: Liz White
Othello, Yaphet Kotto; Iago, Richard Dixon; Desdemona, Audrey Dixon; Cassio, Louis Chisholm
ARC/DHS: Cultural Committee, Howard University, Washington DC

Othello
(GB/USA, 1981): TV, col.
p.c.: BBC/Time-Life TV
pro./dir.: Jonathan Miller
des.: Colin Lowrey
Othello, Anthony Hopkins; Iago, Bob Hos-

kins; Desdemona, Penelope Wilton; Emilia, Rosemary Leach
DHS: BBC, 16mm, v.c.

Othello
(USA, 1981): v.c., col.
p.c.: Bard Productions Ltd
pro.: Jack Nakano
dir.: Franklin Melton
des.: John Retsek
Othello, William Marshall; Desdemona, Jenny Agutter; Iago, Ron Moody; Emilia, Leslie Paxton
DHS: Encyclopedia Britannica, v.c. VHS/BMX

Othello
(USA, 1985): Video, col.
p.c.: Bard Productions
pro.: Jack Manning
dir.: Franklin Melton
Othello, William Marshall; Iago, Ron Moody; Desdemona, Jenny Agutter
ARC/DHS: Bard Productions Ltd. (University of Illinois)

PERICLES, PRINCE OF TYRE

Pericles, Prince of Tyre
(GB, USA, 1983): TV, col.
p.c.: BBC/Time–Life TV
pro.: Shaun Sutton
dir.: David Jones
des.: Don Taylor
Gower, Edward Petherbridge; Antiochus, John Woodvine; Pericles, Mike Gwilym; Marina, Amanda Redman
DHS: BBC, 16mm, v.c.

RICHARD II

Richard II
(GB, 1950): TV, b/w
p.c.: BBC
pro./dir.: Royston Morley/Graham Muir
dir.: Royston Morley
Richard II, Alan Wheatley; Bolingbroke, Clement McCallin; Gaunt, Henry Oscar; York, Arthur Wontner; Queen, Joy Shelton; Mowbray, Leonard Sachs

Richard II
(USA, 1954): Film, b/w
p.c.: Hallmark Hall of Fame/NBC
dir.: Maurice Evans
Richard II, Maurice Evans; Sarah Churchill

An Age of Kings: Part 1, 'The Hollow Crown', Part 2, 'The Deposing of a King'
(GB, 1960): TV, b/w
p.c.: BBC
pro.: Peter Dews
dir.: Michael Hayes
des.: Stanley Morris
Richard II, David William; Bolingbroke, Tom Fleming; John of Gaunt, Edgar Wreford; York, Geoffrey Bayldon
ARC: BBC, 16mm (two parts)

The Tragedy of King Richard II
(GB, 1970): TV, col.
p.c.: BBC/Prospect Theatre Co.
pro.: Mark Shivas
dir.: Richard Cottrell
des.: Tony Abbot
Richard II, Ian McKellen; Bolingbroke, Timothy West; John of Gaunt, Paul Hardwick; Isabella, Lucy Fleming

Richard II
(GB/USA, 1978): TV, col.
p.c.: BBC/Time–Life TV
pro.: Cedric Messina
dir.: David Giles
des.: Tony Abbott
Richard II, Derek Jacobi; John of Gaunt, John Gielgud; Bolingbroke, Jon Finch; York, Charles Gray
DHS: BBC, 16mm, v.c.

Richard II
(USA, 1982): Video, col.
p.c.: Bard Productions
pro.: Jack Nakano/Jack Manning
dir.: William Woodman
Richard II, David Burney; Bolingbroke, Paul Shenar; York, Peter Mclean; Anne, Mary-Joan Negro
DHS: Bard Productions Ltd (University of Illinois)

Richard II
(USA, 1986): Video, col.
p.c.: Old Globe Theatre, San Diego

dir.: Joseph Hardy
ARC: Lincoln Center Library of the Performing Arts

RICHARD III

Richard III
(USA, 1908): Film, b/w, sil.
p.c.: Vitagraph
dir.: William V. Ranous
Richard III, William V. Ranous; Thomas H. Ince, Florence Turner, Julia Swayne-Gordon

Richard III
(GB, 1911): Film, b/w, sil.
p.c.: Co-operative Cinematograph
dir.: Frank R. Benson
Richard III, Frank R. Benson; Moffat Johnston, Constance Benson
ARC: NFA, 35mm

The Life and Death of King Richard III
(USA, 1913); Film, b/w, sil.
p.c.: Sterling
dir.: M. B. Dudley
Richard III, Frederick B. Warde

Richard III
(Germany, 1919): Film, b/w, sil.
dir.: Max Reinhardt
Conrad Veidt and the Reinhardt Co.

Richard III
(GB, 1955): Film, col.
p.c.: London Films
pro.: Laurence Olivier, Alexander Korda
dir.: Laurence Olivier
des.: Roger Furse, Carmen Dillon
Richard III, Laurence Olivier; Buckingham, Ralph Richardson; Clarence, John Gielgud; Lady Anne, Claire Bloom
DHS: RFL, 16mm
ARC: FSL (USA), 35mm

An Age of Kings: Part 14, 'The Dangerous Brother', Part 15, 'The Boar Hunt'
(GB, 1960): TV, b/w
p.c.: BBC
pro.: Peter Dews
dir.: Michael Hayes
des.: Stanley Morris

Richard III, Paul Daneman; Clarence, Patrick Garland; Lady Anne, Jill Dixon; Henry VI, Terry Scully; Buckingham, Edgar Wreford; Margaret, Mary Morris; Henry Tudor, Jerome Willis
ARC: BBC, 16mm

The Wars of the Roses: Part 3 'Richard III'
(GB, 1964): TV, b/w
p.c.: RSC/BBC
pro.: Michael Barry (BBC)
dir.: Peter Hall, John Barton (RSC), Robin Midgley, Michael Hayes (BBC)
des.: John Bury
Richard III, Ian Holm; Margaret, Peggy Ashcroft; Lady Anne, Janet Suzman; Edward IV, Roy Dotrice; Clarence, Charles Kay; Richmond, Eric Porter
ARC: BBC, 35mm

Richard III
(USSR, 1980): Video, col., FL
pro.: Robert Strurua
des.: Mikhail Shveldese
Richard III, Ramaz Chkhikvadze; Buckingham, Giorgi Gegechkovi; Elizabeth, Salome Kancheli
DHS: Rustaveli Theatre, Georgia

Richard III
(GB/USA, 1983)
p.c.: BBC/Time-Life TV
pro.: Shaun Sutton
dir.: Jane Howell
des.: Oliver Bayldon
Richard III, Ron Cook; Edward IV, Brian Protheroe; Buckingham, Michael Byrne; Lady Anne, Zoë Wanamaker; Margaret, Julia Foster
DHS: BBC, v.c.

ROMEO AND JULIET

Romeo and Juliet
(France, 1900): Film, b/w, sil.
dir.: Clement Maurice
Romeo, Emilio Cossira

Romeo and Juliet
(USA, 1908): Film, b/w, sil.
p.c.: Vitagraph

dir.: William V. Ranous
Romeo, Paul Panzer; Juliet, Florence Lawrence; Tybalt, John G. Adolfi; Capulet, Charles Kent; Montague, Charles Chapman; Friar Lawrence, William V. Ranous

Romeo e Giulietta
(Italy, 1908): Film, b/w, sil.
p.c.: Cines
dir.: Mario Caserini
Romeo, Mario Caserini; Juliet, Maria Gasperini

Romeo and Juliet
(GB, 1908)Film, b/w, sil.
p.c.: Gaumont
Romeo, Godfrey Tearle; Juliet, Mary Malone; Tybalt, J. Annard; Mercutio, Gordon Bailey

Romeo and Juliet
(USA, 1911): Film, b/w, sil.
p.c.: Thanhouser
dir.: Barry O'Neill
Romeo, George A. Lessey; Juliet, Julia M. Taylor

Giulietta e Romeo
(Italy, 1911): Film, b/w, sil.
p.c.: Film d'Arte/Italiana-Pathe
dir.: Gerolamo Lo Savio
Romeo, Gustav Serena; Juliet, Francesca Bertini; Ferrucio Garavaglia

Roméo et Juliette
(France, 1914): Film, b/w, sil.
p.c.: Société Cinématographique des Auteurs et Gens de Lettres

Romeo and Juliet
(USA, 1916): Film, b/w, sil.
p.c.: Metro Pictures
dir.: John W. Noble, Francis X. Bushman
Romeo, Francis X. Bushman; Juliet Beverly Bayne; Tybalt, W. Lawson Butt; Friar Lawrence, Robert Cummings

Romeo and Juliet
(USA, 1916): Film, b/w, sil.
p.c.: Fox Film
dir.: J. Gordon Edwards
Juliet, Theda Bara; Romeo, Harry Hilliard; Tybalt, John Webb Dillon; Mercutio, Glen White

Romeo and Juliet
(USA, 1936): Film, b/w
p.c.: MGM
pro.: Irving G. Thalberg
dir.: George Cukor
des.: Cedric Gibbons
Romeo, Leslie Howard; Juliet, Norma Shearer; Mercutio, John Barrymore; Nurse, Edna May Oliver; Friar Lawrence, Henry Kolker
ARC: FSL (USA), 35mm; NFA, 35mm

Julieta y Romeo
(Spain, 1940): Film, b/w, FL
p.c.: Cinedia
dir.: Jose Marie Castellvi
Marta Flores, Enrique Guitart

Shuhaddaa El Gharam
(Egypt, 1942): Film, b/w, FL
p.c.: Les Films el Nil
dir.: Kamal Selim
Leila Mourad, Ibrahim Hamouda

Romeo and Juliet
(GB, 1947): TV, b/w
p.c.: BBC
pro./dir.: Michael Barry
Romeo, John Bailey; Juliet, Rosalie Crutchley; Nurse, Agnes Lauchlan; Tybalt, Michael Goodliffe

Anjuman
(India, 1948): Film, b/w, FL
p.c.: Nargis Art Concern
pro./dir.: Akhtar Hussein
Juliet, Nargis; Romeo, Jaraj; Durga Khole, Raj Rani

Romeo and Juliet
(Italy/GB, 1954): Film, col.
p.c.: Universal-Cine-Verona
pro.: Sandro Ghenzi, Joseph Janni
dir.: Renato Castellani
des.: Leonor Fini
Romeo, Laurence Harvey; Juliet, Susan Shentall; Nurse, Flora Robson; Mercutio, Aldo Zollo; Friar Lawrence, Mervyn Johns
DHS: RFL, 16mm
ARC: FSL (USA) 35mm

Romeo and Juliet
(GB, 1955): TV, b/w
p.c.: BBC

43

pro./dir.: Harold Clayton
des.: Roy Oxlen
Romeo, Tony Britton; Juliet, Virginia
McKenna; Nurse, Flora Robson
ARC: BBC, 35mm

Giulietta e Romeo
(Italy/Spain, 1964): Film, col. FL, dubbed
p.c.: Imprecine/Hispaner Film
dir.: Riccardo Freda
des.: Piero Filipponi
Romeo, Geronimo Meynier; Juliet, Rose-
marie Dexter; Mercutio, Carlos Estrada;
Friar Lawrence, Umberto Raho; Nurse,
Toni Soler
ARC: FSL (USA), 35mm

Romeo and Juliet
(GB, 1965): Film, b/w
p.c.: RADA/Regent Street Polytechnic
pro.: Paul Emerson, John Fernald
dir.: Val Drum, Paul Lee
Romeo, Clive Francis; Juliet, Angela
Scoular
ARC: Royal Academy of Dramatic Art,
16mm

Romeo and Juliet
(GB, 1967): TV, b/w
p.c.: BBC
pro.: Cedric Messina
dir.: Alan Cooke
des.: Eileen Diss
Romeo, Hywel Bennett; Juliet, Kika Markham; Nurse, Thora Hird
ARC: BBC, 35mm

Romeo and Juliet
(Italy/GB, 1968): Film, col.
p.c.: Verona Productions/Cinematografia/
Dino Di Laurentis
pro.: Anthony Havelock-Allen, John
Brabourne
dir.: Franco Zeffirelli
des.: Renzo Mongiardino, Danilo Donati
Romeo, Leonard Whiting; Juliet, Olivia
Hussey; Friar Lawrence, Milo O'Shea;
Nurse, Pat Heywood; Mercutio, John
McEnery; Tybalt, Michael York
DHS: RFL, 16mm
ARC: FSL (USA), 35mm

Romeo and Juliet
(GB, 1976): TV, col.
p.c.: Thames TV (schools production)
pro.: Francis Coleman
dir.: Joan Kemp-Welch
des.: Fred Pusey/Martin Baugh
Romeo, Christopher Neame; Juliet, Ann
Hasson; Capulet, Laurence Payne; Nurse,
Patsy Byrne; Friar Lawrence, Clive Swift
ARC: TTV

Romeo and Juliet
(GB, 1977): TV, col.
p.c.: Television and Educational Classics Ltd
pro.: Paul Bosner
dir.: Paul Bosner, George Murcell
des.: John Wood
Juliet, Sarah Badel; Romeo, Peter McEnery;
Friar Lawrence, Joseph O'Connor; Nurse,
Elvi Hale
ARC: FSL

Romeo and Juliet
(GB/USA, 1978): TV, col.
p.c.: BBC/Time-Life TV
pro.: Cedric Messina
dir.: Alvin Rakoff
des.: Stuart Walker
Chorus, John Gielgud; Romeo, Patrick
Ryecart; Juliet, Rebecca Saire; Mercutio,
Anthony Andrews; Nurse, Celia Johnson
DHS: BBC, 16mm, v.c.

THE TAMING OF THE SHREW

La Bisbetica Domata
(Italy, 1908): Film, b/w, sil.
p.c.: Società Italiana Fratelli Pineschi
dir.: Lamberto and Azeglio Pineschi

The Taming of the Shrew
(USA, 1908): Film, b/w, sil.
p.c.: American Mutoscope, Biograph Co.
dir.: D. W. Griffith
Katherina, Florence Lawrence; Petruchio,
Arthur Johnson; Charles Molee, Linda
Arridson

The Taming of the Shrew
(GB, 1911): Film, b/w, sil.
p.c.: Shakespeare Memorial Theatre Co.

dir.: F. R. Benson
F. R. Benson, SMT Co

La Mégère Apprivoisée
(France, 1911): Film, b/w, sil.
p.c.: Eclipse
dir.: Henri Desfontaines
Cécile Didier, Romuald Joube, Dinis d'Ines

La Bisbetica Domata
(Italy, 1913): Film, b/w, sil.
p.c.: Ambrosio Films
pro.: Arturo Ambrosio
dir.: Arrigo Frusta
Petruchio, Eleuterio Rodolfi; Katherina, Gigotta Morano

The Taming of the Shrew
(GB, 1923): Film, b/w, sil.
p.c.: British and Colonial
dir.: Edwin J. Collins
Petruchio, Landerdale Maitland; Katherina, Mlle Dacia: Bianca, Cynthia Murtagh

The Taming of the Shrew
(USA, 1929): Film, b/w (re-issued 1966, Cinema Classics)
p.c.: Pickford/Elton Corporation
pro.: Matty Kemp (1966)
dir.: Sam Taylor
des.: William Cameron Menzies, Laurence Irving
Petruchio, Douglas Fairbanks; Katherina, Mary Pickford; Baptista, Edwin Maxwell
DHS: BC, 16mm

The Taming of the Shrew
(GB, 1939): TV, b/w
p.c.: BBC
dir.: Dallas Bower
Petruchio, Austin Trevor; Katherina, Margaretta Scott

La Bisbetica Domata
(Italy, 1942): Film, b/w, FL
p.c.: Excelsa Film
dir.: Ferdinando Poggioli
Lilia Silvi, Amadeo Nazzari, Carlo Romano

The Taming of the Shrew
(GB, 1952): TV, b/w
p.c.: BBC
pro./dir.: Desmond Davies

des.: Barry Learoyd
Petruchio, Stanley Baker; Katherina, Margaret Johnston; Baptista, Ernest Jay; Bianca, Sheila Shand-Gibbs

La Mégère Apprivoisée/La Fierecilla Domada
(France/Spain, 1955): Film, col., FL
p.c.: Vascos-Interproduction (Paris), Bonito Perojo (Madrid)
dir.: Antonio Roman
Carmen Serilla, Alberto Closas

The Taming of the Shrew
(USA, 1956): TV, col.
p.c.: Hallmark Hall of Fame
pro.: Maurice Evans/Joseph Cunneff
dir.: George Schaefer/Robert Hartung/ Adrienne Luraschi
Petruchio, Maurice Evans; Katherina, Lilli Palmer

Ukroshchenie Stroptivoi
(USSR, 1961): Film, b/w, FL
p.c.: Mosfilm
dir.: Sergei Kolosov
des.: N. Shyfrin, V. Golikov
Katherina, Ludmila Kasatkina; Petruchio, Andrei Popov

The Taming of the Shrew
(USA/Italy, 1966): Film, col.
p.c.: Royal Films International/FAI
pro.: Elizabeth Taylor, Richard Burton, Franco Zeffirelli
dir.: Franco Zeffirelli
des.: John de Cuir
Petruchio, Richard Burton; Katherina, Elizabeth Taylor; Bianca, Natasha Pyne; Baptista, Michael Hordern
DHS: CEMIW, 16mm
ARC: FSL (USA), 35mm

The Taming of the Shrew
(USA, 1976): TV, col.
p.c.: American Conservatory Group, San Francisco
pro.: Ken Campbell/Charlene Harrington
dir.: William Bell/Kirk Browning
Petruchio, Marc Singer; Katherina, Fredi Olster
ARC: Museum of Broadcasting, New York

The Taming of the Shrew
(GB/USA, 1980): TV, col.
p.c.: BBC/Time-Life TV
pro./dir.: Jonathan Miller
des.: Colin Lowrey
Petruchio, John Cleese; Katherina, Sarah
Badel; Bianca, Susan Penhaligon
DHS: BBC, 16mm, v.c.

THE TEMPEST

The Tempest
(USA, 1911): Film, b/w, sil.
p.c.: Thanhouser
pro./dir.: Edwin Thanhouser

La Tempête
(France, 1912): Film, b/w, sil.
p.c.: Eclair

The Tempest
(GB, 1939): TV, b/w
p.c.: BBC
pro./dir.: Dallas Bower
des.: Malcolm Baker-Smith
Prospero, John Abbot; Miranda, Peggy
Ashcroft; Ariel, Stephen Haggard; Caliban,
George Devine; Ferdinand, Richard Ainley

The Tempest
(GB, 1956): TV, b/w
p.c.: BBC
pro./dir.: Ian Atkins, Robert Atkins
des.: Barry Learoyd
Prospero, Robert Eddison; Miranda, Anna
Barry; Caliban, Robert Atkins; Ariel, Patti
Brooks; Ferdinand, Bernard Brown
ARC: BBC, 35mm; NFA, 35mm

The Tempest
(USA, 1960): Film, col.
p.c.: Hallmark Hall of Fame/NBC
dir.: George Schaefer
Prospero, Maurice Evans; Miranda, Lee
Remick; Caliban, Richard Burton; Ferdinand, Roddy McDowall

The Tempest
(GB, 1968): TV, b/w
p.c.: BBC
pro.: Cedric Messina

dir.: Basil Coleman
des.: Tony Abbott
Prospero, Michael Redgrave; Miranda,
Tessa Wyatt; Caliban, Keith Michell; Ariel,
Ronald Pickup; Ferdinand, Jonathan Dennis

The Tempest
(USA, 1980): Video, col.
p.c.: Berkeley Shakespeare Festival
dir.: Audrey E. Stanley
des.: Gene Angell, Ron Pratt
Ariel, Jane Macfie; Caliban, Peter Fitzsim-
mons; Prospero, Julian Lopez-Morillas
ARC: Lincoln Center Library of the Performing Arts

The Tempest
(GB, 1980): Film, col.
p.c.: Boyd's Company
pro.: Guy Ford, Mordecai Shreiber
dir.: Derek Jarman
des.: Yolanda Sonnabend
Prospero, Heathcote Williams; Miranda,
Toyah Wilcox; Ferdinand, David Meyer;
Caliban, Jack Birkett; Ariel, Karl Johnson
DHS: HF, 16mm, v.c.; AVP, v.c.

The Tempest
(GB/USA, 1980): TV, col.
p.c.: BBC/Time-Life TV
pro.: Cedric Messina
dir.: John Gorrie
des.: Paul Joel
Prospero, Michael Hordern; Miranda,
Pippa Guard; Caliban, Warren Clarke
DHS: BBC, 16mm, v.c.

The Tempest
(USA, 1983): v.c. col.
p.c.: Bard Productions Ltd
pro.: Ken Campbell
dir.: William Woodman
des.: Donald L. Harris
Prospero, Efrem Zimbalist, Jr.; Miranda,
J. E. Taylor; Caliban, William Hootkins;
Ariel, Duane Black; Ferdinand, Nicholas
Hammond
DHS: Encyclopedia Britannica, v.c.
VHS/BMX

The Tempest
(USA, 1986): Video, col.

p.c.: Theatre for a New Audience, New York
dir.: Julie Taymor
ARC: Lincoln Center Library of the Performing Arts

TIMON OF ATHENS

Timon of Athens
(GB/USA, 1981): TV, col.
p.c.: BBC/Time-Life TV
pro./dir.: Jonathan Miller
des.: Tony Abbott
Timon, Jonathan Pryce; Alcibiades, John Shrapnel; Flavius, John Welsh
DHS: BBC, 16mm., v.c.

TITUS ANDRONICUS

Titus Andronicus
(GB/USA, 1985): TV, col.
p.c.: BBC/Time-Life TV
pro.: Shaun Sutton
dir.: Jane Howell
des.: Tony Burrough
Titus, Trevor Peacock; Lavinia, Anna Calder-Marshall; Tamora, Eileen Atkins; Aaron, Hugh Quarshie
DHS: BBC, 16mm, v.c.

Titus Andronicus
(USA, 1986): Video, col.
p.c.: Oregon Shakespeare Festival
dir.: Pat Patton
ARC: Lincoln Center Library of the Performing Arts

TROILUS AND CRESSIDA

Troilus and Cressida
(GB, 1954): TV, b/w
p.c.: BBC
pro.: Douglas Allen
dir.: George Rylands
des.: Michael Yates
Troilus, John Fraser; Cressida, Mary Watson; Hector, William Squire; Paris, Simon Lack; Pandarus, Frank Pettingell; Achilles, Geoffrey Toone; Thersites, Richard Wordsworth

Troilus and Cressida
(GB, 1966): TV, b/w
p.c.: National Youth Theatre/BBC
pro.: Michael Bakewell (BBC)
dir.: Paul Hill, Michael Croft (NYT); Bernard Hepton (BBC)
des.: John Buglir
Troilus, Andrew Murray; Cressida, Charlotte Womersley; Hector, Timothy Block; Achilles, Dennis Marks; Ulysses, Derek Seaton; Helen, Mary Payne; Pandarus, David Stockton
ARC: BBC, 16mm

Troilus and Cressida
(GB/USA): TV, col.
p.c.: BBC/Time-Life TV
pro./dir.: Jonathan Miller
Troilus, Anton Lesser; Cressida, Suzanne Burden; Pandarus, Charles Gray; Achilles, Kenneth Haigh; Ulysses, Benjamin Whitrow; Helen, Ann Pennington; Thersites, Jack Birkett
DHS: BBC, 16mm, v.c.

TWELFTH NIGHT

Twelfth Night
(USA, 1910): Film, b/w, sil.
p.c.: Vitagraph
pro./dir.: Edwin Thanhouser
Julia Swayne-Gordon, Florence Turner

Twelfth Night
(GB, 1939): TV, b/w
p.c.: BBC
pro.: Bronson Albery
dir.: Michel St Denis
Michael Redgrave, Peggy Ashcroft, Esmond Knight, George Hayes, George Devine, Vera Lindsay, Lucille Lisle

Twelfth Night
(GB, 1950): TV, b/w
p.c.: BBC
pro.: Robert Atkins
dir.: Harold Clayton

des.: Barry Learoyd
Orsino, Terence Morgan; Viola, Barbara
Lott; Olivia, Patricia Neale; Malvolio,
Geoffrey Dunn; Feste, John Gatrell

Dvenadtsataia Noch
(USSR, 1955): Film, col., FL
p.c.: Lenfilm
dir.: Jan Fried
des.: S. Malkin
Viola/Sebastian, Katya Luchiko; Olivia,
Anna Lavianova; Sir Toby, M. Yanshim;
Malvolio, V. Morkuriev; Feste, B.
Friendlich
ARC: FSL (USA), 35mm

Twelfth Night
(GB, 1957): TV, b/w
p.c.: BBC
pro.: Michael Elliott
dir.: Caspar Wrede
des.: Stephen Taylor
Orsino, Robert Hardy; Viola, Dilys Ham-
lett; Olivia, Maureen Quinney; Malvolio,
John Moffatt; Feste, James Maxwell

Twelfth Night
(USA, 1957): TV, b/w
p.c.: Hallmark Hall of Fame
pro.: Robert Hartnung
dir.: David Green
Malvolio, Maurice Evans; Viola, Rosemary
Harris; Sir Toby Belch, Dennis King; Sebas-
tian, Denholm Elliot; Aguecheek, Max
Adrian; Olivia, Frances Hyland; Feste,
Howard Morris
ARC: Museum of Broadcasting, New York

Twelfth Night (Was Ihr Wollt)
(FDR, 1962): Film, b/w, FL
p.c.: Bavaria Atelier GmbH
dir.: Franz Peter Wirth
des.: Walter Blokesch
Orsino, Karl Michael Vogler; Viola/Sebas-
tian, Ingrid Andree; Karl Block, Fritz
Wepper

Twelfth Night (Was Ihr Wollt)
(DDR, 1963): TV, b/w, FL
p.c.: DEFA-Studio für Spielfilme (for
Deutscher Fernsehfunk)
dir.: Lothar Bellag

des.: Alfred Tolle
Gerry Wolff, Christel Bodenstein, Johanna
Clas

Twelfth Night
(GB, 1969): TV, col.
p.c.: ITC
pro.: John Dexter, Cecil Clarke
dir.: John Sichel
Malvolio, Alec Guinness; Sir Toby, Ralph
Richardson; Viola/Sebastian, Joan Plowright; Feste, Tommy Steele

Twelfth Night
(GB/USA, 1980): TV, col.
p.c.: BBC/Time-Life TV
pro.: Cedric Messina
dir.: John Gorrie
des.: Don Taylor
Orsino, Clive Arindell; Viola, Felicity Ken-
dal; Olivia, Sinead Cusack; Sir Toby,
Robert Hardy
DHS: BBC, 16mm, v.c.

Twelfth Night
(GB, 1988): Video, col.
p.c.: Renaissance Theatre Company
pro.: Paul Kafno
dir.: Kenneth Branagh
Feste, Anton Lesser; Malvolio, Richard
Briers; Olivia, Caroline Langrishe; Orsino,
Christopher Ravenscroft; Sir Toby Belch,
James Saxon; Viola, Frances Barber

THE TWO GENTLEMEN OF VERONA

Zwei Herren Aus Verona
(FDR, 1963): Film, b/w, FL
p.c.: Bavaria Atelier GmbH
dir.: Hans Dieter Schwarze
des.: Walter Blokesch
Hans Karl Friedrich, Norbert Hansing, Rolf
Becker

The Two Gentlemen of Verona
(GB/USA, 1983): TV, col.
p.c.: BBC/Time-Life TV
pro.: Shaun Sutton
dir.: Don Taylor
des.: Barbara Gosnold

Duke, Paul Daneman; Valentine, John Hudson; Proteus, Tyler Butterworth; Julia, Tessa Peake-Jones: Silvia, Joanne Pearce
DHS: BBC, 16mm, v.c.

THE WINTER'S TALE

The Winter's Tale
(USA, 1910): Film, b/w, sil.
p.c.: Thanhouser
pro./dir.: Barry O'Neill
Leontes, Martin Faust; Hermione, Ms Rosemund; Polixenes, Frank Crane

Tragedia alla Corte di Sicilia
(Italy, 1914): Film, b/w, sil.
p.c.: Milano
pro.: L. Sutto
dir.: Baldessare Negroni
Leontes, V. Cocchi; Pina Fabbri
ARC: NFA, 35mm

Das Wintermärchen
(Germany, 1914): Film, b/w, sil.
p.c.: Belle Alliance
Senta Soneland, Albert Paulig, Richard Sonius

The Winter's Tale
(GB, 1962): TV, b/w
p.c.: BBC
dir.: Don Taylor
des.: Marilyn Taylor
Leontes, Robert Shaw; Hermione, Rosalie Crutchley; Florizel, Brian Smith; Perdita, Sarah Badel
ARC: BBC, 16mm

The Winter's Tale
(GB, 1966): Film, col.
p.c.: Cressida/Hurst Park
pro.: Peter Snell
dir.: Frank Dunlop
des.: Carl Toms
Leontes, Laurence Harvey; Hermione, Moira Redmond; Perdita, Jane Asher; Paulina, Diana Churchill

The Winter's Tale
(GB/USA, 1980): TV, col.
p.c.: BBC/Time-Life TV
pro.: Jonathan Miller
dir.: Jane Howell
des.: Don Homfray
Leontes, Jeremy Kemp; Hermione, Anna Calder-Marshall; Polixenes, Robert Stephens
DHS: BBC, 16mm, v.c.

3

TWO-DIMENSIONAL SHAKESPEARE: 'KING LEAR' ON FILM

PETER HOLLAND

One of the most difficult problems for studying filmed Shakespeare has been finding a taxonomy, a means of organizing and categorizing the differences between the films, a means of distinguishing between the enormous variety of work they constitute in ways that illuminate their forms as films.[1] For the recognition of their specificity as films has most often seemed undervalued since, quite reasonably, the primary concern of most scholars has unquestionably been the films' connections to the original theatre text. The films have risked being seen as effectively indistinguishable from theatre productions, versions to be analysed in the same terms as if the flat screen's two-dimensionality is the same space as the stage's three dimensions. Occasionally, in some recent work, the films have been disconnected from Shakespeare to the extent that the director becomes author or, in the language of traditional film criticism, *auteur*, his/her biography the source of the nature of the film which is redefined as the dominant text for which the Shakespeare play is merely screenplay.[2]

In 1977 Jack Jorgens offered three categories into which Shakespeare films can usefully be divided, categories which mark different and increasing distances from the forms of theatre and, though there has been a positive flood of studies of Shakespeare on film since then, no subsequent writer seems to have been concerned to offer an alternative taxonomic system.[3] He suggested three modes: theatrical, realist and filmic. I want to use and to some extent reformulate his categories to provide a background scheme for looking at four film versions of *King Lear*.

The *theatrical* mode has as its model the camera's record of a theatrical performance, the camera as the eye of the theatre audience. Such films have, Jorgens suggests, 'the look and feel of a performance worked out for a static theatrical space and a live audience' (p. 7). The acting style in such films is essentially that of the theatre, not of film: gestures, for instance, are large and demonstrative, highly theatrical and, when transferred to a cinema screen, somewhat bombastic and excessive. Often such films are direct records of theatre successes, translated quickly and easily to film but without being rethought and reinvented for the different demands of film.

The sets in such films are often the stage sets transferred to the film studio, betraying in their style, design and set construction, their theatrical origins. The opening of Kenneth Branagh's film of *Henry V* (1989), with the Chorus (Derek Jacobi) wandering around and literally illuminating a film studio, by switching the lights on to reveal the debris of the sets, is explicitly designed as a commentary on this transposition, redefining the materials of the film, its sets and costumes, out of which the film will be constructed, alerting us directly to the fact of filming, as the Chorus's own language alerts the theatre audience to the fact of theatrical performance. Indeed, what is surprising and clichéd in Branagh's treatment of Chorus is the subsequent integration of the player into the play's fictive space, so that Jacobi becomes muddy and wet outside Harfleur, precisely the denial of theatrical separation that the treatment of the opening Chorus so well achieves.

The costumes of these 'theatrical' films have often been designed to look right under theatre lights rather than the greater subtleties of film lighting. Everything can appear coarse and badly made when, instead of being viewed from a seat in the stalls, it is revealed in the unyielding, harsh and unforgiving scrutiny of the camera in close-up.

For this reason perhaps, but also because the performances have been conceived in this way, such films are usually made up of very long takes, the camera's long breaths trying to match the sustained acting paragraphs of the theatre rather than the rapidity of shots and the brevity of editing normally used in the cinema. Camera positions in such films are usually medium and long shots rather than close-ups, mimicking as much as possible the position of the theatre audience with its independence and controlled selectivity of observation from its fixed point of view in the auditorium (its individual seat), rather than film's fascination with the detail of a face or a gesture; the style reflects and adopts the theatre's interests in groups of characters seen, now on screen, at once.

The theatrical film is a means of defeating the ephemerality, the horrifyingly temporary nature of the theatre. It marks a considered further stage beyond, say, the videotaping of theatrical performance from a fixed-position camera during an actual performance, a practice that the RSC has adopted for some years with the results deposited for viewing alongside its research collection at the Shakespeare Centre in Stratford-upon-Avon, marking the tapes as scholarly resource, not aimed at a consumer audience.

Yet the result of the theatrical film is often a travesty, an ambiguous creature like Mrs Quickly, neither fish nor flesh. It may be that distance has coloured my views but I still believe Laurence Olivier's stage performance as Othello (directed by John Dexter) is the best I have yet seen. But the film version (directed by Stuart Burge, 1965), which falls so strongly into this first category I am outlining, is intensely disappointing. Students to whom I have shown it are by turns horrified and amused by what they rightly see as its bombast, so magnificent in the theatre but so exaggerated on film. Olivier's voice which thrillingly filled the Old Vic Theatre seems only to rant when heard through a cinema sound-system. The transition of spaces is dependent not on the comparability of size of the auditoriums (theatre or cinema) but on the move to the constriction on the scale of performance permitted by the camera, with its much more intense predilection for the limited scope prescribed by cinematic naturalism.

Occasionally, and intriguingly, theatrical films work better when made for television, rather than the cinema. In 1989, for instance, Trevor Nunn directed a brilliant version of *Othello* for the Royal Shakespeare Company, first shown in The Other Place, their small theatre in Stratford. Nunn's *Othello* moved effortlessly from The Other Place to the television, its domesticity of scale and fascination with the social interaction of the characters in a social circumstance far more detailed, far more realist than the conventions of theatrical Shakespeare. The sustained close attention of the stage-version, conceived for small spaces in which the audience is, in theatrical terms, as close to the action as to a television screen, translated perfectly to television.

The audience's proximity is, in this example, a useful definition of the form of its relationship to the performance but the television has to cope with the essential isolation of the television audience, the absence in the living-room of the theatre audience's community of perception. The scale of Nunn's work fitted the television but it was thus played, in effect, hundreds of thousands of times, each time to an audience of, say, five or fewer. I would suggest that the cinema too reduces the audience's awareness of itself as group by comparison with the theatre; the structure of cinema auditoriums, the black-out necessary because of the projection and the forms of social behaviour at the cinema mean that we rarely have that awareness of participation, of being part of the whole audience that characterizes our experience of theatre. But this isolation is also a consequence of the unyielding nature of the object: film will not, cannot respond to its audience; it cannot allow differing extents for a laugh where theatre, especially the theatre of Shakespearian performance, cannot refuse to acknowledge the presence of the audience, structuring the specific time-scale and rhythm of the particular evening's performance as strongly as the actors themselves. Film and television are oddly isolating experiences. Nonetheless,

Nunn's *Othello* is much more than a record of a stage production; it is a perfect example of filming Shakespeare theatrically.

I have dwelt on this mode because it could so easily and disastrously have been the route Peter Brook took in deciding to film *King Lear* after the success of his stage production for the Royal Shakespeare Company in 1962. Brook's rapid decision to do much more than film a stage production meant that the film took eight years to make, finally appearing in 1971, a process I shall describe in some detail later.

Jorgens' second category is the *realist* film. Most films are realist, though this is not the place to try to explore very far what realism means in film terms. The editing and camera-work of such films usually makes use of the full range of established film techniques. Sequences are constructed conventionally out of establishing long-shots, with the camera then moving in closer to shoot dialogue in the normal sequence of shot and reverse. The rhythm of such films is thoroughly familiar to any regular cinema-goer, rarely drawing attention to itself, simply adopting and accepting the normal grammar of film.

What particularly marks realist film versions of Shakespeare is their design, their fascination with objects, with the things that make up the world of the plays, all those things that the theatre cannot show with the same solidity and in the same quantity but which marks a conventional view of the capabilities of the camera. Such films can show us landscapes and rooms, market-places and battles, processions and shipwrecks in ways that the theatre never can. Stage productions of *Romeo and Juliet* can rarely show life in Verona in the way that Zeffirelli did in his 1968 film, the exact and excited depiction of an imaginary Renaissance Italian reality bearing, of course, scant relation to the truth of history but with a verve and energy that was itself convincing.

At their best such films create a precisely imagined and powerful world in which the actors move, a carefully chosen, imaged and realized reality against which the action is played out. At times, of course, the background can take too much precedence over the foreground, the castles over the people in them, but at others it can create exactly the heightened and interpreted version of reality appropriate to the film's view of the play. In Grigori Kozintsev's *Hamlet* (1964), for instance, Elsinore is a massive castle of threatening battlements, gloomy turrets and oppressive doorways and drawbridges. Hamlet's sense of being trapped in Elsinore, that it, like Denmark, is a prison, is immediately proved true through the filmic language of symbolic place. But the film also proves true Kozintsev's perception of the true nature of Hamlet's imprisonment:

> The theatre sometimes takes too literally the words 'Denmark is a prison,' and proceeds to construct a set reminiscent of a dungeon. The tragedy is in something else. Court life is comfortable. The external trappings are beautiful. But for a person of ideas and feelings this can constitute a prison.[4]

1 *Henry V*, directed by Laurence Olivier: opening panorama showing the Globe Theatre

The dungeon of the opening sequences is a premise which the film treats as metaphor, transforming the opulent court into the prison of the mind. By contrast the castles of Polanski's *Macbeth* (1971) are too characterless, too unrelated to the mood of the play. Nothing in the architecture and atmosphere of Macbeth's castle in this film shows that the murder of King Duncan has turned it into a hell.

Yet cinematic realism is tightly bound-up with a traditional liberal–humanist ideology. It makes assumptions about the essential truth of the humanism of tragedy that many critics (and not only cultural materialists) might well want to argue against. It is striking that Grigori Kozintsev, writing of *King Lear* in his analysis of the process of making his own film (1970), itself a most humane and humanist representation of the play, describes the movement of the play from fiction into realism:

When the King thought that he was the one chosen among many, he was living not in a real world (which he did not know), but in a fictitious world (which he imagined to be reality). Leaving the boundary of the estate where Goneril and Regan now reigned, he went beyond the bounds of the fictitious (what he thought was true); and now he was walking in the world. The bolts had clanged shut by order of the new rulers. It was impossible to leave a world in which he had lived for eighty years; but there was already no turning back. Lear was pushed out not into a new life, but beyond the boundaries of life. There was not even a bush to shelter under. Even the wild animals had crawled into their dens. No one and nothing. The black hole of night. And this was reality. The reality of emptiness.[5]

This definition of the fictitious is also, for Kozintsev, a definition of theatricality:

The play begins with the theatrical – fine dress, pretence, props (the map, coats of arms) contrived speeches and assumed poses. The end of the play has stepped into the real world, on to the dirty blood-soaked earth. (p. 63)

The assumption of the unreality of the world of power makes the world of the heath consoling in its reality. The process is one Kozintsev sees as a stripping away of the social mask, the mask of power, to reveal the 'essential' self beneath.

Some film-makers recognize and avoid the dangers and temptations of the realist mode, seeing the strangeness of the conjunction of a realist world with Shakespeare's unreal language. Laurence Olivier described in interview how he considered setting his film of *Henry V* (1944) against real castles but realized that audiences would only observe the discrepancy between the castle's magnificence in its reality and the artifices and distances created by the language of the text. His choice of design, reproducing in film terms the flat two-dimensionality and false perspectives of medieval paintings like the *Books of Hours*, brilliantly found an analogy between the play's medievalism and the flatness of the film screen. Where Olivier's film opens with a combination of film realism with the representation of theatre in the film's scenes in the Globe Theatre, he keeps back the power of full cinematic realism when it is combined with the realism of performance for the climax of the film, the battle of Agincourt. Branagh's *Henry V*, through the energy of the acting, tries to evade this problem, the tensions of film realism, by using film music at climactic moments, finding the music as a means of justifying the rhetoric, or naturalizing it into a filmic form.

Olivier's decision to medievalize provides a link to the third of Jorgens' categories, the *filmic* mode, the mode, he suggests, 'of the film poet, whose works bear the same relation to the surfaces of reality that poems do to ordinary conversation' (p. 10). Branagh's *Henry V* is filmic in a different sense because the film defines itself in relation to Olivier's film, one film commenting on another. The most famous shot in Branagh's film, the long slow tracking shot across the battle-field of Agincourt after the battle, across the corpses and the survivors, as Henry walks across it with a dead boy in his arms, is a clear definition of the film's central attack on the values of war, a recognition of the cost of battle. But it is also a deliberate inversion of the most famous shot in Olivier's film, the long tracking shot of the charge of the French knights at the beginning of the battle. Olivier showed the exhilaration and medievalized fantasy of the French cavalry. Branagh shows the outcome of the charge. Olivier's knights ride accelerating into a gallop across the screen from right to left. Branagh's King *walks* at the same slow pace across the screen from left to right. The inversion is complete and strongly interdependent.

Filmic films of Jorgens's third type accept the peculiar intensity of the visual over the aural, of sight over sound, that is fundamental to the cinema. Kozintsev defines the problem:

> The problem is not one of finding means to speak the verse in front of the camera, in realistic circumstances ranging from long-shot to close-up. The aural has to be made visual. The poetic texture has itself to be transformed into a visual poetry, into the dynamic organisation of film imagery.[6]

At their worst such filmic films take Shakespeare's images and translate them directly onto the screen. There is a film of *Macbeth* in which, when Macbeth speaks of 'pity, like a naked new-born babe, / Striding the blast, or heaven's cherubin, horsed / Upon the sightless couriers of the air' (1.7.21–3), the film showed, through a window, a ghastly little cherub on a horse riding on the wind. Such literalism is disastrous, an extreme version of the apparently unavoidable temptation to represent Ophelia drowning rather than showing

Gertrude's narration. Instead there must be an imaginative recreation of the language of the play into the terms of the film.

At the same time the filmic mode uses all the resources of the cinema. It makes conscious use of what the *camera* can do, rather than what can be built on the studio sound-stage or found on location. It places its emphasis on montage and demands that we observe what it is doing, what is theatrically impossible and indeed, in some cases, filmically unusual. It finds analogies for the theatricality of Shakespeare's plays in the ways it draws attention to itself as film. In Orson Welles's film of *Othello* (1951), Welles filmed Othello in the senate scene of Act 1 against a different background from the other characters in the same scene so that the two worlds never quite match up and the audience cannot quite see Othello as being in the same room as the Venetian senate; the effect is to demonstrate the complete separation of Othello from the world of Venice.

Such films often make use of the traditions of film: Derek Jarman's brilliant screen version of *The Tempest* (1979), for instance, uses old documentary footage of men coping with sails on a sailing-ship during a storm rather than trying to create afresh the storm which Prospero summons up in the first scene.

The three categories that I have outlined, the theatrical, the realist and the filmic, chart different distances of the film from the theatre. Jorgens also suggests, helpfully, a second and related group of three categories, defining three ways of treating the text of a Shakespeare play, three degrees of distance from the original: presentation, interpretation and adaptation (p. 12).

There is one further category I would wish to add to Jorgens' three: a deconstruction of the text. Amongst film versions of *King Lear* this is represented by Jean-Luc Godard's version of 1988, a film made primarily to honour a contract with Cannon films. Godard's film foregrounds the possibility or rather near-impossibility of making the film at all, opening with the footage shot on the single day that Norman Mailer, originally cast as King Lear, spent on the set before flying back to America in a huff (a repeated intertitle describes the film as 'a picture shot in the back'). Godard juxtaposes the few fragments of the play that are included (with Burgess Meredith as a mafia Lear named Don Learo) with the search by William Shakespeare Jr the Fifth (played by the American theatre director Peter Sellars), to recover the text of his ancestor and an analysis of film by Professor Pluggy (Godard himself). *King Lear* is, in effect, enmeshed by its own appropriation (the work of directors like Sellars) and by the cultural place of Shakespeare as viewed by Godard. As often in late Godard, the potential brilliance of the deconstructive analysis is offset by the perfunctoriness of the film-making, magnified here by the problems with Cannon.[7]

Of course Jorgens' three categories are far from clear-cut but it would be easy to agree that Kurosawa's *Ran* (1985) is an adaptation of Shakespeare's play: the simple transposition of the three daughters of King Lear into the three sons of Lord Hidetora indicates as much, even without the sudden irruption of a Lady Macbeth narrative. Kurosawa does not use the love-test between the children and the notion of dividing the kingdom, altering the whole premise from which the action of Shakespeare's play springs. Instead, Hidetora hands over all power to his eldest son, Taro, making the younger sons, Jiro and Saburo, lords of the second and third castles but demanding from them assurances of fidelity to their brother. It is this notion of trust which Saburo mocks, the mockery leading to his disinheritance. Indeed Kurosawa's whole treatment of the action, the interweaving of the narrative about the Lady Kaede as if Lady Macbeth had suddenly appeared from another play, makes *Ran* a free variation on Shakespeare's text, derived from it but never restricted by it. For this reason, intriguingly, it is a film much disliked by Japanese academics whose culture prizes a notion of fidelity and authenticity in Shakespeare production, even in the wake of the stage productions of Ninagawa.[8] The responsibility of film-maker to Shakespeare is there held to outweigh substantially the responsibility of the film-maker to film.

Peter Brook's *King Lear* is strongly interpretative. Brook's stage production was, of course, deeply influenced by Jan Kott's essay linking the play to Samuel Beckett's *Endgame* and Brook used actors like Jack MacGowran (Fool) and Patrick Magee (Cornwall) with strong links to the performance of Beckett's plays. But there are also numerous details in the film that are alterations of Shakespeare's text. Lines are transferred from one character to another, so that it is Cornwall as he is dying, not Edgar, who tells Edmund of his father 'The dark and vicious place where thee he got / Cost him his eyes' (5.3.163–4); the lines now become, in Brook's film, a dying man's realization of a form of justice and connectedness, a comment from one evil man to another. Brook also makes a number of slight alterations to the action, way beyond the cutting and interweaving of scenes that film finds easier to manage: hence Edmund manages to make Edgar read the forged letter proposing Gloucester's death while Gloucester is concealed and listening. Brook's Goneril (Irene Worth) does not poison Regan but flings her to the ground so that her head hits a rock; in turn, she does not stab herself but throws herself against a rock and brains herself. At what point such adjustments become an adaptation depends on the individual viewer but clearly such changes begin to cross the boundary or at least define the grey area that is both interpretation and adaptation.

The death of Goneril in Brook's film suggests another aspect of the process of film-making. Shakespeare deliberately sets the moment off-stage, partly, I have always assumed, because of a trick he wants to play on the audience with the news of her death. When the breathless and terrified messenger runs onto the stage clutching the bloody knife and tells the audience 'It came even from the heart of – O, she's dead!' (5.3.199), the audience is confused as to the identity of this 'she', imagining for a moment that it is the news of Cordelia's death. Brook instead chooses to show it. He shows Goneril killing Regan, immediately follows it with Goneril killing herself and then, horrifyingly, with a brief shot of Cordelia hanged, swaying. The last shot means that there is no surprise in Lear's entry carrying her dead body, walking along the beach in the film crying out to no one in particular. Instead Brook creates on screen the sequence of death of the three daughters. Films often show what onstage is described. Films of *Hamlet* for instance find it difficult to have Gertrude describe the drowning of Ophelia and instead feel obliged to show her floating in the water. Such a choice seems to me a mistaken response to the cinema's need to show rather than say; it diminishes the fact of the narration and Gertrude's response to the death she is describing. It moves attention from the act of narration to the act that is narrated. Brook's filming of Goneril's death at least has a strong and imaginative reason behind it.

All film versions cut the text savagely. There is no way that a film can include as much language as the theatre accommodates. Film is primarily a visual medium, a form in which language accompanies sight but cannot dominate it. Similarly all the screen versions of *King Lear* are necessarily shorter than theatre performances; none of them lasts even three hours. The BBC television version (directed by Jonathan Miller, 1982) is necessarily an exception with its requirement, from academics and sponsors, that the texts should not be significantly cut but the effect is to produce a tedium, caused by the inability of the television camera to find the variety of image television demands to accompany the immense weight of the text's language.

What is cut in the other examples is of course important and often decisive. But the reasons for the cuts vary. In one extraordinary change, Kozintsev cuts a passage and compensates by filming a scene that is only narrated in the play. Unable to find a cinematic equivalent for the intense theatricality of Gloucester's attempted suicide, a scene that has so often in recent criticism appeared to be the central moment of the play, Kozintsev simply cuts it. What he does show, powerfully and beautifully, is the dying blind Gloucester recognizing Edgar by touch, accomplishing what Shakespeare's Gloucester yearns for, 'Might I but live to see thee in my touch' (4.1.23).

Brook did find a cinematic equivalent to the theatrical ambiguities of Gloucester's attempted suicide. Holding the camera low and eliminating the conventional establishing shot to define the place in which and across which the action is to be played, Brook makes the act of walking itself ambiguous, the audience uncertain whether Edgar and Gloucester are climbing or not. After Gloucester's fall, Brook suddenly cuts to an overhead crane shot, for the first time defining for the spectator the flat landscape and absent cliff.

By contrast with such films, Michael Elliott's television version (1983) is remarkably faithful to the text. It appears simply to want to present the Shakespeare play, avoiding strong lines of directorial interpretation, leaving all its interest focused on Olivier's performance. In effect it understates the extent of the director as author, the auteurism of cinema. In its treatment of the text it is the closest to what Jorgens calls 'presentation'. It is also by far the most conventionally theatrical.

In spite of Olivier's performance which, particularly in the final scenes of the play, is astonishing, this television production is disappointing. An explanation may be found in Robert Hamilton Ball's remarkable account of silent films of Shakespeare.[9] Amongst the dozens of versions of *A Midsummer Night's Dream* and *Hamlet*, Ball documented a number of silent films of *King Lear*. The contemporary reviews of these films identify the problems that the Elliott version fails to overcome. A review of one silent film, made by the Vitagraph studios in 1909, commented

King Lear is not an easy subject to handle, and we think the Vitagraph adapters have made the mistake of trying to adhere too closely to the book . . . The result is that the picture fails to hold the interest of the spectators. The costumes and scenes are faithfully represented, but the photography is dim in parts.[10]

In Elliott's version the photography is never dim but it is always dull. There is nothing that makes us look, nothing that compels our gaze on the action, forces us to watch the horrific events unfold. The costumes are remarkably traditional and, I suppose, in that sense 'faithful' but they are passive. The whole style is the result of 'trying to adhere too closely to the book', of failing to rethink the play from theatre to television.

Peter Brook took a radical step in trying to come to grips with Shakespeare's text, to make the required translation from text to performance for film. Though he had had the full experience of working with the play in the theatre, he recognized that the demands of language in the cinema are very different: it is not enough simply to cut the text until there is the small quantity of spoken language that film can tolerate. Instead he constructed a distance between himself and Shakespeare's language. A non-English director is necessarily distanced from Shakespeare's language by the simple fact of using a translation, as Kozintsev uses one by Boris Pasternak. In order to find the necessary distance,

Brook asked the English poet Ted Hughes to 'translate' Shakespeare, treating it exactly as if it were a foreign classic and translating Shakespeare's language in Ted Hughes's own idiom, trying to find a style which would seem to Hughes 'to be expressive of the story as he saw it, in his own right as a poet'.[11] Brook discarded this strange version but it enabled him to rethink the play, writing his own 'treatment of the play in dialogue form, with no language whatever, simply to seek out its essential nature',[12] without being mesmerized by Shakespeare's language, revaluing the strengths of Shakespeare's poetry in its most important mode for the tightened form of film, its status as an integral part of the play's action.

I suggested that the theatrical mode avoids the reality of cinema, that its set and costumes are usually theatrical in origin. *King Lear* is a play that obviously depends crucially on the contrast between indoors and out, between the shelter found in the castles and the pitiless lack of shelter out on the heath in the storm. Ball comments, of the 1909 film,

> One would have thought that *King Lear* offered ample opportunity for outdoor scenes, but there were none; even Gloucester at the cliff and Lear on the heath were played before painted decorations, the latter a simulacrum of Stonehenge. (p. 51)

There are uncanny anticipations here of the Elliott version made seventy years later. Elliott's version too used a set of Stonehenge as the location for the first and last scenes. Here too there are no outdoor scenes. Every set is clearly built inside a television studio. There is, of course, nothing wrong with that in itself but the sets seem to want to appear realist, to use the conventions of the cinema. It is clear that, no matter how realistic the set may be, it does not exist in a landscape. Returning from hunting to Goneril's house, Olivier rides in on a horse but the horse has clearly only been walked in from the doors of the studio. In the opening sequence of *Ran*, Lord Hidetora and his sons are seen galloping on horseback hunting a wild pig; Brook's Lear is seen riding back from hunting with his hundred knights at high speed across the bleak, wintry landscape. These horsemen arrive into a scene of dialogue from an entire world seen to be adjacent to the castles, tents and rooms in which the drama occurs. Later Olivier catches and guts a real rabbit, offers imaginary cheese to a real mouse, washes himself in a real stream. But the horse, the rabbit and the mouse have no connection with a world. They live awkwardly inside a television studio, awkwardly only because there is an attempt to apply inappropriate techniques of realism to their on-screen existence.

It is the creation of a specific world, a world appropriate to the play, a landscape in which the action belongs that is achieved both by Kozintsev and by Brook. As Kozintsev realized this is an essential possibility within the concept of cinema:

Now I wanted another kind of tragedy which would be achieved not by clearing the screen of all signs of life but on the contrary by swamping it with everyday life.

There is no 'desert' in *Lear*, the world of tragedy is densely populated. And it was just this – a magnetic world humming with reality – which interested me most of all. Lear, the King, in the thick of life, this is what the camera was needed for, this is what the cinema could add to what we knew already, to what the theatre had already revealed.   (p. 82)

This, for Kozintsev, was the direct result of the physical shape of the film. His *King Lear* is shot in 70mm Sovscope, a Russian version of wide-screen cinemascope. The shape of image in the cinema, its aspect ratio, is a rectangle whose sides have been in varying ratios as cinema has developed. Standard formats have varied from 1:1.33 in the early days to 1:1.66 or 1:1.85, the current standard wide-screen format. That is, it is a shape rather broader than it is tall. The ratio for Cinemascope – which I am using as a convenient generic name for wider-screen aspect ratios – has ranged from 1:2.2 (for Todd-AO) up to 1:2.7 (for Ultra-Panavision) but is usually in the range 1:2.35 to 1:2.55 (most commonly the lower ratio), that is, that it is well over twice as wide as it is tall.

On television, where the screen is approximately square, less than half of each frame of a cinemascope film can be shown, unless the whole image is shown using the technique known as 'letter-boxing'. When Ace Pilkington argues for the virtues of the video version of films as an instrument of study,[13] he ignores the problem of the distortion of the image, a particularly acute difficulty in Britain where letterboxed laserdiscs which respect the original aspect ratio are unavailable.

Cinemascope was in the 1970s most commonly used for big epic films; in itself it suggests the massive sweep of action, the colossal scale of Shakespeare's play. Kozintsev's choice of format carries with it an implication for the view of the play. But it has further results. The shape of the cinemascope screen means that a figure is always and necessarily seen in a context, a surrounding place in which the figure lives, through which it moves. It is a world which in Kozintsev's vision of the play is peopled. Hence, for instance, Edgar, transforming himself into Poor Tom, joins a long straggling line of the dispossessed, the poor naked wretches, the underclass of Lear's Kingdom. Later in the film he fights Edmund in a circle made by soldiers of the armies of Edmund and Albany.

Most memorably, perhaps, Kozintsev begins his film in the precredit sequence by showing first a few individuals and then, as the camera draws back, hundreds of people, Lear's subjects, walking across the landscape towards

Lear's castle, drawn together to hear Lear's decision, but remaining excluded, outside the castle walls:

The people without rights, the crowds in their thousands, await their fate outside the confines of the castle . . . In their ignorance they mistake the game for divine providence. The old man, who is no different from them, seems to them like a god.[14]

As Lear, in terrifying fury, screams at the heavens his rage against Cordelia, he appears on the battlements and the people throw themselves prostrate to the ground at the sight of their king. The gulf between the small, wild, mad figure and the symbolic image of the king as some very Russian tyrant, the tsar, this gulf is immense.[15] As Kozintsev comments:

At the beginning of the action one cannot yet recognise Lear: one can see a mask of power in an abstract and illusory form . . . the lifeless eyes of tyranny, the dragon's roar of despotism . . . Lear tears off the mask of power, and throws it away. Only then does his face become visible: suffering has made him beautiful and human.   (pp. 62–3)

I find a similar moment of realization at a different point of the action of the drama in *Ran*. The centrepiece of the whole film is the enormous and terrifying battle at the third castle, an extraordinary depiction of carnage and bloodshed, counterpointed with the sight of Hidetora sitting distraught, inside the stronghold. But the film then concentrates, in a sequence that no one who has seen the film can forget, on Hidetora's near-naked figure, frighteningly vulnerable, walking out of the blazing building, down the steps, pitiable, vulnerable but also alien, a man with whom communication is no longer possible, a man inhabiting his own private world of extreme grief and horror. As the hordes of soldiers fall back and part, he walks between them without seeing them, out of the castle gate, suddenly alone, nothing more than a mad old man, another masked figure, not Kozintsev's Lear shedding the mask of power but now a lord who has replaced the mask of power with the mask of age and madness.[16] Both Kozintsev and Kurosawa achieve their effect by the juxtaposition of the king and the people. Their rulers inhabit a peopled world and the epic scale of their films and the shape of their screens make it possible to show it – for *Ran*, though not shot in cinemascope, is shot in a wide-screen ratio.

Peter Brook's *King Lear* was finally shot in standard format but he had toyed with other possibilities. In an interview he gave while the film was still in preparation, he described the lightning movement of Shakespeare's language:

If you could extract the mental impression made by the Shakespearean strategy of images, you would get a piece of pop collage . . . You see the actor as a man standing in the distance and you also see his face, very close to you – perhaps his profile and the back of his head at the same time – and you also see the background. When Hamlet is doing any one of his soliloquies, the background that Shakespeare can conjure in one line evaporates in the next and new images take over.[17]

Film's antagonism to the density of language has been a running theme throughout this article. Theatre, precisely perhaps because it is less visually urgent than cinema, less active and busy in its images, is the perfect space for language heard by the *audience* as well as watched by the *spectators*. The transition from the page-line to the theatre-voice is far easier than from the page to the screen-sound. Brook was well aware of his need to renegotiate that movement, to move from linearity to film's two-dimensionality rather than theatre's three.

He was fascinated by a multiple-screen cinema he had seen in which three separate projectors were used at the same time on three screens, producing either one colossal picture (with an aspect ratio of 1:5) or three entirely different and disconnected images; it was this possibility of dissociated images that differentiated the form from the better-known Cinerama. He imagined how it might work for *King Lear*:

you can have a heath, and the moment that a soliloquy begins you can drop the heath out of your picture and concentrate on different views of Gloucester. If you like, you can suddenly open one of your screens to a caption, write a line, write a sub-title. If you want, in the middle of a realistic action in colour you could have another or the same in black and white, and the third captioned. You could have statistics or a cartoon parodying the photographic action. This is a film technique which has exactly the possibilities of a Brechtian stage and an Elizabethan one.   (p. 41)

Brook was never able to film *King Lear* in this way. Instead he used the possibilities of editing and of the camera itself to create his unnerving film.

Some of his editing is simple and astonishingly effective. At the start of the reconciliation scene between Lear and Cordelia, for instance, Brook never shows Lear and Cordelia in the same shot, never allows them to appear on screen together until Lear identifies his daughter. As so often in the film the characters seem terrifyingly isolated as they appear alone on the screen, never allowed the comfort and reassurance of sharing the frame with someone else. The characters speak straight out towards us – we are shown them full-face – but that only emphasizes their isolation. Indeed the filming stops us working out how the characters are placed in relation to each other, how far apart Lear and Cordelia are. As Lear slowly and tentatively voices his deeply wished-for thought, 'Do not laugh at me, / For as I am a man, I think this lady / To be my child, Cordelia', Scofield as Lear hardly dares to look up as he speaks, for fear of being laughed at. Suddenly, as Cordelia proves Lear's hope true, 'And so I am, I am', Brook introduces a new shot, showing Lear in profile and now sharing the screen with Cordelia who is unexpectedly shown to be very close to him. The reunion is accomplished, father and daughter are reconciled, by the combination of her verifying of his act of naming her and the camera's act of showing them so physically close together. It is moving and powerful, the language of the scene and the work of the camera perfectly married to chart the coming together of the characters, the translation from text to film performance fully accomplished.

At other points the disjunctive process of such unconventional editing, such denials of film grammar, is used in startling ways. Traditional textual criticism has long observed the irruption of Lear into 4.5, the 'Dover Cliff' scene. The entry is disruptively unexpected, unanticipated, uncontrolled. Brook constructs a bizarre sequence of three shots:

(1) a shot of Edgar looking at Gloucester;
(2) a sudden massive and frightening close-up of two staring eyes, first identified as clearly not Edgar's, then recognized by the audience as being Lear's eyes;
(3) a shot of Lear standing *behind* Edgar.

The effect of the second shot is to make the viewer assume that Lear has somehow appeared within Edgar's field of vision (defined in the first of three shots) whereas Lear is actually (as defined by the third shot) standing behind Edgar looking not into his eyes but staring at the back of his head. The illogicality, the impossibility of reading the sequence in terms of normal film sequence, is part of, indeed central to, the explosion of Lear into the sequence.

One of the most striking aspects of Brook's technique of filming *King Lear* is his willingness to have characters speak directly to the camera. Conventional realist filming is reluctant to accept an actor addressing the camera, in exactly the same way that conventional theatre has found it difficult for the actor to speak directly to the audience. In the Elliott television version, for instance, the only moments at which an actor does speak to camera is when Edmund soliloquizes, making us co-conspirators in the way he confidentially shares his thoughts with us. Throughout Brook's film we are confronted face-to-face by the actors. At the start for instance, Goneril, Regan and Cordelia speak to camera, to us, turning us into King Lears, inviting us to evaluate the truth, sincerity and value of their statements of love in exactly the same way that Lear will. Brook forces us to be present in the action, to engage with the process of understanding that the characters will have to make. As Brook noted,

we are coming to realize that photography is not objective, is not realistic – the reality of the cinema exists at the time of the projection, at the moment when an image is projected on the screen – if there is a spectator, then the interplay of image and spectator is the only reality.

(p. 39)

Kozintsev records a conversation between himself and Brook about their plans for their films of *King Lear*: 'What interested Brook most of all was the delocalization of space. He wanted to film *Lear* without any traces of history showing on the screen' (p. 25). Kozintsev was anxious for his own version about the problems of the genre of history film: 'How is one to portray history on the screen while avoiding the genre of historical film with its elegant external features, its pomp and battle scenes?' (p. 31). In part Brook achieved that by the primitivism of set and costumes, both prehistoric and post-nuclear, but he achieved it above all by the way the spectator becomes an enforced participant in the action, made to watch, as confused and distressed as the characters themselves.

Yet the camera endlessly interrogates the faces of the characters. I know no other film that concentrates quite so inexorably on the faces of the characters, filling the whole screen with a face, desperately trying to understand what lies behind the look. As Cornwall blinds Gloucester, for instance, the screen suddenly goes black – we are not allowed to see the moment, only to hear it – and is then filled with Cornwall's face, the face of a man capable of such an act. What after all does the face of a torturer look like? Brook's interest in this attempt somehow to look through a face derives from an exercise he tried in the theatre:

> I seated one of the actors in front of the group and asked him to think up an elaborate situation for himself and then to live, as an actor, all he could of the inner conditions of this situation. Then the group questioned him to find out what was going on. He was not allowed to answer them. This, of course, created a totally absurd situation . . . The exercise drove home the fact that what the eye sees is often of no narrative value whatsoever . . . [the actors] realised that surface appearances are non-communicative. (pp. 39–40)

Throughout the film, Brook translates this lesson to the screen, teaching us that there is no means to know, to make sense and meaning out of the surfaces of what we see.

As the last sequences of Brook's film unfold, Brook juxtaposes truth and fantasy, shots of Cordelia's corpse with shots of her still alive. At the end, as Lear dies, Scofield as Lear turns and falls back. Brook films this so that Lear seems to fall out of the bottom of the screen but he also films it in slow-motion so that the moment is dragged out for an eternity. The single continuous shot of Lear's fall is broken up into four separate sections, intercutting this endless, unbearable sight of Lear moving from life to death with shots of Albany, Kent and Edgar speaking the last words of the play straight at us. At the end Edgar turns away from the camera, as if to watch the last moment of Lear's fall into

2   *King Lear*, directed by Peter Brook: the face of the King (Paul Scofield)

the oblivion of death. As the last part of Lear's face and arm sink with infinite slowness below the horizon of the screen, the screen is left empty and white for the first time in the whole film. The tragedy is at last over. There is one other aspect of this extraordinary shot of Lear falling back that I want to mention: it is shot without any sound. No music could possibly be adequate to accompany this moment; even Shakespeare recognizes that there is a moment when language stops. Robert Hamilton Ball might have been pleased to know that, as late as 1970, Brook's *King Lear* ended as a silent film.

Notes

1 The problem has been greatly increased by the highly significant development in enumerative filmography, Kenneth S. Rothwell and Annabelle Henkin Melzer's splendid *Shakespeare on Screen: An International Filmography and Videography* (London, 1990).

2 See, for example, Peter S. Donaldson, *Shakespearean Films / Shakespearean Directors* (London, 1990).

3 Jack J. Jorgens, *Shakespeare on Film* (London, 1977), pp. 7–16.

4 Grigori Kozintsev, '*Hamlet* and *King Lear*: Stage and Film' in Clifford Leech and J. M. R. Margeson, eds., *Shakespeare 1971* (Toronto, 1972), p. 192.

5 Grigori Kozintsev, *King Lear: The Space of Tragedy* (London, 1977), p. 191.

6 Kozintsev, '*Hamlet* and *King Lear*: Stage and Film', p. 191.

7 For an interesting attempt to analyse the film see Donaldson, pp. 189–225. Donaldson's auteurist approach yields its best dividends in his work on a film so director-dominated.

8 But see also Frank Kermode's odd definition of Kurosawa's *Kumonosu-jo* (known in England as *Throne of Blood*) as 'an allusion to, rather than a version of, *Macbeth*' (Frank Kermode, 'Shakespeare in the Movies', reprinted in Gerald Mast and Marshall Cohen, eds., *Film Theory and Criticism* (Oxford, 1974), p. 328).

9 Robert Hamilton Ball, *Shakespeare on Silent Film* (London, 1968).

10 Quoted *ibid.*, p. 51.

11 See the discussion by Lord Birkett, the film's producer, in Roger Manvell, *Shakespeare and the Film* (London, 1971), p. 137.

12 *Ibid.*

13 Ace G. Pilkington, *Screening Shakespeare from 'Richard II' to 'Henry V'*, (London, 1991), pp. 14–18.

14 Kozintsev, *King Lear*, p. 36.

15 Lorne M. Buchman argues that a later shot where the castle serves to dwarf Lear proves Lear is 'a king who towers over the world only in his own mind' (*Still in Movement*, New York, 1991, p. 31) but if this is Lear's view of himself it is clearly shared by his subjects.

16 On the connection between *Ran* and the masked forms of Noh theatre, see John Collick, *Shakespeare, Cinema and Society* (Manchester, 1989), pp. 166–87.

17 Geoffrey Reeves, 'Finding Shakespeare on Film: From an Interview with Peter Brook', reprinted in Charles W. Eckert, *Focus on Shakespearean Films* (London, 1972), p. 38.

4

VERBAL-VISUAL, VERBAL-PICTORIAL OR TEXTUAL-TELEVISUAL? REFLECTIONS ON THE BBC SHAKESPEARE SERIES

MICHÈLE WILLEMS

The 1965 issue of *Shakespeare Survey*, entitled 'Shakespeare Then Till Now', included a short article by Laurence Kitchin which must have broken new ground at the time since it dealt with 'Shakespeare on the Screen'.[1] Writing incidentally about what he called television's 'inevitable recourse to Shakespeare', the author remarked ruefully: 'We must learn to live with the results', and concluded that 'as a trendsetter, the screen is potentially a menace. It has given Shakespeare its biggest audience. Up to a point it can lead that audience, but it is a mass audience which demands concessions.'[2]

With the BBC Television Shakespeare completed, not only have we learnt to live with the results but we are learning to teach with them;[3] and we can no longer be content with dealing at one go with 'Shakespeare on the screen'; we must learn to distinguish between Shakespeare on film and Shakespeare on television. Yet, although for many years we have been accustomed to an ever-increasing presence of Shakespeare on the small screen, culminating in what the BBC itself describes as 'the most ambitious and expensive project in the history of television',[4] they have not brought us many equivalents to the full-scale studies of Shakespeare on the big screen provided by Roger Manvell or Jack J. Jorgens.[5] Nor can the student find, on the theoretical front, any reflection on the televising of drama comparable to the analyses conducted by André Bazin or Albert Laffay on the filming of plays, to say nothing of the works of Christian Metz on the semiotics of the cinema.[6] In an age so much concerned with the relation between text and spectacle or script and performance, it is surprising that the transformation of a Shakespearian play into images for the small screen should so often be approached as yet another stage production, its failure or success being mostly attributed to the quality of the acting or to the interpretation of the director.

These, it is true, can also make or mar a television film, but one should not underestimate either the specific problems attached to producing a Shakespeare play for a medium so different from that for which it was written and for the benefit of a public whose expectations and rapport with the play are so different from those of its original audience. The gap between the 'wooden O' – or indeed any modern stage attempting honestly to accommodate a Shakespeare play – and the electronic square is so wide that one may wonder whether the BBC series would not have benefited from a preliminary reflection on the best ways of bridging it, instead of dealing with the problems empirically for better or for worse.[7] As far as analysis is concerned, there is no need to make the same mistake and the very concept of 'Television Shakespeare' calls for an investigation of the two systems of signs informing those two realities which have suddenly been brought together: a Shakespeare play on the one hand, a television film on the other. In both cases, we are dealing with modes of communication, either with an audience or with a viewer, and the functioning of each mode must be investigated before we can appreciate the problems posed by translation from one to the other.

Superficially, the cinema, television and the theatre all appear to rely on the layering of signs to communicate with their publics. Viewer and audience alike must apprehend a variety of signs simultaneously: aural signs such as words spoken by actors, music and other sounds; visual signs such as costumes, setting, lighting and sometimes special effects. But there the similarity ends, because the respective importance and status of these signs vary enormously from one medium to the next. On the stage all the other signs are subordinated to speech (in monologue, dialogue or aside), while on the screen words are secondary; the dialogue follows the image. It is a commonplace to say that the theatre is an aural medium whereas the cinema is primarily a visual one, a characteristic inherited and accentuated by television in spite of its smaller screen. On the stage the spoken word is prevalent; it has a primary function as it conjures up the whole universe of drama, particularly in Shakespearian drama where the language can be oratorical, formalistic, ironical, metaphorical and, on rare occasions only, purely descriptive. (The few cuts in Jane Howell's *Henry VI* do away with descriptions of battles, which are turned into pictures for television.) But most of the time Shakespeare's language is charged with layers of significance; not only does it carry the dramatic energy, it is also fraught with symbols and networks of metaphors. The screen, on the contrary, addresses its public through pictures which often replace words, so much so that words may seem out of place and too much speech may be prejudicial to the effect of a film, as Albert Laffay notes about the end of Chaplin's *The Great Dictator*. And Manvell writes in his first chapter devoted to the problems on moving 'from the open stage to the screen': 'There can be no doubt that the full-scale spoken poetry of Shakespeare's stage and the continuous visual imagery of the cinema can be oil and water' (p. 15). The solution is even more difficult to obtain if the screen is a small screen, as we shall see.

But the tension between text and visuals does not in itself account for the basic incompatibility between the two media, especially as the visual element of stage productions has gained prominence over the centuries. The conversion from play to film comes up against another major contradiction, which is, in many ways, related to the different function of words in each medium: the theatre is a mode of communication based on convention, while the cinema and television are representational media. The cinema, its theoreticians like to explain, produces an impression of reality, the actual two-dimensionality of the image on the screen creating in effect an illusion of three-dimensionality, which encourages the public to enter passively a new world which they perceive as real. But if the cinema thrives on realism, television's proper style is generally described as naturalistic and even domestic, the size of the screen reducing what Bazin calls 'the window open onto the world' (p. 165) offered by the big screen to what amounts to key-hole peeping into a drawing-room. Indeed, the nature of the communication induced by television calls to mind the famous fourth-wall convention which describes so well the functioning of the proscenium arch. In the case of television, the screen stands for some transparent division, which enables the viewer to witness a courtroom quarrel between Hotspur and King Henry IV, or to catch Prince Hal and Falstaff at the tavern in the midst of their plans for robbery. Hence the captivated excitement of the spectator sitting at home in his armchair, but it is passive excitement which does not stop him from getting his cup of coffee in the kitchen. In the theatre, and particularly in the case of a Shakespeare play, the imaginative involvement of a live audience is required. But although active, this participation remains deliberate, complicity is mitigated by detachment. This dual response is a specific characteristic of the theatrical experience which even the confirmed theatre-goer will find difficult to recapture once he is himself in the 'viewing' situation, which, as the very word indicates, does not necessarily include listening or imagining.

Nor does viewing afford the shared experience of the theatre. Even a family of viewers does not make up an audience. The cinema is more akin to the theatre than television as far as communication with a collective public is concerned. Not many people like to see a funny film in an empty auditorium and watching a Shakespeare comedy on television with a crowd of students is preferable to viewing it on one's own. At a symposium on *The Merchant of Venice* held at Rouen University at the beginning of 1985, we showed some eighty colleagues and students the scene between Launcelot Gobbo and his father which had been omitted on French television the previous Sunday.[8] The laughs from the audience drowned part of the dialogue but reconciled Jack

Gold, who was with us to discuss his film, to what he considered as a disappointing performance on the part of his Launcelot (Enn Reitel). He told us how excellent the actor had been in rehearsal as long as he was performing for the benefit of an audience of technicians, cameramen and actors but how, when silence was required in the studio for the actual filming of the scene, he became panic-stricken and the comic quality of his performance went down.

This anecdote points to another opposition between the stage and the screen: however present and real the actor may appear to be on the screen, he is actually absent, unaware of the response of the public and consequently deprived of the possibility of gauging the effect he produces. The interviews collected by Henry Fenwick for publication alongside the BBC Television texts record the frustrations and difficulties of actors normally used to a live audience when they have to perform in a silent studio and when, as Derek Jacobi explains, the experience of acting Hamlet is split up over six or seven days. The essential transience of the stage performance is transformed into something final, encapsulated once and for all, yet to be shown again and again. The advantage of acting for the cinema is the possibility of shooting and reshooting until director and actor are satisfied with the results. But this advantage was lost because of the restrictions imposed on the BBC series. Directors repeatedly bewail the obligation of filming every play in six days, and actors such as Anthony Quayle lament the impossibility of seeing themselves to judge whether the scale of their performance is right.

Even a brief exploration of the specific characteristics of each mode of communication brings to light a number of incompatibilities between a Shakespeare play and television, and points to the necessity of what Kitchin would call concessions, or of what one might choose to call transcoding in the translation from one system of signs to the other.

Now, the BBC's project was to produce the Shakespeare canon, complete and unabridged, and this went together with the decision to use the Peter Alexander text and to take no liberties with it. The initial brief, one reads everywhere, was to cut and alter the text as little as possible, which amounted to stating that the play text would have to serve as film script. The impossibility of rephrasing, of restructuring, of substituting another sign for the prevalent verbal sign of the original meant that the director could not conform to the fundamental necessity of 'shifting the stress from the aural to the visual', as Kozintsev sums up the problem of filming Shakespeare.[9] Both Manvell and Jorgens show how the best Shakespeare films make free with the text the better to adapt it to the exigencies of the medium, the object being to translate the poetical effects of the original into visual imagery. One may argue that the result is another work, but in the best cases it is an adaptation which is faithful to the spirit, if not to the letter, of the original play. And if we turn to precedents in television films, we find that such series as *An Age of Kings* or *The Spread of the Eagle* did not attempt complete or exhaustive productions of the history plays or of the Roman plays. They cut, adapted, restructured, and serialized to meet the demands of the new medium. Can this account for the fact that these series had an average viewing audience of three million some twenty-five years ago, whereas the audience figures for one of the BBC Shakespeares ranged from one to two million, at a time when a Chekhov or an Ibsen could gather five million viewers? Shaun Sutton, the third producer of the series, who provided these figures, offers this explanation: 'Shakespeare's plays are so long . . . one of the main difficulties is the amount of words spoken . . . In television we are used to terseness, to shortness.' Yet to the question: 'What sort of public were you aiming at?', Sutton answers: 'Everybody; students, but also ordinary people; Shakespeare wrote them for everybody.' This may well be true, but nowadays one should also take into account what Jack Gold, who had had no previous experience of directing Shakespeare, stresses in order to explain his primary concern with making his BBC *Macbeth* and *The Merchant of Venice* intelligible to the general viewer: 'When I go to watch Shakespeare, people on the stage seem to be speaking in a foreign language.'[10]

In fact, the BBC's confusion between play text and film script goes together with a confusion about the public aimed at. The production of a 'definitive' version of the Shakespeare canon concerns a limited public of students, teachers, and Shakespeare lovers who may be interested in turning to 'preserved' Shakespeare for want of the real thing. Building up 'a library of Shakespeare video-productions', a definition that was suggested to Cedric Messina in an interview,[11] could justify the ruling out of such tampering with the text as is common even on the stage. But a project which involves a thousand actors, which is supported by well-known financers, widely publicized and sold to thirty-five countries, needs more to justify it than an appeal merely to students. Producing Shakespeare for what Ann Pasternak Slater, in her interview with Jonathan Miller for *Quarto*, refers to as 'the small-screen with the huge audience',[12] implies attracting to Shakespeare a public which rarely or never goes to the theatre and involving viewers who, as David Jones pointed out in a private interview, do not know how the story will end. The basic question connected with the determination of the target is formulated by Stanley Wells, when he writes in an article on 'Television Shakespeare': 'Do we want good television drama or pure Shakespeare?'[13] The fact that this question never received a proper answer is shown by the very diverse reactions of the various directors, some of whom refer to Veronese or Rembrandt to explain to Henry Fenwick how they approached the Shakespearian material, while some others allude to *Dallas* or to Northern Ireland. By not deciding clearly what the target was, which would have entailed a reflection on the best means of reaching it, or rather by aiming at too wide a target, the BBC series ran the risk of satisfying neither the few nor the many. And it had neither the international impact of Olivier's *Richard III*, nor the critical acclaim of his *Henry V* which Bazin described as 'Shakespeare pour tous' (p. 174). Nor does anyone note an increase in the sale of Shakespearian texts comparable to the increase in the sale of recordings of Mozart's symphonies registered in every country after the release of *Amadeus*.[14] As for the few, their enthusiasm was more than muted, as was shown by the results of the poll organized by the Shakespeare Association of America[15] and by the various calls for a remake of the series in the States.[16]

The fluctuations in textual policy also testify to the difficulty of keeping to a party-line which was not theoretically thought out. More freedom to stray from devotion to the text was obviously given by Jonathan Miller than by Cedric Messina. 'It was all talk and no action' became a recurrent excuse for cutting as the series progressed, and it seemed to be more and more recognized that full-length plays acted as a deterrent for the average viewer. The fact, for instance, that *Coriolanus* was submitted to such drastic paring down that it was reduced from $3\frac{1}{2}$ to $2\frac{1}{2}$ hours is not perhaps to be attributed solely to Moshinsky's very personal approach to the text. From the start he contended that a Shakespearian text needed a certain amount of 'doctoring' if it was to be enjoyed by a television public, but even so his 1980 *All's Well that Ends Well* and his 1981 *A Midsummer Night's Dream* were models of textual faithfulness compared to his 1983 *Coriolanus*.[17]

However, taken as a whole, the BBC series offers the original example of using a theatrical text as a film script with only minor changes, thus assuming that a visual medium can somehow accommodate an abundance of verbal signs. This confrontation between the two media is often bypassed – successfully some will argue – by resorting to filmed theatre,[18] which amounts to a superposition of the two media. But in the case of the BBC we are dealing with authentic television films produced in the studio – with the exception of two outside broadcasts – without the support of a live public. The question now is: how do these solve the problem of producing for the small screen a script in which the theatrical mode is to remain prevalent? Given the fact that, as John Wilders explains in his article 'Adjusting the Set', each director was left to find his own solutions, the responses to the problem vary from play to play but they can be classified, roughly, into three categories: naturalistic, pictorial, and stylized.

The naturalistic solution was the most commonly chosen, especially at the beginning of the series. It was presented by the people involved – directors, designers, and costume designers – as the best way of satisfying the expectations of a public who watch the news every night and thus expect battles, fights, and scuffles, among other things, to be presented with a degree of realism. In any case, the brief given by the BBC and its financers, that the plays should be set in a period which Shakespeare would have recognized, did not encourage innovation or invention, but rather threw the directors back on traditional approaches and sent the costume designers searching for reference books and even for a thesis on the clothes worn in Henry IV's reign. Indeed the early publicity for the series was in 'Hollywood style', to take up Jack Jorgens's expression in his review of *Julius Caesar*.[19] It extolled, among other things, the 'authentic recreation of Caesar's Rome', and the filming of *As You Like It* in a 'real forest'. Conversely, it congratulated itself on the exclusion of stylization and 'gimmicks'. Not unsurprisingly, what emerges from the interviews conducted by Henry Fenwick over the first two or three years of the enterprise is the directors' and designers' concern for authenticity, their preoccupation that badges, banners, and weapons should look genuine. Priority was given to historically acceptable reconstitutions: a suitably timbered tavern alternating with a period courtroom for *Henry IV*, a credible Elizabethan mansion and garden for *Twelfth Night* and, even later on in the series, a village square such as Shakespeare might have known for *The Merry Wives of Windsor*, which, much to David Jones's regret, could not be filmed on location like *Henry VIII*. The object of such productions is to present the viewer with a universe which he can accept as an authentic representation of the world of the play. And other choices logically follow: *The Tempest* opens on a real tempest; the actress taking the part of Juliet has to be fourteen – even if this is to be her major asset – because 'on television there's no way in which you can make a 25-year-old look fourteen'; for *Twelfth Night* it seems important 'to get the society of the play right' and thus to make Sir Andrew 'an even faintly plausible suitor for Olivia's hand'. If Jane Howell had opted for this approach in *The Winter's Tale*, her main problem would have been to find a geographically acceptable beach for the coast of Bohemia.

Without denying the attractiveness of many realistic productions or the visual pleasure they can produce, it must be said that the naturalistic approach often aggravates the tensions between the two media instead of solving them. What happens in effect is that each mode of communication imposes its own prevalent signs, which often vie for the spectator's attention without support-ing each other. Shakespeare's idiom is transported wholesale on television. The message is dense, polyvocal; layers of significance qualify and enrich the basic narration. Now naturalism, instead of trying to find ways to transpose this complex language, retaliates by superimposing its own favourite representa-tional idiom. The visuals describe what is said by the text in successions of purely referential shots. The well-meaning desire to make the story absolutely clear often results in the reduction of a play to its story-line and to a number of characters delivering speeches which are received as too long and pointlessly verbose. As with those translations which ignore the various operations of transcoding, only the literal meaning is transcribed. The story, the information, the description get the lavish support of the visuals but the rest of the message is often wasted in the process, if only because the attention of the viewer is channelled towards the visual signs and consequently strays away from the spoken word. The text becomes submerged, devalued. When Old Capulet delivers his lines while shopping in an Italian market, the odds are that the viewer will devote more attention to what Capulet is buying than to what he is saying. The substitution of a real forest for the emblematic Forest of Arden works against the verbal poetry of the play. Real sheep, an oak and magnificent bluebells – an unlikely haunt for a lioness – take first place in the viewer's interest, before Rosalind's love-play and Touchstone's witticisms.

And the conflict between word and picture is complicated by the clash between the conventional mode and the representational one. Prince Hal sitting at a tavern table where he has just finished his breakfast with Falstaff really takes the spectator by surprise when he launches into his monologue: 'I know you all.' When Malvolio airs his dreams of grandeur in a park for the benefit of a few eavesdroppers hiding ineffectively behind a tree, the comic convention of non-discovery comes into conflict with the realistic setting. Throughout the letter scene the conventional status of protagonists-turned-spectators enjoyed by Sir Toby and his crew is totally lost as the camera tries to respond to the comedy of situation with the traditional two-shot technique. When Malvolio is on, the eavesdroppers are off, and when they are all in the picture together the tree adds to the confusion of an already cluttered-up picture. The descriptive sequence of shots characteristic of realistic productions cannot accommodate the conventional play-within-the play.

Indeed it is in comedy that the conflict between the two modes is most marked. This is so true that many directors seem to have thrown in the comic sponge before the struggle to arouse laughter in the living-rooms of thirty-five countries had even begun, preferring to offer the viewer a documentary or sociological study of Elizabethan life instead. David Jones confides to Henry Fenwick about his production of *The Merry Wives of Windsor*: 'I said right from the beginning, I am not concerned at all if the play is not funny'; and Jonathan Miller remarks to Tim Hallinan about *The Taming of the Shrew*: 'As happens with almost all of Shakespeare's comedies, it really is a more serious play than people have taken it for.'[20] Although these may sound like rationalizations after the event, such options are perfectly legitimate, and one must allow that *The Merry Wives of Windsor*, broadcast during the Christmas season, succeeded in its attempt to recreate the Merrie England spirit. But for anyone who saw Ben Kingsley on the stage and enjoyed the hilariously funny effects he drew from the character of Ford, a sense of anticlimax will prevail when watching his Ford on the screen. In fact the importance given to architectural and social realism is probably just as detrimental to the comic effect as the absence of a live public. An actor cannot cultivate his class credibility and his comic performance at the same time; insistence on the first smoothes over the excesses inherent in the second. Again the emphasis is shifted from comic convention to realistic representation. Trying to present Sir Andrew as a plausible suitor for Olivia's hand is basically at odds with the conception of the character; in the same way, the focus on Malvolio's status as a steward cannot easily be reconciled with a truly comic treatment of the character; those yellow stockings and cross-garters cannot be dismissed with a few rather unsuccessful close-ups. The emphasis on social context is part and parcel of the realistic logic. In comedy, particularly, it only reinforces the incompatibility between convention and representation at the expense of laughter.

As in writing, there is a coherence within the style of a production and a number of options are consequential to the initial choice of naturalism. Realistic diction is another one. That the actor can be heard without having to project as far as the last seat in the gallery has been repeatedly hailed as one of the advantages of a medium often described as intimate, the domestic setting being the specific response of television to the necessity of scaling down its naturalistic scenery. The small screen will favour a house rather than a town and an indoor scene rather than a street scene. Now, when speaking in chambers, antechambers or libraries – a recurrent setting in the series – the actor resorts, logically, to a conversational tone of voice to deliver his lines. This may be well adapted to some scenes, such as the beginning of *All's Well that Ends Well* where the reflective mode is served both by the beautiful interiors inspired by Dutch paintings where successive doors open on to successive rooms, and by the quiet diction which is sometimes even used to render part of a monologue voice-over. In *Measure for Measure*, too, the traditional two shots, improved by constantly changing angles of shooting, effectively present the confrontation of Angelo and Isabella, and counter her pleading tones with his quiet determination. But the muted confidential diction does not suit all Shakespeare's speeches. Anthony Quayle shows himself aware of the difficulty of finding the right pitch and of the danger of misgauging his performance on television, and it is true that his Falstaff strikes one as too quiet and too sedate at times. Falstaff is an enormous, larger-than-life character who cannot always give his measure in confidential tones. At the other end of the scale, tragic speeches, with their rhythm, rhetoric, and imagery, hardly benefit either from everyday delivery in naturalistic surroundings. What happens to the famous *Othello* music when it is delivered in conversational tones over a desk in some sort of library? Few tragedies have been treated realistically, and in the case of *Othello* the problem seems to be more one of interpretation. The deliberately domestic bias – rendered among other things by the systematic staging of outdoor scenes in chambers and halls – is meant to stress the fact that, in Miller's terms to Fenwick, the play is not concerned 'with the fall of the great but with the disintegration of the ordinary'.

Whatever Miller's justifications, the realistic approach again results in reductiveness. Its concrete, referential, visual language is certainly effective in story-telling. It makes the most of the advantages offered by the medium in order to smooth over the inconsistencies and deal effectively with the spatial and temporal discontinuity of Shakespearian drama. But it responds to every convention by doing its best to occlude it, at the same time doing away with that unique combination of detachment and involvement which causes dramatic emotion, as well as passing off the poetical density of the blank verse as everyday informative prose.

Another approach was greeted by commentators as possibly *the* answer to the problem of translating a Shakespeare play to television. This was the pictorial solution, initiated by Miller's passion for Renaissance painting and supported by his intimate knowledge of it. In the two interviews he gave on the subject,[21] he explains how he uses paintings as source material not only for setting and costumes but to determine the general organization of space in the studio and consequently on the screen. For *Antony and Cleopatra* he agrees that 'it would have looked ludicrous to place that verse against a realistic Rome and Egypt of the first century AD', so he turned to images of Veronese to recreate a sixteenth-century version of Roman antiquity instead. For *The Taming of the Shrew* he derived his inspiration from Dutch paintings, which gave him a picture of domestic life at the beginning of the seventeenth century. De la Tour was a major influence for the costumes in this play as well as in *Othello*; and more references to Chirico or Caravaggio come to support Miller's contention that he has found a visual counterpart for the 'unscenic stage' that Shakespeare wrote for. It is indeed tempting to consider that this pictorial approach, also favoured by Elijah Moshinsky, particularly in his *All's Well that Ends Well* and in his *A Midsummer Night's Dream*, provides a specific code for the conversion of Shakespearian drama into televisual language. This, one might think, is a specifically visual response adapted to a visual medium. But the question remains of the relation between the text and the visuals. One should not confuse visual richness and visual significance. Titania in her bower beautifully suggests Rembrandt's *Danae's Bower*, and even the spectator who does not recognize the allusion will enjoy the picture, but will this help him to understand a rich and difficult text? Is there not rather a danger that the picture will interfere with the reception of the words? In *A Midsummer Night's Dream*, particularly, the abundance of visual signs would probably be more at home on the big screen than on a small screen. Even systematic filming in depth does not manage to accommodate easily an unusual quantity of visual signs; the result is a picture which is often difficult to decipher and words which are swallowed up in visual abundance. Some unquestionably magnificent pictures seem to use the text as a pretext; they exist at the expense of the words which are often diluted in obtrusive visual detail and interfering sound.

Instead of using music to make a point or underscore an effect ('as a sign-post for the audience', to quote one of Jack Gold's expressions), Moshinsky adds beautiful background music, in keeping with the atmosphere created by the pictures, but often vying with the text for attention. The same goes for his sound effects: bird-songs, evocative of the forest, sounds of water as the lovers wade or splash, neighing when Oberon comes in riding his horse. All these realistic noises blend in with the words which the actors often speak together. The use of overlapping dialogue confirms the priority given to realism at the expense of the text: probable as it is that lovers quarrelling or artisans planning a theatrical performance should speak together and shout to make themselves heard, the result is far less likely to be comprehensible. In the same way, Moon, chanting his part in the hall where the newly married couples are enjoying their meal and passing comments on the performance, has little opportunity of making the most of his text. In such circumstances, it is not surprising that Bottom's most appreciative audience, when he does his party-piece at Ninny's tomb, should be the same Moon, but not the diners or indeed the viewers. The conventional play-within-the-play is a major hurdle for television and one which pictorial productions do not seem to negotiate any better than naturalistic ones. Jonathan Miller chose to film the taming of his shrew without a witness, doing away with the Induction. It is not so much that the size of the screen makes it difficult to show at once the actors and the actors-turned-spectators; what happens is that in a realistic or pictorial context the whole point is lost in any case, the significance of the theatrical metaphor being diluted in attempts to make the situation convincing.

In short, the pictorial solution does not appear as a specific solution at all. It may give more aesthetic and visual attraction to a production, but instead of solving the problem of transcoding from one medium to the other it complicates matters by transcoding twice: once from the theatre into painting and then from painting into television pictures. Instead of reconciling the verbal and the visual, it promotes a predominantly visual mode which may interfere with the reception of the text even more than in a naturalistic production. Whereas in a naturalistic production the visual sign is purely referential and channels the viewer's attention to what the text says (but not to what it means), in a pictorial production it will direct it even more to what is shown. The visual sign is then both referential and aesthetic. Even if the visual quotation is not recognized, the beauty of the picture may become an end in itself and distract from the spoken word, unless it is calculated to reveal it. But referring to pictorial codes to support an interpretation of the text is one thing; this is what Ariane Mnouchkine does when she ends her *Richard II* on a Pieta. But this is not what Miller or Moshinsky are doing when they evoke, or even quote visually, Rembrandt, Veronese, or Caravaggio. They are creating a visual atmosphere, producing a succession of beautifully decorative pictures, but these do not necessarily reveal the meaning of the text or the organic unity of the play.

Both with the naturalistic and pictorial approaches, television responds to the challenge of transposing a Shakespeare play by resorting to a cinemato-graphic mode of expression which, in effect, often brings to light its incapacity to beat the cinema on its own ground. Filming in depth for want of width often results, unless close-ups or head-and-shoulder shots are systematically used, in a confused picture. Visual selection is felt to be a more or less gratuitous intrusion. This is due to the fact that, in a representational mode of expression, what is left out of the picture is felt to be actually missing because one expects a logical chain of references. In another context, what is off-camera can be sensed or imagined as virtually present. A realistic battle scene will only underscore the smallness of the screen, whereas in a stylized universe, like that created by Jane Howell for her *Henry VI*, an archer will be received as representing a whole army. In this case, the metonymic mode of expression brings television much nearer to the theatre. Given the obligation to use a basically unabridged, unmodified text, it appears that an approach where the visual element is used as functional or suggestive is preferable to one in which it is referential or decorative. Instead of vying for pre-eminence with the spoken discourse – when it does not completely interfere with it – the visual discourse can be made to support it or even to reveal it.

Productions like Miller's *King Lear*, Gold's *Macbeth* (and up to a point his *The Merchant of Venice*), Rodney Bennett's *Hamlet*, as well as Jane Howell's *Henry VI*, *Richard III* and *The Winter's Tale*, to name the prominent ones, have this in common: that they resort to the stylization that was the object of so much scorn in the BBC's first publicity for the series. Their settings do not attempt to represent or describe any given location. In fact they often proclaim that they are mere settings, in the first sense of the word: settings for the characters to come to life in, for the words to bounce back on. Bare boards, tall grey walls, columns without tops or even some sort of timeless recreation ground do not make any claim at authenticity (in *Henry VI* a carpet is unrolled under the viewer's eyes and a panel announces 'Part 2' or 'Part 3'); neither do they make a statement descriptive of, or liable to interfere with, the text. They provide a space for the interiorized world of tragedy. In *Macbeth* and in *Hamlet* only slits and holes open onto the outside world. In *King Lear* bare boards and a few props recreate a theatrical space. But these settings also provide a general impression that will support the interpretation of the text. Macbeth's castle is no real castle but an elementary enclosed space where passions will develop and fester. The steps to Duncan's chamber lead to a misty nowhere very suggestive of the everlasting bonfire whereas the scenes in England are filmed against blue skies. The evolution of the setting may also support the progression in the meaning. The colourful playground of *1 Henry VI* becomes gradually boarded up and more oppressive as play follows play, and as the playful skirmishes of the beginning develop into savage battle. The costumes, instead of striving at pure authenticity, fulfil a function; they become darker and more tattered as the war spreads like a disease. This goes beyond the colour coding of naturalistic productions in which the viewer can distinguish between rival factions as in a football match. With Jane Howell, the visual is not only referential, it is supportive, revealing. The same happens in *The Winter's Tale* when the dead tree of the first three acts, set in the middle of the same stylized space which is then looked at through different lenses, is seen in bloom in the second part. Yet at no time is it trying to be a real tree. It provides a visual support to the natural imagery of the play; it reveals the sterility and sickness of Sicilia at the beginning, and suggests the advent of spring and fertility with Perdita in Bohemia. Thus the reversal of tragedy into comedy is made more understandable, supported also by changes in the colours of the costumes, of the setting, and in the lighting.

This is not to say that such productions successfully negotiate all the obstacles. The statue scene in *The Winter's Tale* comes up against the difficulties incident to any last scene of a comedy, complicated in this case by what amounts to a play-within-the-play or a masque-within-the-play. The visual selection that necessarily ensues is not wholly satisfactory. But, on the whole, visual selection is received less as a constraint than as a positive choice in a stylized production. The selection of shots and their arrangement in sequences is what makes up a director's style, his own form of writing, and once the viewer has accepted stylization, he will be prepared to receive elliptic or symbolic shots without feeling frustrated or lost if he is not shown everything and everyone at once. As Jack Gold says: 'Television is not a very democratic

medium; unlike what happens in the theatre, you cannot choose what you see.'
But the inevitability of visual selection can be perceived positively if it is felt to
be part of a pact with the director in the same way as any reader has to play the
game of reading according to a number of rules implicit in the writing from the
beginning. This may result in a form of participation which is still different
from that expected in the theatre, but is nearer to its dual response, as some sort
of active reaction is required if the viewer is to decipher the director's signs and
to let himself be guided towards a better understanding of the play. Thus the
play-within-the-play in *Hamlet* is visually introduced by Hamlet donning a
cloak and covering his face with a mask representing a skull. He walks round
the part of the floor marked by stools that will stand for the stage. The
coexistence of two spaces will now be suggested by filming in depth or more
exactly by layering different planes which are significant as well as descriptive.
In the foreground, to the right and left of the screen are the backs of Gertrude
and Claudius, metonymically standing for the public. The Players are
discovered in the space between them as they walk in along a gallery with a
chequered floor. They are not only distinguished by their masks and clothes but
essentially by their extravagant miming, which survives after the dumb-show.
Their performance is now and again interrupted by reaction shots on Gertrude
and Claudius, laughing and 'paddling palms', but appearing gradually more
worried and closely watched – another series of shots cutting in – by a tense
Hamlet. As the camera either travels over the changing faces of the courtiers or
closes in upon Hamlet shouting his narration of the play from behind the
Players, the whole scene is totally understandable. Reaction shots and close-ups
inserted in a well-thought-out sequence manage to make up for the absence of
space and the whole art consists in first giving the viewer a number of visual
landmarks: the gallery as a background to the performance, the stools as the
limits to the stage, and the public standing on three sides, with Gertrude and
Claudius sitting in a central position facing the corridor. Hamlet can then move
in and out of the theatrical space. The viewer will retain a mental impression of
what is off-camera if its virtual presence has been established by a prior
exploration of the geography of the space in which the drama is to take place.

Most of the time, however, the space provided by the screen will be entirely
devoted to what is said and heard as the important conversations are recorded
in close shots. The close shot, though often decried, remains the basic advantage
of the medium; it helps the viewer to follow the text as the facial expressions
and reactions of speaker and listener can be registered with an intensity that
cannot be equalled on the stage. Many directors use triangular compositions of
faces, or of faces and shoulders, to film dialogue. Both Miller and Gold prefer
their actors to face the camera rather than filming profiles. In *King Lear* the

speaker is often behind the listeners, whose reactions are thus registered in the foreground, as in scenes involving Goneril and Regan. This is often preferred to the not so satisfactory alternative of interrupting the flow of a speech with a reaction shot. But the use of close shots in settings reminiscent of Shakespeare's unfurnished stage will, in any case, encourage a much more theatrical diction. This choice does not exclude the possibility of playing upon a much wider range of voices than in the theatre, where whispering tones cannot be properly used. Nicol Williamson, playing Macbeth, uses a hoarse, rasping voice for the monologues in which he reveals his inner tension and torture, while he remains loud and apparently self-assured in public. But in plays with such abundance of words, the silent shot is a means of getting relief by contrast. Sudden silence, or the use of functional music, accompanies close shots on revealing visual signs: Macbeth's bloody hands; the witches clasping hands in a truce; Lear's tears as the camera closes in on his face at the end of the storm scene; Hamlet suddenly interrupting the verbal and physical violence against Ophelia as the camera registers the realization of his excess, and the fear travelling in his mind before he eventually pronounces, quietly, 'it *hath* made me mad'; or the sudden interruption of loud laughter and noisy reactions that accompanies the transformation of Shylock's well-known plea for his race into a call for revenge. All these are moments of dramatic intensity, which are probably very demanding on the actor but in which the significance of the text can be caught by the camera better than by the wandering and in any case distant eye of the spectator in the auditorium.

Thus visual selection can work as a pedagogy of the text. Using the visual signs that make up the specific mode of expression of television in order to support and reveal the verbal signs which constitute Shakespeare's own mode of expression may allow the director to reconcile the two media. The theatrical and the visual may be made to merge into the televisual. On the whole, although they are often considered as 'just not on on television', stylized productions manage this better than naturalistic ones. Producing Shakespeare with the resources normally expected on the small screen has too often resulted in attracting attention to the fact that Shakespeare did *not* write for television.

Notes

1 L. Kitchin, 'Shakespeare on the Screen', *Shakespeare Survey 18* (Cambridge, 1965), pp. 70–4.
2 Kitchin, 'Shakespeare on the Screen', pp. 70 and 74.
3 For instance, volume 35 (no. 5) of *Shakespeare Quarterly* (1984), devoted to teaching Shakespeare, includes several articles on the use of BBC Shakespeare in the classroom.

4 *The BBC Catalogue for Schools*, p. 20. An expensive project indeed for the school that attempts to buy the series, as the export prices for each play averaged some £400.

5 Roger Manvell, *Shakespeare and the Film* (London, 1971); Jack J. Jorgens, *Shakespeare on Film* (Bloomington, 1977). For studies on Shakespeare on the small screen, see J. C. Bulman & H. R. Coursen, eds., *Shakespeare on Television; An Anthology of Essays and Reviews* (Hanover and London, 1988), and M. Willems, ed., *Shakespeare à la télévision* (Rouen, 1987).

6 André Bazin, *Qu'est-ce que le cinéma* (Paris, 1958); Albert Laffay, *Logique du cinéma* (Paris, 1964); Christian Metz, *Essais sur la signification au cinéma*, vols. 1 and 2 (Paris, 1968).

7 In his article 'Adjusting the Set' (*Times Higher Educational Supplement*, 10 July 1981, p. 13), John Wilders explains that his initial suggestion of holding a seminar before the filming began was rejected for fear of cramping the directors with a 'house style'.

8 This sort of thing often happens because the films have to be reduced to two and a half hours to fit into the programmes. As the plays are subtitled and the credits are not changed, the French viewer is treated at the end to a list of characters some of whom may not have appeared on his screen. Part of the discussion on Gold's *Merchant of Venice* is published in the proceedings of the symposium: *'Le Marchand de Venise' et 'Le Juif de Malte', texte et représentations* (Rouen, 1985), pp. 167–75.

9 Kozintsev, quoted by Jorgens, *Shakespeare on Film*, p. 10.

10 The interview with Shaun Sutton, as well as those with Jack Gold and David Jones, referred to at various times, were collected by our research team, Rouen University's 'Centre d'études du théâtre anglo-saxon' (CETAS). They are published, with other essays, in *Shakespeare à la télévision*.

11 Quoted by Stanley Wells in 'Television Shakespeare', *Shakespeare Quarterly*, 33 (1983), 261–77; p. 263.

12 *Quarto* (September 1980), 9–12; p. 9.

13 Wells, 'Television Shakespeare', p. 266.

14 In France, for instance, an average of 250,000 viewers watched the Sunday afternoon broadcasts of the Shakespeare series, while the viewing figures of French classics were between two and three million and Saturday evening boulevard comedies attracted an audience of up to ten million.

15 The SAA ratings on a scale of 10 ranged from 3.2 for *Romeo and Juliet* to 8.1 for *Henry VIII*. *The Tempest* scored 4.8 and *As You Like It* 5.2.

16 See particularly Maurice Charney, 'Shakespearian Anglophilia: the BBC-TV Series and American Audiences', *Shakespeare Quarterly*, 31 (1980) 287–92; p. 292.

17 At the same time more efforts were made to appeal to the general public. Shaun Sutton confesses 'a show-biz approach' rather different from the more intellectual approach of his predecessor: 'I would have liked to have seen more stars on the series . . . Richardson, Peggy Ashcroft, all these people . . . I think the greater the star, the more chance people will watch.' There was, he explains, no financial reason for not getting the best known actors: 'Even the biggest star only gets so much on television'.

18 This concept means different things for different people. Everyone objects to films of live performances shot from the vantage point of the spectator sitting in the stalls. In his chapter devoted to 'Théâtre et cinéma' (*Qu'est-ce que le cinéma*, pp. 130–78), A. Bazin puts forward his own conception of filmed theatre, which is epitomized by Olivier's *Henry*

V. In a different perspective, in an article entitled 'BBC Television's Dull Shakespeares' (in C. B. Cox and D. J. Palmer, eds., *Shakespeare's Wide and Universal Stage*, Manchester, 1984, pp. 48–56), Martin Banham suggests that the plays could be filmed in front of a live audience.

19 *Shakespeare Quarterly*, 30 (1979), p. 412.
20 In an interview published in *Shakespeare Quarterly*, 32 (1981), 134–45; p. 139.
21 Given to *Quarto* and to *Shakespeare Quarterly*, 32. The subsequent remarks are in *SQ*, 32, p. 137 and then p. 134.

5

TWO TYPES OF TELEVISION
SHAKESPEARE

NEIL TAYLOR

In order to appreciate the significance of The Television Shakespeare (the BBC series which broadcast thirty-seven plays between 3 December 1978 and 27 April 1985), it is necessary to think of it not just as Shakespeare but as television.[1] Derek Longhurst wrote while the series was still in production that it 'needs to be evaluated in terms of the whole determining medium of television' and Graham Holderness has partly taken up this challenge.[2] My intention is more modest and more formalistic.

I shall be looking at the work of two directors, Jane Howell and Elijah Moshinsky, who between them directed eleven of the plays. Much of my evidence will be drawn from Howell's production of the first tetralogy (broadcast in England on 2, 9, 16 and 23 January 1983) and Moshinsky's production of Cymbeline (10 July 1983). In my opinion the originality (and success) of these directors in translating Shakespeare from one medium into another derived from a split in their allegiances. Howell publicly acknowledged a struggle between television and the theatre. Moshinsky's case is more ambiguous, but it can be interpreted that he was frequently attempting to treat television as if it were cinema. In both cases the conventions of television drama were partly assimilated, partly challenged.

Raymond Williams reckoned in 1974 that most people spent more time watching various kinds of drama on television than in preparing and eating food.[3] But if 'Drama' is distinguished, following the BBC's practice, from 'Light Entertainment' and 'Feature Films and Series', the importance of drama on BBC Television has been waning for many years. In 1949–50 it represented 17.8 per cent of all broadcasting, in 1973–4 only 6.1 per cent, and in 1984–5 it was down to a mere 3.2 per cent. At the time of preparing this essay for republication (1992) the latest figure stands at 3.1 per cent. If one distinguishes between plays written originally for the stage and plays written specially for television, television's output of the former category has always been dominated, as one would expect, by Shakespeare. But there has been a recent marked decline in the number of broadcasts of this category of play. In 1964 there were seventy-three such broadcasts on BBC Television. When it is taken into account that some of these were serialized episodes, excerpts, or repeats, the number of different plays broadcast in that year turns out to have been fifty-three. In 1984, however, only eight different plays were broadcast – and of these fifty per cent were part of The Television Shakespeare.[4]

There is thus an institutional commitment to Shakespeare (no doubt because he seems to be ideologically safe and sound[5]) and yet he forms part of a genre, the stage play translated into television, whose importance is steadily diminishing. The odds would seem to be that, in terms of production-style, Shakespeare will always be subject to the predominant conventions of the medium.

What, then, are these conventions? John Ellis has argued that, instead of the single, coherent text that is found in the cinema or theatre,

broadcast TV offers relatively discrete segments: small sequential unities of images and sounds . . . organised into groups, which are either simply cumulative, like news broadcast items and advertisements, or have some kind of repetitive or sequential connection, like the groups of segments that make up the serial or series.[6]

But the conventions also derive from the conditions under which programmes are made and viewing takes place. The use of multiple cameras and cross-cutting in studio time creates a sense of 'real time'. The use of direct address in non-dramatic programmes, along with the continuity of radiating sound for all broadcasts, combines with the illusion of real time to establish a very direct relationship between the image and the viewer. The result is an aesthetic which emphasizes the close-up and fast cutting. At the same time, viewing is assumed to be casual, domestic, and familial, and this affects programme content. Ellis concludes that television 'massively centres its fictional representations around the question of the family. Hence TV produces its effect of immediacy even within dramas of historically remote periods by reproducing the audience's view of itself within its fictions.'[7]

If these are, indeed, the conventions, then Shakespeare would seem to be both highly suitable and highly unsuitable for television. Jonathan Miller, who produced thirteen plays in the series, revealed his suitability for such a role when he remarked in an interview, published in 1981, that 'Shakespeare is the great playwright of the family.'[8] Furthermore, one can see immediately that Shakespeare's plays can be regarded as costume pieces and the canon as a series. But the sustained concentration demanded by the individual plays as discrete units runs counter to television's rhythms of very short, ateleological segments. And who, had they never been put on, could have predicted that the first tetralogy and *Cymbeline* would have proved so royally as to attract an average audience for each broadcast of over half a million viewers?[9]

I

Jane Howell's productions within the series were *The Winter's Tale* (broadcast on 8 February 1981), the first tetralogy, and *Titus Andronicus* (27 April 1985). Her attitude to the printed text was the same in all six productions: a remarkable fidelity, both to its letter and to its spirit. In the case of *Titus Andronicus*, for example, she made two significant editorial interventions, opening at line 70 and thereby introducing Titus before Saturninus, and inserting a silent Young Lucius into this and a number of other scenes. But, as Stanley Wells wrote at the time, 'the text is altered here less than in most stage productions'.[10]

Furthermore, she resisted television's normal pattern of segments. The original 1965 television version of *The Wars of the Roses* kept to John Barton's heavily cut and reworked tripartite division, but it was also shown in fifty-minute episodes.[11] Cedric Messina, who conceived The Television Shakespeare and produced the first twelve plays, had begun by wanting to compress the *Henry VI* plays into two episodes.[12] His script editor was of the opinion that about $2\frac{1}{2}$ hours is 'the maximum length for a television play to hold the viewer's attention'.[13] But Howell's production of the first tetralogy was four complete plays shown on consecutive Sunday nights, each broadcast averaging about $3\frac{1}{2}$ hours of peak viewing time.

A consequence of playing the full tetralogy was that, when *Richard III* was reached, the usual pressure to cut it on grounds of obscurity was less forceful. David Snodin, the script editor on her production, pointed out that

Whereas in most productions of the play several references to the reign of Henry VI are omitted, they have naturally been allowed to remain in this version – as has, of course, the haunting figure of old Queen Margaret, who so dominates the *Henry VI* trilogy, but who is often removed altogether from productions of *Richard III*.[14]

Howell cut only five per cent of the text of the tetralogy (613 out of 11,601 lines). Such respect for the writer may be regarded as revealing theatrical thinking – after all, in the cinema the actors and the director have almost always eclipsed the author of the screenplay – but Stanley Wells believed that in the case of this production the texts were 'probably purer than any given in the theatre since Shakespeare's time'.[15]

Because of its financial resources and because of its fragmented rehearsal and shooting schedules television can employ large, talented casts. Messina promised in 1978 that The Television Shakespeare would employ 'some of the greatest classical actors of our time'.[16] Effectively, he played the star-system, signing up big names in television, the cinema and the theatre: Claire Bloom, John Gielgud, Derek Jacobi, Celia Johnson, Penelope Keith, Alec McCowen, Keith Michell, Helen Mirren, Kate Nelligan, Anthony Quayle, John Stride, Michael York, and so on. For the tetralogy, Howell drew on eighty-one different actors but created a hard-core company of thirty-nine whom she used throughout. Despite the BBC publicity, which spoke of a 'star-studded cast',[17] her company had no stars and only one or two faces familiar to television viewers.

Instead of stars she chose actors with whom she had worked before, added to them, and tried to create 'a strong sense of family'.[18] Her target was a company whose unity derived from a corporate experience during production; the willingness and versatility to double parts enabled actors to become far more involved in the play as a whole than is normally the case in the disintegrated process of television filming. Altogether, twenty-six actors were required to double. The actor playing Henry (Peter Benson) appeared in all the plays in that role, but also played two other minor parts. The actor playing Richard (Ron Cook) took three other minor roles. Another actor (Derek Farr) played sixteen different roles!

Howell intended the viewer to recognize, and think about, the doubling.[19] And the actors were themselves forced to acknowledge the puzzling effects of televising the tetralogy, of exposing the plays to viewing conditions. David Burke, who played Gloucester, Dick the Butcher, and Cade, talked to Henry Fenwick about the differences between the Gloucester of *Part 1* and the Gloucester of *Part 2*:

Watching it all in one evening an audience would say, 'That actor's changed his style'. But I know that there will be a gap between the two episodes and therefore people will just have a vague memory of what he was like; hopefully they won't see a change in style, they'll just see a different aspect of him.[20]

The approach to casting was thus practical, in that it encouraged integration and cohesion between actors, and interpretative, in that the doubling exposed relationships between one role and another, and between the community of roles and the community of actors. Howell remarked that her *Richard III* was a play 'haunted by the other three plays and also by the presence of the same actors'.[21]

Part of the strength of her company derived from the conditions under which rehearsals and filming took place. Whereas most productions in the series had to make do with a month's rehearsals and a week's filming, Howell worked with her company over six months. Furthermore, the plays were made in the right chronological order and, although they were shot in the normal stretches of a week each, the same company was actually filming together for a total of twenty-nine days. Such conditions improved ensemble playing. As she herself put it, 'courage grows and people get better'.[22]

Fenwick called Howell's use of a permanent company, and the device of doubling, a 'theatrical approach' from a director with a 'strong theatrical background'.[23] Another of her decisions which was more characteristic of the theatre than of either television or the cinema was the choice of a permanent set. Indeed, in all her productions in the series, Howell used some form of permanent, semi-abstract and semicircular structure, surrounding an open acting space. It was most abstract in her first production, *The Winter's Tale*. In *Titus Andronicus* (her last) it was clearly intended to suggest the Colosseum – a theatre of cruelty. In the tetralogy the size, complexity, and flexibility of the crude wooden structure, punctuated by a number of openings, ramps, and swing-doors, created an equivalent of medieval multiple staging. The shape, bareness, and twin levels of the structure encouraged a use equivalent to Shakespeare's own experience of an Elizabethan public theatre. Finally, modernity was provided by the avowed inspiration of an urban adventure playground[24] and the use of anachronistic features – not just the swing-doors but a vast area of parquet flooring for the ground level.

Beyond all this, the set for the tetralogy called attention to itself *as a set*. Its patent artificiality was intended to help the viewer 'accept the play's artificiality of language and action'.[25] The swing-doors and the fact that, throughout the first scene of *Part Two*, the words 'HENRY VI Part Two' were written on the set itself, were sources of a Brechtian alienation. Finally, the parquet flooring openly proclaimed the actual conditions under which the production was being filmed: it seemed to be saying, 'This is a television studio.'[26] Such frankness was part of a strategy to educate the viewer into an understanding of the spatial conditions under which the performance was taking place.

As well as providing an immense range of different settings, the tetralogy's set allowed Howell the pace and flexibility of the medieval or Elizabethan stages. But, as John Wilders has pointed out, television itself can 'restore to Shakespeare's plays the unbroken flow and continuity they almost certainly achieved in the renaissance theatre. By the simple process of cutting, the director can shift from one scene to another even more swiftly than was possible in Shakespeare's time.'[27] Furthermore, the camera is mobile. Thus Howell had at her disposal the physical opportunities of her set, permitting her the spatial strategies of the theatre, and the cinematic possibilities of cutting from one shot to another and, by means of the camera's own movements, 'discovering' or 'losing' an actor or a portion of the set. In the theatre the set is all there before us, but in film and television each new shot creates a new set. Howell achieved *two* sets, the *known* permanent set and the *framed* set, and she played them off against each other.

On the other hand, her spatial manipulation of the three elements – actors, camera, and permanent set – privileged the first two over the third. Although the set's residual force was part of a possible metatheatrical statement ('This is a play'), the fact that it was inconsistently naturalistic, and susceptible of merely abstract or geometrical readings, suppressed its denotative and spatial significance.

Instead, the camera concentrated on the actors and their relationships. They were blocked primarily in relation to one another and to the camera itself, and only rarely in relation to a detail of the set, such as an entrance, or a level, or a property. The set merely created an acting space, and a space for the camera to move in.

Because the camera was so mobile in this production Howell could create fertile spatial relationships not only within the studio but also within the frame. But the source of that fertility was primarily her knowledge of what can be done with blocking in the theatre.

I do find the transition from one medium to another an extra worry and burden and problem. The scenes themselves need so much work and I get so involved that often at the end of a scene I think, 'Oh blast it, Jane, you were supposed to be dashing around looking for camera shots!' But actually I was thinking about what the scene means.[28]

And, for all that on occasion Howell could use filmic techniques (there were slow-motion sequences in both the tetralogy and *Titus Andronicus*), her notion of meaning was always theatrical before it was filmic. For example, she had a problem with Act 3, Scene 1 of *Henry VI Part 2*.

The Parliament scene where Gloucester is baited by his enemies was a nightmare . . . There is something foreign about doing it on telly because you need to see them all. What is lovely is seeing all the group at once, but I know I can't do that a lot of the time. And you can't ask the actors to be somewhere just because of the camera: they've got to have their own reality.[29]

This statement makes three important points. In the first place she seems to feel that the scene is at home on the stage but not on television which, by contrast, is restricting and denying. Secondly, the actors must have their own reality, i.e. they are not Eisenstein's *types* to be co-ordinated in pictorial terms by the solely autonomous director. Thirdly, 'you need to see them all'.

This phrase surely indicates that Howell would like television to do what the theatre has to do, namely provide the viewer with a visible account of those present throughout a scene. And in all her productions in the series she tried to find gaps in a composition which she could fill with the heads of the silent participants in a scene. By moving the camera or moving the actors a sense of the complete cast for a particular scene could be built up. The composition of the frame was rapidly and continuously changing, through a combination of actors' regrouping, camera movement, and cutting between cameras. The actors' movements were theatrical, the camera's movements were cinematic, but the constant impulse to change the composition or the shot was televisual.

Commitment to 'seeing them all' was part of Howell's consistent desire to relate individual experience to social experience and social facts, and not to read human history in terms of those few individuals with power and authority.[30] Even in *Titus Andronicus* sympathetic identification was deflected away from the suffering Titus and on to the viewer's representative she had constructed for her production – Young Lucius. Her adherence to attitudes and techniques drawn from the theatre was both a commitment to a 'committed' theatre and an attempt to make television communal in the way that all theatre inevitably is.

II

In his attitude to the text, to casting, to *mise-en-scène*, and to the individual, Elijah Moshinsky provided a distinct contrast to Jane Howell. His productions in the series were *All's Well that Ends Well* (4 January 1981). *A Midsummer Night's Dream* (13 December 1981), *Cymbeline, Coriolanus* (21 April 1984) and *Love's Labour's Lost* (5 January 1985). These were his first work in television, but from the beginning he enunciated some bold principles: 'People think the plays should "speak for themselves"! . . . Plays *don't* speak for themselves – you interpret them by casting, by editing, by designing. They *need* interpretation . . .'[31]

'Interpretation' is a radical procedure in Moshinsky's hands. In *Cymbeline*, which may be regarded as typical of his method, he set about creating a new structure for the play, and to this end removed twenty-five per cent of the lines (820 out of 3,272). Furthermore, he transposed speeches, divided scenes into smaller units and then staged them in different settings.

The cutting of speeches is not to do with the overall length of a production . . . but with the internal rhythm and excitement of it. For example when you're trying to balance different parts and different points of view it's not very good if you have long development takes . . . The best thing to do is not to have long speeches but to intercut them, so you get four or five speeches, cut in the middle and relocated in different places so that they can be done as it were simultaneously. I also think time-lapse is vital in all this because it's got to do with rhythm . . . In television I can cut within a speech to a different location and not worry about continuity: it's like a time jump.[32]

This degree of editing had ceased to be a matter of interpretation of someone else's text. A new text, effectively the product of the cinema's cutting room, had displaced Shakespeare. Moshinsky had become *l'auteur*.

The contrast between the two directors continued into the area of casting. Moshinsky went for stars, particularly in *Cymbeline*, whose cast included Claire Bloom, Richard Johnson, Robert Lindsay, Helen Mirren, and Michael Pennington. The BBC's pre-publicity used a close-up of Mirren on the *Radio Times* cover ('Helen Mirren stars as Imogen . . .') and a two-page article inside included a second photograph of her, occupying almost a whole page. This article, entitled 'Mirren's Imogen', took as its theme the seeming inappropriateness of her playing the part of a long-suffering, patient, and pure wife. 'But then, director Elijah Moshinsky does not see the play the way the Victorians saw it. "I wanted an actress of great sexual voltage," he declares.'[33] Thus, the star-system offered Moshinsky the opportunity to establish a tension between the actor's public image and the conventional reading of her/his role.

The producer of Moshinsky's first two plays in the series was Jonathan Miller, and Moshinsky's ideas for settings for all his productions showed the clear influence of Miller's theory and practice. In Miller's opinion, the way to unlock Shakespeare's imagination is to immerse oneself in 'the themes in which he was immersed. And the only way you can do that is by looking at the pictures which reflect the visual world of which he was a part.'[34] The television frame became a picture-frame in Moshinsky's productions, and the viewer was invited to recognize in the sets and compositions the worlds of Rembrandt, Hals, Vermeer, and other Dutch masters (*All's Well that Ends Well* and *Cymbeline*), and of Watteau (*Love's Labour's Lost*). In *A Midsummer Night's Dream*, the picture-frame became a picture-frame stage and even a cinema screen as the exterior scenes invoked the productions of Beerbohm Tree and Max Reinhardt. But on the whole Moshinsky's pictorialism concentrated on naturalistic interiors. Naturalistic exteriors, argued his designer for *All's Well*, 'look dreadful in the studio, so phoney. We deliberately eschewed any sort of exterior – not even landscapes through windows.'[35] In *Love's Labour's Lost* the famous eavesdropping scene in the park was set in a library and in *Cymbeline* so much exterior setting was lost that one reviewer complained that the play's ideas of pastoral were lost too.[36]

Naturalistic interiors in the manner of the Dutch masters not only look authentic on television but suit television's conventional pressure towards domestication. In *Cymbeline* even Jupiter was dressed as a Rembrandt nobleman, and merely had the advantage over the mortals of meriting a tilted camera angle – in other words, of being looked up to. Jane Howell is quoted as saying that 'Everything you put on stage is a political statement.'[37] In *Coriolanus* Moshinsky could see 'a curious mixture of the domestic and the political' and decided that the central theme he wanted was 'the non-political one'.[38]

Moshinsky's directorial style was also quite opposed to Howell's: it involved keeping actors and camera comparatively still and providing movement through montage. The drastic editing of the text and modernist fracturing of the narrative were reflected in the use of montage and rejection of development shots. Henry Fenwick remarked that, in the case of *Cymbeline*, this was 'a style worked out carefully to gibe with his vision of the play as a dream'.[39]

Convinced that the play is a psychological study of 'very dark motives'[40] Moshinsky provided his *Cymbeline* with two texts, an objective level of action and 'a subjective level of action . . . [which] is like a series of nightmares . . . The play centres round these therapeutic dreams.'[41] Moshinsky cast the viewer in the role of voyeur-cum-analyst, observing and overhearing the conscious and unconscious actions of the play. Whereas Howell had deployed two modes of verbal discourse – open dialogue and soliloquy addressed directly to the camera – Moshinsky opted for three: open dialogue, voice-over, and soliloquy directed at an angle to the camera.

We have a simple relationship to characters who are engaged in open dialogue. We witness the dialogue but our existence is not acknowledged; we are voyeurs, eavesdroppers, in a way absent. Our relationship to voice-over is one in which we seem to be privileged, in direct communication with the characters' thoughts. But in the third of Moshinsky's modes, soliloquy not addressed to the camera, the viewer is in an ambiguous position, possibly absent but equally possibly known to be present but being evaded. The complex of all three modes created a gulf between viewer and actors. The concentrated study of the characters was intimate, but the viewers were unacknowledged voyeurs. Such a relationship characterizes cinema rather than theatre or television.

In order to signal the beginnings of dream sequences (Iachimo, for instance, came out of the trunk in Imogen's bedchamber both literally and, the viewer was encouraged to believe, within Imogen's dreams), naturalism was overlaid with conventional signs drawn from the cinema: 'We're very close and we move in and we do all the filmic technique of close-up and time-lapse and silhouettes and menacing shots and the suggestion of his nakedness, so he has a rather potent sexual force.'[42]

In comparison with Howell, Moshinsky went for closer shots. Her characters were almost always standing, his frequently seated and often at tables. Whereas in *Henry VI Part 2*, for example, there were 315 medium and long shots, in *Cymbeline* there were only 226; whereas *Part 2* had only 88 close-ups, *Cymbeline* had 231. The effect in *Cymbeline* was to reinforce Moshinsky's emphasis on individuals, psychological interpretations of behaviour, and subjective experience.

This emphasis was also noticeable in his *Coriolanus*. David Snodin, the script editor, explained that the massive cuts and changes to the text were effected 'in order to sustain the story's narrative energy by concentrating on the thoughts and actions of the principals'.[43] Moshinsky wished to stress the central character's intensifying isolation:

> when you read it it looks as though the play has no internal monologues or discussions at all, whereas actually on television you can extract lots of Coriolanus' speeches where the sense of internal disenchantment grows; he becomes alienated . . . we have these incredible close-ups where he's off-centre and we can hear the monologue of disenchantment which goes throughout the play.[44]

In his *Cymbeline* he deployed a series of devices to suggest the isolation of all the characters. As well as using the close-up he ensured that one character would be separated from another by being reflected in a mirror, or he deliberately broke the flow of the action by breaking up the text. He conceived of Posthumus as a man who 'labours entirely under guilt, the guilt of his existence . . . a bitter, existential and Dostoevskian character'.[45] This existential isolation of the characters was often reinforced by the set. The windows offered no views of the outside world, and many of the characters had their backs to the walls and were out of direct communication with others. Silent, oppressively obsequious, standing or bowing, the servants and anonymous courtiers might be present but served only to focus attention on the principals.

Where Moshinsky's approach was under the greatest strain was in the final scene.

> On the stage, of course, it's the whole cast assembling and telling each other what they've experienced and how their relationships have changed . . . I came to the conclusion that how to do this on television . . . is to deal with it not as a group scene but as a series of individual small scenes . . . It's all either close-ups or two shots . . . without too many geographical establishings of where people are. Iachimo as it were disappears out of the scene after he's said his piece and Posthumus comes in – he literally walks off camera and isn't seen again until he's needed. And we're not meant to know where he is – he's somewhere off camera.[46]

So, this way of shooting the final scene ensured that the architecture and topography of the shooting conditions were not finally intelligible to the viewer. The emphasis was on individual characters and on the smallest units of human interaction. Howell's tetralogy had given a social reading within a simulated real time (often employing long takes on a single camera) and real place (the known set in an implied studio). Moshinsky's *Cymbeline* was thoroughly subjective, exploring dream interiors in dream time.

III

Stanley Wells wrote, after The Television Shakespeare was complete, that few of the productions had tackled, let alone solved, the problems of adapting Shakespeare to the television medium.[47] Howell and Moshinsky may not have solved all the problems, but they certainly tackled some of them, boldly. Both drew on some of the conventions of television (in Howell's case, the primacy of talk and a rapid alteration of the image, for instance; in Moshinsky's case, a preference for the seated figure and the close-up) but rejected others (Howell opted for stylized acting, Moshinsky for images of intense visual detail). In addition, Howell discovered in television's immediacy and intimacy an equivalent to the stage actor's direct relationship with the audience. Television's ability to simulate real time was combined with its frankness about the physicality of things, so that a pact was made with the viewer: these are the actors, this is the text, this is the set, this is the space in which we shall all be working. She operated within the known.

Moshinsky, on the other hand, discovered in television's sealed, iconic screen a denial of immediacy and intimacy. He deconstructed the text and remade it. His *mise-en-scène* ensured that the space which the viewer saw became a puzzle. He used television's preference for segmentation, and its ability to cut between shots, to create a cinematic montage that challenged the known.

Their joint achievement derived from their ability to combine an initial conception of the cultural form to which television could best be assimilated – for Howell, theatre, for Moshinsky, cinema – with a sensitivity to the character of television as a cultural form in itself.

Notes

1 In the preparatory work for this article I was very grateful for the encouragement of Dr T. P. Matheson of the Shakespeare Institute.

2 Derek Longhurst, 'Not For All Time, But For an Age', in *Re-reading English*, ed. P. Widdowson (London, 1982), p. 163; Graham Holderness, 'Radical Potentiality and Institutional Closure: Shakespeare in Film and Television', in *Political Shakespeare: New Essays in Cultural Materialism*, ed. Jonathan Dollimore and Alan Sinfield (Manchester, 1985), pp. 182–201.

3 *Television: Technology and Cultural Form* (London, 1974), p. 60.

4 The statistics in this paragraph derive from the *BBC Annual Report and Handbook* (1951; 1975; 1986), *Radio Times* (1964; 1984) and *Guide to the BBC 1992*.

5 See, for instance, Rod Allen, 'International Co-Production: Cash for the Concept', *Edinburgh International Television Festival Magazine* (1978), pp. 22–4; Carl Gardner and John Wyver, 'The Single Play: From Reithian Reverence to Cost Accounting and Censorship', *EITFM* (1980), pp. 48–9. At the opening press conference for the series the

Managing Director of BBC TV promised that it would be 'straight' (*Birmingham Post*, 2 November 1978, p. 2).

6   *Visible Fictions: Cinema, Television, Video* (London, 1982), p. 112.

7   *Ibid.*, p. 135.

8   Quoted in Tim Hallinan, 'Interview: Jonathan Miller on The Shakespeare Plays', *Shakespeare Quarterly*, 32 (1981), 134–45; p. 140.

9   *Henry VI Part 1*: 800,000; *Part 2*: 500,000; *Part 3*: 500,000; *Richard III*: 500,000; *Cymbeline*: 400,000. (Source: BBC Broadcasting Research Department.) These figures must surely outstrip the total size of audience for any production of any Shakespeare play ever performed in the British theatre.

10 'The Canon in the Can', *Times Literary Supplement* (10 May 1985), p. 522.

11 Stanley Wells, 'Television Shakespeare', *Shakespeare Quarterly*, 33 (1982), 261–77; p. 261.

12 Cedric Messina, 'Cedric Messina Discusses *The Shakespeare Plays*', *Shakespeare Quarterly*, 30 (1979), p. 135.

13 Alan Shallcross, 'The Text', *Romeo and Juliet*, The BBC TV Shakespeare (1978), p. 21.

14 'The Text', *Richard III*, The BBC TV Shakespeare (1983), p. 34.

15 'The History of the Whole Contention', *Times Literary Supplement*, 4 February 1983, p. 105.

16 Preface to *Richard II*, The BBC TV Shakespeare (1978), p. 8.

17 *Radio Times*, 24 December 1982.

18 Henry Fenwick, 'The Production', *Henry VI Part 2*, The BBC TV Shakespeare (1983), p. 26.

19 Fenwick, 'The Production', *Richard III*, The BBC TV Shakespeare (1983), p. 27.

20 Fenwick, *Henry VI Part 2*, p. 29.

21 Fenwick, *Richard III*, p. 27.

22 Fenwick, *Henry VI Part 2*, p. 24.

23 Fenwick, 'The Production', *Henry VI Part 1*, The BBC TV Shakespeare (1983), p. 29.

24 *Ibid.*, p. 24.

25 Wells, 'The History of the Whole Contention', p. 105.

26 In fact, as Fenwick pointed out in *Henry VI Part 2*, p. 20, the parquet was not the studio floor but was laid specially for the production!

27 'Adjusting the Set', *Times Higher Educational Supplement*, 10 July 1981, p. 13.

28 Fenwick, *Henry VI Part 2*, p. 23.

29 *Ibid.*, p. 22.

30 See her remarks on Richard quoted in Fenwick, *Richard III*, p. 30.

31 Fenwick, 'The Production', *All's Well that Ends Well*, The BBC TV Shakespeare (1980), p. 17.

32 Fenwick, 'The Production', *Cymbeline*, The BBC TV Shakespeare (1983), p. 20.

33 Fenwick, 'Mirren's Imogen', *Radio Times*, 9–15 July 1983, p. 4.

34 Hallinan, 'Interview', p. 140.

35 David Myerscough-Jones quoted in Fenwick, *All's Well that Ends Well*, p. 25.

36 Katherine Duncan-Jones, 'Sitting Pretty', *Times Literary Supplement*, 22 July 1983, p. 773.

37 Quoted in Ultz, *Plays and Players* (September 1983), p. 15.

38 Fenwick, 'The Production', *Coriolanus*, The BBC TV Shakespeare (1984), p. 21.

39 Fenwick, *Cymbeline*, p. 26.

40 *Ibid.*, p. 19.
41 *Ibid.*, p. 17.
42 *Ibid.*, p. 17.
43 'The Text', *Coriolanus*, The BBC TV Shakespeare (1984), p. 31.
44 Fenwick, *Coriolanus*, p. 22.
45 Fenwick, *Cymbeline*, p. 25.
46 *Ibid.*, p. 26.
47 'The Canon in the Can', p. 522.

6

SHAKESPEARE'S COMEDIES ON FILM

RUSSELL JACKSON

I

What happens when films are made from Shakespeare's comedies? They have been less attractive to film-makers than his tragedies and histories: limiting the reckoning to full-length sound films in English, there have been productions of *As You Like It*, *A Midsummer Night's Dream*, *The Taming of the Shrew* and *The Tempest*, all of them filmed twice. Kenneth Branagh's *Much Ado about Nothing* was released in 1993.[1] This essay discusses aspects of the filming of Shakespearian comedies, referring for the most part to films currently available for viewing and study, and concentrating on productions that seek cinematic expression for what their makers see as the qualities of the original texts. This is a purposely loose definition of the notion of 'fidelity' to the plays, that requires a film to tell the play's story more or less fully and to try to achieve some of its effects. The professed 'Adaptation' of *The Tempest* by Peter Greenaway is a powerful and rich film, but it remains an adaptation, and I refer to it only in passing. My main concern is with the difficulties and opportunities that present themselves when filmmakers attempt to bring Shakespeare into 'mainstream' and 'popular' cinema. No doubt because my own experience (as a consultant for Branagh's two Shakespeare films to date) has been in this area, I find the problems that arise in such circumstances particularly interesting, and I favour Derek Jarman's *Tempest* more than, say, Christine Edzard's *As You Like It* or Peter Hall's *Dream* because his film seems to manage 'mainstream' appeal ('gothic' horror, camp humour, a sense of festivity) on a 'fringe' budget. Journalistic writing about Shakespeare films often raises the spectre of the 'purist' who may be affronted by what films 'do to' the cultural commodity of Shakespeare. This repressive figure seems to me to be as imaginary as many others conjured up in film publicity: in what follows I am concerned with some of the results of attempting to make Shakespeare's comedies into films, and my principal motive is the desire to see good films rather than to make sure that some sort of homage has been paid to 'Shakespeare'.

The uneasy relationship between filmic and theatrical genres probably only broadens in the cinema the diversity of generic definitions that in any case become apparent when the comedies are played before diverse modern theatre audiences. The two *Shrews* (Sam Taylor, USA, 1929 and Franco Zeffirelli, Italy, 1967) are farcical comedies featuring popular stars; the *Dreams* (William Dieterle and Max Reinhardt, USA, 1935 and Peter Hall, Great Britain, 1968) differ markedly from one another in production values and outlook. Like Max Reinhardt, Paul Czinner was a refugee from Hitler's Germany, and his *As You Like It* (Great Britain, 1936) may have more in common with Reinhardt and Dieterle's 1935 *Dream* than with Christine Edzard's production (Great Britain, 1992). This in turn shares some common ground with Derek Jarman's *Tempest* (Great Britain, 1980), which clearly has its context among the director's other contributions to a British counter-culture and the desire to redefine cinema. Peter Greenaway's *Prospero's Books* (Great Britain, 1991) has comparable intentions, and a corresponding target audience that can be defined as 'art-house'. The *Shrews*, the 1935 *Dream*, the 1936 *As You Like It* and Branagh's *Much Ado about Nothing* (Great Britain, 1993) aim for the popular market, although (as usual) it is not always easy to identify who is catered for and how successful the strategy has proved. Appeal to the nature of the audience catered for on the film's initial release ('popular' or 'art-house') is made insecure by the fact that Shakespeare films have always had a peculiar and privileged 'afterlife', accentuated since the late 1970s by their greater availability in video form for home consumption and school and university study.

Comparisons with the familiar kinds of film comedy are not easily made, given the constantly shifting kinds of appeal that define 'popular' cinema. Although certain elements of popular film comedy appear in Zeffirelli's *Shrew* (the chase, the slapstick combat) both it and Branagh's *Much Ado* may draw on the cinema's long tradition of comedies based on the 'battle of the sexes'. The 1929 *Shrew* had direct links with silent film comedy, and the 1935 *Dream* with fantasy film: both have elements of other film conventions. In any case, it is one thing to speak of film 'conventions' and genres as patterns evident to the student and another to contemplate films with the producers' eye for what the public has seen before and what kinds of surprise it will take. The financers of films have a notorious tendency to think of innovation as consisting in novel combinations of what has already worked, and of characterization as the calculated combination of stars and the effects they are known to deliver in the box office. It is tempting to consider Shakespearian films as constituting a distinctive genre of their own, claiming kinship with various other kinds of film but always distinguished by their origins in texts that are at once theatre scripts and cultural icons. Perhaps to the 'front office' of the old studios or the production companies of the present day their only predictable potential is for bestowing *kudos* on their makers.

Nevertheless, we can usefully distinguish kinds of films of Shakespearian comedies on the basis of the qualities of the original texts that film-makers have responded to. The present essay discusses two such genres of Shakespearian film comedy, fantasy and farce, and glances briefly at the comedy of manners. It should be said that whenever Shakespeare's language is spoken in a film, the artificiality of the production is foregrounded. Film's need for images, for movement, and for a rhythm of the physical world makes elaborately patterned and expansive eloquence hard to dramatize or even to accommodate. Even when the script has been composed by whittling down the play's text to an absolute minimum, the dominance of language among the sign-systems of the plays makes it inevitable that in Shakespearian films characters will simply talk more, as well as more quaintly, than in comparable films with contemporary dialogue. Tragedies and histories suffer less than comedies from the consequences of this, and the chance to use Shakespeare's words can only help film-makers who are saved the anxieties of finding an idiom that will suit the antique setting but can still be achieved by modern scriptwriters and accepted by audiences. 'Modern dress', now a commonplace in stage Shakespeare, is rare in film Shakespeare.

Christine Edzard's *As You Like It* is the exception here. Set in contemporary Britain, and making deliberate use of the distance between language and its social context, it is likely to speak to the cultural experience of those who have undergone an education in the arts during the last two decades, but in so doing (as its rapid disappearance from commercial cinemas seems to suggest) it sets itself apart from the films aimed at a more conservative 'popular' audience, for whom old-fashioned speech still requires passably old-fashioned clothes and settings. Unfortunately Edzard's film is a poor representative of the vigour and sense of relevance that 'modern dress' can bring. In the dockside wasteland that stands for Arden the references to trees, streams and deer are allowed to stand, and the contemporary social focus is hopelessly vague. The characters are either bankers in an echoey office-block foyer or drop-outs who huddle in cardboard boxes. The play's mixture of pastoral vagueness and social precision is lost, to be replaced with modern pieties rather than analysis and argument. Money-dealers are bad, destitution is a blight, so we should throw into neglect the pompous court. What occupation can Corin or Touchstone have in this landscape? Constant traffic and aircraft noise in the background obscure the voices, which sometimes reach us from figures stranded in the middle distance.

There are some happy inventions (sprayed graffiti for Orlando's poems, Audrey's mobile snack bar, the cocktail party of the first 'court' scenes) but they lack coherence. The film refuses to show the wrestling match and omits Hymen altogether: it takes pains to avoid wooing us with entertainment. The accomplished performances are flatly filmed, and an audience without knowledge of the play would surely miss the point of most of what happens. On this evidence *As You Like It* is hardly the best vehicle for criticism of present-day Britain, and the suppression of its joyousness and sense of recuperation through love makes the choice seem especially perverse. Paradoxically, this film uses more of the text of its play and captures less of its spirit than other more radically adapted versions of the comedies.

The physical and temporal isolation of the screen action from its audience has a particular significance for comedy: the performance cannot respond directly to their mood, and the normal theatrical mechanisms that produce comic rhythm and timing have to function in a vacuum, or indeed cease to operate at all so far as the actors are concerned: timing is largely created in the editing suite. Film comedy rarely builds long scenes and patterns of scenes on the 'literary' quality of dialogue, but has ways of dramatizing the actions and relationships of which such speeches are the verbal evidence: the 'gesture' of the scene is shown, with more precision and economy than is usually required on the stage. Repartee in American comedies of the 1930s, for example, or in Neil Simon's work in the same tradition, is funny more by rhythm and aptness than by elaboration of some witty conceit. The need for movement and variety of setting – usually clearest when a stage script is 'opened out' by having characters go on journeys – is only one symptom of the need to tell stories by a range of devices of which dialogue is not paramount. We listen in the theatre, but eavesdrop in the cinema, according to a professional scriptwriter, whose book on technique offers some useful definitions of the commonplaces of feature-film writing in Hollywood: 'Both the theatre and the novel base their use of speech on articulacy; and again, this is where film dialogue suffers, for at its most effective it is based on an essential inarticulacy.'[2]

Such 'rules' are of course not accepted by every filmmaker, but a consequence of the predominance of the 'realistic' mode in popular cinema is that a Shakespearian comedy will immediately seem to be unfolding in an unreal world in which speech has formidable power and value. This suggests one overall alignment with cinematic genres themselves: Shakespeare in the cinema is always some kind of fantasy film. As a starting-point for a discussion of the films of Shakespeare's comedies, I begin with films based on plays whose theatrical mode and subject matter gives them the clearest claim to be considered fantasy: *A Midsummer Night's Dream* and *The Tempest*.

II

Fantasy may be defined (to adopt Tzvetan Todorov's formulation) as fiction that evokes the response, 'I nearly believed it.' Todorov suggest that absolute belief and total incredulity both lead us away from the fantastic: its vitality comes from our hesitation between assent and disbelief.[3]

A Midsummer Night's Dream and *The Tempest* invite exploration of the film medium's inextricable but divergent tendencies: to create convincing representations of reality, and to offer new ways of showing the unreal. In the films of these plays design techniques that would denote self-conscious Expressionism in other contexts are the norm: the light of common day, an illusion so painstakingly sought after in other films, is scarcely required here. The supernatural element in the plays can be accommodated with little sense of dislocation between theatrical origins and the new medium, because in fantasy films the cinema is not emphasizing its ability to imitate reality. At the same time the conventions of popular cinema might easily accommodate the prose-speaking comic characters – the Mechanicals or Trinculo and Stefano. In the 1935 version of *A Midsummer Night's Dream*, it is the lovers, occupying a middle ground of stylized speech and behaviour between mechanicals and fairies, who seem to present the most difficulty. Theseus and Hippolyta, existing in a world of legend and courtly ceremony, are in this respect unproblematic: there is no need for them to display 'natural' behaviour (and if they do, it comes as a pleasantly surprising bonus). The 'star' (and non-Shakespearian) status of most of the performers makes this film a particularly interesting example for study.[4]

Puck mediates between the supernatural and the ordinary, becoming through Mickey Rooney's hyperactive performance at once a satyr and the boy next door who, like his generic equivalent in modern comedy, gets into scrapes but is to be forgiven. Puck, however, has supernatural powers into the bargain. The fact that he is unashamedly American in speech aligns him with a tradition in American culture that goes back, via the actor's own film roles, to Mark Twain's juvenile heroes. The mechanicals are so self-evidently and quaintly comic that their area of the film seems stylized, and the elaboration of the gags makes it clear that we are watching behaviour which has an interesting relationship with reality rather than offering to imitate it precisely. Among the gallery of verbal and physical tics (such as Flute's constant nibbling of nuts) James Cagney's performance as Bottom seems paradoxically restrained, subtle and ironic. Bottom is the least histrionic of the would-be actors, except when he is acting or talking about it, or when he is under the influence of powers not his own (as Titania's bridegroom he has an absurd mincing walk, and pinches her cheek in a mannered display of uxoriousness). His reactions to seeing he has become an ass are mannered: his body trembles convulsively, and the camera travels down to show his knees and legs twitching; but this is the furthest reach of what reads as artifice in Cagney's performance.

It is impossible to see Cagney as Bottom without a sense of his other, more usual, roles: the effect of ordinary gestures and gait being as it were 'put on', in self-conscious cocksure swagger, is common to his driven but insecure tough guys. In *A Midsummer Night's Dream* Cagney's presence, like that of Mickey Rooney, refers the audience to another kind of fictional world in which the actor's performances are read as a 'realistic' or flatteringly 'special' enactment of ordinary behaviour. They are lifelike and lively but more vivid than life itself. They usually refer directly to the real rather than simply enacting it. The context of Shakespearian comedy brings out the artifice that usually achieves that effect and, paradoxically, helps to sustain the stylizing of the mode of performance throughout the film. With little more adjustment than a change of clothing this Puck and Bottom could respectively cheek the grown-ups in a small town or order a beer in a bar-room. Both these performances anchor the film in the area of doubt: they are and are not Rooney and Cagney, just as the events both are and are not taking place in the Wood outside Athens.

By contrast, the lovers seem to exist in no coherent framework of believability. The contemporary cinema has a mode of self-consciously stylized performance which might suit their poetic eloquence and patterned behaviour, and it is the one which allows characters in musicals to move into song. The film does precisely that with Dick Powell's performance, suggesting a brave acceptance of the consequences of casting him as Demetrius. But Powell's technique is already in its own no-man's land of the real–unreal. He is empowered to burst into song, but he also plays the character with a wise-guy, leering humour that resists the verbal medium imposed by the lines themselves. Of the four lovers he is the one who has the clearest idea of what a night in the woods might lead to. The film's opening sequence cuts most of the lyrical passages about love, but even 'the course of true love never did run smooth' (which is more or less all he has to say on the subject) as spoken by Powell implies that he knows this is the kind of line to shoot to a girl like this.

The most immediate appeal of this production of the *Dream* lies in special effects, which offered Reinhardt opportunities not available even in the most lavish of the many theatrical productions he had staged of the play. The effects range between elaborate artifice (optical effects, matte painting, filters, flying rigs, set-construction) and nature itself (real sky and landscape, animals and birds). The film establishes a fantasy Athens as its starting-point. After the titles, a written proclamation is shown, commanding the citizens of Athens to celebrate Theseus' return to Athens, and we witness the triumphant arrival of the conquering army, which features Lysander and Demetrius and marks their relationships with Helena and Hermia. The oratorio-like chorus that accompanies this seems to be presented in all seriousness, although it is dangerously reminiscent of the 'Hail Freedonia' number in the Marx Brothers' *Duck Soup*. All this moves economically into the main strands of the plot and establishes the levels of performance among the mortals: eloquent and stately for the rulers, 'smart' for the lovers, and quaintly comic for the workmen.

The spacious settings and breadth of histrionic effect establish a scale for the mortal world that will be surpassed only by the lavishness of the wood when we come to it – and when we see fairies swirling and dancing across the huge expanse of territory that had been built on two adjacent sound stages. The opening says clearly that Theseus' world has a grandeur that only cinema can manage convincingly. The film then proceeds to the revelation of the 'dream' world that implicitly insists 'Only the cinema can realize dreams so fully.'

The virtuoso display of cinematic tricks in the first 'fairy' scene, marking arrival in the wood, bears some resemblance to the elaborate set-ups and choreography of song-and-dance numbers in contemporary musicals, but unlike the chorines in Busby Berkeley routines, these dancers never acknowledge an audience. The fairy rites are witnessed by the audience rather than offered to them, and the element of voyeurism is strengthened by the unabashedly erotic presentation of the fairies, achieved by soft, glowing photography of diaphanous veils and long flowing hair over apparently naked bodies, optical effects that cover the screen with twinkling stars and bounce light off sequins on faces and clothing, and a performance of Mendelssohn's music that accompanies quasi-sexual surrender with swooning cadences. The impression of a specifically sexual fantasy is furthered in the retention when so much else is cut of Titania's lines at the end of Act 3, Scene 1 – 'Methinks the moon looks with a wat'ry eye . . .' – and in the sequence which shows Oberon's bat-like attendants rounding up fairies in what seems a cross between the original choreography of the Rite of Spring (the dance director for the film was Bronislava Nijinska) and an old-fashioned painting of the Rape of the Sabines. Reinhardt repeated from his stage presentations the famous effect of the First Fairy's hands, which are seen fluttering together in diminishing spotlight as a muscular agent of Oberon carries her away into the dark. The image of sexual conquest is reminiscent at once of Anna Pavlova's 'Dying Swan' and (less exaltedly) the 'Adagio' dance acts once so popular on Variety bills.

When the immortals in the dream find voices, the trouble starts. Titania's painfully affected voice and wooden gestures are mitigated to some extent by photography, staging and music (Bottom is seduced chastely but Korngold's score veers from Mendelssohn to something in the ecstatic manner of Richard Strauss). Victor Jory's Oberon is also vocally staid and pompous, and his movements consist mainly of standing still in an imposing manner: his physicality does not correspond to Titania's. Cagney's ass-head does not allow him to use any of his enjoyable subtlety of expression in responding to Titania's blandishments, and the skittish 'bridegroom' behaviour referred to above does not imply any degree of erotic response. Moreover, when Titania starts coying Bottom's amiable cheeks, it is made clear that he has taken the place of the Indian Boy in her bower – and that relationship is clearly chaste. (The boy, sobbing at this rejection, is consequently glad to take up with Oberon.)

The Reinhardt–Dieterle *Dream* is a notable example of a Hollywood studio's desire to enhance its public image by presenting Shakespeare (the opening credit states that 'Warner Brothers is Honoured to Present . . .'). It makes clear some of the ways in which the techniques and scope of some of Hollywood's popular film genres might correspond to dimensions of the play. Deriving so directly from Reinhardt's long theatrical experience, and the incredible variety of his productions of the *Dream*, it has an exploratory spirit that amply compensates for such limitations as the presentation of the lovers and the arch inadequacy of its Titania. It has a fresh, ambitious quality. If the directors had been able to use colour photography the result might seem more obviously comparable with the most successful live-action fantasy films of the subsequent decade: *The Wizard of Oz*, Korda's *The Thief of Baghdad*, Powell and Pressburger's *The Red Shoes* and *The Tales of Hoffman*. Like them, it plays on the cinema's enjoyable tension between assent and the knowledge that its effects are only illusion. The elaborate contrivances that create a fairy wood are appropriate to the play's own self-consciousness. (An interesting contrast is provided by Czinner's 1936 *As You Like It* in which the sound-staginess of the Forest of Arden is hardly less artificial than the elaborate palace gardens of the world Rosalind and Celia flee.) For all its occasional vulgarities and absurdities – or perhaps because it is not afraid to embrace such effects – it seems to engage with the medium to which the play has been adapted.

Peter Hall's film of the play (Great Britain, 1968) has disappeared from circulation in Great Britain. It followed a successful and much-revived stage production for the Royal Shakespeare Company, but seems to hold the film medium at arm's length. The idea of showing the play performed in a 'great hall' which (being wooden and rush-strewn) is metamorphosed into both the Elizabethan theatre and the woodland, has somehow failed to achieve vitality in its transposition to a 'real' location for the film. An accomplished cast traipses through woods in a very imperfectly rendered day-for-night Midsummer's eve. The immortals are naked, except for strategic leaves and a coating of greenish body-paint, and the mortals wear an odd combination of Elizabethan and modern dress (the women, including Hippolyta, are in mini-skirts). Simple stop-frame devices and jump-cuts make the immortals appear and disappear, but it is hard to credit the gaucheries of camera technique and direction as innovative devices of an *avant-garde* film. The roughness of technique seems inadvertent rather than experimental. The film preserves some excellent stage performances, in particular those of David Warner, Helen Mirren and Diana Rigg among the mortals and Judi Dench as Titania, Ian Richardson as Oberon and Ian Holm as Puck, but the outdoor world seems drab, cold and far from magical while the great house itself is poorly used. There are many incidental felicities of acting and direction (such as a 'second audience' of servants at the performance of 'Pyramus and Thisbe') but these seem theatrical rather than filmic. The camera picks out reactions and line-readings doggedly with little sense of rhythm (or, at times, continuity) and the comedy is a ghost of what amused theatre audiences. Only the erotic force of Judi Dench's Titania and the blank devotion of David Warner's Lysander survive the translation. It is notable that both follow the old cinema-actor's rule of seeming to do less and let the camera observe them: for much of the time the other performances seem over-projected on the screen.

Like Hall's 'country house' *Dream*, Derek Jarman's film of *The Tempest* (Great Britain, 1980) uses very little of the trick technology of the cinema, and its self-consciousness differs from that of Reinhardt and Dieterle. But it is the work of an image-maker.[5] There are no flying effects or glass shots, and the most elaborate optical effects are those used to present the image of Ariel in a mirror over a fireplace or the sight of scenes and characters through the magic glass on Prospero's staff. Despite this, the film has plenty of extraordinary visions, but they are produced for the most part by staging tableaux and filming them. The sophisticated trick effects of Hollywood were used habitually to create effects of greater space than had been staged on the studio floor: Jarman's film, with a budget far smaller than a Hollywood fantasy, achieves a different but comparable disorientation of the viewer's sense of space by shooting for the most part on location within the rooms of a real mansion.

The film begins with the heavy breathing of deep sleep, the words of the mariners in Shakespeare's storm, blue-filtered shots of a sailing ship in a stormy sea and the figure we come to know as Prospero (Heathcote Williams) evidently dreaming the nightmare. As we are allowed to get our bearings, locating him in a bed (rather than on the ship) and then seeing Miranda lying awkwardly across her bed and evidently having the same dream, we are gradually granted the ability to make sense of what we see and hear. The world we enter is not so much an island whose magical properties are drawn on by a magus, as the realm of a magus who has withdrawn into a house which his magic has since made special. The predominant sense is of seclusion that will prove the prelude to knowledge. This house is haunted, like Satis in *Great Expectations*, by human emotions turned grotesque rather than ghosts themselves.

Miranda (Toyah Wilcox) has clearly been kept in childishness well beyond the time of physical maturing: there is no self-conscious eroticism in her behaviour, but her body speaks for itself, and the child's fantasy world is established deftly in such scenes as that in which she stands on a rocking-horse, thinking the lines of the masque (not used elsewhere in Jarman's script) or trying out a stately and balletic progress down a grand but unswept staircase. She puts on a tattered ballgown and crinoline hoop, and the general effect is of an adolescent Miss Havisham. Caliban, seen ogling her as she bathes, is a bald swarthy creature in a butler's tail-coat and over-size boots, and since the floors of the mansion's rooms are covered in hay and loam, he is at once the indoor and outdoor servant. Prospero's island is therefore implicitly a retreat indoors – Ferdinand splits his logs in a drawing-room, Caliban wheels fuel around in a wheelbarrow – and it is the 'Old Dark House' of gothic fiction in print and in the cinema, with its concomitant vampirish overtones of sexuality and the female as predator, prey or prize. Trinculo and Stefano are led by Caliban (whom they encounter on the beach) through the shuttered corridors and back staircases of the mansion, with the usual suspense of such journeys in the cinema. The 'frippery' they are tempted by is a grotesque display of tattered finery (more of Miss Havisham's cast-offs) on tailor's dummies with skeleton masks, and they are frozen into a tableau of terrified grotesqueness rather than literally pursued by Ariel's 'hounds'. Prospero lures the courtiers along corridors towards the sounds of a ball in full swing (with a Viennese waltz) but they encounter an empty room in which they are pinched and harried by dwarfs (whose vanishing and appearance is one of the film's few optical tricks). After turning them into a waxwork-like tableau, Prospero is persuaded by Ariel to relent, and the celebratory masque ensues. A chorus line of enthusiastic (and not very polished) sailors are dancing to what sounds like *bouzouki* music, and their gaiety is the prelude to a stunning and simply filmed rendition by Elizabeth Welch of 'Stormy Weather'.

Most of the film takes place in darkened interiors, lit with Jarman's characteristic painterly chiaroscuro, or in blue-filtered exteriors with a day-for-night effect that is so clearly artificial that it reads as self-conscious artifice. The cinematography 'convinces' in the sense of securing the audience's assent to actions and words that are clearly unreal. By using real rooms, fantastically lit, furnished, and peopled, Jarman is transforming a pre-existing 'reality,' creating a 'magic' of the film itself that suggests a redefinition of the magic of Prospero and, implicitly, of the play. The modern (or Victorian) dress puts the characters into a world whose relationship with that of the viewer is more direct than that established by the comic-opera baroque of the 1935 Theseus and Hippolyta. As a reclusive magician Prospero has filmic relatives who might not inspire confidence in his good will, for they include Drs Caligari, Moreau and Frankenstein, as well as many less illustrious 'mad' and manipulative scientists. His control over the house places him in a position of social dominance more immediately comprehensible than that of a Crusoe-like Prospero on a desert island. Ariel's white boiler-suit and Caliban's tail-coat suggest modern versions of the servant–master relationship, and the fact that they are the most eloquent speakers of verse in the film suggests an equality of rank in them. In the finale Ariel has changed into a white tuxedo to preside over the masque, and Prospero, moving back a century rather than forward with Ariel, has adopted more of the Regency finery we previously glimpsed in a flashback showing him with the infant Miranda. The young couple are seen to have adopted eighteenth-century fancy dress.

The film's fantasy, dependent as it is on costume, lighting and set-dressing rather than filmic tricks, is the kind that might be achieved in real life: the eclectic clothing has a closer relationship to contemporary fashions than anything worn in the Reinhardt–Dieterle film, where modernity was in Dick Powell's gosh-darn amorousness and Cagney's wise-guy insecurity rather than their clothes. Most of the cast might have gone for a walk down the King's Road without scandal. Although this might suggest a kind of art-school Shakespeare, cheap, showy, and cheerful, it does tell the play's story forcefully and engagingly, moving with the text through illusion, threats, vengeance, and comedy to a joyous sense of release. This is more than can be said for Peter Greenaway's *Prospero's Books*, which is art-historians' Shakespeare, a stately progress through the seemingly infinite appendices and footnotes of a sumptuously illustrated edition of the play. It uses the most advanced video techniques available to achieve a many-layered imaging of the text, often strikingly beautiful and disturbing but sometimes oddly literal (we see the rats turning up their noses at the leaky boat that saved Prospero and Miranda, we see his wife Susannah, and when Alonso imagines Ferdinand's drowning, we see that too). In terms of *milieu*, Greenaway's film sometimes seems like a deluxe version of Jarman's (both show us Sycorax, for example), but its refusal to tell the play's story simply is its undoing as anything other than the 'adaptation' it claims to be. Oddly enough, its reverence for the text is extreme: Gielgud speaks it (taking *all* the parts) with wonderful eloquence and feeling, and sometimes we see the words being written or are shown them on screen alongside the images they suggest.[6] Perhaps the film's admiration for the text is the key to its treatment of the play: it illustrates the story rather than playing it out. The most eloquent individual in the film, apart from Gielgud's Prospero, is Caliban – in Michael Clark's astonishing embodiment of an ideally expressive but purely physical being. The 'low' comedy scenes go for little, and the film disrupts the play's economy of showing and telling by offering from the very beginning a series of shows far grander than most directors ever achieve for the masque. When Juno and Ceres arrive, the audience have spent over an hour in far stranger company.

III

The Taming of the Shrew has no scope for displays of the supernatural but both the sound films made from it have lavishly indulged the play's opportunities for physical action, largely bypassed the wit of the spoken text and offered fantasy of another order: Zeffirelli in particular creates a convincingly detailed social picture of a world of sexual and social success, in which people can better themselves and each other. Neither film version has made any use of the play's framing device, in which Sly the drunken tinker is convinced that he is a lord and is entertained by the play proper, but both have their own ready-made 'frame' of the audience's expectations of the stars, as well as distancing devices that operate variously within the two films.

The 1929 film, directed by Sam Taylor, was the first full-length sound film of a Shakespeare play, and the first occasion on which Douglas Fairbanks and Mary Pickford appeared together in major roles. The plot of this 'most admirable adaptation of Shakespeare's comedy, played in broad slapstick as he would have had it played', was summarized as follows in a British trade paper, the *Kinematograph Weekly*:

Petruchio comes to Padua to find a rich bride, and agrees to marry Katharina, a notorious shrew. He uses her methods of violence against herself, and carries her off, after a whirlwind wedding, to his home. Here he rants and raves until finally she hits him on the head with a stool and takes him in her arms. Next morning, she appears subdued, and gives a lecture on wifely duty, winking the while at her friends. (21 November 1929)

This is a fair resumé of the film, which omits the wooing of Bianca and the corresponding master–servant disguise element, and has Katharina's 'lecture' follow immediately on the events of the night at Petruchio's house, with no journey back to Padua, no 'supposed' or real Vincentio, and no wager. In interviews Fairbanks and Pickford had emphasized the film's reverence for Shakespeare, the simple knockabout nature of the original play, and the fact that the film was (in Fairbanks' words to a British reporter) 'a typical American comedy' that would 'go down all right' (*Daily Telegraph*, 11 September 1929). Taylor (whose experience included Harold Lloyd comedies) seems to have employed two 'gagmen', silent film functionaries who specialized in physical rather than verbal joking.[7] With their help (supported by plentiful repetition of words and phrases and accompanying mugging) the film was stuffed with extra comedy without breaking too radically its claim to have stuck to Shakespeare's words. Katharina and Petruchio are defined largely through physical behaviour and facial expression, which leads to showy athleticism on his part and absurd acts of vandalism on hers. The keynote of the film is given by the opening sequence: in a crude Punch-and-Judy show a woman beats a would-be admirer but is herself beaten by another wooer whom she embraces. Then the camera tracks along a busy Paduan street before moving (via an establishing shot of its exterior) to Baptista's villa, where he insists to Bianca that his other daughter, Katharina, must be married before he will consent to her wedding. The camera then follows the sound of a raised voice and crashing furniture to a hall dominated by a steep open staircase. Two servants are ejected from the doorway at the top and roll comically down the stair, and the camera moves up, into the room, past the wreckage of furniture, to close in on Katharina at bay, glowering and holding a whip ready for further action.

Little of this depends on words, and it is possible to imagine that a silent version (such as appears to have been released concurrently with the 'talkie') would work perfectly well. The opening's travelling shot incorporated 'real' street sounds, which seem to have been as much of a novelty as the dialogue itself. Publicity made much of the new-found ability to bring Shakespeare's words to the masses and Fairbanks was alleged to be a lifelong devotee of the dramatist. Much discussion of the film turned on his strengths and weakness as a speaker of the lines, but his characterization is broadly physical – a variant of his familiar athleticism and gaiety. On a technical level, it can be noted that the rhythm of many sequences seems that of a silent film, with long gaps in the dialogue for reactions that are either purely physical or merely supported by exclamations or laughter.

In the two final sections of the film – the night at Petruchio's house and the 'submission' speech – Pickford seems to be in a more congenial vein than in the straightforward brutalities of the 'taming' (where they fight each other with whips) and the farcical wedding scenes. After arriving at Petruchio's country house and being tipped into the mire of the courtyard Katharina is denied food and sent off to bed. Petruchio comes back to the table and eats heartily, informing his dog, Troilus, of the politic moves with which he has begun his reign. Katharina, who has overheard this, now turns the tables on her husband, matching him in eccentricity as he opens the windows and flings bedding around. She throws his whip in the fire, and some kind of turning point has obviously been reached. Finally she brains him with a well-flung stool and ends up cradling his wounded head in her arms. We cut immediately to the feast where she stands by the bandaged Petruchio, who lolls happily in his chair as she lectures the company on the duties of women towards their husbands. Pickford directs a notorious wink at the camera, qualifying all she has said – although within the film's story the gesture is directed not to the cinema audience but to Bianca, who smiles in happy complicity.

In all this part of the film, Pickford has a winsome knowingness quite different from the pasteboard termagant she presents earlier, and it seems as though the sly looks and 'takes' (lovingly caught in reaction shots and unseen by Petruchio) are part of the actress's more familiar repertoire of effects. This Katharina prevails by simulating submission, and has merely learned a lesson in 'politic' behaviour. The famous wink is in fact stronger in its effect than her vocal delivery of the speech. It might be argued in retrospect that the speech belonged to one medium, and the wink to its new successor.

The wink's significance for contemporary audiences went beyond its effect within the story of Katharina and Petruchio. Fairbanks and Pickford were rumoured to have quarrelled during the making of the film, but Pickford's autobiography indicates that things were in fact worse than the press knew: the rumours that this might be their last as well as their first picture together were well founded.[8] Pickford was commonly known to be a shrewd business-woman as well as 'America's Sweetheart'. The wink brings the film into the modern world and, consequently, into the publicity's story of Pickford's relationship with Fairbanks and her status as a modern woman. As one British reviewer expressed it, this moment reverses the original intention of the taming, making it clear that Petruchio has been duped, and 'the independent womanhood of the United States has been placated, for no American woman could fall for her husband as her head and sovereign. If it is not Shakespeare it is modern and brings the farce up to date' (*Daily News*, London, 15 November 1929).

Franco Zeffirelli's *The Taming of the Shrew* (Italy, 1966) offers a fuller version of the play's text than Taylor's, finding space for the 'winning Bianca' plot as well as the central 'taming'. As Jack Jorgens has observed, although Zeffirelli discards the play's framing device he substitutes one of his own: the carnivales-que setting that effectively presents Petruchio and Katharina as a Lord and Lady of Misrule.[9] The film opens with Lucentio and Tranio making their way to Padua through a setting that is so obviously a superimposed scene-painting as to be self-consciously painterly, and has them arrive in a city overflowing with

3   *The Taming of the Shrew*, directed by Franco Zeffirelli: Elizabeth Taylor as a destructive Kate

picturesque local colour. At this point in the film, it seems that *milieu* is to be everything. At Padua University an impressive religious ceremony is in progress, but it suddenly turns from solemnity to extravagant farce, erupting into a feast of fools. This is the context in which we encounter Katharina's destructive temperament and Petruchio's sozzled roistering. Bianca, the island of calm and beauty among all this, is not immune: she is serenaded bawdily by a gaggle of street musicians and seems to enjoy the experience.

In the midst of all this, among ornately 'comic' performances of the smaller parts, Richard Burton's Petruchio seems at first simply to share the relentless tumbling of the Paduan world, and Katharina looks as though she has a slightly more wilful and dangerous version of the prevailing taste for knockabout. But the film in fact claims sanity for the pair of them by placing moments of perception – quiet epiphanies among the hullabaloo. They are comic characters who, so to speak, 'wise up'.

Petruchio is florid, drunken and gross during the sequence in which he undertakes to woo Katharina, and in weighing up the situation he does not hesitate to ascertain the quality of Baptista's silverware (only the camera sees this, so his interest in wealth seems real). But as he prepares for his first encounter with Katharina he looks at his reflection in a window ('Say that she rail . . .') and becomes both thoughtful and eloquent. He unthinkingly smooths his hair and beard, and then on further consideration ruffles them up again – suggesting for the first time that his roughness is a strategy rather than involuntary. As he turns to look at her for the first time we see him from her point of view with light in his hair – not quite a halo but definitely an aura. In one episode of the furious chase that prolongs the 'taming' sequence Katharina and Petruchio come close to sustaining real injuries – but as a result of their equal powers of boisterousness rather than any cruelty by him. At the end of the sequence, she is locked into a room while Petruchio claims that they have agreed she will pretend to be curst when they are in company. She climbs onto a table and gazes down through the fanlight to watch the scene on the stairs: her eyes are seen through the window from the hall below – recalling the film's first glimpse of her as flashing eyes behind a shuttered window – the stained glass reflects on her face when she hears Petruchio waft a kiss in her direction ('Kiss me, Kate'). The camera dwells on her beauty and music identifies a thoughtful rather than simply scheming Kate. She sinks down onto the table, deep in thought, and there is a cross-fade to the animated street on the morning of the wedding.

Moments of this kind are placed carefully to suggest stiller, deeper waters running silently beneath the surface behaviour of the pair. At Petruchio's house a comic scene involving the preparation and destruction of a meal is followed by a scene in the bridal chamber where the sexual dimension of the couple's relationship is emphasized.[10] Katharina begins to undress gingerly, with what seems like real modesty, and she pulls away from Petruchio when he kisses her shoulder with apparent tenderness. She sits on the bed alluringly, but when he approaches she hits him on the head with the warming pan. He flings the bedding around, and then makes a pretence of blaming the servants, going out onto the balcony to tell them that 'this is the way to kill a wife with kindness'. The camera 'finds' Katharina on the bed (perhaps like a husband finding his bride), where she lies sobbing into the pillow. Something occurs to her, and her sobbing ceases and she begins to smile. The music suggests a degree of serenity – the 'love' theme as it has now been established. We cannot tell what the idea might be, but when Petruchio wakes in the morning he finds that the servants are lowering the chandelier in the hall to give it the cleaning it seems not to have had for many years – and Katharina is supervising the housework, with a scarf tied round her hair. Is this what made her smile – realizing the power she could achieve in his home?

In the final section of the film, Katharina's address to the wives is preceded by a long, effectively wordless sequence of looks and thoughts between her and Petruchio, including a moment when (again to serenity in the music) she gazes at a group of children playing with a dog – she's getting broody. She clearly registers distaste for the meanness and triviality of Bianca and the widow. In Jorgens' understanding of the scene this motivates her to seize the opportunity of the wager to make a pact with Petruchio.

By underlining the general crassness of Paduan society, Zeffirelli presents the central pair as superior creatures, for all her killing looks and his over-hearty laughter. Moreover, Burton and Taylor do not have to do very much less elaborate 'acting' than those around them in order to achieve the film actor's goal of seeming more interesting simply by doing less than other people. At the end of the film they speak more eloquently than the others, and her long 'submission' speech is heard without any extraneous merrymaking on the soundtrack, as though it commands a silence more absolute than anything we have heard before. The scene is a big public display of their authority, and when Katharina brings the errant wives into the room she leads them to the most formal, balanced composition yet seen in the film: she is in the centre, and they are placed on either side of the screen. Brief reaction shots establish the onlookers and Petruchio during the speech, and on 'True obedience' music supports a direct look between Katharina and Petruchio. As she speaks 'My hand is ready', a medium shot of her is followed by a reaction shot, then a close up on her again for 'may it do him ease'. Katharina is made the still centre of the crowded room, her serenity emphasized by the camera as it becomes more intimate with her than has previously been possible. Like Petruchio, the camera (on the viewer's behalf) has achieved intimacy with Katharina.

The journey of both Katharina and Petruchio through the film is from absurd indecorum to what seems to be the truly decorous. Katharina's eloquent silences may well denote an awakening to sexual desire and the prospect of its satisfaction, a 1960s liberation more likely to appeal to Lawrentians than present-day feminists. Katharina and Petruchio are special, sensual beings, capable of smouldering while Padua fiddles. Comparison with the emotional careers of the film's stars was irresistible. As represented to its potential audiences through press reports and publicity, the film was part of a whole series of interrelated narratives: Burton's return to Shakespeare and Taylor's début in the works; the saga of the stormy relationship, with Burton's notorious drinking echoed in Petruchio's early behaviour; echoes of previous films, specifically *Who's Afraid of Virginia Woolf?*; the fact that this was Zeffirelli's first venture as sole director of a feature film – not to mention the eternal debate as to whether Shakespeare could or should be filmed. As with Pickford and Fairbanks, some of this still affects responses to the film. Pickford's famous wink seems to have undermined the eloquence of the speech in a way that reflected the truth about her and her real-life husband. Taylor's serenity and authority allegedly derived from her love for Burton with an appropriately different effect. According to Zeffirelli, Burton was deeply moved by the speech: 'I saw him wipe away a tear. "All right, my girl, I wish you'd put that into practice." She looked him straight in the eye. "Of course, I can't say it in words like that, but my heart is there." '[11]

Zeffirelli's choice of this play largely circumvents the problem of comic dialogue but several of the cast seem to have been chosen on account of their theatrical background and experience in speaking Shakespeare's lines. The contribution made in the film to the range of effects available to cinematic Shakespeare consists to a considerable extent in Zeffirelli's achievement of a comic world for the play, rather than simply a naturalistic one, but the use of eloquence in the final scene suggests another remarkable achievement – it shows how the speaking of the language can be turned to account in a way that is legitimately cinematic. Despite this, it cannot be denied that the 'wooing' and 'taming' sections rely less on verbal skill than on action, particularly the long chase sequence in the middle of Petruchio's first interview with Katharina and the Church Scene (comparable with that in the 1929 version) that makes Gremio's narration redundant. This Padua seems to be a Renaissance ancestor of the *Mad, Mad, Mad, Mad World* of Stanley Kramer's 1963 extravaganza.

Zeffirelli offers a happily resolved version of erotic antagonism – a romantic alternative to the grimmer humour of *Who's Afraid of Virginia Woolf?* The economy of popular film's dealings with character and plot is carefully adhered to: rough diamonds are shown to be smooth by a gradual revelation of their true qualities; the sensation of getting to know vivid and warm persons is complemented by a 'double' sense of growing acquaintance with the stars themselves; the setting is gratifyingly 'authentic' and picturesque – and at times lavish on a scale rarely available elsewhere in performing art. Quite apart from the requirement that an audience should forgo some of its modern convictions about relations between men and women, like the Screwball Comedies of the 1930s, the film calls for a return to a time 'when irritation could be, and was, an exhilarating sign of love.'[12]

This definition of the *mores* of Screwball Comedy clearly has a bearing on the presentation of *Much Ado About Nothing* for the cinema. In this play, however, the evil men can do to women is located outside Benedick and Beatrice (who irritate one another without doing actual harm), the demands made on the audience's ability to imagine other moral sensibilities than its own are less formidable. The confronting of the leading couple with uncomfortable truths about what men may say and do, just at the point where they are ready to admit their love for one another, provides a scene that might have been designed for the cinema. The greater range of this play's emotional and moral situations, and the sense that the characters are more like the 'rounded' and 'knowable' beings favoured alike by popular cinema and classic realist novels makes it easier to assimilate to modern sensibilities: even if their codes of honour are not ours, the characters display sensitivity and can be shown to *worry* in ways that we recognize. The collision of 'feminine' and 'masculine' worlds may resemble some modern preoccupations enough to make Benedick seem like a 'new man' – a fate never possible with either of the film Petruchios. It might be claimed that in Kenneth Branagh's film by textual adjustments and by the camera's ability to register feeling in an actor's face, Claudio is done more favours than is usually the case on stage, but it is noteworthy that the film makes few alterations to the rhythm and pace of the Beatrice–Benedick encounters. In the business of 'showing and telling' it is not surprising that the audience should witness with Claudio the apparent treachery of Hero, and that the film's grander visual gestures should be in the area of the masked ball, the wedding, the scene at Hero's tomb and the final dance. The problem of Margaret's complicity with the deception of Claudio can be negotiated more deftly in the cinema (with some cutting and the placing of reaction shots) than is usual on stage. As with Zeffirelli's *Shrew*, casting alone makes it clear that the film seeks to be considered popular cinema, and the *milieu* it creates shows a sympathetic rather than ironic attitude towards the romance of the play. Branagh's Tuscan location for Antonio's household could not be further in spirit from Edzard's bleakly urban Forest of Arden, but the play chosen affords less potential for readings in terms of class and gender conflict. Don John's stagey villainy has proved an inadequate vehicle for angst in stage productions by companies that have found little difficulty in showing the winter winds blowing through Arden. *Much Ado* is a play in which people with the means of happiness at their disposal sort themselves out: *As You Like It*, with couples who have only got to know each other in disguise, has less assurance of the future. The influence of Jaques on audiences is less easily contained than the more superficial menace of Don John.

My involvement with the film of *Much Ado* makes it inappropriate for me to comment on its effectiveness, but it seems legitimate to point to aspects of it that might be considered alongside the sequences from other films referred to above. The first is the festive environment, which might be compared with that of Zeffirelli's *Shrew* but which seems much less determinedly picturesque. Comparison of the opening sequences in terms of the screenplay's need to 'grab' an audience and engage interest and attention shows that both Zeffirelli and Branagh offer what is effectively a prologue in sights and sounds – with differing uses of text. In the 'overhearing' scenes for Benedick and Beatrice the tactics of using visual humour go beyond what is available in the theatre, but in different ways: readers and viewers have to decide whether the treatment seems inventively cinematic. A further test-case for the director's ability to use the play's material would be that of the Dogberry sequences, here redistributed in order to make better use of the material and the characters in terms of a film audience's attention, and less dependent than might be expected on the verbal joke of Dogberry's mistaken vocabulary.

Most important, in the terms suggested in this essay, is the film's ability to accommodate verbal wit, the fantasy of happy articulacy. Does it *dramatize* for film the scenes in which characters speak to each other, and does it make the subtextual currents evident and absorbing? In Zeffirelli's *Shrew* the text is so simplified and the physicality so pronounced that the moments of stillness noted above suggest more depth in Katharina and Petruchio than is really present. The longer, subtler transactions of the scenes between Beatrice and Benedick may seem less assimilable to the idioms of popular film, but it should be remembered that the range might include (in comedies alone) Woody Allen's best New York films. Few of the cinema versions of Shakespearian comedy so far made have had to deal with this kind of material at the centre of the play: the nearest approach to sustained comedy of wit is probably to be found in the treatment of the Katharine scenes in the versions of *Henry V* by Olivier and Branagh. 'High Comedy' wit is a sort of conquest, and like the social and amatory success of the witty couple (Restoration, Wildean, or Screwball) it has social connotations that perhaps disturb critics more than audiences. Edzard and Branagh (and, with little success, Czinner in his *As You Like It*), are the only directors who have so far tackled it in Shakespearian films. Whether the Shakespearian comedy of wit has found cinematic exponents in Edzard and Branagh is the question this essay must end with.

Notes

1 To these might be added a Czech puppet version of the *Dream* (1958: released in Britain with dialogue and narration in English), a Russian *Twelfth Night* (Yakov Fried, USSR, 1955) and various films owing their outline or some major element to a Shakespearian comedy – for example, Paul Mazursky's *Tempest* (USA, 1982) or Fred Wilcox' *Forbidden Planet* (USA, 1956), both derived from *The Tempest*. The present article is very much concerned with what might be considered the 'mainstream' or 'canonical' body of Shakespearian film: for an alternative view of the 'canon' of filmed Shakespeare see Graham Holderness, 'Shakespeare Rewound', *Shakespeare Survey 45: 'Hamlet' and its Afterlife*, ed. Stanley Wells (Cambridge, 1993), pp. 63–74.

2 Wolf Rilla, *The Writer and the Screen. On Writing for Film and Television* (London, 1973), p. 89.

3 Tzvetan Todorov, *Introduction à la Littérature Fantastique* (Paris, 1970), p. 35.

4 In 'Babes in the Woods. Shakespearean Comedy on Film', in *Shakespeare Observed. Studies in Performance on Stage and Screen* (Athens, Ohio, 1992), Samuel Crowl identifies a Barriesque element in the 1935 *Dream* and other films. Reinhardt's *Dream* is also discussed by John Collick in *Shakespeare, Cinema and Society* (Manchester, 1989). On Reinhardt's Hollywood stage production, with Mickey Rooney as Puck, see Kurt Pinthus, 'Max Reinhardt and the USA,' *Theatre Research/ Recherches Théâtrales*, v, 3 (1963) 151–63. The *Dream* productions are also considered by Leonhard M. Fiedler, 'Reinhardt, Shakespeare and the *Dreams*' (in Margaret Jacobs and John Warren, eds., *Max Reinhardt. The Oxford Symposium*, Oxford, 1986, pp. 79–95) and J. L. Styan, *Max Reinhardt* (Cambridge, 1982).

5 Jarman described the making of *The Tempest* in *Dancing Ledge* (London, 1984). By his account the process of making the film in Stoneleigh Abbey resembled a long party, and he gives particular credit for the film's 'look' to the designer, Yolanda Sonnabend. Jarman's visual conception of the play's theatricality can be compared with Hall's approach to the metatheatre of the *Dream*, summarized by Michael Mullin, 'Peter Hall's *Midsummer Night's Dream* on Film', *Educational Theatre Journal*, 27 (1975), 529–34. On Jarman's film see also Collick, *Shakespeare, Cinema and Society*, and Holderness, 'Shakespeare Unwound'.

6 The script is available in Peter Greenaway, *Prospero's Books. A Film of Shakespeare's 'The Tempest'* (London, 1991).

7 On Taylor and the 'gagmen', see Roger Manvell, *Shakespeare and the Film* (London, 1971), pp. 24–5.

8 Mary Pickford, *Sunshine and Shadow* (London, 1956), pp. 311–12. She claims that Taylor told her dramatic coach, Constance Collier, 'We don't want any of this heavy stage drama; we want the old Pickford tricks,' and that as a result 'instead of being a forceful tigercat, [she] was a spitting little kitten'.

9 Jack Jorgens, *Shakespeare on Film* (Bloomington and London, 1977), chapter 4. Graham Holderness's chapter on the film in *Shakespeare in Performance: The Taming of the Shrew* (Manchester, 1989) explores further the dimension of 'carnival' in the film, and examines the relationship between this and the media celebrity of the two principal actors. The distancing effect of Zeffirelli's cinematography and designs is discussed by Michael Pursell, 'Zeffirelli's Shakespeare. The Visual Realization of Tone and Theme', *Literature/Film Quarterly*, 8 (1980), 210–18.

10 Conceptions of sexuality and gender in this and other versions of the play are discussed by Barbara Hodgdon, 'Katharina Bound; or, Play(K)ating the Strictures of Everyday Life', *PMLA* 107/3 (1992) 538–53; see also William Van Watson, 'Shakespeare, Zeffirelli, and the Homosexual Gaze', *Literature/Film Quarterly*, 20 /4 (1992), 308–25.

11 The incident is described in *Zeffirelli. The Autobiography of Franco Zeffirelli* (London, 1986), p. 216.

12 Ed Skirov, *Screwball. Hollywood's Madcap Romantic Comedies* (New York, 1989), p. 29. Analogies between one film of this period and Shakespearian comedy are suggested by Lelanda Poague in '*As You Like It* and *It Happened One Night*: the Generic Pattern of Comedy', *Literature/Film Quarterly*, 5 (1977), 346–50.

7

THE ENGLISH HISTORY PLAY ON SCREEN

MICHAEL MANHEIM

The chief television screening of Shakespeare's second tetralogy, that by David Giles, has been extensively discussed,[1] and there is strong argument to be made for the idea that the plays of the earlier tetralogy (along with *King John*) are Shakespeare's quintessential English histories, focusing as they do more on the turmoil of events than on strong individual personalities (the infamous Richard of Gloucester excepted). Those terrible fifteenth-century events that come under the rubric 'Wars of the Roses' have also lent themselves well to the kind of sweeping multi-part television series we are familiar with. So, while I shall begin with a relatively brief discussion of the well-known feature-length film versions of the English histories – Olivier's *Henry V* and *Richard III*, and Branagh's *Henry V*[2] – these remarks will concentrate chiefly on three television versions between the 1960s and 1990s of the young Shakespeare's first historical tetralogy. But first, the better-known films.

OLIVIER AND BRANAGH

The usual procedure in recent criticism of Kenneth Branagh's *Henry V* has been to compare it directly with Olivier's film, pointing out ways in which the youthful Branagh of the 1980s both leans on and departs from his not-quite-so youthful predecessor of the 1940s. What has not been done is to look first at Olivier's *Henry V* in relation to his *Richard III*, with which, from a perspective of forty years, it has notable similarities, then look at the Branagh film. While the two Olivier films provide a sense of the English history play made for a film audience of the mid-1940s and early fifties, Branagh's provides a sense of what is appropriate for a film audience late in the century. The chief difference, as we shall see, is in the contrasting perception of the kingly figure.

As for the plays themselves, despite their obvious differences, there are similarities between the Elizabethan Shakespeare's treatment of the popularly conceived greatest of English medieval heroes, Henry V, and the popularly conceived greatest of English medieval villains, Richard III, similarities that are emphasized in the films. They may quickly be recognized if one sees the two plays as representing the two faces of the Elizabethan Machiavel. While Richard is of course the obvious Machiavel, chiefly associated with standard anti-Machiavellian propaganda of the period, and concomitantly with popular theatrical representations of that figure, Henry is also a Machiavel in the new image of that figure coming to be shared, though they might be hesitant to admit it, by more educated people of the 1590s, especially those actually familiar with *The Prince* itself.[3] In fact, if one considers which of the two dramatic images the author of *The Prince* might have preferred, it would undoubtedly be Henry – in part because of his more successful image-making, in part because of the greater subtlety of his intimidation, and in part because of his success.

That Olivier plays both roles in films he directed little more than a decade apart brings the similarities of the two figures into sharper-than-usual focus. The genius of his *Henry V* is not that it portrays the heroic English king so dashingly for a wartime audience quite disposed to approving the triumph of an English leader on the European continent, but that, even though Olivier cuts most of the action revealing the violent side of Henry's nature – his threats before Harfleur, his hanging of Bardolph, his command to kill the prisoners – his heroic king can today be so easily recognized as a consummate politician. The very 1940s leading-man dash of his gestures and facial expressions tends to suggest that now if it did not then; and if some of the overt threats are missing, his violence seems all the more effective now for being intimated. Nowhere is this more apparent than in the amused irony of his Henry's telling Princess Katharine that she need have no concern whether her father will consent to their marriage.[4]

The passage in *The Prince* that best suggests why Olivier's Henry fits the Machiavellian mould is the following '. . . [I]t will be well for him [the prince] to seem, and actually, to be merciful, faithful, humane, frank, and religious. But he should preserve a disposition which will make a reversal of conduct possible in case the need arises . . . He must stick to the good so long as he can, but, being compelled by necessity, he must be ready to take the way of evil.'[5] Olivier's Henry clearly possesses the good qualities Machiavelli lists, but he also 'preserves a disposition which will make a reversal of conduct possible'. That is why he can command such admiration. Especially does the adjective 'frank' capture the tenor of Olivier's performance: the easy familiarity of his oft-mentioned gesture of tossing his crown over the post of his throne, the steely mercy concerning the railing courtier, the superb camaraderie inherent in the

'Crispin Crispian' speech, the genuine quality of his prayers. Yet always the sense of his control is present, as well as the suspicion that, except in his famous Act 4 soliloquy, what we are seeing is a magnificent façade.

Since Olivier omits the actions of Henry that are morally suspect, one must infer the capacity for duplicity and violence. It is, surprisingly, most evident in the comic touches he gives the role. While it may be thought that Olivier obscures the Machiavellian implications of Henry's claim to France in the opening scene by treating it farcically, the comedy of the sequence makes the orchestrated nature of the 'salique law' argument obviously Machiavellian. The farce involving the two bishops and the dropped pages of parchment has the effect of reinforcing the clownishness of the claim itself. Olivier's mock-serious behaviour, among other things in helping Canterbury pick up the dropped pages, makes very clear a Henry so totally in charge of this situation that he can subtly mock its trumpery. And the close-ups of the sleek Renaissance lords making their supportive speeches make them (today) seem manipulated. What we see is Olivier playing the fox and the lion in this scene – the fox as he makes his bishops and courtiers 'persuade' him to make war on France, the lion as, following the tennis balls insult, he speaks Henry's most threateningly leonine speech of all using his patented medium-shot echo-chamber effect to full advantage. Not only is Henry's duplicity strongly intimated in this scene but also his willingness to create havoc to achieve ends that have more to do with his power and greed than with the 'salique law'. Olivier's Henry is indeed 'merciful, faithful, humane, frank, and religious', but demonstrates here and elsewhere 'a disposition to be otherwise in case the need arises'.

Olivier's treatment of the all-important figure of the Chorus further emphasizes the image the successful Machiavellian prince must create. While the chorus is obviously not a character in an Elizabethan play, one gets the impression in the film that Olivier's Henry and Leslie Banks's Chorus work as a team dedicated to the creation and advertising of a magnificent royal personality. Especially at the beginning and before Southampton, we sense the Chorus describing a royal image that Henry will shortly illustrate.

The sense of Machiavellian artifice that dominates this film works in other ways as well. I am thinking of the tripartite structure of settings Anthony Davies has identified,[6] a structure that moves us from the world of the playhouse, to the world of the French court, to the world of the battlefield, then back to a defeated French court. The playhouse set that occupies the film through the play's first two acts, while intended for the instruction of the modern audience, also lends a sense of the artificially theatrical to the proceedings, and hence to the artificiality of the tale itself. These scenes *feel*

4 *Henry V*, directed by Laurence Olivier: Renée Asherson, as the French Princess, in a book-of-hours setting

constructed, including this king's model image and behaviour – especially as he 'takes his bows' at the conclusion of the first scene. Then, rather than countering this feeling, the film's move out of the playhouse into the larger world reinforces it. What we chiefly see pictured in this world is the glorious departure for France, an imagined 'fleet majestical', and a highly ornate French court. As Davies makes clear, this is really no real world either, but another constructed world drawn in part from late medieval court painting and tapestry, trappings even more artificial than those of the playhouse.

But the third world Davies sees in the play, which one might assume would lend a sense of something akin to a real world to the film, is ultimately the most artificial of all. The images of battle, of Agincourt and victory, suggest the American film western with its inevitably triumphant hero, supplementing the cinematically overwhelming advance of the cavalry in Eisenstein's film *1812*. This Henry's prowess as a leader seems almost to grow out of his prowess as a master image-maker. (Or his director's prowess, which in this case amounts to the same thing.) We are flooded with cinematic contrivances insisted upon by the popular heroic film: cuts from advancing horsemen, to spruce drummers, to archers with bows raised, to the king with his sword on high ready to give the command to shoot, to a magnificent tableau of battle itself (again drawn from images in art) culminating in the hero's victory over the evil knight. All these effects invite the film audience to relish the victory and its splendid achiever. But all these effects also add to the effect of something manufactured to please.

By combining his role as actor and film-maker with the artifices of setting, Olivier strongly intimates the idea of Henry as actor and image-maker, as creator of political illusions. His Henry is from beginning to end the perfect embodiment of the new Machiavellian prince – not a figure to be hated, feared, and scorned (that would come later with *Richard III*) – but one who could strengthen and preserve the state, the declared objective of *The Prince*. In short, in his efforts to create the image of a victorious wartime English leader for a country at war in a noble cause, Olivier, perhaps unwittingly, created what is probably the sole instance in drama of what Machiavelli really had in mind – and he did it by means of the medium most suited to the creation of illusion.

All that is implicit in Olivier's Machiavellism as Henry is explicit in his Machiavellism as Richard, the one probably deriving from a sophisticated reading of *The Prince*, the other from a stage tradition that blended the traditional figure of the medieval 'Vice' with the officially approved popular stage image of the villainous *Machiavel*. Davies (78–9) actually sees Olivier's Richard as a 'grotesque parody' of his Henry. Richard's Machiavellism begins, as does Henry's, with a chorus-figure, only this time that figure is the central character himself, whose opening soliloquy in the play, and succeeding soliloquies and asides, serve to set the stage for the political Richard as the Chorus in *Henry V* sets the stage for Henry. In each case the chorus figure serves not only as narrator but also chief raisonneur. Olivier emphasizes Richard's function as Chorus, as Davies points out (69ff.), by speaking directly to the camera during his soliloquies, which has the effect of inviting the film audience to be co-conspirators, just as Leslie Banks, the Chorus in *Henry V*, grandiosely invites both mock-playhouse and implicitly film audiences to be Henry's. Olivier's Richard thus works his crowd very much as Banks's Chorus works Henry's.

To emphasize Richard's function as chorus early in the play, Olivier devises a set whereby Richard can observe what is going on without being seen. What we get is a throne room seen from above, over which is an enclosed encircling corridor. The camera tracks Richard as he walks this corridor observing what is going on below through periodic openings. He thus observes and comments on action Olivier interpolates into the play like King Edward condemning Clarence, responding to Jane Shore, and showing signs of advancing illness. Few stage productions have so deftly called attention to Richard's choric function, inviting us for a time to share Richard's perspective.

Like Olivier's Henry, his Richard is aware of, and more than slightly amused by, his superiority in both courage and intellect to those around him. For example, as Olivier's Henry mockingly plays the clown in the 'salique law' scene, his Richard mockingly plays the clown as he flatters and fawns, literally leaping about the screen in his efforts to seem accommodating to the Queen and her faction early in the play. But the comedy that is one of Olivier's chief means of realizing the special qualities of both Richard's and Henry's mastery significantly disappears once Richard turns bloody. That Richard becomes not more but less the effective Machiavel once the slaughter begins is made eminently clear by the savage madness of Olivier's portrayal of Richard later in the film. While a great deal of wit is implicit in Richard's and Buckingham's deception of first Hastings and then the commoners (whom the film sees as a good deal less deceivable than the nobles), the wit suddenly disappears at the moment of Richard's crazed demand that Buckingham bow down and kiss his hand. With that gesture, Olivier's Richard ceases to be, like his Henry, the effective Machiavel. That is, he loses his audience, relinquishing entirely those superficial graces Machivaelli's prince must never relinquish.

A comparison of Olivier's wooing of Princess Katharine with his wooing of Lady Anne further supports a treatment of the two monarchs that emphasizes their similarity. In both, Olivier plays the same vigorous, overpowering lover, convincingly winning a lady many of whose relatives have lost their lives because of him. If his Henry's sexuality in the scene is obvious, his Richard's is also,[7] as Olivier disregards the play's text to include two prolonged kisses – in both of which Olivier has the actress firmly in his grasp – that ensure the same kind of sexual dependency on the part of Anne as Henry achieves over Katharine. (It has often been observed how firmly his Henry clutches the princess's hand as he kisses her.) Claire Bloom's finely-wrought, highly vulnerable Anne seems mesmerized by Richard, drawn to him in part by her

5   *Richard III* directed by Laurence Olivier: Richard (Laurence Olivier) woos Anne (Claire Bloom)

immaturity and insecurity, partly by his sexuality. Renée Asherson as Princess Katharine seems comparably drawn to Henry by her immaturity, and by the powerful sexuality of her good-looking, not to mention witty, conqueror. In both films, Olivier stresses, along with the sheer masculine strength of his heroes, the quickness of mind inherent in their wooing. The amused imperialism of Olivier's Henry as he assures Katharine that he loves France so much that he will not part with an inch of her is paralleled by his Richard's casuistry as he tells Anne that since he has murdered her husband and her father he will make amends by marrying her. In both cases, true logic falters before the amusement and self-awareness of Olivier's pressing lover. And what we see in both his figures as lovers is again their essential Machiavellism – the one to be adored, perhaps, and the other loathed, but Machiavellism nonetheless.

As Olivier's Henry takes its lead from the medieval romance, as well as the American film western, his Richard takes its lead from traditional nineteenth-century melodrama, with menacing music in the background, snide asides, and lengthening shadows of the villain. In this sense both fit conventional moulds. But what is not conventional is that, especially when the same actor plays the two leads in films made relatively close to one another in time, the traditional villain can be recognized as quite similar to the traditional hero. Both jest, both smile, both ingratiate, both keep a jump ahead of the opposition, both have little trouble charming women (especially vulnerable ones), both easily master those around them. And both appear genuinely to enjoy what they are doing. After the passage of years since these films were made, we begin to realize that while we applaud the one who is attractive and hiss the one who is repulsive, Olivier reveals both to be masters of the new political art associated with the name of the disgruntled Florentine civil servant whose message provoked such overwhelming response, not all of it negative, in Renaissance Europe. Especially from Olivier's acting and directing of both films, we get a sense of political leaders who are ahead of their time in depending more upon their talent for creating images of themselves than upon the modes of morality and behaviour they were born into.

The chief respect in which Kenneth Branagh distinguishes his Henry from Olivier's is that his is not Machiavellian, and it is chiefly in this that he creates a Henry for *our* time. There is not the hint of duplicity in Branagh's presentation of this character. If Canterbury and the lords dissemble about the 'salique law', Branagh's Henry does not. Young (a bit pimply) and rather callow, he seems genuinely interested in whether in fact he does have a claim on the French throne. His ensuing threats to the French ambassador are made because he has been genuinely hurt by the Dauphin's tennis balls insult, and he is still more deeply hurt by the treachery of false friends revealed at Southampton. And finally, of Branagh's wooing of the princess, no better remark has been made than that by a (woman) student, who observed that whereas Olivier's Henry is the lover every man would like to be, Branagh's is the lover every woman would like him to be. Not glamour but sincerity is the word for this Henry.

There seems, in fact, little to add to what several reviewers, notably Peter Donaldson and Samuel Crowl,[8] have already said about this film. Heavily influenced by Adrian Noble's 1984–5 RSC production, in which Branagh also played the leading role, it sees in Henry's achievements a tale of personal development. Unlike Olivier, who presents a Henry whose 'personality is already complete at the start' (Donaldson 68), Branagh gives us a Henry who is at the beginning little more than a boy seeking his appropriate voice and direction. In the opening scene, in place of the comic posturing of the shrewd Henry and fatuous Bishops of the 'salique law' passage in the Olivier film, we get an image, largely from Branagh's eyes and posture, of a Henry lonely, still unsure of himself, capable of being led. His lords, most of whom seem little older than him, do not seem his companions. In this atmosphere the older figures obviously wield great influence. From beginning to end, he appears to follow the lead of a fatherly Exeter (capaciously played by Brian Blessed) and the Bishops, who are the conspiratorial ones. When Branagh's Henry asks Canterbury whether he 'with right and conscience' can make his claim on France, the question feels genuine.

Branagh's Henry seems more the contriver when he tricks the hapless traitors at Southampton, but even here Exeter seems in part instigator of the scheme, fully cognizant of what the king has in mind. The emphasis in the scene is clearly more on Henry's rage at Scroop, his erstwhile 'bedfellow', than on making a political point. It seems more than incidental that the scene is played in private – secure on shipboard among the chief lords – rather than in public, where the Machiavellian leader might wish to demonstrate his control performatively, for all to see. Olivier, who omits the traitors, nevertheless presents this scene as a public spectacle. We get a sense in Branagh more of a young man still caught up in his personal feelings than of Olivier's princely master of all situations.

When this king's developed personality emerges from the Henry we see in France, that personality is as passionate and uncontriving as the undeveloped one. Olivier's image of Henry is that of a king who knows ahead of time what needs to be accomplished, cognizant of the value of appearances and of the need for occasional deception in achieving his ends. When Olivier speaks the line, in response to the treacherous murder of the boys by the French, 'I was not angry since I came to France / Until this instant', we believe him. His seeming anger up to this point has been part of his facade. Branagh's anger, on the other hand, feels spontaneous, guided by his emotions. He has been *always* angry since he came to France, and his response to the murdered boys seems as genuine as was his response to the Dauphin's insult and Scroop's betrayal. He convincingly feels the atrocity.

Yet herein lies the complexity of Branagh's acting of Henry. He is the Henry for our time basically because along with his ingenuousness, sincerity, and apparent decency – he is also a ruthless murderer. Branagh's characterization radically divides our sympathies. As I suggest in a recent paper,[9] it is not that we cannot make a decision about him; we tend to make opposing decisions about him. On the one hand, we get the image of the searching youth developed into the fearless warrior and selfless leader. We get a sense of once-repressed passions turned loose in what the protagonist (and part of us) believes to be a noble cause. This sense culminates in the emotions elicited by hard-won total victory for the English – culminates really in Patrick Doyle's unforgettable 'Non Nobis' music, which builds from a single raw voice singing in the midst of carnage to the massive chorus so reminiscent of Promenade Concerts at the Royal Albert Hall, where a thousand voices join as one in singing 'Rule, Britannia'. All this plays on passions responding to the sincere boy grown into a champion, into a St George who defeats the dragon of France.

But on the other hand, there is the opposing sense, marvellously realized by Branagh, of the senselessness of warfare (medieval or modern), of its inherent cruelty – one cannot view the execution of Bardoph in this film with equanimity – and of the powerful soporific effect of the kind of patriotic sentiment exemplified by the music. One simply cannot cling to the first set of reactions in the face of Branagh's muddy, bloody slaughter on screen. In recent films, only the battle scenes in Kurosawa's Shakespeare-based 'histories' of the 1980s, his *Kagemusha* and his *Ran*, so graphically represent the horror of medieval battle. And the jarring of our first set of reactions with our second results in the complexity of this film. It elicits contradictions in audience response far deeper than that between the two sides of the Machiavel. This is a juxtaposition that focuses our eternal schizophrenia about wars and heroes.

Kenneth Branagh realizes depths in *Henry V* that have rarely been acknowledged. If the function of the Chorus has, in spite of Derek Jacobi's acting, been rendered uncertain, Branagh's film is nevertheless great because it considers the overpowering human instinct to admire a chivalrous hero alongside the still more overpowering need to rid the world of the horror of war. It is very much a Henry for our time because what once seemed to us like noble image and sentiment – the wartime utterances of a Winston Churchill or a Franklin Roosevelt, the charms of a John Kennedy (who, significantly, much admired Olivier's film) – now seem to many like facades. Knowing that political leaders, to one extent or another, all have followed the precepts of *The Prince* in order to succeed, Machiavellism as a theme of political drama no longer has the appeal it did at mid-century. What now strikes home more deeply than the story of the subtle leader making war is that of the sincere leader making war. The battles that lie ahead in our time are very likely those between sincere, noble, and quite possibly youthful leaders willing to massacre all before them for principles that make about as much sense as resistance to the 'salique law'. It is our anxiety about the future that makes Kenneth Branagh's film finally so telling.

And now to the far-more-numerous televised versions of Shakespeare's English histories, versions that culminate in one with an outlook not far different from that of Branagh's film.

THE ENGLISH HISTORY PLAY ON TELEVISION: THE FIRST TETRALOGY

Four versions of Shakespeare's first historical tetralogy have been televised since the early 1960s, of which I shall here discuss the three that have been available to me.[10] These are the 'Wars of the Roses' adapted by John Barton[11] and directed by Peter Hall for the RSC in the mid-1960s, the BBC/Time-Life treatment of the series directed by Jane Howell in the early 1980s, and one by the English Shakespeare Company under Michael Bogdanov and Michael Pennington in the early 1990s.[12] The three are eminently comparable. Hall/Barton and Bogdanov/Pennington are television productions based on actual stage versions of the plays, while Howell uses a television studio that very much conveys the effect of a stage production adapted for television. All three television versions are comparably inventive in their minimal and flexible scenery, multiple cameras, and their tracking, lighting, and special effects. Hall/Barton makes the movement from scene to scene faster than possible on stage, showing how effectively the screen can convey turmoil and sweep, though this version does not avoid confusion as to what is going on. Howell builds on Hall/Barton with her device of swinging doors that make clear the rapid divisions between everything from opposing sides in battle to events far removed in time and place. And Bogdanov/Pennington introduces unexpected changes in historical costume and setting that suggest what historical forces individual characters represent and underscore present-day parallels.

But it comes as no surprise that these productions are also quite different from one another, particularly in their underlying political and moral perspectives. They seem in some measure guided by philosophical fashions prevailing at the time they were made. Hall, and especially his adapter Barton, appear influenced by the 1960s passion for 'absurdity', that code-word for the somewhat pop existentialism associated often in regard to Shakespeare with the criticism of Jan Kott (Hodgdon 77) and the drama of Samuel Beckett. What comes through most emphatically in their production is a sense of arrogant, self-centred swagger in a senseless political maelstrom. Touchy, arrogant noblemen (and women) quite literally 'whirl' a kingdom 'asunder'.[13] The fog and smoke that dominate the battle scenes in this production emit very much the sense of a world in which 'ignorant armies clash by night'. There seems little attempt by the characters to understand the meaning of what is going on – politically or morally. Rather, they all seem to rush pell-mell into a foggy abyss. And just as foggy, but divorced entirely from any of the arrogance and ego of the others, is the hapless king (superbly played by a young David Warner), whose frustration and inability to grasp the significance of events serves well until Part 3 of *Henry VI*, where Shakespeare's lines and Warner's acting are an endorsement of a Jesus-like forbearance leading to wisdom that seems at odds with the absurdist basis of this production. An equally young Ian Holm's Richard of Gloucester, however, seems the full flowering of that absurdity. Always cool, almost always calm, this Richard is not a villain in the traditional sense so much as a pleasant alien creature, a visitor from a planet where matters such as conscience and compassion are unknown.

Jane Howell, who keeps, not incidentally, closest to the text (the 1951 Peter Alexander edition), seems rooted in an outlook, identifiable most recently with the immediate post-Vietnam War period, that has not given up on the human spirit.[14] Her nobles are egotists certainly, but not so overbearing. Each possesses sparks of decency, and each appears to know the meaning of honour. The topoi of atonement as each approaches death seem spoken from the heart. Good Duke Humphrey, who seems all but lost in the fog of the earlier version, comes through in Howell as what I have elsewhere put forward as a martyred prototype of the Christian humanist.[15] And out of her Henry's callowness grows a maturity that is fully in keeping with the play's repeated variations of the suffering Jesus' response: 'They know not what they do.' Rob Benson's Henry, while not so affecting as Warner's, is nevertheless central to this version. Henry's vision in Part 3, which in the other versions seems pointless, becomes in Howell *the* point. The king's instinctive pacifism becomes the sole opposing force to the senseless blood and carnage that Howell epitomizes in the stacks of corpses concluding each battle sequence and culminating in the image of the crazed old Queen Margaret cackling atop a veritable mountain of corpses at the conclusion of *Richard III*. Howell, it should be noted in this context, makes the most effective use of the physical limitations all three directors work under in her battle scenes, which move from images of boys marching gaily into battle to the bloody disarray that makes it increasingly difficult to distinguish victors from losers as the plays progress. Her quasi-balletic, blood-on-snow, Battle of Tewkesbury in *3 Henry VI* rivals even the battle scenes in Kurosawa's histories in representing the horrible beauty of medieval warfare.

Bogdanov/Pennington appears at times to be consciously countering

Howell, especially in the respect that its characters, from start to finish, lack any sense whatsoever of true honour. The semblances of honour that appear on the surface of the lords are strictly part of the veneer of rulers, masking always the unalloyed ruthlessness that, in the view of this production, has accompanied the acquisition and maintaining of political power from the opening of the bourgeois/Machiavellian era (i.e. Shakespeare's late sixteenth century) down to the present day. To maintain their power, the powerful suppress the powerless – all appearances of conscience, loyalty, or fear of divine retribution being but self-serving poses. In this version, King Henry is a total dupe, and something of a fop, whose Christian forbearance and 'wisdom' in Part 3 seem particularly naive. He is made to look a true royal weakling – his early costuming interestingly suggesting the image of Edward VIII at the time of his abdication in the late 1930s. The climax of this version is the rise of Richard of Gloucester, the fullest embodiment of bourgeois Machiavellism. Richard's increasing pre-eminence can hardly be down-played in any version of these plays, but in this one he is overwhelming, the monster that two generations of unmitigated competitive greed have spawned. It is hard to imagine any Richard today out-doing his many famous predecessors in the role, but Andrew Jarvis, with his pronounced northern accent, his oversize Al Capone-like striped suit, and his deep sense of mockery, gives new dimensions to the figure.

Paralleling the 1950s/60s existentialism of Hall/Barton and the 1970s post-Vietnam War humanism of Howell is the 1980s/90s Neo-Marxism of the Bogdanov/Pennington version. The shifts in military costume – from the Royal Dragoon red of Talbot battling the French in Part 1, to the plainer first world war uniforms of the Lancastrians set against the spiffy RAF-style garb of the Yorkists in Parts 2 and 3, to the Falkland and Gulf War military fatigues of *Richard III* – suggest a progression paralleling the stages of Marxist historical determinism. If the Royal Dragoon images of Part 1 may be said to stand for the fashions of English feudalism, then the successive progressions surely represent the changing fashions of bourgeois domination. While hardly precise, the parallels are clear and effective, accompanied as they are by similar shifts in the background music – which progresses from fashionable Edwardian garden party music in Parts 1 and 2 to Gatsby-ish cocktail party jazz in Part 3.

While the above is a brief set of impressions of what the three productions convey, I think their differences can be seen more precisely in a few, significant individual scenic images from them that seem particularly inviting to compare.

Differences, for example, in the treatment of the 'Temple Garden' scene in *1 Henry VI* (2.4) nicely illustrate the approaches to the plays these directors take to the entire tetralogy. There is little factual substance to this Garden scene, even though it is where the conflict of the 'Roses' originates. Since the legal issues that separate the two factions are never made explicit in the text, the emphasis must be on the conflicting egos of the participants. In Hall/Barton, the scene is purely one of individual conflict. What we see on screen as white or red roses are chosen is not so much a choosing of sides in a conflict as a muddle of individual, hostile warlords more concerned with their own interests than with the good of the land. There is less sense of two powerful factions coming into existence than of secretiveness and rampant self-interest. Warwick (Brewster Mason) and York (Donald Sinden) are each made to appear distracted; each appears to have his mind more on what is to come than on matters at hand. Both seem little more than stubborn embodiments of arrogant individualism.

Howell's treatment of the scene differs sharply. In place of the anger and suspicion of the Hall/Barton version, we get a group of exuberant youths, snickering in adolescent ways, emerging drunkenly from what has more the feel of a late-night fraternity party than a parliamentary gathering. It almost seems the drink more than the legal disagreement that leads to the quarrel involving the roses here, the hostility emerging rather as the effect of high spirits than of old grudges. But that very high-spiritedness in time makes the scene the most overtly violent of the three. Here, York (Bernard Hill) and Somerset (Brian Deacon) seem youthfully desirous of some kind of on-the-spot action to settle the issue; and if Mark Wing-Davey's Warwick seems appropriately crafty in his attempts to pacify York, he also seems something of a sixth-form king-maker. Most important, and in keeping with Howell's treatment of these characters throughout, they are likable – as competing schoolboys are likable. The incipient grace and even honour each will ultimately reveal is intimated here, in part in the very nature of a violence that seems so youthful and spontaneous.

There is nothing likable about these figures in Bogdanov/Pennington. They are introduced by darkly discordant twentieth-century music, and they appear from the start embodiments of duplicity and suspicion. In his defiance of York, Sion Probert's tough, unyielding Somerset (which strongly suggests characterizations in the BBC productions of John Le Carré's spy thrillers) sets the tone of the encounter. The participants are in a single line across the screen identically costumed in early twentieth-century evening dress, intended perhaps to suggest how little they basically differ from one another, and the plucking of the roses takes place with a fierce and smouldering but inexplicable rancour. This is an image of nascent political power struggle that is essentially meaningless, the director not so much interested in uncontrolled egos as in the development of factions within a system where all factions ultimately stand for the same thing: the plundering of the weak by the strong.

A significant point of contrast among the three versions is also evident in the 'hawking' scene in 2 *Henry VI* (2.1), that lull before the storm that will bring down Duke Humphrey, the only true crutch for the young king's very shaky reign. The three are not equally clear that the scene is intended to demonstrate the precise nature of the Lord Protector's sagacity as he reveals the false miracle of a supposedly blind peasant recovering his sight. Their differences are evident in what the camera tells us. Hardly interested in Humphrey at all, Hall's camera emphasizes King Henry going through the first of many disillusionments. His face in extreme close-up appears tortured – more so than the essentially trivial revelation might seem to call for. Thus, this treatment seems more a critique of the king's inability to understand what is going on around him than of Humphrey's wisdom. In Howell, on the other hand, the king appears merely gullible, and the camera focuses chiefly on the Lord Protector, whose downfall is played as outright tragedy. (David Burke's Duke Humphrey is throughout reminiscent of Paul Scofield's Christian humanist Thomas More in Robert Bolt's *A Man for All Seasons*.) Finally, even more than in Hall/Barton, Humphrey's heroism is vitiated in Bogdanov/Pennington. As in Howell, the camera focuses chiefly on Humphrey, but true to what seems an underlying principle that all the nobility must appear corrupt, stupid, or both, Colin Farrell's Humphrey here appears a self-righteous, somewhat fussy legalist – not corrupt perhaps, but not very bright either, and distinctly smug. It is interesting to note that Farrell in other scenes acts fools or dupes – the unfortunately literate clerk Emanuel in the Jack Cade sequence, for example – while Howell's Burke plays strong figures, like the perceptive if violent Butcher among Cade's followers.

The episode involving those Jack Cade scenes (2 *Henry VI*: 4.2, 4.3, and 4.6–8) – surely among the most telling representations of political insurrection in literature – illustrates the central differences among the three versions in still more complex terms. All three versions suggest the repressions and deprivations that bring such violence into being, and all three are effective in bringing its hideous senselessness to life. It is not just the close-ups of the physical atrocities that are so telling – the brutal images of emasculation, the kissing of two victims' heads on poles, the suggestions of mass rape – but the wit and two-way-cutting ironies as well: the (in)famous 'Let's kill all the lawyers', and all Cade's comments on the 'political incorrectness' of literacy.

Cade himself is an effective demagogue in all three versions. Roy Dotrice in Hall/Barton is a crafty schemer who is so clearly linked to the absent and scheming Duke of York that his personal cadre of defenders (which neither of the other Cades have) wear a crest centred on a white rose. Howell's Cade, played by the redoubtable Trevor Peacock (who plays an unexpectedly similar

Lord Talbot in Part 1) seems a more independent rabble-rouser, a loud-mouth rough who might actually have qualities of genuine leadership, were there rationally conceived ends to his venture. (Again, Howell's tendency to find likable, if not redeeming, qualities.) And, true to form, the Bogdanov/ Pennington Cade, skinny Pennington himself, is a bona-fide revolutionary terrorist, who wears an unlaundered sleeveless Union Jack T-shirt with a white rose at its centre, and flashes a head, and very exposed underarms, of dirty red hair (suggesting popular images of the IRA bomber.)

That the relevance of the Jack Cade scenes to the rest of 2 Henry VI goes beyond the Yorkist rebellion is directly related to the character and sorry fate of Lord Saye, the stand-in during these scenes for the lately martyred Duke Humphrey, is emphasized in the Howell version. In these scenes in the text it is the palsied Saye who embodies the idea of education in the service of moral action – the hallmark of Erasmian humanism. And the play, through the martyrdom of Saye and its essentially sympathetic treatment of individuals within the mob, makes clear the humanist idea that it is not inherent wickedness but ignorance that invites the outrages done by the multitude. 'They know not what they do.' Howell's treatment of Saye, played by Derek Farr as an old man made the more sympathetic by his infirmities, renders the old lord's courage in the face of martyrdom central to what the Cade scenes stand for. Despite his weakness, Saye's verbal skills and wisdom almost win the day. Farr, shaking from palsy rather than from fear, is particularly persuasive in Saye's eleventh hour appeal to the mob that almost saves his life and almost undoes Cade.

Saye is omitted entirely from Hall/Barton and badly distorted in Bogdanov/ Pennington. In the latter, Saye is one more aristocrat exploiting the masses, literacy for these directors being one of the means by which the illiterate were suppressed. When confronted by the rebels this Saye appears detached, amused, and superior; but when assaulted, he becomes craven. In all respects the very opposite of Saye's rather saintly image in Howell, this Saye's shaking is directly related to his fear. It is significant that Clyde Pollitt, the actor who portrays Saye in this version, is also the cold-hearted, hypocritical Cardinal Winchester earlier in the play. Bogdanov and Pennington appear duty-bound to discredit aristocrats. Even the memory of Henry V is not immune, as Pennington's Cade's mocking tone in referring to the late hero of Agincourt indicates.

It is similarly instructive to compare the treatments of the soliloquies late in 3 Henry VI spoken by King Henry (2.5.1–124) and Richard of Gloucester (3.2.124–95), the two characters whose increasing polarity becomes central to these plays. That polarity, of course, can be viewed in several ways: one, that it reveals two extremes that result in bad government, and another that it suggests the necessity for one or the other extreme in a land where unrestrained ambition, greed, and corruption have led to something resembling anarchy. Hall/Barton appears to endorse the first idea. Their Henry is too soft and impractical in his soliloquy, as in his reign, however great and genuine his compassion; Richard is too ruthless and bloody, however great his perspicacity and intelligence. In this view, something in between seems called for, a middle ground that York and Warwick might have provided had overblown ego, arrogance, and in the case of York an early death not destroyed the opportunity. Their failure seems central to the despair underlying the Hall/Barton version.

Howell, on the other hand, clearly endorses Henry's view. In his soliloquy, her Henry (Peter Benson), in medieval monastic terms, describes the ordered existence of the humble shepherd with a directness and clarity that suggest just what the kingdom needs: 'So many hours must I tend my flock, So many hours must I take my rest, . . .' (*3 Henry VI*: 2. 5: 31–40) Despite its seeming political irrelevance, the genuine practicality of Henry's speech is driven home by her close-up realism of the action Henry witnesses during his speech: the lamentations of the father discovering he has murdered his son, and those of the son discovering he has murdered his father.[16] Only Christian forbearance, in this view, can begin the process of healing a state in such disarray.

Since Henry's speech is secondary in Bogdanov/Pennington, there is little point in discussing it. Henry is not the centre in this version, but Richard, whose outlook the directors come close to endorsing in their impatience with the obtuseness and hypocrisy of the other nobles. So it is Richard's soliloquy we must look at here. Richard works better for Bogdanov/Pennington in part because while they know what to do with Richard, they do not with Henry. And they have Andrew Jarvis. In the soliloquy in question, it is not so much that Ian Holm in Hall/Barton and Ron Cook in Howell fail – Holm ingeniously makes the hypocrisy mixed with sudden violence that Richard envisions in it the literal basis of his postures and attitudes to follow – as that Jarvis brings to it an uncanny mixture of middle-class north country candour with a more self-aware 'murderous' Machiavellism. Treated as a long aside during a 1920s black-tie reception to honour the newly victorious, now *King*, Edward, the speech is spoken by Jarvis to the background rhythms of slow cocktail-party piano jazz, Jarvis allowing its long, somewhat drowsy cadences to reflect precisely his inner state as he muses on how to get a crown.[17] Further, in the extreme close-ups in which we view Richard throughout, the camera often shoots him from below, dwelling extensively, as it did on Pennington's Cade, on the speaker's chin, mouth and even saliva to intensify the effect of his villainy. The actor then adds uniquely varied, sometimes clownish, facial expressions that lace the speech with a vicious mockery that is relished by the speaker. By such means, the close-ups of Jarvis give the prospect of Richard's rule a perverse and frightening appeal.[18] His confidence infects us.

And so we have moved from a production that sees both Henry and Richard as representing extremes to be avoided, to one that supports Henry's view, to one that, in spite of itself, almost supports Richard's.

More specific scenes need fuller treatment in this fashion than space affords. Nevertheless, a few additional points should be made. For one thing, it is disappointing that Howell's clear, convincing treatment of the three parts of *Henry VI* is not equalled by her *Richard III*. Perhaps she really is not that interested in Richard. It is obvious that in her Henry VI plays, she likes the contradictory nature of the internally as well as externally struggling nobles, or the almost primitive nature of Henry's Christianity, or the polarity that develops between Christian Henry and Machiavellian Richard. And she likes expressing her own pacifism through her explorations of medieval warfare. But her *Richard III* is not so effective in 'descanting' on a tyrant's evil. The other directors are more engaged with the inventions of the arch-villain than she. And perhaps as a result, Ron Cook is the least effective Richard. Almost likable in his ruthless energy, Cook is not quite up to the subtleties of the soliloquies, and Howell does not help him. In her *Richard III*, Hastings and Buckingham are more effective in their confrontations with death than is Richard confronting his evil in 5.3. Howell is more engaged with old Margaret's cacklings as she sits on her mountains of corpses during the credits – fine pacifism, but not really the point of *this* play.

The acting of Queen Margaret also requires some further notice. All three of the actresses – Peggy Ashcroft in Hall/Barton, Julia Foster in Howell, and June Watson in Bogdanov/Pennington – are suitably terrifying, but none quite matches Mary Morris's Margaret on the Marlowe Society sound recordings of these plays. (Morris also played the role in the 1950s BBC 'Age of Kings' series.) Her menacing metallic tones make Margaret's shrill rages unvaryingly penetrating. Despite their best efforts, the other three seem too gentle for the witch-like Queen, though Howell's costuming of Foster in military dress following the death of Margaret's lover Suffolk does give a special force to Foster's playing of the role.

More should also be said about individual performances in these productions. Charles Kay's Dauphin of France in *1 Henry VI* and Clarence in *Richard III* in Hall/Barton stand out (even in the face of Gielgud's Clarence in the Olivier film). Howell's Antony Brown, who plays a wide variety of minor roles, excels as the terrifying Ratcliffe in *Richard III*, with his eternally scratching quill pen. And as Janet Suzman plays a thoughtful and self-contained Joan la Pucelle in the Hall/Barton *1 Henry VI*, she is an unexpectedly intelligent Lady Anne in their *Richard III*. Her love-hate relationship with Holm's Richard injects a fascinating cerebral quality into the seduction.

KING JOHN

Now to turn to brief examinations of *King John* and the second tetralogy. *King John*, probably written between the two tetralogies, deals with political turmoil and ineffective leadership in terms even more pointed than the Henry VI plays. At no point, until the very end, is there the promise of peace in *King John*; at no point is there a relative stasis, a feeling of stability. The turmoil of the second and third acts, which portray the three-cornered struggle involving England, France, and Rome over John's legitimacy and the claim of young Arthur to England's throne, characterize the play as a whole. No agreements, no pacts, no loyalties last long – and endless bloody war seems the permanent destiny of mighty powers in conflict. But the difference between *King John* and the first tetralogy is focused in Philip Faulconbridge, reputed bastard son of Richard the Lion-Hearted, who both as part of the turmoil and as student of it makes that turmoil the means of his transition from idealistic but also ambitious youth to the knowing political professional who saves the realm. The Bastard's role, like the play itself, bridges the gap, as seen by the young Shakespeare, between Henry VI's medieval asceticism as solution to the turmoil and the solution implicit in the new-Machiavellian patriotism of Henry V. In the end it is the Bastard's astuteness alone that can restore stability to the realm.

Infrequently performed on stage or screen, *King John* in David Giles's BBC/Time-Life production of 1985 treats the values I discuss above with the solid realism that characterizes Giles's direction of the second tetralogy in the same series. The images one takes away from the production are those of relentless instability: the royal succession in disorder, and a mother-dominated, infirm, and highly insecure monarch (played with suitable quirks by Leonard Rossiter) who progresses from deep insecurity to a state of mental collapse by the end of the play. But all is finally righted by George Costigan's Bastard, a dashing young knight who goes beyond his time in the science of politics. Costigan does not quite capture the studied verbal music that is the means by which that figure imposes an illusion of stability upon the land (that music foreshadowing the triumphant patriotic speeches of Henry V), but the music is there, particularly in Costigan's rendition of the Bastard's famous concluding speech.

Giles was most fortunate in the cast he had available for this production, especially for the women characters. Mary Morris as the troublesome Queen

Mother (Elinor of Acquitaine) is matched by Claire Bloom as the equally troublesome Lady Constance, mother of the pretender Prince Arthur – the one still capable of an erotic twinge in the direction of the attractive Bastard despite her advanced age, the other effectively articulating in the charged language of her speeches how the sudden shifts in the winds of politics 'whirl' the individual 'asunder'. Janet Maw's playing of the Lady Blanche who speaks that great line gives deserved place to what is not really so minor a role as it may seem.

If intelligence in conception and the availability of good performers were the only measure, this *King John* should be among the best English histories on screen. But the production overall tends to be sterile, and the reason is to be found in what Giles chooses to include visually. The production is much less rich in action than in costuming and décor. Giles includes no battle scenes whatsoever, though the absurdity of meaningless violent conflict is essential to what this play is about. At the very least the twice-defeated French should appear bloodied. Jane Howell's brilliant battle scenes help give life to the chief issues of the plays in her first tetralogy. In Giles's *King John*, there is much lamentation, but any sense of real brutality and carnage is absent. And hence, too, the real point about the shifting ground of politics is lost. Even the poignant Hubert-Arthur scene suffers in this sense. Effectively performed by John Thaw as Hubert and especially Luc Owen as the adolescent prince, the episode centring on Hubert's threat to blind the boy, in the absence of any previous evidence of such bloody mutilation in the play, does not ring true. By contrast, one calls to mind the devasting effect of Kurosawa's violently blinded princely youth in his *Ran*. When Lady Blanche talks about the *dismemberment* in war, she means something not merely figurative but terribly literal, and that all-important terror is distinctly missing in Giles's production. It is, after all, alleviation of the terror that makes the peace and unity achieved by the bright new patriotic imagery of the Bastard so attractive.

THE SECOND TETRALOGY

Television screenings of the plays of the second tetralogy deserve more probing treatment than I can devote to them here. Ace Pilkington in particular has written a careful and detailed book-length study of David Giles's versions of them in the BBC/Time-Life series.[19] But the screen version that has scarcely been touched on is the one by Bogdanov and Pennington – a version that is quite comparable to their work with the first tetralogy, with which it is of a piece. Thus it is to that version that I direct my concluding remarks.

The chief respect in which the Bogdanov/Pennington second tetralogy is comparable to their first is that the plays are treated as something other than simply vehicles for the acting of such time-honoured roles as Richard II, Falstaff, Hotspur, and Prince Hal. The primary interest is political; once again the emphasis is on the old giving way to the new, and the weak giving way to the strong. The emphasis is on the idea that the more surfaces change, the more the same objective of power and subjugation prevails. Michael Cronin's Bolingbroke easily tears into the mystically ordained line of royal succession because he is so obviously stronger and more politically shrewd than Pennington's at first foppish, then Werther-like Richard (performed in Goethe-period dress and acted to the strains of Haydn and Beethoven). And a not-so-stable but politically more imaginative Hal (Pennington) has no trouble sweeping aside his father's David Lloyd George image with a 'reformation' that 'glitters o'er his fault'. Bogdanov/Pennington lays great stress on the idea of a Hal who must learn, painfully, not to be over-sensitive and neurotic like Richard, but to give free rein to the side of him represented in the 'I know you all' speech of 1 Henry IV: 1.2. Having finally overcome self-disgust in Part 2, this Hal goes on to reign as a new kind of monarch capable of declaring English hegemony as never before. Pennington's Henry V is a good deal less callow than Branagh's.

Of the acting of the other two notables of the Henriad, we get a restrained Falstaff from Barry Stanton, and a Hotspur from Andrew Jarvis that is too much like his Richard of Gloucester for the good of the role. (Jarvis fares better in Henry V as a very quirky Dauphin of France.) Certainly a counter to the Welles and Anthony Quayle near-tragic Falstaffs, Stanton also seems to realize that while Falstaff is first and foremost a clown, he should be played more for the wit that is 'the cause of wit in others' than for the slapstick that characterizes him in many productions. Jarvis, on the other hand, fails to realize that Hotspur's quixoticism represents Shakespeare's essential critique of feudal honour. For all its energy, Jarvis's posturing Hotspur is too much north country agrarian bluster and not enough the 'chivalry' that Hal acknowledges having been 'a truant to'.

Unusual features of this production tend to support some of the same misanthropy on the part of the directors evident in their first tetralogy. In a gesture Crowl calls 'powerful and puzzling' (152), a disarmed Hal cowers before Hotspur gives him back his 'sword' (dagger, actually) and Hal delivers the fatal thrust. This cowering, possibly intended to be a ruse, has the effect of suggesting a genuine lack of honour on Hal's part, which is inconsistent with much in the text as well as with Pennington's overall acting of the role. Also jarring is the re-arrangement of the conclusion of 1 Henry IV so as to make the king and a very snippy Prince John actually accept Falstaff's claim to have himself murdered Hotspur. This revision, obviously intended to serve as motive for an offended Hal's back-sliding in Part 2,[20] is inappropriate on the face of it – Falstaff's word would never be taken over Hal's – and the humour inherent in the preposterousness of the claim (so preposterous that Hal jokingly will 'gild it with the happiest terms' he has) is totally undermined. The claim is the culmination of Falstaffian pretences going back to his bare-faced lying about the robbery at Gadshill, and the whole point is that no one believes them.

Others of Bogdanov/Pennington's surprises work better. Pennington's repeated indications that Henry V is in the early stages of the dysentery that was to kill him is an effective reminder that Henry's 'famous victories' were but transitory. And if it seems unlikely that the English might be wearing twentieth-century military dress to battle while the French wear Napoleonic costumes, the effect is to suggest quickly what it takes Olivier and Branagh many elaborate (and expensive) scenes to suggest: the inventiveness of Henry's tactics at Agincourt versus the glamorous but essentially tired militarism of the French. Finally, that Bogdanov and Pennington are at their most imaginative in their use of music is nowhere better exemplified than when the English troops set out for France to the competing strains of Beatles-style Rock music and the profound tones of Parry's setting of William Blake's 'Jerusalem'. A musical symbolism is here created to anticipate Henry's encounter with the soldiers the night before battle, just as a musical counterpoint in jazz is created for Richard of Gloucester's great soliloquy in *3 Henry VI*.

Among the qualities in the Bogdanov/Pennington second tetralogy that are missing from the Giles version is the feeling we get at the end of the former that we are about to begin the whole senseless story over again. By presenting the whole of the two tetralogies in the order written, Bogdanov/Pennington gives us an awesome sense not only of the rise and fall of kings, but of the rise and fall of great nations – which may in the final analysis constitute the real immediacy of this production. Theirs is indeed a *political* reading of these plays, and as such at the close of the twentieth century, a reading that leaves us profoundly bewildered and even disheartened. As our world, like that of the hapless Henry VI, seems on the threshold of new, ever-more-terrible re-enactments of factional violence on every continent, and with the growing certainty that political 'saviours' are at best chimerical and at worst terribly threatening, the Bogdanov/Pennington interpretation of Shakespeare's historical cycle, like Branagh's *Henry V*, invites thoughts of a future even more forbidding than the twentieth century, with all its terrors.

The appropriate note on which to close is the wish that all these television recreations of the English histories were more readily available to the public. They are obviously none of them glossy productions; they deal with little-known historical figures; they boast few star actors; they are produced under the greatest constraints. But they speak to us even more directly than the Olivier and Branagh *Henry V* films because they are so focused on unpredictables in violent flux. They never really give us the shape of things; they rather leave us with the suspicion that history is shapeless. And their deepest political insight, realized in all three versions, is that apparent security is never permanent. They are like Sophocles' greatest 'history play' in warning that none should feel confident of good fortune until the moment of death.

Notes

1 See Ace Pilkington, *Screening Shakespeare from 'Richard II' to 'Henry V'* (Delaware, 1991), pp. 22–99. See also Peter Saccio, 'The Historicity of the BBC Shakespeare Plays', in J. C. Bulman and H. R. Coursen, eds., *Shakespeare on Television* (New England, 1988), pp. 208–13; and Martin Banham, 'BBC Television's Dull Shakespeare', in the same collection, pp. 213–21; as well as reviews by Michael Manheim, Samuel Crowl, Peter Saccio, and Paul M. Cubeta in *Shakespeare/Film Newsletter*, 4.1 (1979), 5.1 (1980), and 6.1 (1981).

2 I have not included Orson Welles's *Chimes at Midnight* (also entitled *Falstaff*) as it is considered in Robert Hapgood's ' "Chimes at Midnight" from Stage to Screen: The Art of Adaptation' in *Shakespeare Survey 39* (Cambridge, 1987), pp. 39–52. For other discussion of that film, see Pilkington, *Screening Shakespeare*, pp. 130–55; and Samuel Crowl, *Shakespeare Observed* (Ohio, 1992), pp. 35–50.

3 An excellent discussion of the influence of *The Prince* among young, educated Elizabethans is still Felix Raab, *The English Face of Machiavelli* (Toronto, 1964), especially pp. 51–76, upon which is based much of my approach in *The Weak King Dilemma in the Shakespearean History Play* (Syracuse, 1972). The acceptance of my approach, and that of Moody Prior in *The Drama of Power* (Northwestern, 1973) *et al.*, has waned since the 1970s, new historicists like Stephen Greenblatt, Gary Taylor and others preferring a Shakespeare who accommodated to the will of the authorities (who would in no way sanction Machiavelli, even if they used his methods). Henry undoubtedly was an unsubtle ideal of Tudor political virtue for some in the audience, but probably not for, say, the young Inns of Court men who recalled their surreptitious readings of Machiavelli in college and recognized the closeness of Shakespeare's Henry to the Machiavellian ideal.

4 The line in question is 'Nay, it will please him well, Kate; it shall please him, Kate' (*Henry V*: 5.2.262–3). Interestingly, Kenneth Branagh speaks the line quite differently from Olivier. Neither amused nor ironic, Branagh's Henry speaks it reassuringly to an uneasy princess.

5 *The Prince and Selected Discourses*, translated by Daniel Donno (New York, 1966), p. 63.

6 *Filming Shakespeare's Plays* (Cambridge, 1988). Davies's chapter on Olivier's *Henry V* is on pp. 26–39, while his chapter on Olivier's *Richard III* is on pp. 65–82.

7 The first article on the film to call attention to the nature of Olivier's extraordinary sexuality as Richard is Constance Brown, 'Olivier's *Richard III*: A Reevaluation', in Charles W. Eckert, ed., *Focus on Shakespearean Films* (New Jersey, 1972), pp. 131–46.

8 Donaldson, 'Taking on Shakespeare: Kenneth Branagh's *Henry V*', in *Shakespeare Quarterly*, 42 (1991), 60–71; and Crowl, *Shakespeare Observed*, pp. 165–74.

9 'The Function of Battle Imagery in Kurosawa's "Histories" and the *Henry V* Films', World Shakespeare Congress, Tokyo, 1991.

10 The series I have been unable to see without a visit to England is the early 1960s BBC 'Age of Kings'. I did watch parts of it at the time on what was then called Educational Television and have faint recollections of young Sean Connery as a dashing Hotspur, and of Mary Morris's Queen Margaret.

11 For a discussion of Barton's extensive adaptations, see Barbara Hodgdon, *The End Crowns All* (Princeton, 1991), pp. 76–81.

12 For discussions of this series on stage, see Crowl, *Shakespeare Observed*, pp. 142–64; and Hodgdon, pp. 87–99.

13 The line is spoken by Lady Blanche in *King John*: 3.1.255.

14 For a most perceptive discussion of Howell's version, see Dennis Bingham, 'Jane Howell's First Tetralogy: Brechtian Break-Out or Just Good Television', in *Shakespeare on Television*, pp. 221–9. Among other things, Bingham identifies the highly original use Howell makes of her close-ups. See also reviews by Stanley Wells, *TLS*, 4 (February 1983), 105; and Manheim, *SF/NL* (April 1984), 2.

15 For a discussion of Duke Humphrey's image as precursor and prototype of the Christian humanists, see Manheim, 'Duke Humphrey and the Machiavels', *The American Benedictine Review*, 23 (1972), 249–57.

16 The problem of whether or not Henry's soliloquy should be treated in realistic fashion is best resolved in Hall/Barton, where the lamenting father and son are strictly images in Henry's mind, appearing in balloon-like insets at upper corners of the screen, with Henry in extreme close-up apparently mouthing what they are saying. These insets, which accord with the medieval feel of the speech, are an original way to screen a Shakespearian soliloquy. The artifice also makes clear that for Hall/Barton the scene is not realism. The shrill and bloody battle shots in the background of Henry's soliloquy in both Howell and Bogdanov/Pennington, on the other hand, leave it uncertain whether the action surrounding Henry's words actually takes place. If it does, then some acknowledgement of Henry's presence by father and son would seem in order; if it does not, why the literal blood and the trappings of battle?

17 See Crowl's discussion of the delivery of this passage on stage, in *Shakespeare Observed*, p. 161.

18 It should be added that not only does Jarvis go beyond Holm and Cook with this speech, but he transcends Olivier as well, whose acting of the role the ever-inventive Jarvis at times subtly parodies. (Olivier incorporates a large portion of Richard's *3 Henry VI* soliloquy into Richard's speech opening *Richard III*.) Both Olivier and Jarvis possess the 'alacrity of spirit' called for. Both are master-contrivers, both mock the absence of alertness and intelligence in those around them, both treat their deformity as a means of intimidating others at appropriate moments; but in this speech, as throughout his playing of the role, it is Jarvis who 'set[s] the murderous Machiavel to school'.

19 See Pilkington citation in Note 1.

20 No distortion of the play is necessary to account for Hal's back-sliding in the second part. Without any immediate battles to fight and with Henry IV still alive, there would be

little for Hal to do but back-slide. As for the Chief Justice's praising Falstaff's 'day's service' at Shrewsbury (*Henry IV*: 1.2.147), Falstaff's simply having been at the battle in the Prince's company would be sufficient for that response. In fact, no reference is made in Part 2 to Falstaff's having killed Hotspur, and that no reference is made either to Hal's having killed him is insufficient reason to assume that Falstaff's claim has been accepted. That the battle has been won is all that matters to the court, and that Lady Percy does not mention Hal (or Falstaff) in her lament for her dead husband only suggests that all she cares about is Hotspur, not who killed him.

Such distortions by Bogdanov/Pennington of the second tetralogy are consistent with their omission, in *Richard III*: 2.3.27, of the third citizen's remark 'O, full of danger is the Duke of Gloucester.' Without that line, all the citizens appear to be dupes; with it, one gets the important idea that not everyone is taken in.

8

A WORLD ELSEWHERE: THE ROMAN PLAYS ON FILM AND TELEVISION

SAMUEL CROWL

Shakespeare's interest in Plutarch's *Lives* as a source for his drama stretched throughout his career. As Shakespeare found Rome an appealing spark to his imagination, so modern producers have been equally attracted to Shakespeare's Roman plays as a source for film and television adaptations. There have been nine major productions on film and video in the past forty years: four each of *Julius Caesar* and *Antony and Cleopatra* and one of *Coriolanus*.[1] These versions reveal an instructive range of the potent possibilities and potential liabilities of translating Shakespeare into the technologies which dominate popular entertainment in our time.

Film, in the hands of directors as varied as Welles, Olivier, Zeffirelli, and Branagh, has repeatedly demonstrated a startling capacity to absorb and transform Shakespeare in aesthetically and intellectually fascinating ways. Television, in a half century of existence, has not. However, only the most ardent admirer of Shakespeare on the screen would refuse to trade films of the quality of Stuart Burge's *Julius Caesar* or Charlton Heston's *Antony and Cleopatra* for Trevor Nunn's and Jon Scoffield's magnificent television version of *Antony and Cleopatra*.[2] Imagination, intelligence, and taste (and their opposites) can flow through many forms and as James Bulman has wisely observed, 'for pedagogical purposes, even the worst productions can be useful'.[3] Bulman is here speaking about Shakespeare on television, but his insight holds true for film and stage Shakespeare as well.

Shakespeare's imagination kept circling back to Rome throughout his career: first to explore the tragic crisis in the struggle over heritage and authority in *Julius Caesar*, and then to offer two complicated and remarkable female challenges to Rome's masculine hegemony in *Antony and Cleopatra* and *Coriolanus*. In each play a central masculine figure closely identified with Roman values – Brutus, Antony, and Coriolanus – is destroyed precisely because he is psychologically and politically incapable of regarding Rome unambiguously, even in the case of Coriolanus, who appears on the surface to be the most absolute Roman of them all.

The three films of *Julius Caesar* present an interesting stylistic progression, moving from David Bradley's youthful experimentalism, through Joseph Mankiewicz's mainstream formalist approach, to Stuart Burge's view of the play through a postmodern lens. Bradley's film (1949) overflows with filmic invention; Mankiewicz's (1953) reflects the talents of a Hollywood professional working at the height of his career; and Burge's (1970) attempts to interpret the play in light of the explosive decade of the sixties.

Bradley's film is remarkable student work made with a group of friends who met at Northwestern University. The film is interesting on three accounts: its clever use of some of Chicago's famous neo-classical architecture for location shooting; its introduction to the screen of Charlton Heston who plays Mark Antony; and Bradley's highly imaginative way with his camera. Viewing the film is like watching an experimental, fringe theatre company performance of Shakespeare where our pleasure derives more from the radical inspiration of individual moments than from the coherence and polish of the entire production.

From the stunning opening with the Soothsayer's face in close-up going in and out of focus as he utters his famous prophecy, to the camera's first discovery of Heston – practically naked – leaning majestically against one of the huge Romanesque columns at Chicago's Soldier's Field with his arms folded across his chest, to the dazzling chiaroscuro effect Bradley achieves in Cassius' seduction of Brutus, to Heston's taking his sword and striking off the eagle affixed to the back of Caesar's chair on 'Cry "Havoc", and let slip the dogs of war', to shooting the riot engendered by Antony's oration and the subsequent death of Cinna the poet through a ring of fire eating at the edges of the frame, the film provides a wealth of stimulating details. Bradley's most sustained cinematic achievement is his handling of Grosvenor Glenn, the actor who plays Cassius. Glenn has a wonderfully appropriate face: long and lean with deep-set eyes and full lips. The face is powerful and nasty. Bradley shoots Cassius' 'I know that virtue to be in you, Brutus' speech in extreme close-up as though we were moving into the deep recesses of Cassius' mind. As Cassius begins his tale of swimming in the Tiber with Caesar, Bradley shifts to a flashback and gives us the scene of the two struggling swimmers. The moment isn't perfectly realized, but the idea is a good one as this *image* of the physically inadequate Caesar is powerfully present in Cassius' memory.

Daringly, Bradley shoots just Glenn's eyes in extreme close-up on 'Why man, he doth bestride the narrow world / Like a Colossus . . .' with the camera capturing in them Cassius' deep and dangerous envy of Caesar's undeserved

6   *Julius Caesar*, directed by David Bradley: Mark Antony's oration (Charlton Heston as Mark Antony)

prominence. Bradley follows this shot with an equally arresting cut to a similar close-up of Cassius' mouth as he spits out 'upon what meat does this our Caesar feed, / That he is grown so great?' The screen filled with just Cassius' eyes and then his mouth provides a powerful image for the character's dependency upon Caesar, the necessity for him to sustain himself, to feed upon his vision of Caesar's inadequacies. These are instances of what Lorne Buchman calls film's 'spectacle of multiplicity' in which the camera can provide an infinite variety of visual images and spatial perspectives in trying to capture the Shakespearian dynamic on film.[4]

Bradley clearly sees his Brutus as the noble victim trapped between Cassius' powerful envy and Mark Antony's latent ambition. Heston's Antony displays a wonderful physical arrogance, but he is gamesome only in the athletic sense. Bradley's invention flags during the funeral oration as he fails to find a radical camera and editing style to match his earlier work with Cassius, and the battle scenes are beyond his technical and financial resources.

Bradley's film is a collection of moments, some more riveting than others, but does not provide us with a sustained interpretation of the play; for that we can turn to Joseph Mankiewicz's sadly neglected formalist masterpiece released in 1953. Mankiewicz is well known for his literate films – ones which deftly employ literary devices like the flashback and multiple points of view with rare film success. Mankiewicz came to directing after a long career as a screenwriter and producer, and he came to *Julius Caesar* fresh from writing and directing his two greatest films – *A Letter to Three Wives* (1949) and *All About Eve* (1950) – both of which won him Oscars for best direction and best screenplay.

John Houseman, the film's producer, recalls that he and Mankiewicz successfully battled the studio executives at Metro-Goldwyn-Mayer to be allowed to shoot the film in black and white because they were eager 'to stress the historical parallel between the political intrigues of the last years of the Roman Republic and recent European events' captured in the public's imagination by press photos and newsreels.[5] Houseman believed that the Forum scenes would inevitably 'evoke memories of the Fuhrer at Nuremberg and of Mussolini ranting from his high balcony overlooking the wildly cheering crowd that would presently spit on his dead body as it hung by its feet outside of a gas station'.[6]

Unfortunately nothing in the film works to specifically remind us (unlike Olivier's startling death in his portrayal of Coriolanus at Stratford in 1959) of these contemporary parallels, and one might as easily suppose that the play was selected for its parallels not with pre-war Europe, but with post-war America. America was left, by war's end, as the inheritor of the power and problems associated with European imperialism. By the early 1950s the country was being internally consumed by the communist witch-hunts sponsored by the House Un-American Activities Committee and Senator Joseph McCarthy. Hollywood was intimately involved in both the extension of America's international influence and the internal hysteria about supposed subversives. Mankiewicz explicitly refuses to give us the spectacle version of Rome we might expect from Hollywood to concentrate instead on a tightly focused

formalist approach eager to explore the play's irony and ambiguity. Mankiewicz's ironic design is apparent from the film's first cut as we move from the roar
of the MGM lion to a close-up of a military standard bearing the Roman eagle:
the symbol of a cultural empire in the making laying claim to the still powerful
legacy of a political empire long dead.

The style of Mankiewicz's film neatly mirrors its interpretative intentions. In
contrast to the often disorienting perspectives provided by Bradley's camera,
Mankiewicz's shots, as Jack Jorgens has accurately described them, are 'rigidly
frontal and composed in geometric patterns: circles, triangles, and squares. In
general . . . individual shots call little attention to themselves . . . [their] force
and movement are linear as the action is propelled forward and emphasis placed
on the actors and their lines.'[7] For instance, in the opening procession into the
Forum for the running of the Lupercal, Mankiewicz's camera quickly cranes
down from capturing the crowded spectacle to concentrate on two moments
when Caesar stops the procession: first to greet Mark Antony, then to hear the
words of the Soothsayer. In each instance Mankiewicz's camera catches a
solitary figure, first Casca and then Cassius, circling behind Caesar who has
turned towards the camera. Here is one of Jorgens' geometric patterns at work,
visually anticipating the way in which Caesar will be encircled by these two
prominent conspirators at his assassination.

Not surprisingly for its historical moment, the film presents James Mason's
brooding, softly spoken Brutus as the classic conscientious liberal trapped
between his pure ideals and dirty politics. Mankiewicz provides an ambiguous
qualification to Brutus' nobility by first shooting his capitulation to Cassius'
promptings in 1.2 with the camera looking down over the shoulder of a
massive statue of Caesar. Here Mankiewicz's camera captures Caesar's looming
presence and reminds us of his inescapable centrality to the play and to the lives
of these very conspirators who seek to topple him.[8] Later, Mankiewicz
similarly complicates several moments in Brutus' famous 'it must be by his
death' soliloquy by shooting him first through the limbs of a barren tree and
then with the shadows cast by an overhead arbour falling across his face, each
image suggesting the dry and tangled nature of Brutus' tortured reasoning.

A production which seeks to emphasize the play's irony and ambiguity will
inevitably come to centre on the play's most ironic and ambiguous figure:
Mark Antony. Marlon Brando's performance is a stunning example of
controlled, calculating intelligence and is film acting at its finest. His eyes are
the key to his performance, from the way in which they absorb and
comprehend Caesar's treatment of Calpurnia on the way into the Forum, to
their refusal to acknowledge Brutus and the conspirators until they have
looked long on Caesar's fallen body, to their movement up from the corpse to

take the measure of each conspirator as Brando shakes each of their hands and then glances with disgust down at his own, now bloody hand, to the manner in which he gives and then withdraws his gaze from the mob during the funeral oration, to the smile that plays about his eyes and lips as he takes in the view of Rome from Caesar's balcony (in 4.1) and slightly readjusts the position of Caesar's bust gazing back at him. When Mankiewicz shoots Brutus and Cassius from down over Caesar's shoulder his camera creates the ambiguity of the moment; here it is Antony, in his repositioning of Caesar's bust, who is in control and relishing the irony of his triumph. These are just a sampling of the many examples which could be cited as evidence of the cool, formalist intelligence which distinguishes Mankiewicz's film.

Almost twenty years later the play would be revisited on film in a very different historical moment. Stuart Burge's film appeared at the end of the decade dominated by the assassination of John Kennedy, the war in Vietnam, and the student revolt in Europe and America. The film's look and tone and feel reflect its times. The opening shot captures an eagle soaring over a battlefield in Spain littered with fallen bodies. The film then cuts to a ravaged skull still wearing its helmet and as the camera closes in on the skull's gruesome expression we hear the shouts of 'Caesar . . . Caesar . . . Caesar' on the sound track as we segue to Caesar's triumphant procession.

The film seems intentionally ugly; nothing quite matches from the satiny sheen and gaudy colours of the costumes, to the graffiti carelessly carved on the wall in an ante-chamber to the Forum, to the seedy look of Casca's untrimmed beard, to the ridiculously mannered spit curls which deck Brutus' forehead, to the embarrassing way in which the four principal performances fail to cohere. For example, John Gielgud's performance of Caesar is – along with Diana Rigg's Portia – the most interesting in the film, but it bears no resemblance to the opening images of military carnage. It is impossible to imagine Gielgud's vain, slightly daft, Caesar as a great general or as a powerful politician. Charlton Heston's reprise of Mark Antony is all grunt and grimace done without a trace of irony, and Jason Robards' Brutus speaks in a relentless monotone and only comes to life in the quarrel scene with Cassius in 4.3 where Shakespeare's material most resembles Eugene O'Neill's. Even Richard Johnson's solid Cassius is demeaned by having to perform such tacky gestures as scratching out Caesar's name with his dagger on a graffiti-covered wall and carving Brutus' next to it.

The film struggles towards presenting the play from a postimperialist, postmodern perspective. Its elements consist of a garish collection of details which jangle and jar with one another in an attempt to make the play speak to a time clearly out of joint. By reducing all of the play's central characters to unattractive stereotypes: Gielgud's effete Caesar, Heston's crass Antony, Johnson's radical Cassius, and Robards' dim, mumbling Brutus the film fails to make a convincing case for its approach to Shakespeare's Rome. Only Diana Rigg's Portia, perhaps intentionally, is allowed to escape with her intelligence, nobility, and genuine concern for her husband intact.

Film's infinite technical resources coupled with its long history of directorial innovation have provided it with many avenues of imaginatively translating Shakespeare in ways denied to television. Anthony Davies well understands how the Shakespearian dynamic responds to 'the psychological effect of the modern camera's spatial versatility . . . to break down the constant of distance between the viewer and the detail in the framed image. Not only is the image itself in sustained movement, but so also is the viewpoint, for the camera's function is one of exploration rather than presentation; one of making the spectator conscious of the dynamics of space in breadth as well as depth.'[9] Studio television, with its basic three floor cameras, is much more earthbound than film and generally incapable of making camera work and editing as central and significant an interpretative tool as they are in the world of film. Davies' distinction is helpful here as television is decidedly a medium of presentation rather than exploration. The successes and failures of the BBC Shakespeare series have amply demonstrated that Shakespeare must be as carefully re-imagined for television (an aesthetic we take for granted with film) and not just left to speak for himself when the red light goes on. Eventually, the BBC series – particularly in the work of Jane Howell and Elijah Moshinsky – had some stunning successes, but the first seasons under Cedric Messina's leadership largely produced disasters, among them Herbert Wise's *Julius Caesar* (1979).[10]

By trying to follow Messina's dictum to produce Shakespeare 'straight' Wise ended up by creating a deadly museum piece; 'a mediocre piece of television', in the words of Jack Jorgens, 'full of disorganized, banal, ugly images'.[11] Every aspect of the production is musty from the studio sets with their painted backdrops, to the unimaginative and stilted camera work where five or six actors are jammed in front of a camera to suggest a crowd or another camera lingers for a puzzlingly long time on the back of an actor's head just so he can make an unnatural pivot to speak directly into the lens, to the pompous poses struck by many of the actors and their failure to find an effective means of delivering very public oratory over a very private medium.[12] Because Wise's production lacks both style and vision it is the least interesting of this quartet of *Caesar*s, though it does serve to provide an example from the conservative end of the interpretative spectrum when considering Shakespeare on television. We shall soon encounter a production from the opposite end of that spectrum when we examine Jonathan Miller's production of *Antony and Cleopatra* from the same series.

If film dominates video in productions of *Julius Caesar*, the reverse is true for versions of *Antony and Cleopatra* where the wide range of the empire has been most often imagined on the small screen rather than in cinemascope. *Antony and Cleopatra*'s geographical, political, and emotional expanse and excess would seem to make it a natural candidate for effective treatment on film. By the same token, its vastness would seem to be confined by television's limitations. Paradoxically, the three television versions we have of the play are all superior to Charlton Heston's film which seeks to translate the play into the sweep of a Hollywood epic and like Heston's Antony becomes quite un-ravelled in the process.

The brilliant success of Trevor Nunn's television version of *Antony and Cleopatra* (1974) clearly reveals that the failure of Wise's *Julius Caesar* owes more to the messenger than the medium. Like his more recent *Othello* (1990) and *Macbeth* (1979) done with Philip Casson, Nunn's television version of the play flowed out from a highly successful Royal Shakespeare Company stage production. Thus his principal actors: Janet Suzman (Cleopatra), Richard Johnson (Antony), Patrick Stewart (Enobarbus), and Corin Redgrave (Octa-vius Caesar) were fully at ease with their carefully nuanced performances and alert to their necessary modification for the camera. At the heart of any production of *Antony and Cleopatra* is the way it seeks to capture the polarities of Egypt and Rome and the judgements it makes about the images and values Shakespeare associates with each world. For Nunn, Egypt is golden and languorous; less a place than a state-of-mind. Cleopatra's palace could be either tent or barge defined by oriental rugs, huge soft yellow and brown cushions, transparent curtains in yellow and white, and the loose, flowing caftans and burnouses worn by Cleopatra, Antony, and Enobarbus. The music which distinguishes this Egypt is decidedly Eastern provided by Mardian and his quartet of plump, bald eunuchs playing exotic-looking wind and string instruments. Nunn even creates a technical equivalent for Shakespeare's images of Egypt as fluid, melting, indistinct, and discandying by often distorting the edges of the camera's lens so that only figures in the centre of the shot are held in a clear focus. This creates a shimmering, hazy texture to Nunn's evocation of Egypt which perfectly matches Antony's inability to hold either Cleopatra or himself in a steady focus,.

Richard Johnson's Antony is a large, generous, bear-like man who is by turns delighted, perplexed, and ultimately baffled by Suzman's Cleopatra. His delivery of 'she is cunning past men's thoughts' with a deeply puzzled expression on his face precisely captures his Roman sense of fascination and frustration. Nunn shoots this exchange between Antony and Enobarbus with both men in their burnouses comfortably spread out upon giant red cushions. He uses an overhead shot – a device he repeats with effect several times in the production to break the standard eye-level perspective so common on television – to capture the easy intimacy of the two men. This Enobarbus is clearly Antony's close friend and confidant and a fellow Roman fully at ease with Egyptian life.

Suzman is the only one of our four Cleopatras to have a 'tawny front', and Nunn makes her complexion conspicuous by having his camera catch her

7   *Antony and Cleopatra*, directed by Trevor Nunn: Janet Suzman as Cleopatra

reflection in a hand mirror as she observes that she is 'with Phoebus' amorous pinches black / And wrinkled deep in time'. Suzman's Cleopatra manages to be both playfully erotic and politically quixotic as she seeks to have her Antony and to tilt at Roman windmills as well. As a reminder of her power, Nunn fills her court with a collection of richly garbed Eastern kings.

In contrast to the rich textures associated with Egypt, Nunn's Rome is seen all in bright white, both in background and costume. Here the camera prefers the static close-up capturing a series of Roman heads, particularly Corin Redgrave's pale, blond, arrogant Caesar, in profile. The music is dominated by the trumpet blast. Without sentimentalizing either Antony or Cleopatra, Nunn's production gives full weight to depicting the delights of Egyptian excess in contrast to the powerful but barren images of Roman efficiency and restraint. Patrick Stewart's Enobarbus provides us with a Roman guide to Egypt both in his response to Antony's complaint 'Would that I had never seen her' which he delivers very quietly with his eyes closed as he summons up the images of that wonderful piece of work in his mind and in his exquisite version of 'The barge she sat in' where he leans his head back into his hands and drops the lids of his eyes as he sees again – and relishes the vision – Cleopatra hop forty paces through the public streets and with her loss of breath, make defect perfection.

As Kenneth Rothwell has noted, Nunn's production features a remarkable sound track: dogs bark, horses neigh and whinny, flies buzz, thunder growls, crickets drone, and the sound of the Nile washes gently against the shore.[13] The ultimate example of the production's use of sound comes with the great wind which blows and howls as Antony is hoisted up into Cleopatra's monument. The wind whips Suzman's hair as she tries to quicken her Antony with kissing. It whistles plaintively in counterpoint to her huge scream after 'My lord' when she realizes that Antony has died.

Nunn also cleverly uses the camera to achieve a fine effect in Cleopatra's final moments. He shoots the first lines of 'Give me my robe . . .' in close-up so we see only the stunning beauty of Cleopatra's royal headdress and gown – all blue and gold and red – when he slowly pulls the camera back as she reaches 'my other elements / I give to baser life' and stands before us sheathed as Isis. Suzman then lies down on a golden bier, takes the asp to her breast, and with a little wince between 'un' and 'policied' subtly lets us know the moment of its fatal pinch, reminding us of the politics as well as the romance ('Husband, I come') of her death.

Nunn's production of *Antony and Cleopatra* set a standard which has not been matched, though Jonathan Miller's BBC version (1980) provides an interesting interpretative contrast. Miller counters Nunn's exotic Egyptian excess with classical Roman restraint. Miller's version is formal, even chaste – Antony and Cleopatra rarely touch and never kiss, even when the text tells them to do so, until Antony's dying moments – inspired by the depiction of the classical world in Renaissance paintings.[14] As a result the production provides no distinction between Egypt and Rome. The same rich deep blue drapes, similar costuming of the characters in both landscapes, and typical Renaissance music (a violin and cello provide the musical background for our opening introduction to *Antony and Cleopatra*) are used to create both worlds. Miller's precocious directorial intelligence prides itself in overturning stereotype, but surely it works mightily against the contrasting images associated with Rome and Egypt – Caesar and Cleopatra – in Shakespeare's text to have Antony and Enobarbus welcomed in Rome to a meal far more splendid than anything we encounter in Egypt.

Miller's use of the camera, in contrast to Nunn's, is intentionally static. He shoots most scenes in medium close-up – this is truly an *Antony and Cleopatra* from the waist up – and will often hold a single shot for fifty lines of dialogue or more. Jane Lapotaire's sharp, pale, extremely ironic Cleopatra, with a strand of pearls tight at her neck and exquisite matching earrings, might have stepped right out of a Bronzino portrait. Her Cleopatra, in keeping with Miller's intentions, is more a 'belle dame sans merci' than a sensuous serpent of old Nile. The virtue of her performance is in discovering in Cleopatra a deeply ironic and mocking intelligence. It is impossible to imagine her Cleopatra ever hopping forty paces through the public street; the power she breathes forth is all verbal, delivered with a cutting nasal edge. By creating a Cleopatra more a match for Ian Charleson's aristocratic and emotionally repressed Caesar than for Colin Blakely's straightforward and hearty Antony, Miller dismisses the Egyptian flavour from his production as surely as he dismisses it from the decor. In so doing he misses the play's entire tragic tension as noted by reviewers of the production ranging from the cautiously sympathetic (Richard David) to the openly hostile (H. R. Coursen).[15]

Because Miller is of Caesar's party regarding Egypt, he must find a way to undercut the viewpoint of that Roman observer who provides us with another picture of the Egyptian scene and its queen: Enobarbus. Emrys James brilliantly accomplishes this task for his director by creating a garrulous windbag who is always willing to stick his nose in other people's business – particularly in the confrontation in Rome between Antony and Caesar where he literally squeezes himself into the frame to offer his unwelcomed advice. James appropriates the camera by speaking directly to us in a gossipy manner meant to set us straight on the play's events and personalities. This cheerful, comic approach is an inventive means of undercutting and thus discounting Enobarbus' Egyptian enthusiasms, but it is certainly at odds with the tragic manner in which this Roman ultimately earns a place in the story. Nunn's production strives to realize the emotional and political transcendence Cleopatra reaches in her final moments while Miller's settles for being an intellectually clever misreading transforming Shakespeare's most poetically and spatially flamboyant play into something small and oddly barren.

The Bard version (1985), done on a studio constructed open stage with wooden steps descending on two sides from an upper platform, lacks both Nunn's sure feel for the play's festive and tragic rhythms and Miller's radical reassessment.[16] Lawrence Carra's production has the virtue, for a novice audience, of being a less complicated reading of the play than Miller's, and it allows Lynn Redgrave (Cleopatra) and Timothy Dalton (Antony) to give full rein to the play's passionate moments. If Jane Lapotaire and Colin Blakely rarely touch, this pair are almost always in one another's arms. The production's finest visual moment comes at the conclusion of Antony and Cleopatra's fatal love-making. Redgrave, kneeling, has held her Antony to her breast in his final moments and after her cry of realization that he has died, she very slowly and carefully lowers his upper torso to the floor as she delivers: 'The soldier's pole is fall'n: young boys and girls / Are level now with men.' Otherwise, Redgrave's Cleopatra is too pleasant; she lacks depth and allure. Dalton is too young for Antony and plays him as a dashing buccaneer – more like the swashbuckling Pompey than the grizzled military veteran.

The production proceeds at a furious clip, a horse without a rider, except when Barrie Ingham's Enobarbus has the stage. He is all soldier, neither confidant nor clown, but a wise senior counsellor to Dalton's impetuous Antony. The most interesting touch of costuming in the production is the colourful North African weave Enobarbus wears over his Roman breastplate in the Egyptian scenes indicating that he has gone just slightly native. If Miller's production reveals the potential dangers of director's Shakespeare, Carra's, like Wise's *Julius Caesar*, reveals the dangers of empty Shakespeare produced without a compelling desire or reason to make a complex play speak to a contemporary audience.

We owe Orson Welles' direction of the marvellous film noir *Touch of Evil* to Charlton Heston's intervention with the producer. Would that Heston had exercised such imaginative wisdom when he set out to produce and direct his film version of *Antony and Cleopatra* (1972).[17] The film has a promising opening as we watch a red-sailed ship moving across a sparkling blue sea carrying a Roman soldier into port. When the ship lands the soldier quickly mounts a horse and spurs by several camels and plunges up through a narrow North African street, carelessly overturning produce from a bazaar as he urges his horse forward. Only an overwrought film score pulsing with violins detracts from this image of Roman haste and power bursting through a much more somnolent world. In a quick succession of visual images the film establishes the play's expanse and its clash of cultures. Unfortunately, those suggestive images dissolve as soon as the rider reaches Cleopatra's palace. Here our messenger from Rome is greeted not with one of the greatest opening lines in our dramatic literature ('Nay, but this dotage of our general's / O'erflows the measure'), but by his own enquiry: 'Where is mine Antony?' To which the reply is, 'Walking in the garden', and one's expectations sink.

This moment is typical of Heston's way with his Shakespearian material; he tries to domesticate it. He provides a version of Egypt-as-Hollywood with Cleopatra's palace an ugly fortress all decorated in hideous blue and green and pink pastels. When the camera finally discovers Antony he isn't walking in the garden but is stretched out in Cleopatra's arms as she paints his mouth with lipstick. No wonder Heston's Antony seems more than a little glad to be summoned back to Rome. In fact, Hildegard Neil's Cleopatra is almost always discovered at her make-up table, or being massaged, or – most egregiously –

8   *Antony and Cleopatra*, directed by Charlton Heston: an episode in the domestic life of Antony (Charlton Heston) and Cleopatra (Hildegard Neil)

doing a little interior decorating when Antony – having miraculously fought his way out of being surrounded by Caesar's entire army – rides his horse right into her palace only to be brought down by becoming entangled in the bolts of cloth she has been inspecting. Neil's queen doesn't wrangle; she pouts. She never breathes forth power; she only stamps her foot petulantly when Antony is in a Roman mood – which is most of the time.

If Egypt, complete with a coffee table containing a miniature pool filled with gold fish and model ships, is imagined as a version of tasteless Hollywood opulence, Heston's Rome also draws upon Hollywood sources. Heston is more successful with his creation of Rome because he is more at home there and because he gets a fine Octavius Caesar from John Castle. However, their initial scene is compromised by being shot as they watch two gladiators fight. This visual metaphor is lifted from Stanley Kubrick's *Spartacus* and then ruined by clumsy and obvious cutting between the two fighters and Antony and Caesar.

The film's saddest casualty is Enobarbus. He is conceived as Antony's steward, and Eric Porter plays him with a worried scowl. The script gives Porter an intolerable burden by assigning him Philo's opening lines (they do eventually get delivered) and having the great 'The barge she sat in . . .' description of Cleopatra delivered in Athens to a household servant! This comes just after Antony's advances to Octavia have been spurned and as he descends the stairs from her bedroom he overhears Enobarbus' account of Egyptian life which suddenly reminds him of Cleopatra's charms and sends him sailing off to her arms where he is greeted with, 'Lord of lords . . . Comest thou from / The world's great snare uncaught?'

As these brief examples are meant to suggest, Heston's film not only fails, visually and verbally, to capture the dynamics of Shakespeare's play but also fails to create an interesting epic inspired by a Shakespearian source. Nunn's production is the only one of the four to create an Egypt – through decor, direction, and Suzman's wily performance – which truly becomes a world elsewhere to rival Rome and thus create the necessary tension in Antony's tragic vacillation. It also allows us an understanding of all that Cleopatra abandons when she decides to die after the high Roman fashion. The remarkable poetry Shakespeare gives to Antony and Cleopatra in their final moments is awash with images of transcendence. Caesar has Rome and the world, but even he is momentarily awestruck as he gazes at Cleopatra who looks 'As though she would catch another Antony / In her strong toil of grace.'

Coriolanus marks Shakespeare's final return to Rome, this time with a vision so astringent as to scour any trace of transcendence or grace possible within its context. Elijah Moshinsky's *Coriolanus* (1983) completes the trio of Roman plays in the BBC series, with each production being representative of the work done during the tenure of the three producers of the series: Cedric Messina, Jonathan Miller, and Shaun Sutton. Moshinsky was recruited by Miller and his productions reflect the painterly style introduced by his mentor, but his *Coriolanus* also demonstrates the greater freedom allowed in the trimming of the text under Sutton's leadership. I find Moshinsky's production technically arresting and persuasively performed, the very best of the Roman plays produced in the series.[18] Following Miller's lead of finding inspiration at the National Gallery, Moshinsky's interiors are inspired by Van Dyck and Holbein in their colours and composition with an added depth of perspective created by our seeing rooms beyond rooms through open doorways or portals.[19] If Rome is imagined as a series of confining interiors hedging in Coriolanus' desire to be self-created and unlimited – even his appearance before the citizens in Act 2, Scene 3 is shot in an enclosed square with people leaning out of windows and doorways – then Corioli and the battle scenes are presented in a much more stylized and choreographed manner. Corioli's exterior is one massive soot-stained stone wall while its interior is seen as a roaring inferno before which Coriolanus and Aufidius, bare-chested, clash swords for the first time. These are crucible images: no eagle in a dovecote fluttering the Volscians here. This scene and Coriolanus' later revealing of himself to Aufidius in Act 4, Scene 5 are played by Alan Howard and Mike Gwilym as strongly homoerotic.

Moshinsky's reading of the play concentrates on the psychological with his textual cuts excising politics to focus on the personal, most obviously in Coriolanus' struggle to define himself caught as he is between Volumnia and Aufidius. Howard's Coriolanus, a role he played with great success in Terry Hands' heralded production for the RSC in 1977, manages in voice and bearing to project the necessary haughty arrogance while offering occasional clues that his carefully constructed persona is built on quicksand. This Coriolanus, except when he reveals himself to Aufidius and eventually capitulates to Volumnia, can only express himself in anger and aggression. He dies giving vent to both as the conspirators' chant of 'Kill, kill, kill' is reassigned first to Coriolanus and then to Aufidius to echo as the two men lock themselves in a deadly embrace.

Irene Worth is our age's definitive Volumnia, and she remarkably makes her character's perverse internalization of Rome's masculine values seem positively maternal. She is an iron vase with a brilliantly glazed porcelain exterior. When she melts, Coriolanus is lost. He has attempted to fashion a uniquely independent identity and when challenged he contemptuously insists that there is a world elsewhere; in his case Corioli. But for Coriolanus all roads inevitably lead back to Rome and Volumnia where, as Janet Adelman observes, his 'rage, like his hunger, is properly directed . . . [for] Rome and his mother are finally one'.[20]

Shakespeare's Rome is stern, powerful, masculine and cunning and those who underestimate that power and that cunning as Brutus does in his liberal dream of blood sacrifice without butchery, or Antony in the hopes of enjoying both pleasure and power, or Coriolanus in his insistence on fashioning an absolutely independent self, all come tragically to discover that the only world elsewhere is death. Mankiewicz's film of *Julius Caesar*, Nunn's television version of his RSC stage production of *Antony and Cleopatra*, and Elijah Moshinsky's *Coriolanus* in the BBC series, in their very individual ways, make palpable the dynamic tragic tensions Shakespeare's imagination seized upon when engaged in conceiving Rome and its legacy.

Notes

1 I follow Maurice Charney's lead and argument in excluding *Titus Andronicus* and *Cymbeline* from this discussion. See his *Shakespeare's Roman Plays* (Cambridge, 1961), pp. 207–18. I have chosen to discuss those film and television productions of the Roman plays which remain in general circulation.

2 Television directors, unlike their film counterparts, are culturally inconspicuous. Jon Scofield was the television director who worked with Trevor Nunn in reconceiving his Royal Shakespeare Company stage production for the small screen. I recognize his contribution here, though I will refer to the production by the name of its originator in the body of my essay.

3 'The BBC Shakespeare and "House Style"', *Shakespeare Quarterly*, 35 (Special issue, 1984), p. 580.

4 *Still in Movement: Shakespeare on Screen* (Oxford, 1991), p. 12.

5 *Unfinished Business: Memoirs: 1902–1988* (New York, 1989), p. 324.

6 Houseman, *Unfinished Business*, p. 324.

7 *Shakespeare on Film* (Bloomington, 1977), p. 101.

8 As C. L. Barber and Richard Wheeler perceptively observe, when 'the rivalry erupts between Brutus and Cassius [it can] be reconciled only on the common recognition that they are both bereft, lost inwardly without the center Caesar gave their lives'. *The Whole Journey: Shakespeare's Power of Development* (Berkeley, 1986), p. 36.

9 *Filming Shakespeare's Plays* (Cambridge, 1988), p. 7.

10 For an instructive account of the political and aesthetic issues involved in producing and directing Shakespeare for the BBC series, see Stanley Wells, 'Television Shakespeare', *Shakespeare Quarterly*, 33 (Autumn, 1982), 261–77.

11 'The BBC-TV Shakespeare Series', *Shakespeare Quarterly*, 30 (Summer, 1979), p. 412.

12 The production's most interesting performance is Richard Pasco's Brutus. Against tradition, Pasco's Brutus is testy and quick to anger, particularly when his decisions are challenged by Cassius. In the quarrel scene he literally explodes, overturning his camp table and hurling the scroll he is reading at his friend.

13 Kenneth S. Rothwell and Annabelle Henkin Melzer, *Shakespeare on Screen* (London and New York, 1990), p. 29.

14 See the introduction to the BBC edition of *Antony and Cleopatra* (London, 1981), p. 18 for Miller's rationale for using Veronese's *The Family of Darius at the Feet of Alexander* as the inspiration for his visual conception of the play. Interestingly, Peter Hall's fine stage production of the play at the National Theatre in 1987 also had its design source in a Veronese painting; in this instance the more appropriate *Mars and Venus Bound by Cupid*.

15 'Shakespeare in Miniature: The BBC *Antony and Cleopatra*', pp. 139–44 and 'The BBC-TV *Antony and Cleopatra*: Far More Harm Than Good', pp. 272–3, both in *Shakespeare on Television*, ed. J. C. Bulman and H. R. Coursen (Hanover and London, 1988).

16 The Bard series originated in Los Angeles as an American challenge to the BBC Shakespeares. It collapsed after producing just five of the plays: *Antony*, *Merry Wives*, *Othello*, *Richard II*, and *The Tempest*. Curiously, for an American series, it featured as many British actors as American. For example, three of the four principals in *Antony* were British: Lynn Redgrave, Timothy Dalton, and Barrie Ingham.

17 Heston did have the good sense to realize the film was seriously flawed and it never went into commercial release, though it is now widely available on video.

18 For a contrary view, particularly relating to Moshinsky's reshaping of the text, see Gordon P. Jones, 'Nahum Tate is Alive and Well: Elijah Moshinsky's BBC Shakespeare Productions', in Bulman and Coursen, *Shakespeare on Television*, pp. 192–200.

19 The Dutch inspiration carries over to inform Joss Ackland's excellent Menenius. His stout bearing, beard, and dress – which features an open white linen collar over a black shirt – makes him resemble the anonymous Dutch portrait of Ben Jonson which hangs in the National Portrait Gallery. Ackland's Menenius looms in the background of many of Moshinsky's shots as though presiding over this most Jonsonian of Shakespeare's major tragedies.

20 ' "Anger's My Meat": Feeding, Dependency, and Aggression in *Coriolanus*', in *Representing Shakespeare: New Psychoanalytic Essays*, ed. Murray M. Schwartz and Coppélia Kahn (Baltimore and London, 1980), p. 140.

9

ZEFFIRELLI'S SHAKESPEARE

ACE G. PILKINGTON

In the late twentieth century, most scholars have abandoned the hostility to productions of Shakespeare typified by Charles Lamb and, instead, regard performance texts as useful resources with dimensions and possible explications often unavailable from printed sources. More and more editions of Shakespeare include performance histories and comments on recent productions from stage and screen. Even the old prejudice which saw the theatre as superior to – because more Shakespearian than – film is breaking down as a result of recent insights. As Peter Hall said in 1970, 'In a sense any production or even any criticism of a play is an adaptation of the original.'[1] Obviously, Shakespeare in the contemporary theatre (with the use of lights, sound effects, actresses, and modern pronunciations) is adapted, no matter how much like the Globe the stage may look or how closely the production adheres to its chosen version of Shakespeare's text. Indeed, as Bernice W. Kliman and Kenneth Rothwell insisted in 1986, in a tenth-anniversary editorial for the *Shakespeare on Film Newsletter*, 'the attitude toward films as texts coincides with new critical movements that have made suspect the idea of *one* Shakespeare text'.[2]

Those directors who cut and rearrange Shakespeare have the support of influential scholars who assure them that the Bard himself rewrote and restructured. Stanley Wells and Gary Taylor in *The Complete Oxford Shakespeare* (1987) judged the changes in *King Lear* to be 'not simply local but structural, too',[3] and so printed the Quarto and Folio versions separately. Directors and scholars such as Laurence Olivier and John Wilders have maintained that the sixteenth-century stage was a medium much like film, that the screen 'can restore to Shakespeare's plays the unbroken flow and continuity they almost certainly achieved in the Renaissance theatre'.[4] Presumably the result of these changed attitudes should be a golden age of praise for Shakespearian film-makers, who will gather accolades from both the general and the judicious.

However, if the war between scholars and directors seems to be over, the peace terms have not yet been agreed, and there is a large no-man's-land into which film-makers wander at their peril. The principal combatants in this guerrilla conflict might perhaps be called the purists and the popularizers, and no modern director has a better claim to the dangerous title of popularizer-in-chief than Franco Zeffirelli.

Ironically, it is the new parity which film has achieved with the stage and the new fluidity of the term *adaptation* which have put film-makers at risk. While few critics worry over the liberties taken in obvious re-writings such as a science fiction version of *The Tempest* (*Forbidden Planet*) or *Othello* as Western (*Jubal*), both produced in 1956, any screen version of a Shakespeare play that also uses his words is held to a higher standard, no matter what disclaimers it may contain. As a result, Kurosawa's Japanese *Macbeth* (1957), Kozintsev's Russian *Hamlet* (1964), and even Zeffirelli's own stage *Hamlet* (1964) in Italian have fared better with many critics than Zeffirelli's Shakespeare films. He labels his productions adaptations, but where all is perceived as adaptation, that claim offers little protection.

Writing in 1990, Charles Boyce records the typical reaction: Zeffirelli 'is often criticised for the lavish spectacle of his productions, which are said to distract from the underlying play, but he has undeniably brought Shakespeare to a very wide audience'.[5] Similar comments have been directed at his stage Shakespeare, for example, his 1961 *Othello*, which Stanley Wells summed up in 1985 as 'visually splendid but less successful dramatically'.[6] Some assessments have not been as balanced as these or at least have seemed more vituperative. In a 1989 review for *The New York Times*, Donal Henahan wrote, 'At one time, Franco Zeffirelli was an opera director of artistic significance . . . [but] he is most charitably thought of nowadays as a fashion designer and interior decorator.'[7] And the condemnation of Zeffirelli's work in other media or his non-Shakespearian films may also affect critical responses to his Shakespeare. Commenting on *Brother Sun, Sister Moon* (1973), Stanley Kauffmann said, 'Essentially Zeffirelli is up to the same game here as in his *Romeo and Juliet* (1968): flatter the young and swamp them in Beeyootiful Color.'[8]

Zeffirelli got his start as an artist and stage designer who was influenced by Vittorio De Sica, Roberto Rossellini, and Luchino Visconti. 'With Visconti, Zeffirelli was one of the first to introduce the style known in Italy as *riesumazione*, the return to nineteenth-century realistic sets and costumes.'[9] He would defend his stage and film sets as more than background and pleasant pictures to attract the masses. In a 1990 seminar, he said, 'an actor cannot hold the stage alone; he needs to be helped by . . . a beauty around him . . . It becomes a kind of additional character.'[10]

More than that, the beauty and meaning of Renaissance Italy sometimes became Zeffirelli's justification as a director of Shakespeare, at once a starting point and a cultural bridge that linked him to his material. He was, he said in a 1968 interview for *Vogue*, telling the story of Romeo and Juliet, but 'it will really be a documentary of the period as well. . . . I know my Romeo and Juliet; but, oh, how I also know my Italy.'[11] He had found a yet larger significance in this blending of Italian and English culture, what he called in a programme note for his 1960 stage production of *Romeo and Juliet*, a 'combination of Italian feelings applied to a masterpiece of the classical English theatre which might prove . . . that times have changed in Europe and people of different backgrounds can easily work together for creating a new European conscience'.[12]

However, purists have criticized not only Zeffirelli's cultivation of scenic design but also his pruning of Shakespearian texts. Lewis Grossberger complains in his *Vogue* review of Zeffirelli's filmed *Hamlet* (1990), 'Frankly, Franco, that ain't cutting; it's axplay.'[13] And while other reviewers were less colloquial, they were equally annoyed. For Richard Corliss, with the elimination of material such as Claudius' confessional scene, 'Sometimes the movie forgets that it's *Hamlet*.'[14] James Bowman wrote, 'It is not *Hamlet* without the prince that I mind so much as *Hamlet* without the words.'[15] According to Mel Gibson, the slashing was even worse with the initial script. He 'called the early draft . . . "famous quotes from Hamlet"'.[16] Julia Wilson-Dickson, voice coach on the film, said of the final cut, '"It is, slightly, the comic-book version."'[17]

Similarly, Zeffirelli's filmed *Romeo and Juliet* is usually praised for its action and spirit and blamed for its elimination of the poetry, a choice necessitated by the inexperience of his young stars, and his version of *The Taming of the Shrew* (1967) has also been criticized for minimizing the text. In fact, Zeffirelli's cuts are more than usually harsh. He kept only 773.5 lines in *The Taming of the Shrew*, 1,044.5 lines in *Romeo and Juliet*, and 1,242.5 lines in *Hamlet*. Using *The Complete Oxford Shakespeare* and counting all lines which it includes from the Folio and Quartos, that would mean approximately thirty per cent of *Shrew*, thirty-five per cent of *Romeo and Juliet*, and thirty-seven per cent of *Hamlet*.

In addition to cutting, Zeffirelli also rearranges and rewrites. He has, for instance, shifted the scenes in his *Hamlet* to match Olivier's, in part, no doubt, because of his long-standing admiration. It was, Zeffirelli says in his 1986 autobiography, Olivier's *Henry V* (1944) which inspired him to decide that 'architecture was not for me; it had to be the stage'.[18] When he premiered *The Taming of the Shrew* in Italy, he says he showed 'it first at the Odeon in Florence, where all those years ago I had seen Olivier's *Henry V*'.[19] Zeffirelli declares that 'The main pleasure' for him in his 1965 stage version of *Much Ado About*

Nothing was that 'it brought me close to Larry Olivier, who had been my hero since I was a boy'.[20] It was Olivier's opening shot for *Henry V* that Zeffirelli echoed at the beginning of his *Romeo and Juliet*, a film in which Olivier voiced the Chorus, Lord Montague, numerous small parts, and even crowd noises.[21]

It is not difficult to find Olivier's influence either on the screen or behind it. Brad Darrach quotes Zeffirelli as saying, ' "I wanted a new kind of Hamlet. We haven't had one on the screen since Larry Olivier played him in 1948." '[22] Even giving Zeffirelli the benefit of the doubt and assuming he means the big screen, that is an extraordinary statement; it is as though other filmed *Hamlet*s in England and elsewhere simply did not exist. It may also be an indication of how little attention Zeffirelli has devoted to the filmed Shakespeare of other directors.

A further example of the impact of the Olivier version comes from Glenn Close in the short HBO film *The Making of Hamlet*: 'The first day of shooting he [Mel Gibson] was given by one of the producers the actual shirt that Olivier wore in his famous Hamlet.' And Gibson tells of making 'sure that I was in the hotel room by myself, with the lights out, and I tried this shirt on. Gradually, I got the courage to turn the lights on, and I found that it was probably a little too small, but it fit well enough.'[23]

In fact, the relationship between the two films is rather like Mel Gibson's experience with Olivier's shirt: the Zeffirelli version may deal with slightly larger issues and include more characters, but the fabric of the interpretation fits both well enough. The similarities come not single spies but in battalions. Just as in the Olivier, Laertes' leavetaking at 1.3 is interchanged with 1.2, Horatio and Marcellus' report to Hamlet on their ghostly encounter. Hamlet comes to Ophelia's closet in disarray in this film too, but here Polonius spies on them, and Ophelia's report is unnecessary. Hamlet's 'To be or not to be' soliloquy follows his confrontation with Ophelia as does his meeting with the players, though Rosencrantz and Guildenstern are (briefly) alive here. Hamlet is shown on shipboard as he journeys toward England; we see him changing the letters, but the pirates do not appear. We also, as in the Olivier, see Ophelia's drowning while Gertrude does a voice-over.

There are, of course, independent cuttings and rearrangings in Zeffirelli's *Hamlet*, most spectacularly the elimination of the entire first scene, ghost and all, and the removal of both the politics and the Hamlet/Claudius opposition from the second scene, which is then filmed in eight different parts, a simultaneous simplification and illustration of the material, stretching the visuals to keep the audience watching.

Zeffirelli's first scene (as opposed to Shakespeare's) is in a royal mausoleum at the burial of Hamlet's father, with Claudius speaking the opening words:

'Hamlet, think of us / As of a father . . .' (1.2.107–8). The scene shifts to the court for the announcement of the wedding of Claudius and Gertrude, then shifts again to a library/book bindery for the business with Laertes. Zeffirelli's fourth scene is the exterior of the castle for a wordless conference between Claudius and Gertrude, and scene 5 takes us inside to still another room, where Hamlet, who has been off screen since the court scene, discusses his college plans with his aunt/mother and uncle/father and then, after Gertrude signals Claudius to leave, with his mother alone. To conclude this segment of the action without the new king, Gertrude, who has become the film's co-star, has been given some of his lines. Scene 6 features Gertrude running downstairs and skipping off with two ladies-in-waiting, and we next return to Hamlet and his interior room for Scene 7, the 'O that this too too solid flesh would melt' (1.2.129) soliloquy, which also contains scene 8 when Hamlet looks out of a window and sees Claudius on horseback with Gertrude reaching up to kiss him. One is left with the impression that this court is not only equestrian but also peripatetic.

Unlike his *Hamlet*, most of the rearranging in Zeffirelli's *Romeo and Juliet* is the shifting of lines within scenes, but in *The Taming of the Shrew*, he has larger changes, following an unusual pattern similar to Tom Stoppard's *Rosencrantz and Guildenstern Are Dead*. As Petruchio chases Kate through the rooms and over the roof of Baptista's house, he also chases her in and out of other scenes, which are overheard and spied on rather than straightforwardly presented. The chase has become a metaphor for Zeffirelli's treatment of the Bianca subplot and perhaps even for his treatment of text.

After Katherine retorts, 'Too light for such a swain as you to catch' (2.1.204), she pretends she sees her father standing behind Petruchio and says, 'Father, this man . . .' and as Petruchio turns around to look for Baptista, she ducks behind a curtain and exits through a passageway. In his pursuit, Petruchio opens a door behind which Gremio and Tranio (as Lucentio) are making bids for Bianca's hand in marriage, and Tranio says, in Zeffirelli's simplified version of Shakespeare's lines, 'Vincentio, my father hath no less / Than three great argosies, besides two merchant ships / And twelve light galleys' (2.1.373–5). Petruchio leaves them and wanders into a courtyard where Hortensio is attempting to drag Bianca away from Cambio/Lucentio's lecture. The lines from Act 3, Scene 1 Zeffirelli uses here in the order he uses them are: 28, 1–5, 9, 57, 25, 37, 39, 24, 25, and again 28. Petruchio then continues his search for Katherine, and when he finds her, he says, 'Good morrow, Kate. Good Kate, I am a gentleman' (2.1.182, 217). This last is spoken without Shakespeare's cue and with no discernible visual substitute.

Zeffirelli, like Olivier in his *Hamlet*, is also guilty of another sin in the purists' catalogue of seven deadly edits – rewriting. He does this in two ways, by replacing words with others which are supposedly easier for his audience to grasp and by inserting entirely new lines for the same reason. Some of the changes indicate that Zeffirelli has a distressingly low estimate of his audience's intelligence. At 3.2.49, for instance, 'stirrups of no kindred' becomes 'stirrups of different families'. At 1.1.84, 'Minerva' is replaced by 'goddess'.

Longer replacements follow the same pattern. Tranio's lines at 1.1.31–3, 'Let's be no stoics nor no stocks, I pray, / Or so devote to Aristotle's checks / As Ovid be an outcast quite abjured', turns into 'But let us not be so confined by learning that love becomes an outcast.' Petruchio proclaims, 'I won the battle you have yet to fight' rather than ''Twas I won the wager, though you hit the white' at 5.2.191. Capulet cries out, 'Juliet! My baby, where is she?' This, presumably, is meant to replace Lady Capulet's 'O me, O me, my child, my only life! / Revive, look up, or I will die with thee' (4.4.46–7).

And some material is simply added in, for example, Romeo and Juliet's theme song – sung first at Capulet's banquet – which begins 'What is a youth? Impetuous fire. / What is a maid? Ice and desire. / The world drags on.' After 3.2.155 in *Hamlet*, Zeffirelli interpolates for the Player King, 'But should I die before a new sun shine, / You might another husband soon entwine'.

Zeffirelli's defence against these charges (and he has answered them repeatedly) is that he is bringing Shakespeare to the masses. He says, 'With the cinema, you have to make up your mind whether you do a film for a small number of people who know it all – and it's not very exciting to work for them – or really make some sacrifices and compromises but bring culture to a mass audience.'[24] In spite of his enormous admiration for all things English, he has little faith in Shakespeare's ability to move a modern audience without directorial intervention. Speaking of the type of full-text production that the National Theatre might do, he maintains, 'You inform your audience that this is it, but don't expect them to cry with you – they might laugh, as a relief.'[25]

Zeffirelli has little respect for scholars or for the discipline which produces scholarship. He tells, in his autobiography, of his uneasiness when he met Richard Burton's mentor, 'a Shakespearean scholar'; 'I wondered', he says, 'if I was going to find myself arguing with some sort of dusty Welsh bookworm with petty notions of how the Bard should be preserved.'[26] His advice in a seminar on filming Shakespeare was, 'If you want to be a Shakespearean director, I don't think it's necessary to bog down for three years and exclusively study that. You might get a bit confused.'[27]

In spite of his frequently expressed intention to popularize Shakespeare, Zeffirelli does not have much faith in the audience to which he caters. He says in *The Making of Hamlet*, 'Think of it, nobody knows anything about *Hamlet*, about Shakespeare; they don't know anything. They go there, in a dark room, and they see something on the screen and that's what?' Here, Zeffirelli rolls his eyes upward in an expression of vapid confusion. The result of these twin denigrations is a kind of isolation for the director. The concerns of scholars are ruled out as an impediment to making 'the audience understand that the classics are living flesh',[28] and that same audience is perceived as a *tabula rasa* on which the director must write in broad strokes. Even Shakespeare is to some extent deemed irrelevant because, as Zeffirelli says, 'The poetry of the original language, the original poetical language of Shakespeare, is not what makes it internationally unbetterable, with no peers.'[29]

The film, then, becomes a simple matter of the story Zeffirelli is telling to his unsophisticated audience. For Jill L. Levenson, in her 1987 study of *Romeo and Juliet* in performance, the result was 'a version of the Romeo and Juliet narrative more like Shakespeare's sources'.[30] Lawrence Frascella reacts similarly, in a review for *US*, arguing that with his *Hamlet*, Zeffirelli 'has succeeded in turning literature's greatest tragedy into a rip-roaring melodrama'.[31]

In fairness to Zeffirelli, however, he has, using minimalist budgets, conjured Shakespeare films that made both profits and audiences. His seventy-day shooting schedule for *Hamlet* cost slightly more than $15.5 million;[32] *Romeo and Juliet* came in at $1.5 million and 'grossed $50 million'.[33] Also, some of Zeffirelli's concentration on visuals and unwillingness to challenge full texts has less to do with directorial ego than personal insecurity and perhaps even an accurate evaluation of his own strengths and weaknesses. In contrasting two of his stage productions, he writes, '*Romeo* has this wonderful universal story, so marvellously structured it survives any translation . . . In the end, with *Othello* the language is all . . . Thus what had been forgivable oversights in my *Romeo* when set against the vivacity and the drama would . . . be inflated into major errors in *Othello*.'[34]

Zeffirelli might argue with some justice that he is 'translating' Shakespeare into film, and point to comments such as Michael Pursell's in *Literature/Film Quarterly* that 'In each of his Shakespearean films, Zeffirelli offers a lucid and subtle visual interpretation of the particular text.'[35] Nor is the visual interpretation all. It might also be argued that while Zeffirelli has avoided some textual difficulties (and created others) by pruning his Shakespeare films, he has not shirked the major directorial challenges and confrontations in any of them.

The central problem of *The Taming of the Shrew*, for example, is what to make of Petruchio's taming. While the play does not demand brutality and is not a sixteenth-century tract for the subjugation of women, it is frequently played as though it does and is. Directors who see the play as a man's violent domination of a woman have manipulated the text in two main ways. One is to foreground the violence à la Charles Marowitz, who declares that 'The modern technique for brainwashing is, almost to the letter, what Petruchio makes Katherine undergo.'[36] Another and more 'popular means of not dealing directly with the main story has been', as Tice L. Miller writes, 'to mock it by turning the production into a knockabout farce'.[37]

Farce is seemingly Zeffirelli's choice, but his plot manipulations produce something subtler and less threatening to Katherine than is usual, while at the same time presenting a Petruchio who has greater difficulties and therefore more room to grow. Part of Zeffirelli's success comes from his retaining a sort of Induction, not Shakespeare's story of Christopher Sly, but what Jack Jorgens called in his seminal 1979 study, 'the saturnalian revels of the students of Padua',[38] which gives his farce a Renaissance backdrop and an almost mythic undertone.

Petruchio's wooing of and confrontation with Katherine (mentioned earlier) becomes in this festive context a chase scene through Baptista's house and over the rooftop with opportunities for swinging on ropes, smashing wooden structures, and repeatedly falling into a large pile of wool. Kate in her turn becomes the pursuer after the wedding, tracking her new husband over rough country during a storm.

As a result of this filmic revision, Zeffirelli's *Shrew* avoided the direct violence usually included in 2.1 by turning the scene into a series of chases. There is in Jorgens' words, 'harmless violence and festive destruction'[39] such as Kate breaking a music stand, throwing a small lute at Petruchio when he says he has heard her 'mildness praised in every town' (2.1.191), and kicking his stool out from under him at line 198. But after she insists that she is 'Too light for such a swain as you to catch' (2.1.204), she slips out of the room, initiating the chase.

This less violent Petruchio is, however, obsessed with money. When Hortensio says, in lines which exist only in the screenplay, 'Now, Petruchio, if I do plot thy match with Katherine, there is a favor I would ask of thee to help me woo her younger sister, Bianca', Petruchio responds, 'Ask it, and so it be not gold, 'tis granted.' When he enters Baptista's home, he eagerly inspects a silver serving set. Zeffirelli has shifted lines so that the first thing Petruchio says to his future father-in-law is, 'What dowry shall I have with her as wife?' He repeats the question in its rightful place (2.1.120), and when Baptista tells him he shall have twenty thousand crowns, he utters an 'Ah!' of pleasure, and smiles. After he tells Kate, 'Will you, nill you, I will marry you' (2.1.265), she says, 'I'd rather die' and jumps out a high window (onto a roof, we soon discover); he shows no concern for Katherine personally, but mutters anxiously, 'My twenty thousand crowns', looking exceedingly relieved when he finds that he has not lost her dowry.

Zeffirelli darkens Petruchio in other ways. After the marriage, Petruchio puts Kate on a mule, and he and Grumio gallop off toward his house without waiting for her. Kate chases after them in the rain and finds a shortcut over a mountain; on the other side, her mule is startled by Petruchio's horse and throws her into a pond. Petruchio chortles and rides on without offering assistance, leaving her to survive the rain (which soon turns to snow) alone.

Reaching his home, Petruchio celebrates by throwing gold to his servants. He looks disappointed and disgruntled when the bedraggled Kate walks through the door, as though he had hoped she was dead and the dowry his with no further trouble. His complaints to his servants concerning the lack of preparation for his bride's arrival seem a desperate attempt to cover his surprise and excuse his boorishness.

Petruchio's world is an exclusively male one similar to the environment which Romeo must abandon in order to love Juliet. While Petruchio educates Kate, she domesticates him, reordering his life as he is reintegrating her into the society which she feels has rejected her, and which she, in turn, has rejected. In fact, both the lovers have operated outside the bounds of society. As Jack Jorgens points out, 'Petruchio and Kate are allied with the saturnalian forces which stand the everyday on its head and turn reason inside out. As Zeffirelli sees it, the comedy is not primarily about a taming, but about a release of Dionysian energies.'[40]

Of course, it is those very energies in the lovers which are tamed or at least redirected; Kate's shrewishness and Petruchio's wildness make a new domestic dynamic. As Graham Holderness wrote in 1989, endorsing and extending Jack Jorgens' commentary on Zeffirelli's film, 'The function of carnival is to promote social integration . . . Kate's subversive energy of resistance and Petruchio's parodic exposure of commercialised relationship both serve ulti-mately, and paradoxically, to reintegrate the disrupted order of Paduan society.'[41]

Ironically, the section of the film which summarizes this message, Kate's reading the speech on obedience as though she means it and then slipping away at the end to begin the chase all over again, was not entirely a matter of directorial choice. As Zeffirelli says, 'I had assumed, as I imagine had Richard, that when we did the notoriously controversial final scene in which Katherine makes her act of submission . . . she would do it in the now accepted ironical way . . . Amazingly, Liz did nothing of the kind; she played it straight.'[42] However, if not all of this message originated with Zeffirelli in a film that was to some extent the on-screen continuation of its stars' off-screen lives, it was his inspiration which brought them into the production in the first place and his direction that brought a tenuous order to the saturnalia in front of and behind the cameras.

With *Romeo and Juliet*, Zeffirelli took his biggest gamble and came up against one of the greatest dangers for the adapter. On Shakespeare's stage, the boy actor removed the play from the precincts of verisimilitude and freed the audience to use its collective imagination. Modern productions face the formidable choice of a Juliet too young to act or too old to be believed. Perhaps part of Zeffirelli's success in *The Taming of the Shrew* and *Hamlet* is his substitution of one kind of distancing device for another. If a boy actor is not Juliet, a recognizable movie star is not Kate or Hamlet. If no one expects a boy playing a girl to inspire absolute conviction, no one expects a movie star playing Shakespeare to do it either, and the plays or films around them benefit from the air of unreality, the lowered expectations of believability.

But in *Romeo and Juliet*, Zeffirelli followed his own stage precedent, employing young actors and a realistic set. He was also following the road travelled by Castellani in his 1954 film of the play, where he had used 'a hilltop town in northern Italy as an authentic backdrop'.[43] However, a comparison between Castellani and Zeffirelli's results indicates some of the reasons for Zeffirelli's success. Though both employed real locations, they were not equally successful in meeting what Anthony Davies defined in his ground breaking 1988 study of the use of space in Shakespearian films as 'the most formidable challenge to the film maker who adapts Shakespeare for the screen', that is 'reconciling the heightened utterance and increased density of poetic dialogue with the convincing realism of cinematic space'.[44] Ultimately, Castellani's Verona is as much a backdrop as any nineteenth-century set, with the added disadvantage that real buildings can upstage the actors, making them seem as static as figures in the Renaissance paintings from which the film drew its visual inspiration.

For Zeffirelli, the Italian towns which became his Verona (Tuscania, Pienza, and Gubbio)[45] are part of the plot, an 'additional character' indeed, with the beauty of Renaissance Italy but also a sinister energy which drives the tragedy inexorably on. The town seems to crowd and compress the characters so that the individual violence and the riots look like attempts to escape from a maze, and the briefly deserted squares and streets provide a chance to breathe before the tension builds again to critical mass. Even the crane shots do not give a feeling of openness so much as the dwarfing of the characters in their monumental prisons.

If Zeffirelli loses the sense of Fate as an outside force driving the play, he actually increases the tension created by Shakespeare, 'who does not emphasize quite so early the depth and the terror of the feud'.[46] In this film, it is family which is Fate, and Romeo and Juliet's struggle to find their individual identities apart from the world of Capulet and Montague and 'thereby' as John Wilders says, introducing the 1978 BBC film of the play, 'to become exclusively themselves' is doomed from the start.[47]

Of all Zeffirelli's films, *Romeo and Juliet* comes closest to the essence of the Shakespeare play on which it is based, perhaps in part because the beauty of Zeffirelli's actors and camerawork echoes (even as it replaces) the formal ornamentation of Shakespeare's verse. Although many of the lines are sacrificed and some appear in new contexts, there is no radical rewriting either in terms of plot (as in *The Taming of the Shrew*) or interpretation (as in *Hamlet*). Zeffirelli did drop the apothecary scene and the killing of Paris (both of which he had shot) to avoid awkward questions in the first case and additional blood on Romeo's hands in the second,[48] but, in general, he rearranges and cuts line by line, often making the camera do the work of the missing text. For example, 'Say "better". Here comes one of my master's kinsmen' (1.1.55–6) is eliminated, and it is Abraham who looks into the crowd for help before he precipitates the fight with, 'You lie' (1.1.58).

Perhaps most notable in Zeffirelli's substitution of shot for text is his equating of male sexuality with the weapons of the feud. Of course, the message remains in the lines of the film, but Zeffirelli's camera provides a graphic and repetitive emphasis on codpiece and sword. As Peter S. Donaldson points out in his excellent 1990 analysis, *Shakespearean Films/Shakespearean Directors*, Romeo is distinguished from this wholesale equation as a symbol of 'pacific masculinity ... There is only one moment ... in which the film presents Romeo in terms of the sword/phallus metaphor.'[49] It is, of course, when Romeo is drawn into the cycle of violence, just before his duel with Tybalt.

Zeffirelli has also foregrounded the Tybalt–Capulet rivalry, with a suggestion of an incestuous relationship between Lady Capulet and Tybalt and a widening circle of ripples through both families to indicate that the feud, begun by the older generation, 'permits indulgence in fantasies of youthfulness, potency, and control at the expense of younger male rivals'.[50]

Finally, though I must reject Jill L. Levenson's judgement that the film is 'a version of the famous legend more uniform in tone, beautiful in conception, and passionate in mood than Shakespeare's',[51] I believe that Zeffirelli has created a film which provides at once a respectable critical interpretation and a believably fiery incarnation of Shakespeare's text.

Between *Romeo and Juliet* in 1968 and *Hamlet* in 1990, Zeffirelli's career had contained almost as many traumas as triumphs. In part as a result of severe injuries in a 1969 automobile accident and a difficult and prolonged recovery, Zeffirelli made two religious biographies, *Brother Sun, Sister Moon* (1973) and the mini-series *Jesus of Nazareth* (1977). His other films in the period included *The Champ* (1979) and *Endless Love* (1981), which were more successful financially than critically, and two operas, *La Traviata* in 1982 and *Otello* in 1986. They were followed in 1988 by another biography *Young Toscanini*, which remains unreleased.[52] Also in 1988, Zeffirelli 'denounced *The Last*

Temptation of Christ',[53] alienating some members of the film community and creating a controversy over whether his remarks about the Scorsese film were anti-Semitic, an accusation he emphatically denies.

Zeffirelli had wanted to direct Shakespeare, but his two attempts in this period, a musical version of *Much Ado About Nothing* with Liza Minnelli and a theatrical *Hamlet* with Richard Gere, failed in the planning stages.[54] In spite of his continued interest in Shakespearian production, Zeffirelli does not seem to have drawn inspiration from or changed his production style as a result of the filmed Shakespeare which appeared between his *Romeo and Juliet* and *Hamlet*. His autobiography, in some ways a *Who's Who* of the film and theatre world, contains no references to Kozintsev, Kurosawa, Peter Brook, or even Orson Welles. 'Zeffirelli says he sees *Hamlet* as his ticket back to dramatic cinema',[55] and he drew on his two earlier successes as well as Olivier's film for inspiration. Zeffirelli's *Hamlet* has the appeal to youth of his *Romeo and Juliet* coupled with the star power (for generating production money, distribution contracts, and audiences) of his *Taming of the Shrew*.

In *Hamlet*, Zeffirelli confronted one of the greatest mysteries in the canon, the nature and motivation of the Prince, a role he had played himself 'in a university production right after World War II'.[56] Although in an interview for *Parade*, Mel Gibson described Hamlet as 'introspective' and 'thinking too much',[57] the character who emerged had, in the words of Cathleen McGuigan's *Newsweek* review, 'vitality and edginess'.[58] It was, Caryn James wrote in *The New York Times*, 'a shrewd, intelligent performance'.[59] Zeffirelli's sudden inspiration as he watched Mel Gibson in *Lethal Weapon*, that here was a young actor who could play a new kind of Hamlet,[60] had paid off in a return to the roots of Shakespeare's play – the revenge tragedy and *Hamlet* as thriller. As *Sight and Sound* reviewer Jonathan Romney observed, 'This Hamlet is unequivocally a man of action.'[61]

There is an air of manic desperation in almost all of Gibson's characters, from which his Hamlet benefits. He is believable as the obsessed Prince, and Zeffirelli's medieval backgrounds of real and manufactured castles give him an effective context for violent action. If Gibson's stint doing stage Shakespeare in Australia did not quite prepare him to hold his own with Paul Scofield, Alan Bates, Trevor Peacock, and Ian Holm, his time as an action hero allows him to swashbuckle through the part, and his star quality keeps him from fading into Zeffirelli's sumptuous but subdued landscapes.

Though they are mostly visual, there are some first-rate ideas in this film: Hamlet lying on the graveyard grass, head to head with Yorick's skull; Hamlet looking down on and overhearing much of the plotting against him, a spy in a world of spies; the sheer vitality and happiness of Claudius and Gertrude,

9   *Hamlet*, directed by Franco Zeffirelli: Hamlet (Mel Gibson) with Yorick's skull

paired and contrasted with the cautious shuffling of Polonius and the sullen skulking of Ophelia; and over the whole film the blue dimness of distance, the colour equivalent of black and white but with a suggestion that the characters are receding from the audience into a kind of mythic mistiness.

It is unfortunate that Zeffirelli, following Olivier in this as in so much else, chose to explain Hamlet with Freud, foregrounding the incest theme and almost making the film what Edward Quinn called it in the *Shakespeare on Film Newsletter*, 'a fluid, excitingly paced movie about two middle-aged, star-crossed lovers'.[62] Partly this is the fault of Glenn Close's refusal to act her age or anything close to it. She says in *The Making of Hamlet*, 'My Gertrude is very alive. I think she had Hamlet at a very early age, married a much older man. And all her sensuality, all her kind of physical comfort, she got from her son . . . She's a kind of woman that three men are revolving around.'

Franco Zeffirelli comments that Hamlet is 'mad about this creature, this mother. He's jealous of the wind that touches her cheeks', and Mel Gibson's version of the same sentiment is, 'When she abandons him and runs off with his uncle . . . He's lost his gal, in a way.'[63] The result of this wrongheadedness is a bed scene where Hamlet's wrestling with his mother, his movements mimic-king the sex act, and the passionate kiss Gertrude gives him prompted some of my Shakespeare students to conclude that the Ghost entered not to hurry Hamlet on to his revenge or to chide him for being too rough with his mother, but to prevent him from having sex with her, a situation that Mary Z. Maher labelled 'ghostus interruptus'.[64]

In this production, incest does not stop with Claudius and Gertrude or even with Hamlet and Gertrude. According to Mel Gibson, 'Ophelia is fourteen years old and just beginning to awaken sexually . . . in the scene where she hugs her brother (1.3), Bonham-Carter "does something with her eye" that tells the viewer she is experiencing her first sexual moment.'[65]

It is Zeffirelli's contention that he is 'using a language that will make clear and accessible every single word of William Shakespeare'.[66] But with most of the politics gone, while sex and violence are foregrounded, what is left of the plot can be somewhat confusing, sending the audience to other versions or even to the text, which could arguably be part of Zeffirelli's intention in this film and the others, not only to popularize but to energize and even to tantalize. For Zeffirelli, Hamlet was a big risk as well as a satisfying challenge, his only Shakespeare film without the comfort of an Italian setting. In light of his remarks about the 'errors' in his stage Othello and his troubles with the 'language',[67] his dependence on the Olivier version may, in some ways, have seemed a safety net for him as he walked the criss-crossing tightropes of text in Shakespeare's longest play.

Finally, against large difficulties (such as being 'contractually obligated to keep the running time at about two hours' with Hamlet),[68] Franco Zeffirelli has produced a body of work that is always interesting and sometimes splendid, that cuts but does not shirk, rewrites but does not abandon. Zeffirelli's films are particularly valuable at a time when 'Shakespearean critics' are 'more willing to examine each film in terms of its own assumptions' since it is 'one in a series, yet another taped essay on and journey into the play'.[69] Multiple incarnations of a play, on stage and film, make possible the broadest possible perspective for Shakespeare, and Zeffirelli with his insistence on the Bard's links to the Italian Renaissance and the whole culture of Europe has helped immeasurably in the creation of that perspective.

Notes

1 Peter Hall, 'Introduction', The Wars of the Roses: Adapted for the Royal Shakespeare Company from William Shakespeare's 'Henry VI', Parts I, II, and III and 'Richard III', by John Barton, in collaboration with Peter Hall (London, 1970), p. viii.
2 Bernice W. Kliman and Kenneth S. Rothwell, 'A Tenth Anniversary Editorial', Shakespeare on Film Newsletter, vol. 11, no. 1 (1986), 1, 6, 12; p. 6.

3 Stanley Wells and Gary Taylor, *The Complete Oxford Shakespeare*, 3 vols. (Oxford, 1987), vol. 3, p. 1233.

4 John Wilders, 'Shakespeare on the Small Screen', *Deutsche Shakespeare-Gesellschaft West Jahrbuch* (1982), 56–62; p. 61.

5 Charles Boyce, *Shakespeare A to Z: The Essential Reference to his Plays, his Poems, his Life and Times, and More* (Oxford and New York, 1990), p. 724.

6 Stanley Wells, *Shakespeare: An Illustrated Dictionary* (Oxford, 1985), p. 191.

7 Donal Henahan, 'More Zeffirelli on the Grand Scale in the Met's New "Traviata" ', *The New York Times*, 18 October 1989, C-15, col. 4.

8 Stanley Kauffmann, 'Stanley Kauffmann on Films', *The New Republic*, 168 (7 April 1973), 24 and 33; p. 33.

9 William Weaver, 'Franco Zeffirelli: The Patience for Infinite Detail that makes Dramatic Miracles', *High Fidelity Magazine*, 14 (March 1964), 30 and 34; p. 30.

10 Franco Zeffirelli, 'Filming Shakespeare', *Staging Shakespeare: Seminars on Production Problems*, ed. Glenn Loney (London and New York, 1990), pp. 239–70; p. 269.

11 Polly Devlin, ' "I Know My Romeo and Juliet" ', *Vogue*, 151 (1 April 1968): 34, 52, 69, 80; p. 52.

12 Programme note to Zeffirelli's production of *Romeo and Juliet* with the Old Vic Company, 1960, cited in Jill L. Levenson, 'Translation, 1960–1968: Franco Zeffirelli', *Romeo and Juliet (Shakespeare in Performance)* (Manchester and Wolfeboro, New Hampshire, 1987), pp. 82–123; p. 85.

13 Lewis Grossberger, 'Movies: Shakespeare Goes Hollywood', *Vogue*, 181 (February 1991), 214 and 220; p. 220.

14 Richard Corliss, 'Wanna Be . . . or Wanna Not Be?', *Time*, 137 (7 January 1991), 73.

15 James Bowman, 'This Great Dane's a Dog', *The American Spectator*, 24 (March 1991), 30–1; p. 30.

16 Michael P. Jensen, 'Mel Gibson on Hamlet', *Shakespeare on Film Newsletter*, vol. 15, no. 2 (April 1991), 1, 2, 6; p. 1.

17 Cyndi Stivers, 'Hamlet Revisited', *Premiere*, 4 (February 1991), 50–4, 56; p. 54.

18 Franco Zeffirelli, *Zeffirelli: The Autobiography of Franco Zeffirelli* (New York, 1986), p. 61.

19 *Ibid.*, p. 224.

20 *Ibid.*, p. 201.

21 *Ibid.*, p. 229.

22 Brad Darrach, 'Mad Max Plays Hamlet: Mel Gibson, a great Dane from Down Under', *Life*, vol. 14, no. 2 (February 1991), 36–42, 46; p. 38.

23 *Classic Mel Gibson: The Making of Hamlet*, narr. Mel Gibson, HBO, 1991.

24 Zeffirelli, 'Filming Shakespeare', p. 244.

25 *Ibid.*, p. 262.

26 Zeffirelli, *Zeffirelli*, p. 212.

27 Zeffirelli, 'Filming Shakespeare', p. 243.

28 *Ibid.*, p. 252.

29 *Classic Mel Gibson: The Making of Hamlet*, 1991.

30 Levenson, 'Translation, 1960–1968: Franco Zeffirelli', p. 116.

31 Lawrence Frascella, 'Reviews: Hamlet', *US*, 24 January 1991, 55–6; p. 56.

32 Stivers, 'Hamlet Revisited', p. 52.

33 Zeffirelli, *Zeffirelli*, p. 229.

34 *Ibid.*, pp. 165–6.

35 Michael Pursell, 'Artifice and Authenticity in Zeffirelli's *Romeo and Juliet*', *Literature/Film Quarterly*, 14 (1986), 173–8; p. 173.

36 Charles Marowitz, 'Introduction', *The Marowitz Shakespeare* (London, 1978), pp. 7–27; p. 18.

37 Tice L. Miller, 'The Taming of the Shrew', *Shakespeare Around the Globe*, ed. Samuel L. Leiter (New York, 1986), pp. 661–6; p. 662.

38 Jack Jorgens, *Shakespeare on Film* (Bloomington, Indiana, 1979), p. 73.

39 *Ibid.*, p. 71.

40 *Ibid.*, pp. 73–4.

41 Graham Holderness, 'Franco Zeffirelli (1966)', *The Taming of the Shrew (Shakespeare in Performance)* (Manchester and New York, 1989), pp. 49–72; p. 59.

42 Zeffirelli, *Zeffirelli*, p. 216.

43 Kenneth S. Rothwell and Annabelle Henkin Melzer, *Shakespeare on Screen: An International Filmography and Videography* (London and New York, 1990), p. 252.

44 Anthony Davies, *Filming Shakespeare's Plays: The Adaptations of Laurence Olivier, Orson Welles, Peter Brook and Akira Kurosawa* (Cambridge and New York, 1988), p. 15.

45 Zeffirelli, *Zeffirelli*, p. 227.

46 J. L. Halio, 'Zeffirelli's *Romeo and Juliet*: The Camera *versus* the Text', *Literature/Film Quarterly*, vol. 5, no. 4 (1977), 322–5; p. 323.

47 John Wilders, 'Romeo and Juliet', *New Prefaces to Shakespeare* (Oxford and New York, 1988), pp. 88–94; p. 89.

48 Zeffirelli, 'Filming Shakespeare', pp. 244–5.

49 Peter S. Donaldson, *Shakespearean Films/Shakespearean Directors* (London, 1990), p. 156.

50 Donaldson, *Shakespearean Films/Shakespearean Directors*, p. 161.

51 Levenson, 'Translation, 1960–1968: Franco Zeffirelli', p. 123.

52 See Stivers, 'Hamlet Revisited', pp. 51–2, 54, 56. For comment on individual films see Zeffirelli, *Zeffirelli*, pp. 233–40 (for information on Zeffirelli's accident, its religious aftermath, and *Brother Sun, Sister Moon*), 304–8 (*The Champ*), 310–18 (*Endless Love*).

53 Stivers, 'Hamlet Revisited', p. 56.

54 Zeffirelli, *Zeffirelli*, p. 266; Stivers, 'Hamlet Revisited', p. 52.

55 *Ibid.*, p. 52.

56 *Ibid.*, p. 51.

57 Michael Ryan, ' "I Admire People with Self-Control": An Interview with Mel Gibson', *Parade: The Sunday Newspaper Magazine*, 3 March 1991, 8 and 10; p. 8.

58 Cathleen McGuigan, 'Melancholy Mel Goes to Elsinore', *Newsweek*, vol. 116, no. 27 (31 December 1990), p. 61.

59 Caryn James, 'Too Oft, Fault Lies in the Stars', *The New York Times*, 6 January 1991, sec. 2, p. 13, col. 1 and sec. 2, p. 19; p. 19.

60 Stivers, 'Hamlet Revisited', p. 51.

61 Jonathan Romney, 'Hamlet', *Sight and Sound*, May 1991, 48–9; p. 49.

62 Edward Quinn, 'Zeffirelli's *Hamlet*', *Shakespeare on Film Newsletter*, vol. 15, no. 2 (April 1991), 1–2, 12; p. 1.

63 *Classic Mel Gibson: The Making of Hamlet*, 1991.

64 Mary Z. Maher, 'The Un-Hamlet', unpublished paper delivered at the Western Conference on Literature, Film and the Humanities, University of Arizona, 3 January 1992, p. 4.

65 Jensen, 'Mel Gibson on Hamlet', p. 1.

66 *Classic Mel Gibson: The Making of Hamlet*, 1991.

67 Zeffirelli, *Zeffirelli*, pp. 165–6.

68 Jensen, 'Mel Gibson on Hamlet', p. 1.

69 Ace G. Pilkington, *Screening Shakespeare from Richard II to Henry V* (Cranbury, New Jersey, and London, 1991), p. 162.

THE FILMS OF *HAMLET*

NEIL TAYLOR

No Shakespeare play has generated more films than *Hamlet*. At the latest count there have been forty-seven film-versions of the play or part of the play, and at least ninety-three other films alluding to it – educational films in which extracts from *Hamlet* appear, feature films which derive from the Hamlet story, or feature films which happen to include extracts from *Hamlet* as part of their story.[1]

The bulk of these films have been British or American, but other have come from countries as diverse as Italy and India, Ghana and Brazil, Poland and Japan. The films preserve for posterity performances by classical actors such as Johnston Forbes-Robertson, John Barrymore, Jean-Louis Barrault, Laurence Olivier, Richard Burton, John Gielgud, Michael Redgrave, David Warner, Michael Pennington, Jonathan Pryce, Ian McKellen, Helen Mirren and Mark Rylance, and by Hollywood stars such as Buster Keaton, Katherine Hepburn, Jack Benny, Michael Caine, Mel Brooks and Arnold Schwarzenegger. The forty-seven 'pure' *Hamlet*s begin with Sarah Bernhardt's silent black and white version of the duel scene shot in the theatre of Mme Chenin at the Paris Exposition of 1900. They end, at least by the time of this essay's composition, with a three-hour version of the play issued in 1993 by King Alfred's College in Southampton, England.

Six 'pure' *Hamlet*s are currently widely available on video. Four were made originally for the cinema (those directed by Laurence Olivier, Grigori Kozintsev, Tony Richardson and Franco Zeffirelli) and one for television (Rodney Bennett), while the sixth, a thirty-minute Russian cartoon version for the *Shakespeare: Animated Tales* series and first shown on BBC Television on 7 December 1992, was made to be marketed as a video as much as a television film. Each has a claim to be regarded as both a worthy exercise in film adaptation and a useful educational tool.[2] This essay offers the opportunity to

consider these very different realizations of *Hamlet* within the simple comparative framework provided by the analysis of certain technical features of their
directors' *mise en scène*, the number and nature of the camera shots, and the
nature of the cutting of the text.[3]

In 1947, BBC television made the first ever attempt at a relatively full
production of *Hamlet*, directed by Basil Adams.[4] A year later, Laurence Olivier
brought out the first relatively full commercial film of *Hamlet*. It is not only the
first, it is one of the longest of all *Hamlets* produced for the cinema.[5] Yet, in
order to be marketable, it had to conform to cinematic conventions, and these
included a conventional maximum length. By being 'ruthlessly bold' and
turning it into 'An Essay in Hamlet' rather than a compressed version of the
play,[6] Olivier kept it down to 155 minutes, losing more than half of
Shakespeare's lines.

The cuts are fairly evenly spread – in each of eighteen of the play's twenty
scenes, Olivier removes more than a third of the lines and in even the least cut
scene (1.2) a quarter of the lines disappear. But three whole scenes – 4.1, 4.2 and
4.4 – are dropped in their entirety, and so are five whole characters – Reynaldo,
Rosencrantz and Guildenstern, Voltemand and Fortinbras. Of the six films,
four adopt readings which stress personal relationships within the court of
Elsinore, the individuality of the Prince and, in particular, his distinctive
psychological condition. The most extreme example is Olivier's, whose
interpretation is reflected in these cuts. 4.1 explores Claudius' relationship with
Gertrude, 4.2 involves Rosencrantz and Guildenstern, and 4.4 concerns
Fortinbras. Reynaldo's function is to establish ideas about Polonius' view of
Laertes; Rosencrantz and Guildenstern illustrate the corrupting power of
Claudius; Voltemand tells us about Fortinbras. By cutting them, Olivier
diminishes interest in Laertes and Claudius and completes his elimination of
Fortinbras, all of whom are models of decisive action and operate as alternative
foci to the object of Olivier's interest: Hamlet's individual personality and
mental state.

By opting for a psychological rather than a political reading of the play,
Olivier is not obliged to adopt a continuous use of close-up. Hamlet's centrality
is ensured by other means. Although he is on camera a great deal (he features in
forty-six per cent of the shots), Olivier is seen less than Nicol Williamson in
Tony Richardson's film, and not a great deal more than the other Hamlets
under discussion. Films of the play inevitably provide audiences with less visual
evidence of the actor playing Hamlet than do theatrical productions. A stage
Hamlet will be visible even when he is not speaking, whereas all film directors

are committed to some extent to establishing shots and to reaction shots, which will almost always involve cutting away from Hamlet at the end of his speeches and thereby rendering him invisible.

However, in Olivier's treatment, whatever else is in shot redirects attention to Hamlet's psychological state. This means not only that his blond hair stands out against the dark sets but that, as Foster Hirsch puts it, the sets themselves, those 'dark, mostly bare rooms, and the vast, empty spaces', express his 'tormented consciousness'.[7] The impression that the film as a whole explores Hamlet's inner life is reinforced by using voice-over in order to realize almost the whole of Hamlet's soliloquies.

In only one aspect of his camera work is Olivier the leader of the pack, and that is in his use of the high-angle shot, to which he devotes thirteen per cent of his shots. Olivier trails Kozintsev in the mobility of his camera work and, although Anthony Davies has referred to the 'long, uninterrupted takes' which characterize this *Hamlet*,[8] the average length of Olivier's shots is twenty-one seconds – which is not much more than Grigori Kozintsev's and a long way short of Tony Richardson's (twenty-seven seconds).

The high-angle shot can easily communicate moral significance. Thus Hamlet criticizes the style of Claudius' court while literally looking down on it from above (the device is copied by Zeffirelli in his film), and Davies cites the scene in which the camera moves up and away from Claudius and Laertes as they sit plotting Hamlet's death: 'the movement, and particularly the high angle of the camera, make a moral judgement upon its own picture'.[9]

Sometimes the high-angle shot communicates tragic significance. An aerial view of Hamlet's pall-bearers reaching the top of the tower in Elsinore castle provides the opening to the film, and a companion low-angle shot of the same ascent provides the closing to the film. Between them they establish a cyclical structure[10] which may be read as symbolic of either regeneration[11] or futility.

Olivier not only directed the film, he spoke his own invented prologue, he played Hamlet and he provided the voice of Hamlet's father. Alan Dent may be credited with the screenplay but whenever Olivier wrote about responsibility for the cuts he used the pronoun 'we': Dent himself explains how Olivier removed 'How all occasions do inform against me' during the making of the film.[12] One could say, therefore, that Olivier effectively wrote the film, played its major roles, and, as director, determined every aspect of its final realization. At the same time, as well as being engaged in the scrutiny and presentation of his own image as actor by directing himself on celluloid, Olivier was also scrutinizing and presenting himself as director. This he achieves, first during the Players scene where Olivier the director directs himself as Hamlet the director, and secondly through his involvement in the production of two books about the making of the film and a six-minute film documentary on the set and costumes used in the film, all of which came out in the same year as *Hamlet*.[13] The result is an intensely and complexly personal film, and one in which Olivier is observed holding the mirror up to Olivier.

As part of his preparation for a 1937 Old Vic production, Tyrone Guthrie took his Hamlet, Laurence Olivier, to talk to Ernest Jones, Freud's disciple, about the Prince's motivation. Critics regularly assert that Olivier's film interpretation derives strongly from what he learnt from Jones.[14] In the closet scene, Olivier certainly attempts to stress the sexual and infantile roles Hamlet plays as he adopts the postures of rapist, romantic lover and babe in arms. But, in Graham Holderness's opinion at least, the result is 'a film-text that resembles an analyst's report more than it does an imaginative exploration of the unconscious'.[15] This may be true of Hamlet's unconscious, but Olivier's film can be read as exploration of another unconscious – his own.

At least one critic, Peter S. Donaldson, subjects not only the film but Olivier himself to readings which have their roots in psychoanalysis.[16] Donaldson argues that the film expresses Olivier's personal need to rework both his own oedipal experience and the trauma of a particular childhood incident, for

Olivier's account of being raped, or nearly raped, on a staircase at All Saints School at age nine . . . associates paternal gifts and sexual abuse.[17]

Roger Furse's set is dominated by staircases – formal, ceremonial stairways and a linking series of steep steps running from the depths of his Elsinore to the top of the top-most tower – and Olivier uses them for any number of conscious effects. One, at least, is comic: Osric is shown tripping and tumbling down some steps. But Donaldson argues persuasively that the incident on the All Saints staircase is working through Olivier's unconscious to create tragic statements.

In a series of shots involving Hamlet with the Ghost, with Ophelia, with Claudius and with Gertrude, the camera pulls away and upwards from the victim, who has been thrust to the ground but stretches out a hand to his or her abuser. Together they contribute to a statement about 'the compulsively cyclical character of abuse'.[18] The result is a *Hamlet* read as the 'tragedy . . . of a son unable to find a nonabusive relation to his father'.[19]

Donaldson argues that Olivier's Hamlet, oscillating between grandiose assertiveness and passive, self-destructive depression, is a narcissist. One might add to such a reading the observation that the complex entanglement of Olivier with the processes of making his *Hamlet* (he was even having to cope with the knowledge that Vivien Leigh mistakenly believed him to be conducting an affair with Ophelia, the eighteen-year-old Jean Simmons)[20] was a narcissistic exercise in self-scrutiny and self-celebration. When, in the final scene, the camera looks up to shoot the famous fourteen-foot leap from a staircase onto Claudius – a leap which knocked out the stuntman standing in for Claudius and which Olivier recognized as a major personal risk to his own life[21] – it records Hamlet and Olivier in a gesture which is simultaneously heroic, self-annihilating and over the top.

Throughout the nineteenth century, Russian intellectuals alienated from their society had turned to *Hamlet* as an expression of their political disaffection and thwarted idealism and, once the conditions of tyranny created by an Alexander III had been revived through the tyranny of a Josef Stalin, parallels with the court of Claudius became again apparent.[22]

They can still be seen in Grigori Kozintsev's film of 1964. Even in the period of comparative thaw associated with Kruschev, the memory of Stalinism was such that Kozintsev regarded Hamlet as 'a man of our time'.[23] The film derives from a 1954 production Kozintsev staged at the Pushkin Academic Theatre of Drama in Leningrad, and the seeds of that production probably go back at least nine years to discussions about the play which Kozintsev was then having with Meyerhold's most talented disciple, Nikolai Okhlopkov. When, by a coincidence, Okhlopkov came also to direct the play in 1954 (at the Mayakovsky Theatre), his set was dominated by a huge metal grille that clearly indicated that Elsinore was a prison. The opening sequence of Kozintsev's film depicts Hamlet riding urgently into the jaws of a castle whose portcullis closes on him as if he, too, were entering prison. Once inside, he is obliged to live under a tyrant with a court full of puppets and spies.

Kozintsev's Elsinore, like Olivier's, is full of staircases. Stairways are hardly a unique feature in Russian *Hamlet* design: almost the whole of the action in Kote Mardzhanishvili's 1925 Tbilisi production took place on an enormous stairway symbolic of Hamlet's fluctuating fortunes.[24] On the other hand, it could be argued that the staircases derive from Olivier, to whom Kozintsev's film is strongly indebted. But Olivier's steep staircases are often the setting for very private, isolating encounters, whereas Kozintsev's broader stairways are all too public, dotted as they are with courtiers, 'flatterers and frightened dignitaries'.[25] Their significance lies in the nature of the framed image.

Kozintsev's roots go back to Constructivism and the Factory of the Eccentric Actor (FEKS) which he founded in 1922 and whose project was to subvert bourgeois realism by reassembling images, sounds and text in a new order. Kozintsev's film is thirteen minutes shorter than Olivier's and despite omitting only three scenes in their entirety, he is far more radical than Olivier in his pruning of the text. Out of the twenty scenes, sixteen are more than fifty per cent cut and a total of sixty-five per cent of the play's lines experience cuts of one kind or another. But he also reinstates material dropped by Olivier. He brings back Rosencrantz and Guildenstern, and above all Fortinbras. As he himself explained, 'Olivier cut the theme of government, which I find extremely interesting.'[26]

The extent of the cuts he and his screen-play writer, Boris Pasternak, make in their film amount to a reconstruction of the play as a new art-work. In some respects it could be argued that it becomes not just a play but a symbolist poem which foregrounds a non-verbal, visual and musical text. Dmitri Shostakovitch's score, which accompanies 236 out of the film's 434 shots, stirs deep emotions while reinforcing, or acting in counterpoint to, other rhythmic patterns. Raymond Ingram describes how 'the billowing movement of banners is repeated not only in the Ghost's cloak, the curtains in Gertrude's closet and the enveloping mourning veil into which Ophelia is forced after her father's death, but in flames, breaking waves and streaming clouds'.[27]

Each frame is an aesthetic composition worthy of exhibition in its own right and the average length of shot is long enough (just under twenty seconds) to allow the spectator time to appreciate the beauty of the image. At the same time, of the six directors, Kozintsev's is the most active camera. In forty-six per cent of his shots it is either zooming or panning and this mobility means that the composition is often evolving and changing within a shot. Characteristic of the compositional complexity which Kozintsev aims for is his treatment of Ophelia's drowning. The camera pans slowly across the surface of a river, uncovering a cross-patterning of ripples and reflected images of trees and clouds. Mist is blowing across the water and Shostakovich's music is playing over the pictorial images. Ophelia's almost submerged body slips into the frame. We then follow the flight of a bird across mountains, the cloud-ribbed sky and, finally, the wave-torn sea. The camera finally discovers Hamlet, alone on a sterile promontory.

In his indoor shots, the combination of a mobile camera, a set involving foregrounded abstract patterning (chiefly, stairways), and a predilection for medium and long shots, creates constant movement within the frame: it is criss-crossed, from side to side and up and down, by a mass of unindividuated courtiers. We are never allowed to concentrate on Hamlet alone: his isolation is defined as being political rather than merely psychological or emotional, and he is subject to larger and stronger currents than those of one Family Romance.

Kozintsev uses more low-angle-shots than any other of the five directors. As his fellow Constructivist Aleksandr Rodchenko (1891–1956) put it, 'The most instructive viewpoints from which to depict modern life are those from above, from below, and on the diagonal'.[28] Kozintsev eschews the diagonal, but when

10 *Hamlet*, directed by Grigori Kozintsev: a typical low-angle shot: Gertrude (Elza Radzin-Szolkonis) and Hamlet (Innokenti Smoktounovski)

his camera looks up or down at Hamlet, as he strides above or below the seemingly huge Gothic ghost, we are being informed of many things at once – Hamlet's ambivalence towards his father, his state of personal alienation, the ambiguous status of his princely power, and 'the inescapable and implacable weight of history'.[29]

The narrative coherence of Kozintsev's film co-exists with an incoherence deriving, not only from his conflicting allegiances to social realism and visual formalism, but from the conflicting allegiances involved in his own political identity as an artist who had survived Stalin to live under Kruschev. The film can be read both as a critique of a specific political situation in Russia and as a fatalistic statement about the individual's experience of history. By riding into Claudius' castle, Hamlet engages in an action of self-destructive futility. Inside, his first soliloquy is in voice-over as he strides through crowds of 'bland, . . . sleek, artificial, permanently intimidated' courtiers,[30] alone and lonely in his head. But Hamlet's death is followed immediately by the arrival of Fortinbras and his new but equally oppressive regime. Hamlet's corpse is soon lost in the crowd outside the castle walls.

Hamlet is not thereby lost. The crowd outside the walls of Elsinore includes you and me. By making 'the rest is silence' the last words of his film Kozintsev opens up as many possibilities as he closes down. Hamlet conducts himself with dignity throughout the action. The director's decision to remove material which suggests a moral darkening of Hamlet's character (the scene in which he comes across Claudius at prayer and considers how best to ensure that Claudius suffers in hell) continues a process which, at least for Russian audiences in the 1960s, had begun with the decision to cast in the role Innokenti Smoktou-novksi, a man known to have endured imprisonment both by the Germans in World War II and then by the Russians themselves in the Gulag Archipelago.[31] Similarly, a pessimistic reading of the film such as Bernice Kliman's (it 'begins and ends on the same note of political hopelessness')[32] is partially countered by the intervening wit and subversive vigour of the wandering players who represent, for John Collick at least,[33] a Bakhtinian assertion of the revolution-ary potential of peasant culture.

Of the six directors, only Zeffirelli works primarily within the naturalistic traditions of film. But Kozintsev's political text is at its most eloquent when the mobile camera documents in medium and long tracking shots the manoeuvres of Fortinbras' army, or when, on his return from England, Hamlet meets Horatio against the backdrop of a peasant village.[34] Beyond Olivier's Elsinore there is nothing, but beyond Kozintsev's there is everything else – not only much more of the same, but also, in his own words, 'out-of-the-way places, where there is rubbish scattered around, where hens are cackling and the grooms are unharnessing horses'.[35]

Tony Richardson's *Hamlet* was made for Woodfall Films in 1969.[36] It is the shortest of the five full-length films under discussion (112 minutes). Yet, despite making cuts in forty-eight per cent of the text and removing Fortinbras and at least thirty per cent of every scene except 3.1, he retains more of the text than any of the five directors except Bennett.

The speed with which the film processes its text is largely a function of the speed with which its Hamlet, Nicol Williamson, delivers his speeches. Whereas

Laurence Olivier, Derek Jacobi and Mel Gibson take over three minutes to deliver the 'To be or not to be' soliloquy (the only soliloquy preserved intact in all five full-length films), Williamson has finished with it in 150 seconds.[37] His idiosyncratic delivery – muttering nasally, sometimes gabbling – is an element of characterization: this Hamlet is full of a half-repressed infantile anger which renders him a neurotic outsider, spasmodically distressed and overwrought. And that characterization is the heart of the film, for, like Olivier, Richardson opts for a psychological *Hamlet*.

The conditions for sustained and intense psychological analysis are established by Richardson's exclusion of all reference to a material setting beyond the actions of the actors. Although his film is a record of his own stage production mounted at the Round House theatre in London's Chalk Farm, he had intended to film the production from the start. He chose the Round House to 'free the theatre from the tyranny of the proscenium arch and the social habits which go with it'.[38]

There is no clearly defined set, no attempt at creating an architectural Elsinore. Characters are sometimes to be found up against expanses of Victorian brick wall or exploring the lower levels or outside of the Round House, but these are just stage properties, the equivalent of the throne, double bed and hammock which also emerge from the black void in which the production operates. Elsinore is like the true Elizabethan court, a collection of courtiers following the King, a network of relations and values.

Richardson's camera-style is also geared to the exploration of the minutiae of inter-personal activity. Close-ups and medium close-ups account for ninety-six per cent of his shots, far more than in any other of the five films. By means of the close-up he recreates his Elsinore in every shot. He packs the frame with key players, holding in one composition, for example, not just Hamlet but Laertes, Gertrude, Claudius and Horatio too. It is as if the camera were not just an intrusive journalist but itself a member of the court.

The film has fewer shots per minute (2.2) than any of the other five. Through persistent use of long takes in close-up Richardson creates a claustrophobic milieu of enforced intimacy. His hand-held camera is not especially mobile in the sense that Olivier or Kozintsev's camera tracks left and right or zooms in and out to create new compositions; but it *is* mobile in that it follows the actors' faces as if the director were a member of the paparazzi pursuing royals in the news.

This Elsinore is ostensibly ruled by a version of the Pleasure Principle. The relative youthfulness and sexuality of Claudius and Gertrude's relationship is emphasized – they and their courtiers laugh uproariously at the idea that the King of Norway should be 'impotent and bed-rid' (1.2.29) and in 2.2 they choose to hold court from their own nuptial bed. Ophelia is played by

Marianne Faithfull, a current pop star with a high-profile sexual image thanks to her media roles as Mick Jagger's girl friend and the star of Jack Cardiff's 1968 erotic fantasy, *Girl on a Motorbike*. Lest Claudius and Gertrude feel embarrassed about the nature of their marriage, Ophelia and Laertes kiss and fondle each other incestuously. As if in reaction to this Sixties ethos Hamlet not only acts the puritan but fails to display any sexual involvement with his mother.

In the stage production Williamson addressed every soliloquy to the audience, hectoring them in an aggressive, aggrieved and whining tone. The majority of the audience was necessarily always experiencing Hamlet's direct address indirectly, observing it rather than being subject to it. In the film that relationship cannot be established in the same way. Richardson still requires Williamson to address the camera directly and the effect is far more winning and controlling, because there is no escaping his gaze. Yet, Hamlet cannot sustain an engagement with the camera's attention for more than a few lines – he drops his gaze, his head shifts away, and the viewer is left scrutinizing him as an object of, by turns, admiration, concern, pity and distaste.

Williamson's eccentric delivery, and the degree of his alienation from the superficially good-humoured atmosphere of the court, turns him into something of a freak. On the other hand, the audience is encouraged to identify with Hamlet by Richardson's attempts to defuse moral hostility to his actions. Like Kozintsev, he drops the sub-scene in which Hamlet comes across Claudius at prayer. Like Olivier, he has Hamlet turn on Ophelia only when he notices that Polonius and Claudius are playing peeping toms. Horatio's respect and affection for Hamlet is reinforced through the repeated use of reaction shots displaying Horatio's concern for his friend; the film's final shot begins with Horatio's head in profile intimately juxtaposed with Hamlet's.

Furthermore, Richardson devotes a greater proportion of his shots (forty-nine per cent) to Hamlet than does any other of the five directors. Alone among the five directors, Richardson decides not to make the Ghost visible to the viewer. Its presence is signalled by a bright light being shone in the face of those who can see it. While this might sometimes encourage in us Gertrude's opinion that Hamlet is deluded and talking to thin air, its chief effect is to put the spotlight literally on to Hamlet. The film ends with the moment of Hamlet's death. Then the camera closes in on Williamson's face in extreme close-up. This frame is frozen, and the credits are read aloud so that visual attention remains undistracted from the face. Hamlet is defined as being, not just the hero, but the total subject of the film.

In 1980 Rodney Bennett was a television director with no experience of directing Shakespeare. In order to direct *Hamlet* for the BBC Television Shakespeare series, he therefore had to establish a relationship between the conventions of the classic text with which he was confronted and the conventions of television as he knew them.

Unlike Richardson, who had to move into the awkward, inflexible space of the Round House (never even intended to be a theatre, let alone a film studio), in which a well-established stage production was being recorded for posterity, Bennett, by contrast, was working from scratch in a large, purpose-built television studio, where the shooting script could be created at comparative leisure well in advance.

Faced with this challenge and this freedom, he decided to reject television's normal commitment to naturalism. Hamlet's soliloquies are all addressed directly to the camera: Susan Willis describes Derek Jacobi confiding his thoughts 'as a means of self-expression and self-explanation in a world where he must hide or obscure what he thinks, what he feels, what he suspects'.[39] Richardson had already used this device, but Bennett is more original in his decision to encapsulate each soliloquy in a single, long take.

By contrast, Claudius does not have direct access to the camera, even during his prayer scene. This treatment of soliloquy is an attempt to avoid the naturalistic conventions of television drama and brings together instead the conventions of Elizabethan stage-craft and the conventions of those television talking heads who are *not* characters in drama – presenters, newscasters and so on. But the trick had already been used by earlier directors in the BBC series (and, in the British cinema, in such films as Lewis Gilbert's 1966 film, *Alfie*).

Bennett did not want a naturalistic set, but he could not bring himself to undermine the convention whereby the twentieth-century material reality of the television studio is suppressed: that, he felt, would be to create a conflict with the series' commitment to period costume. He turned for inspiration to other television genres. Thus, as far as narrative was concerned, Bennett 'approached it like a thriller'.[40] As for setting, he turned to television Light Entertainment, i.e. that descendant of Music Hall in which a number of cameras rove freely around non-naturalistic scenery set against huge cycloramas in vast studios. 'Studio 1, it's a wonderful volume to use and one can so rarely get a chance to use it as a totality.'[41]

In other respects, Bennett espouses the naturalism which operates in soap opera and sit com: 'it's such a relief to play it domestically for the camera, to scale it down and let the camera play it for you'.[42] He allowed Eric Porter, Claire Bloom and Patrick Stewart to play Polonius, Gertrude and Claudius as essentially warm, sensitive, reasonable people. Indeed, through sustained use of close-up and reaction shots, he handles all his characters with compassion. He came to the conclusion that television provided him with opportunities for psychological and moral analysis which a stage production would have denied him. Speaking of Horatio's function in certain scenes with Hamlet, he commented 'One can get much more out of the relationship on television than on stage. Whereas on stage Horatio is *around* quite a lot, on television you can keep seeing him, keep cutting to him looking at Hamlet, Hamlet looking at him, building up a relationship that is much more striking than that on stage.'[43]

H. R. Coursen calls Bennett's film 'probably the best version of the play we are likely to see this side of the stage'.[44] The fullness of such praise probably derives from pleasure at the fullness of the text. Although film *Hamlets* tend to be heavily cut, and although very long *Hamlets* are not unknown in the theatre, Bennett's film outdoes normal practice on the commercial stage. Derek Jacobi was signed up to play Hamlet when he was in a 1979 production at the Old Vic in London; he was to discover that he had far more lines to learn for Bennett than he had ever had to deliver on the stage. *Branagh's now?*

At 225 minutes Bennett's is the longest film *Hamlet* ever made. It is all the more remarkable that a television production should challenge all the conventions of television programming and emerge as 3 hours 45 minutes, with just one interruption. It preserves far more of the text than any of the other films under discussion. Bennett retains all the characters, and his is the only film which preserves *any* scenes entirely uncut. But, even so, there are only two such scenes and even in this version, only eighty-seven per cent of the play remains intact. For all its pedagogical ambitions, the BBC Television Shakespeare series which broadcast the complete canon between 1978 and 1985 and then went on to target the educational market by selling the video, as well as a booklet containing the text and essays on the play, ended up marketing somewhat less than the scholar's ideal *Hamlet*.

The 1990s have already produced two remarkably successful attempts to extend the market for *Hamlet*. Franco Zeffirelli's 1990 film, starring Mel Gibson and Glenn Close, and the 1992 Russian series of videos, *Shakespeare: The Animated Tales*, have not only targetted a world-market but a youthful market as well. And, just as Olivier's film was accompanied by a film and two supporting books describing the making of the film, so Zeffirelli's *Hamlet* was followed up immediately by what proved to be a best-selling video, marketed with a glossy little booklet on the director, the stars and the play,[45] while, by the time they began to appear on BBC Television in late 1992, the *Animated Tales* had been sold to television stations in thirty countries, and were going into the shops as videos and in book-form.[46]

Of the six directors, Natalia Orlova, having to create a film of only thirty minutes, necessarily cuts more lines than anyone else. Her poignant, understated *Hamlet* follows the conventions of animated television films in frequently simulating extreme camera angles and shifting 'shot' at a steady, fast pace (the average length is seven seconds). Leon Garfield's simplified narrative (he follows Olivier in dispensing with characters such as Rosencrantz, Guilden-stern and Fortinbras) recasts the story in ten scenes of snatches of Shakespeare's dialogue linked by a narrator. Hamlet is almost a child, robbed at his conception of his divine verbosity, hiding miserably in corners and under blankets, trapped in a bat-infested castle and catching tantalizing glimpses through its windows of sea-birds in their freedom. Although derivative of both Olivier and Kozintsev in its use of the castle-setting and in its presentation of the Ghost, Orlova's film succeeds in creating a distinctive folk-tale *Hamlet*, arresting in its dream-like imagery and in its concentration on youthful suffering.

Zeffirelli, on the other hand, has adopted the shooting style and, to some extent the narrative conventions, of a quite different *genre* – 1980s cinema and television action movies. In such films a slightly antisocial, often humorous, male hero (or pair of buddies) challenges a corrupt and evil male villain, finally outwitting and then killing him after scenes of extraordinary violence. The text of *Hamlet* can release such a story but only with some directorial manipulation. Zeffirelli is by far the most radical reshaper of the text. His 129-minute film contains only thirty-one per cent of the lines, but he cavalierly re-organizes the order of the text that remains, advancing and delaying speeches in a bewilder-ing manner. The longer speeches and scenes are broken down into bite-sized pieces. This process of segmentation complements his shooting style, which involves frequent changes of image. Zeffirelli moves the camera very little but uses far more shots per minute than any of the other directors – his average shot lasts less than six seconds.

Such an interventionist directorial style affects the power-relations between characters (cutting to reaction shots can divert attention from the character whom Shakespeare's language would prioritize on stage) and between actors and audience (the effect of rapid cutting on a soliloquy like 'To be or not to be', which involves sixteen different shots, is to prioritize the role of the director over the character). Like Garfield, although not to the same extent, Zeffirelli's prime purpose is to simplify the narrative. 'To be or not to be', being in voice-over, can be disentangled from the question of being overheard by Ophelia, Polonius or Claudius, and is delivered later in its own discrete scene. Next, Mel Gibson's Hamlet follows the conventions of Beverly Hills cops and rides out of town into the open countryside in order to commune with nature. Only then does he meet Rosencrantz and Guildenstern, whom he treats to a cook-out and a few beers. This sub-scene itself precedes a truncated version of 'O what a rogue' which, ending as it does with the decision to put on a play, leads directly into the play scene.

Here is a Hamlet who can make up his mind, and who is, in the words of the video blurb, 'more macho than melancholy'.[47] Zeffirelli saw him in Richard Donner's 1987 film, *Lethal Weapon*, in which Gibson plays a suicidal young detective. 'There was a scene in which there's a kind of "to be or not to be" speech. Mel Gibson is sitting there with a gun in his mouth but he can't pull the trigger. When I saw that I said *This is Hamlet! This boy is Hamlet!*'.[48] And this Hamlet is 'a man who likes sex, likes to drink, likes riding horses . . .', but who suffers from the modern condition of being unable to find God.[49]

Perhaps because of the frequent cross-cutting between shots, Mel Gibson appears in a smaller proportion of shots than any of the other Hamlets in these five films (only forty per cent). Gibson's acting is psychologically unexpressive, but his function in the simplified Zeffirelli narrative, combined with his star status, reasserts his prioritized role in the film. At the same time, the casting of Glenn Close as Gertrude encourages the reading into her performance of both an unusual importance (Raymond Ingram argues that she is 'the centre of this film'[50]) and a sexual authority derived, at least for early audiences of the film, from her roles in Adrian Lyne's *Fatal Attraction* (1987) and Stephen Frears's *Dangerous Liaisons* (1988). Murray Biggs asserts that 'Zeffirelli makes no bones about translating the Oedipal theme into a full-blown, vulgarized, traditional screen romance between coevals, in which the viewer is less aware of Shakespeare's mother and son than of the Hollywood stars who have transformed them into other types altogether.'[51]

Zeffirelli wishes not only to 'bring the movie to young people'[52] but to do for Elsinore what he did for Verona in his 1968 film of *Romeo and Juliet* – create an a-tragic world of people going about their daily business in a glamorous, open, sunlit, cinematogenic environment, and then tell the unglamorous story of that society's ability to waste its young. His may be the slightest of the six films but, like each of the other directors, Zeffirelli succeeds in expanding our sense of the world which Hamlet dies from.

Notes

1 I have conflated and up-dated the entries on *Hamlet* in Graham Holderness and Christopher McCulloch's 'Shakespeare on the Screen: A Selective Filmography', *Shakespeare Survey 39* (Cambridge, 1987), pp. 13–37, Kenneth Rothwell and Annabelle Henkin Melzer's *Shakespeare on Screen* (London, 1990), Cathy Grant, ed., *As You Like It: Audio Visual Shakespeare* (London, 1992) and Luke McKernan and Olwen Terris, eds., *Walking Shadows: Shakespeare in the National Film and Television Archive* (London, 1994).

2 Many of them have already been extensively analysed as independent artefacts – for example, in Bernice Kliman, *Hamlet: Film, Television and Audio Performance* (London and Toronto, 1988).

3 Each of the six directors has worked on a screenplay which departs noticeably from any existing edition of the play. I have taken T. J. B. Spencer's New Penguin edition of the play (Harmondsworth, 1980) as my control text (at 3,835 lines, it is a fairly full eclectic edition).

4 Although it lasted 180 minutes it was shown in two halves, first at 8.30 pm on consecutive Sundays (7 and 12 December) and then again on at 8.30 pm on consecutive Tuesdays (9 and 14 December). Since these were all live performances, it must have been peculiarly demanding on John Byron, who played Hamlet.

5 Those which are longer tend to be either television productions or else recordings of stage productions (such as the Electronovision attempt to market Richard Burton in John Gielgud's 1964 New York production, which ran to 199 minutes, and Liviu Ciuler's video of Kevin Klein in Joseph Papp's 1986 New York production, which lasts 214 minutes).

6 Laurence Olivier, 'An Essay in Hamlet', in Brenda Cross, ed., *The Film Hamlet: a Record of its Production* (London, 1948), p. 11.

7 Foster Hirsch, *Laurence Olivier on Screen* (New York, 1984 edition), p. 80.

8 *Filming Shakespeare's Plays* (Cambridge, 1988), p. 45.

9 *Ibid.*, p. 51.

10 *Ibid.*, p. 43.

11 Hirsch, *Laurence Olivier on Screen*, p. 87.

12 Alan Dent, 'Text-Editing Shakespeare, with Particular Reference to *Hamlet*', in Alan Dent, ed., *'Hamlet': the Film and the Play* (London, 1948) (pages unnumbered).

13 Dent, *'Hamlet', the Film and the Play*; Cross, *The Film Hamlet*; Set and Costumes for *'Hamlet'*, six-minute black-and-white documentary film directed by Laurence Olivier in 1948 (no. 99 in Rothwell and Melzer, p. 62).

14 E.g. Murray Biggs, '"He's Going to his Mother's Closet": Hamlet and Gertrude on Screen', in Stanley Wells, ed., *Shakespeare Survey 45: 'Hamlet' and its Afterlife* (Cambridge, 1993), pp. 54–7.

15 'Shakespeare Unwound', in Wells, *Shakespeare Survey 45*, p. 65.

16 *Shakespearean Films/Shakespearean Directors* (Boston, 1990), pp. 31–67.

17 *Ibid.*, p. 35.

18 *Ibid.*, p. 49.

19 *Ibid.*, p. 63.

20 Donald Spoto, *Laurence Olivier: a Biography* (London, 1991), p. 177.

21 *Ibid.*, p. 178.

22 John Collick, *Shakespeare, Cinema and Society* (Manchester, 1989), p. 127.

23 Grigori Kozintsev, *Shakespeare: Time and Conscience* (London, 1967), introductory note.

24 Konstantin Rudnitsky, *Russia and Soviet Theatre: Tradition and the Avant-Garde* (London, 1988), p. 114–15.

25 Kozintsev, *Shakespeare, Time and Conscience*, p. 251.

26 *Ibid.*, p. 234.

27 'Angles of Perception', in Grant, *As You Like It*, p. 17.

28 'The paths of contemporary photography', *Novyi Lef* (1928), no. 9, quoted in Grigory Shudakov, *Pioneers of Soviet Photography* (London, 1983), p. 17.

29 Collick, *Shakespeare, Cinema and Society*, p. 139.

30 Kozintsev, *Shakespeare, Time and Conscience*, p. 257.

31 Jan Kott, 'On Kozintsev's *Hamlet*', *The Literary Review*, vol. 22, no. 4 (Summer, 1979), p. 404.

32 Kliman, *Hamlet: Film, Television and Audio Performance*, p. 113.

33 Collick, *Shakespeare, Cinema and Society*, p. 140.

34 On the basis that there is no smoke without fire, Collick thinks he can see evidence of a 'ruined, burning village' (*Shakespeare, Cinema and Society*, p. 140), but where he sees smoke I see only mist.

35 Kozintsev, *Shakespeare, Time and Conscience*, p. 249.

36 In *Hamlet, Film, Television and Audio Performance*, Kliman referred to 'Richardson's television *Hamlet*' (p. 167). In *Shakespeare on Screen*, published two years later, Rothwell and Melzer repeated this idea ('The film version, actually made for television', p. 72). Certainly Richardson's *Hamlet* has many of the characteristics of a televised play – Kliman describes 'the tightness of its shots' (p. 167) and one might also note the absence of a musical score – but neither Kliman nor Rothwell and Melzer produce any evidence for their assertions that the film was made for television broadcasting.

37 Only Kozintsev, at 143 seconds, is quicker. Williamson takes 120 seconds over 'How all occasions do inform against me', whereas Jacobi drops 1½ lines but still takes 142 seconds. Williamson takes 228 seconds over ninety per cent of 'O what a rogue' (six of its lines are cut), whereas Jacobi takes 285 seconds over the full speech.

38 Interview with Sheridan Morley in *The Times*, quoted in Roger Manvell, *Shakespeare and the Film* (London, 1971), p. 127.

39 *The BBC Shakespeare Plays: Making the Television Canon* (Chapel Hill and London, 1991), p. 213.

40 Henry Fenwick, 'The Production', *Hamlet: The BBC TV Shakespeare* (London, 1980), p. 22.

41 *Ibid.*, p. 18.

42 *Ibid.*, p. 28.

43 *Ibid.*, p. 27.

44 *Shakespearean Performance as Interpretation* (Newark, 1992), p. 103.

45 Alasdair Brown, *Hamlet* (London, 1990).

46 Robin Buss, 'A Palpable Hit', *The Independent on Sunday* (8 November 1992), p. 33.

47 Brown, *Hamlet*, p. 9.

48 *Ibid.*, p. 8.

49 *Ibid.*, p. 8.

50 Grant, *As You Like It*, p. 18.

51 Biggs, ' "He's Going to his Mother's Closet" ', pp. 61–2.

52 Brown, *Hamlet*, p. 8.

11

FILMING *OTHELLO*

ANTHONY DAVIES

I

The three most widely known films of *Othello* are the Welles film of 1952/3, the Yutkevich film of 1955, and the Burge/Dexter film with Olivier in the title role (1965). It is more helpful in an aesthetic sense not to discuss these in their chronological order, but to start with the stage-based film of 1965 and to conclude with that which has been most discussed: the Welles version first released in 1952 and restored and re-released in 1992.

The 1965 film emerges as one of a sub-genre of Shakespearian film produced in England during the 1960s, others being Peter Hall's *A Midsummer Night's Dream* (1969) and Tony Richardson's *Hamlet* (1969). And it is possible to argue that Peter Brook's *King Lear* (1971), while its filmic dimensions are much more sophisticated, also springs from the same principle.[1] The intention was to base cinematic presentation upon an earlier successful theatre production and to capture on film as far as possible the essence of theatrical performance. The cinematic dimension of these presentations – with the exception of Brook's – tends to take the form of an overlay and to be, at best, unevenly integrated with the more dominant dramatic conventions and aesthetics of the theatre.

Despite this unevenness, which is especially noticeable in the Burge/Dexter *Othello*, the film can legitimately claim a position of importance in the field of our interest. One of the perceived intentions behind John Dexter's 1964 Old Vic production (which is the substance from which the film selects its images) was to stress the contemporary social relevance of Othello as a black man in an established white society, and to base the precariousness of his self-image in large measure upon that.[2] An interesting irony arises from this, for while the natural ephemerality of immediate social relevance is ideally suited to theatre, the film has an added value in being both a record of Olivier's unique performance and a historical document revealing an interaction of theatre with society.

In analysing some of its aesthetic shortcomings as cinema, however, there is much that can be learned from it about the distinction between the presentation of Shakespeare as filmed drama on the one hand, and as dramatic film on the other.

Peter Brook has observed that the particular power of theatrical expression arises from the proximity of event to audience. 'What happens in the theatre affects an audience in the same room.'[3] There were bound to be disappointments, then, when Anthony Havelock-Allan pronounced that 'the whole object [of the producers] was to capture the absolute magic of the theatre'.[4] For while the cinema can bring images apparently closer in magnification, the distancing effect of the frame, its two-dimensionality and the film's independence of audience reaction reduces the involvement of the viewer, bringing about that 'self-satisfaction', that 'concession to solitude', that 'betrayal of action by refusal of social responsibility' of which Bazin writes in his essay on 'Theatre and Cinema'.[5]

One such disappointment arises from the tendency of the camera to isolate in its frame individual characters, so that at moments when we should be presented with a meta-theatrical situation, the dramatic complexity is diminished with the reciprocity of tension between individual character and an audience within the play being lost. In focusing so insistently upon individual performance, the visual strategy of the film sets up a relationship between specific character and the film viewer rather than one between character and a dramatic ambience created on-stage. This deficiency is most manifest when Brabantio arrives to interrupt the Senate in its midnight deliberations and when Othello tells the story of how he won the heart of Desdemona. In the former sequence, the Duke's reassurances to Brabantio gather no resonance from the presence of the other senators, whose figures in the dim background of the composition do not radiate any sense of involvement. In the latter, the camera remains almost wholly concentrated upon Othello's head and shoulders as he unfolds his spell-binding narrative, so that the Duke's 'I think this tale would win my daughter, too' carries no endorsement from the formal occasion of its utterance.

Again, when Othello is roused to restore order and demote Cassio, the camera cuts to and from Othello keeping him separate from the brawling activity so that the dramatic impact of his entrance is reduced from its theatrical intention.

The final piece of meta-theatre which will illustrate the point being made here is the behaviour of Othello to Desdemona in the presence of Lodovico and the emissaries from Venice. The gentlemen from Venice enter the Cyprus environment with its intense inter-personal stresses. The contrast between their sophisticated control and the smouldering despair of Othello was no doubt adroitly established in the theatre. Yet the moment and its culmination in Othello's striking Desdemona are strangely muted in their cinematic impact. There is no strongly visualized sense of incredulity and shock at Othello's action. Again the camera concentrates upon the central action but the frame divorces from that action the peripheral response of those who are its witnesses.

An explanation for these unsatisfying moments would seem to be that dramatic focus in the theatre is achieved through means that are different from those resorted to in cinema; that there is an aesthetic clash between the centripetal function of the actor on the theatre stage and the centrifugal dynamic of the cinema frame. Perhaps, too, the desire to advance the prominence of the actor on the screen prompted a deliberate reduction of peripheral interaction – an attempt to compensate for the fact that in film, both actor and background become no longer distinguished in substance. They are given a pictorial equality.[6]

If it is possible to select moments as illustrative of the film's failure to satisfy in terms of cinematic drama, it is also possible to cite sequences at which the dramatic language of both theatre and cinema coalesce. One such is the opening sequence where Iago and Roderigo are established facially and vocally in the dark shadowy area under arches below Brabantio's house. There is a nicely captured natural alliance of the two characters with their affinitive elements. Another dramatically effective moment is Iago's 'Hell and night / Must bring this monstrous birth to the world's light' with which he brings to a close Act 1. The fade on the set to fill the cinema frame with total blackness after the word 'light' is a masterly blend of theatre and cinema. Cassio's drunken exit in Act 2, too, is dramatically strong on the film because the camera holds our concentration where it would, in the theatre, naturally be.

Such effective sequences are short and thinly scattered in the film, but they serve to suggest that when the placing and concentration of the camera work is in line with the theatrical intentions of the original production, the film is both compelling and satisfying.

There are also moments where the cinema frame's concentration on inanimate objects gives to them a prominence which the theatre production could not have intended. Sometimes this distortion of perspective imposes a distracting emphasis, not merely on the object itself, but on some aspect of the character with whom it is associated. Other instances, perhaps by lucky chance, allow the magnification of an object to work quite positively. Both the bracelet blade which Othello wears and, more importantly, the handkerchief lose their subtle qualities in being given such visual prominence in the frame, the handkerchief being deprived of its particular wisp-like lightness which so strongly contrasts with the terrible consequences which it precipitates. On the

11 *Othello*, directed by Stuart Burge after the stage production by John Dexter: 'There's magic in the web of it'; Othello (Laurence Olivier) and Desdemona (Maggie Smith)

other hand, the medallion and cross which hang around Othello's neck are given a visual emphasis which is not dramatically inappropriate as a reminder of Othello's dependence upon the importance of symbols in the Venetian culture with which he strives to identify. A part of Othello's tragedy is arguably his readiness to make symbols more important than the abstractions for which they stand.

In its treatment of the original stage production, the camera work (directed by Stuart Burge) is intensely selective. One does not have the sense of witnessing production in its fullness. One is constantly aware that one's concentration is being restricted to only a part of a theatrical presentation designed for a different audience receiving continuity of performance through a medium which deals in total effects. While one is captivated – and held so – by Olivier's performance, the uneasiness produced by the aesthetic clash of cinematic centrifugality with theatrical centripetality is never far below the surface.

That there are ways of compensating for the losses suffered in filming a staged version of *Othello* is evident from the strategies employed in the television film of Janet Suzman's production staged in the Market Theatre, Johannesburg in 1988. In the camera's following Othello as he moves in front of the listening senators so that the frame not only holds him in medium-close foreground, but also one or other of the senators in the background, the meta-theatricality of Othello's narrative is effectively enhanced. The somewhat under-powered playing of John Kani, too, is suited to the medium of close-up television in a way that Olivier's powerful stage projection is not, so that the Duke's 'I think this tale would win my daughter too' gives a convincing stamp of authority to Othello's tale, and makes the proportional weight of the tale to its endorsement dramatically right.

The moment when Othello strikes Desdemona in the presence of Lodovico and the emissaries from Venice, too, is memorably effective in this adaptation. The moment is subtly prepared for with Desdemona moving towards Othello so that her pitying and anxious face is well lit in the frame. Othello's blow is delivered with brutal force and with resounding impact. Instead of turning away, Desdemona stands facing Othello, shattered with disbelief, bewilderment and pain. The camera holds her face in the frame as she holds a hand to her cheek and says, with restraint and inner certainty, 'I have not deserved this.' By holding our concentration on Desdemona, the camera unites the viewers with Lodovico and the others on stage as witnesses of a shocking moment, and obviates the need to register shock in the Venetian onlookers.

A moment which works well enough in the Burge/Dexter *Othello* is made even more dramatically powerful in this film. There is no fading of light at the end of Act 1. Instead, Iago's

> I have't. It is engendered. Hell and night
> Must bring this monstrous birth to the world's light.

is delivered directly to the camera, Iago accompanying his words with movement and gesture which hint at crude animal sexuality. The lines are heralded, too, and accompanied by the peals and rumbles of thunder which introduce the storm for the next scene, as Iago reaches for and holds in front of himself a blazing torch, his face lit grotesquely by its flames as he continues to face straight into the camera.

As if to heighten the sense of the handkerchief's apparent insubstantiality, Iago places it over his upturned face and blows it into the air where, with the aid of a glimpse of slow-motion photography, the 'ocular proof' appears almost subliminally to float in the air.

The successful transposition of this *Othello* from stage to film is accomplished through two other important strategies. Firstly the stage set for the production allows both horizontal and vertical distances to be photographically exploited, as, for instance, when Bianca returns the handkerchief to Cassio in Othello's hearing. Secondly, the camera work is both subtle and adventurous, moving about the stage to dramatize the action and managing unobtrusively to break down the rigid sense of theatrical frontality. The ecstatic meeting of Othello and Desdemona in 2.1 is shot from where the theatre audience would not see it, but along the slope of the steps which Desdemona climbs to clasp the descending Othello.

The agility of the camera work is evidenced again when Othello in 3.3 puts his trust in Iago, and in the location of the handkerchief. His

> . . . Now by yond marble heaven,
> In the due reverence of a sacred vow
> I here engage my words

is filmed from close below with the camera tilted up to him, his head and shoulders filling the frame and so giving his vow a double authority.

II

Serge Yutkevich's *Othello* released in 1955 is a very different experience. In many ways, *Othello* is necessarily a claustrophobic play both in its spatial confinement and in the nature of its character relationships. Othello, Desdemona, Iago, Cassio, Roderigo, Emilia, each one's personal territory is constantly threatened by another's. People are followed, they are overheard, their intimate secrets are known so that when Iago assures Othello that

> There are a kind of men so loose of soul
> That in their sleeps will mutter their affairs:
> One of this kind is Cassio,

Othello, the general who knows about how men live together in close proximity, has no difficulty in finding the evidence revealed in Cassio's somniloquence wholly credible. Yet despite the play's constant stress on the interlocking of people's most intimate movements (of mind and body) Yutkevich gives us a film of blue skies, open sea and spaciousness. In terms of a spatial strategy for filming *Othello*, we are about as far from the close camera work and the theatrical confinement of the Burge/Dexter *Othello* as one can legitimately go. The film is arguably over-indulgent in its ventilation of the *Othello* tragedy. Yet what Yutkevich attempts is the deployment of the natural world as a dramatic chorus. In his own words, he 'broadened the frame of the tragedy by introducing a new element: nature, which can play a much bigger role on the screen than in the theatre'.[7] The extent to which he achieves an integrated dramatization of nature, and the extent to which there is an ironic relationship between exterior and interior (psychological) action are perhaps the most profitable lines along which to discuss this film.

Yutkevich's prelude to the *Othello* drama establishes this latter relationship. The 'globe' beside which Desdemona stands during the opening sequences of the film (which runs for some minutes without dialogue) is essentially a spherical grating. On the convex surface it represents a world and the world-travelled experience of Othello. But within the concave curvature of the sphere it is a cage. We are taken through a close-up of Desdemona into her own reconstruction of the Othello narrative in visual terms. There are shots of Othello commanding gunners in battle, of his being captured and caged, of his being enslaved as an oarsman and of the ship then being wrecked and of his being washed ashore naked, on rocks. The sequence ends with an up-tilted shot giving Othello, now magnificently robed on a ship, full dominance in the frame as he stands, noble and composed, against a background of masts and sails. The cycle suggests the progress of Othello's adventurous journey over the earth's surface within Desdemona's mind, and we are finally brought back to her face in close-up.

Like Desdemona's globe, the Cyprus fortress has both an exterior and an interior dramatic function. One of the great climactic moments early in the film is the arrival of Othello at the fortress and his long-awaited reunion with Desdemona. Between the lines, 'O my fair warrior!' and 'It gives me wonder, great as my content / To see you here before me . . .' (Desdemona's line is omitted) Yutkevich gives Othello six flights of steps to climb at the run, his red cloak billowing out behind him, before he meets Desdemona descending the steps from top-left of the frame. Their embrace is shot with an up-tilted camera, against the bright blue sky. This strong upward movement with all its suggestions that in *Othello* the lover and the soldier are at this moment triumphantly unified is almost immediately juxtaposed with a descent which reveals something of the nature of the interior dimensions of the fortresses as well as the forces at work there. The camera follows Iago down to a small recess in the lower reaches inside the fortress wall where, with the camera uncomfortably close, he assures Roderigo that Desdemona 'loved the Moor but for his

12   *Othello*, directed by Serge Yutkevich: 'O my fair warrior!': Othello's arrival in Cyprus; Othello
(Serge Bondarchuk) and Desdemona (Irina Skobtseva)

bragging', his words deriving a grotesque and malicious contortion from the
pressures exerted by the confined space.

Stone recesses within the fortress become increasingly associated with
Roderigo as his affinitive space. It is in one of them that he is ultimately trapped
and stabbed by Iago. As the drunken fight spreads after the provocation of
Cassio, it is Roderigo who, wedged between the stone supports, jerks the bell
rope with a manic and uncontrolled lust for chaos, his whole body writhing in
an ecstasy of perverted passion. And Othello's challenge, 'Are we turned Turks
and to ourselves do that / Which Heaven hath forbid the Ottomites?' is given
an unusual inner quality. It is spoken like a soliloquy, as though even at this
early stage, opposing forces of order and chaos have become internalized.

In a more general sense, too, there is a shift from outer to inner articulation as
the action moves forward from this point. Iago's

I'll pour this pestilence into his ear:
That she repeals him for her body's lust,
And by how much she strives to do him good,
She shall undo her credit with the Moor.
So will I turn her virtue into pitch
And out of her own goodness make the net
That shall enmesh them all

whispered to his reflection from the water surface in a well propels this shift, his narcissistic pleasure darkened by the enclosing walls of stone. While much of the ensuing action from this point on is shot on exterior locations beneath open skies, what is openly expressed no longer directly corresponds with the inner psychological developments of the drama. The bright openness is deceptive and has about it a cruel irony. And when Othello, much later, is confronted by his own image in the well, it is as though Iago has somehow poisoned the water. Othello can no longer see beyond the reflected images that Iago has constructed for him, both of himself and of Desdemona.

The sea, the sky, and stone are the dominant natural features which make up Yutkevich's dramatic chorus. Subtlety of colour nuances he saw to be essential in the treatment of these elements. Manvell notes Yutkevich's making known his particular liking for the Sovcolor 'sensitivity to half-lights, to subtle greys and purples of dawn and dusk'.[8]

The stone of the fortress, to which we are introduced, is suggestive of power, decisiveness and certainty. But as the dramatic action proceeds, it is replaced by stone which functions along less reassuring lines. During the sequence where Desdemona promises Cassio that she will restore him in Othello's favour, the surrounding spatial detail changes from a background of lush, leafy foliage as Emilia is seen plucking grapes, to distant pines as Desdemona reassures Cassio. The frame then includes a stark foreground of harshly lit, sharp-edged boulders through which Othello and Iago approach. Othello soon afterwards is seen in his agony against pillars of stone, one with an immense face carved into it; stone which asserts itself as the ruins of an age past.

In the later development of the action, there is a recurrent appearance of rocky backgrounds devoid of any growth. A typical moment is when Othello asks Desdemona for the handkerchief. She puts into his hand the one she holds at that moment. Othello, without looking at it, believes it to be the one which will disprove his suspicion and he embraces Desdemona with passionate relief, against a background which is diagonally divided into sky and barren rock. Another is when Othello (aboard an anchored ship from which he has overheard the conversation between Cassio and Bianca) contemplates the killing of Cassio. His line, 'How shall I murder him?' initiates a sequence against

13 *Othello*, directed by Serge Yutkevich: Othello (Serge Bondarchuk) and Desdemona (Irina Skobtseva) against a rocky background

a background of sunlit rock rising out of a dramatically lit sea, with Desdemona's singing voice as a background on the sound track.

From suggestions of the refined architecture of Venice, we are shown a change in the dramatic character of stone through the massive functionality of the Cyprus fortress, to weather-worn pillars of a past age, and finally to stone backgrounds and foregrounds in which the architect and sculptor would seem to have been elemental forces: a visualization of Othello's 'My heart is turned to stone: I strike it and it hurts my hand.'

The pivotal shot in the film is the long tracking shot during which Iago destroys Othello's certainties. We move alongside Othello and Iago as they become increasingly surrounded by the fishing nets hung out along the shore to dry. It has somewhat obvious implications and despite its effectiveness on a purely visual and associative level, it lacks the compelling complexity of the famous Welles shot which covers the same dialogue, and integrates the dramatic moment so powerfully with the elements of stone, sea and sky.

Yutkevich makes the moment crucial, too, for not only does his dramatization of stone undergo a change after this sequence, but so also do the dramatic functions of the sea and the sky. The sea, which can be given such powerful visual associations in a film, is never far from the action, but until Othello's certainties are destroyed, it would seem to suggest qualities against which Othello would naturally stand. However, Othello's agonized farewell to his former self ends with his falling headlong on a beach so that the final 'Othello's occupation's gone' is accompanied by a massive wave breaking and throwing up its white spume into the darkness. The ensuing violent sequence with Iago, in which Othello demands that he (Iago) 'prove my love a whore', is played around a massive anchor with the sea's white edges creeping around and momentarily covering Othello's black cloak as he and Iago kneel and Iago promises to rid him of his uncertainty; to

> so prove it
> That the probation bear no hinge nor loop
> To hang a doubt on . . .

Since the character of the sea is so influenced by the lighting effects thrown upon it, the atmospheric dimensions of the film's later stages are increasingly conveyed by the colour combinations of both sea and sky. Dark clouds split the sunlight into rays striking the surface of the sea, as Othello is torn between his instincts and his rationality, Desdemona singing across the water from a distant boat and her song accompanying the dialogue:

OTHELLO . . . A fine woman, a fair woman, a sweet woman!
IAGO Nay, you must forget that.
OTHELLO Ay, let her rot and perish . . . No, my heart is turned to stone.

After the conspiracy between Othello and Roderigo to kill Cassio, the coming on of night is heralded by a blood-red sun setting beneath clouds over the sea. And it is towards a cloud-darkened sunset reflected on a vast rippled sea surface that the ship sails carrying the dead bodies of Othello and Desdemona in the film's closing shot.

In discussing these films we have covered two very different cinematic strategies, the first of which is to use film as a medium for recording performance on the theatre stage. At the other end of the spatial spectrum, we find Yutkevich setting the tragedy in an organic and elemental world, and being thus enabled to exploit cinematic resources with much more freedom, if not always with an integrated inventiveness, and clearly to aspire to – if not consistently to achieve – a dramatization of the natural world. Bela Balazs poses the question, 'How is the countryside turned into a landscape?' and then goes on to distinguish between the mere incorporation of nature on the one hand, and, on the other, the integration of nature as an articulation.

Not every bit of nature is a landscape in itself. The countryside has only a topography . . . But the landscape has a mood which is not merely objectively given: it needs the co-operation of subjective factors before it can come into existence.[9]

And Kozintsev has noted that 'A film landscape is concealed, hidden under another sort of covering. At first you do not so much see it as feel the possibility of its existence.'[10] Despite the many visually memorable moments in this film, one questions firstly whether nature in Yutkevich's film is transformed into 'a landscape' and secondly, whether there is a sufficiently focused 'feeling' beneath what is visualized.

III

It is not wholly fair to dismiss, as Jorgens does, Yutkevich's *Othello* as a 'lush colour imitation of Welles's *Othello*'.[11] Manvell maintains that Yutkevich's intention to make an *Othello* film dated from 'before the war',[12] and Derek Prouse refers to an article based on Yutkevich's *Othello* conception 'written by the director as early as 1938'.[13] The Welles *Othello*, does, however, come persistently to mind as one views Yutkevich's film, not merely because many of Yutkevich's devices do tend to echo Welles, but more particularly because of the sheer memorability of the Welles images, and because one is aware of a major difference in overall effect. The cinematic language of Welles's film suggests, as Jorgens has observed, the cosmic sense of a fallen world.[14] For Yutkevich, the tragedy is not so cataclysmic. His view of the play makes it about the search for harmony and the loss of faith. Othello's trust in Iago is part of his faith in mankind, and his discovery of Iago's treachery is the climax of the tragedy.[15] Indeed, this seems to have been a traditionally established view of the play in Russia. Jan Kott maintains that

The tragedy of jealousy became, there, a tragedy of betrayed confidence, in which Othello fell victim, not only to Iago's intrigues, but to the envy of the Doge and the entire Venetian Senate.[16]

In an unpublished doctoral thesis written in 1967, Donald Skoller suggests that the film conveys an overall sense that the tragedy might have been avoided 'with better planning', and that the film reflects 'a prevailing and politically acceptable doctrine in the Soviet Union at the time'.[17]

It is certainly true that Yutkevich's film is dramatically less complex than Welles's. Where Welles tends to juxtapose images and allow the composite effect to mature in the mind of the viewer, Yutkevich seeks, perhaps, to make too many issues explicit. However, the colour in his film presents us with some unforgettable images in which natural elements – stone, sky, and sea – do become a chorus to the dramatic development. Most potent in this respect is the sea, images of which, in Jack Jorgens's words, 'saturate' the film, 'demonstrating that a motif can work as powerfully in setting as it can in poetry'.[18]

What, then, is it that Welles's *Othello* has which makes it at once a more filmic and a more profoundly penetrating treatment of the play? In a fine essay on this film, Lorne Buchman argues that one of the merits of a significant Shakespeare film is its capacity to illuminate structures that are not immediately apparent, but which underpin the action in the Shakespeare play. 'What is perhaps the most interesting aspect of Welles's [*Othello*] is the way in which he exploits the concept of time inherent in the text.'[19] He goes on to analyse the opening sequences, and to propose that in these sequences Welles establishes a major vein along which the film will penetrate into the play.

In the opening sequence, Welles intersplices the funeral processions of Othello and Desdemona with shots of Iago dragged by chains through crowds of screaming Cypriots. Guards throw him into an iron cage and haul him to the top of the castle walls. We witness the world momentarily from Iago's perspective; the cage spins as it hangs, the crowd screams, and, as long as we are with Iago, the stately rhythm of the processions is lost. In the prologue, Welles develops his temporal theme by realising the opposing rhythms of Othello and Desdemona on the one hand and Iago on the other.[20]

There are, too, the immense oppositions which Welles manages to incorporate into the film: the apparent disappearance of the funeral procession into darkness at the end of the opening sequence, set against the hoisting of the caged Iago into the merciless glare of Mediterranean sunlight. And there is the superbly inventive use which Welles makes of his Mogador location so that the play becomes truly filmic in its dramatization of space and the relation of sea, sky, stone, light, shadow and darkness to character and momentary situation. Welles's ability to keep alive motifs – like Iago's cage – at important moments in the film gives the whole work suggestions of a visual opera, and there are thematic developments which move through intricate and finely wrought variations, like the trap motif which recurs in the shadowed bars that cut across the frame or the pattern of links on the stone floor where for a moment the solitary Desdemona stands, a motif which culminates in the closely woven cloth stretched over Desdemona's face as Othello smothers her on the bed.

All these contribute to making Welles's *Othello* an unforgettable filmic experience. Yet, for all that, the film – even the newly restored version – is further removed from the play in the nature of its impact than are most other Shakespeare film adaptations from their source plays. Despite the brilliance of Welles's cinematic resourcefulness, the film lacks an intensity of theatricality which, at its core, the play demands. Welles arranges Othello's striking Desdemona in the presence of Lodovico and the emissaries from Venice so that Othello's hand moves across the frame to slap Desdemona's face as she approaches looking directly into the camera. It is ingenious, unexpected and effective. But it does not stop one's breath as does the same moment in the television film of Trevor Nunn's 1989 RSC production, with Imogen Stubbs's young, almost girlish Desdemona actually felled by Othello's blow. Welles's *Othello* invites us to respond primarily to the image. Shakespeare's *Othello*, more perhaps than any other of his plays, insists that we relate – at times obsessively – with actor and with character.

Notes

1 'Paul Scofield himself was one of our reasons for undertaking *King Lear* in the first place.' Michael Birkett in Roger Manvell, *Shakespeare and the Film* (London, 1971), p. 140.

2 James E. Fisher, 'Olivier and the Realistic OTHELLO', *Literature Film Quarterly*, 1 (1973), 325, and Jack J. Jorgens, *Shakespeare on Film* (Bloomington, 1977), p. 192.

3 Peter Brook, Public Lecture, The Warehouse, London, 20 January 1982.

4 Anthony Havelock-Allan in Manvell, p. 117.

5 André Bazin, *What is Cinema*, 1 (Berkeley, California, 1967) p. 102.

6 See Bela Balazs, *Theory of the Film: Character and Growth of a New Art* (London, 1952), pp. 93, 96.

7 Serge Yutkevich, 'OTHELLO vu par Serge Youtkevitch', *Cinema 56*, Vol. II, No. 10, p. 19.

8 Roger Manvell, *Shakespeare and the Film* (London, 1971), p. 73. Two versions of the film were released: the original one in Sovcolor with Russian dialogue, and a slightly later version in Technicolor with dubbed English dialogue on the soundtrack.

9 Balazs, *Theory of the Film*, pp. 96–7.

10 Grigori Kozintsev, *King Lear: The Space of Tragedy* (London, 1977), p. 128.

11 Jack Jorgens, *Shakespeare on Film* (Bloomington, 1977), p. 26.

12 Roger Manvell, *Shakespeare and the Film* (London, 1971), p. 73.

13 Derek Prouse, *Sight and Sound* (Summer, 1956), p. 30. See also *Cinema 56*, pp. 10–19.

14 Jorgens, *Shakespeare on Film*, p. 175.

15 Yutkevich, 'Othello', *Cinema 56*, Vol. II, No. 10, p. 13.

16 Jan Kott, *Shakespeare Our Contemporary* (London, 1975), p. 81.

17 Donald Skoller, 'Problems of Transformation in the Adaptations of Shakespeare's Tragedies from Playscript to Cinema' (unpublished PhD dissertation, New York University, 1968), p. 292.

18 Jorgens, *Shakespeare on Film*, p. 26.

19 Lorne M. Buchman, 'Orson Welles's *Othello*: A Study of Time in Shakespeare's Tragedy', *Shakespeare Survey 39* (Cambridge, 1987), pp. 53–65.

20 *Ibid.*, p. 54.

21 Jorgens, *Shakespeare on Film*, p. 26.

12

REPRESENTING *KING LEAR* ON SCREEN: FROM METATHEATRE TO 'META-CINEMA'

KENNETH S. ROTHWELL

The advantage of the cinema over the theatre is not that you can even have horses, but that you can stare closer into a man's eyes; otherwise it is pointless to set up a cine camera for Shakespeare . . .   Grigori Kozintsev[1]

Representing *King Lear* on screen, representing almost any Shakespearian play on film or videotape, means broadening the ancient trope of the world as stage to include the world as screen. As the idea of the screen as screen takes its place alongside the idea of the play as play, so 'meta-cinema' inevitably emerges alongside metatheatre. In making the means of representation a subject of representation, film-makers have only mimicked their stage forebears.[2] Like theatre, film may also self-referentially draw attention to itself through ironic devices, or alternatively, it may even have sequences that are essentially movies-within-movies. Olivier's *Henry V*, by shifting from a documentary mode in the Globe playhouse to a stylized medievalism at the court of France, gives an example of the former; while the Polanski *Macbeth*, in embedding a silent movie about Ross within the talking picture about Macbeth, illustrates the latter.

In Shakespeare films, 'meta-cinema' may or may not assume the additional burden of apologizing for the film's not being a page in a printed book or a play on the public stage. The history of screened Shakespeare furnishes a special reason for this directorial breast-beating. Ever since those early silents, such as the 1911 'epoch-making picture of *Henry VIII*, as given by Sir Herbert Tree',[3] or Sir Johnston Forbes-Robertson's 1913 *Hamlet*, for which at enormous expense a castle was constructed in Dorset's Lulworth Cove,[4] film-makers have been guilt-ridden. Movies, it was thought, were an unsuitable vehicle for the masterpieces of Shakespeare. Stanley Kauffmann, while excoriating Franco Zeffirelli's 1966 *The Taming of the Shrew* as an 'abomination', expressed a consensus when he wrote that 'the film medium and Shakespeare are born antagonists'.[5] Laurence Kitchin uttered much the same thought, though less abrasively, twenty years ago: 'Shakespeare's plays were written to be used by live actors in the presence of a crowd. It follows that all screen versions of them are subject to the limitations of the screen.'[6] Sensitive to these concerns, directors have sought to appease Shakespeare's praetorians in the libraries and theatres with gestures of obeisance. Insofar as these defensive strategies draw attention to the way that the film is being made, they emerge in a meta-cinematic context.

I

Edwin Thanhouser's 1916 *King Lear*,[7] one of the best of the silents, offers a paradigm. Its opening sequence takes the 'forelock-tugging' approach. Director Ernest Warde's concern about tampering with the written text of Shakespeare's play is privileged over the *diegesis* (film narrative) itself. The opening shot reveals a man in a smoking jacket who affects a wing collar. Seated bolt upright in a wingback chair, he is reading a book. These codes signal a stereotypical Victorian gentleman – learned, haughty and stuffy. The film's anxiety about removing a Shakespearian tragedy from that context into the vulgarity of the Nickelodeon is betrayed by the very next shot, a close-up of the first page of *King Lear* in what could pass for the Globe edition.

The actor seated in the chair, it so happens, is Frederick Warde, who in his day resembled an American clone to Albert Finney's 'Sir' in Peter Yates's 1983 film version of *The Dresser*, with Tom Courtenay as Norman, or Fool. Warde, described by his biographer as 'an old-fashioned, ranting performer', was an expatriate Englishman born in 1851, who toured the hinterlands of the United States as an itinerant Shakespearian, never quite making it on the New York Stage, until he 'drifted' into a film career.[8] In his regal appearance Warde embodied every nineteenth-century Bardolator's ideal of an authentic Shakespearian actor. And in the next sequence of the film Warde gradually begins to dissolve in front of the audience's eyes and to turn into King Lear.[9] Once transformed into the king, Warde's position in the frame is then usurped by a lengthy explanatory title:

King Lear was written in 1607 during the time when the immortal dramatist was at the height of his creative power. King Lear, a proud old man in his dotage, listened to the flattery of his treacherous daughters, and divided his kingdom between them, while he banished Cordelia, his youngest child, the only one who really loved him. On the day that King Lear assembles his court to tell them of his proposed abdication in favour of his daughters . . . [etc.]

The film struggles to free itself from the constraints of page and stage. It moves from the opening *mise-en-scène* with a man reading in a chair (which is

14 Frederick B. Warde as King Lear on tour in the United States in the early part of this century

spatial), to the close-up of the *Lear* text (which involves montage), to the Méliès-like stunt of dissolving Warde into Lear, and then to the narrative device of subtitles for telling the plot of the play. The director has privileged the world of the library (the page); used a well-known actor of the time in the title role (the stage); and literally framed his movie (the screen) between the pages of a book. Page, stage and screen, the triad of Shakespearian incarnations, momentarily interface, though the tension generated among the three inevitably favours disconnection of the filmic from page and stage. To accomplish that, the book and the reader are figuratively and literally dissolved to make room for the movie.

15 Frederick B. Warde as King Lear banishes Cordelia (Lorraine Huling), while the Fool (Ernest Warde) looks on

Admittedly, to sensible persons the whole idea of Shakespeare on silent film must seem nothing short of crazy.[10] How could Shakespeare, whose essence is the spoken English language, plausibly be represented in silent moving pictures? As the old silent Shakespeare films with a Forbes-Robertson or a Frederick Warde show, to derive any pleasure from them the audience was expected to be, or at least had to be, familiar with the text. It has so often been said that the early film-makers exploited Shakespeare only to legitimize a sleazy art form that this point has been virtually lost to view. Forbes-Robertson's *Hamlet*, for example, was played on screen much as it was acted at the Theatre Royal, Haymarket, and in 1914 in America at Boston's Shubert Theatre and Chicago's Blackstone. Warde's Lear resembled what he had done on stage all over America in transforming himself into the very incarnation of the noblest and most monarchial-looking of kings. The silent Shakespeare films challenge the spectator to recollect what words go with what lip movements, facial expressions, and body language of the on-screen players. Thus very early in the history of filmed Shakespeare, there was a proleptic fulfilment of John Russell Taylor's belief that often the best filmed Shakespeare is based on the assumption that the audience knows the play. The film 'affirms' but does not 'record'.[11] Today's avant-garde Shakespeare films, such as the 1980 Derek Jarman *Tempest* and the 1991 Peter Greenaway *Prospero's Books*, also attempt to affirm rather than record, though their roots lie in the underground films of an Andy Warhol rather than in the classical movies of a George Cukor. The audience should know better than to assess these films as literal representations of Shakespeare's text.

In Warde's *King Lear*, however, the visual treatment alone, even without the imagined dialogue, shows again, as it did in the eighteenth century for John Boydell's Shakespeare Gallery of engravings, the power of Shakespeare's verbal imagination to inspire pictorial representation. For example, the 'division of the kingdom' scene is framed around the admonishing hand of the old king pointing at a Cordelia who shrinks from her father's abuse behind her protector, France. The empty space between father and daughter, contrasted with the clasped hands of Cordelia and France, signifies the shattered bond between father and daughter. In the foreground, conspicuously inconspicuous, as though he did indeed belong inside Lear's head, is the Fool. The frame thus positions the severing of the bond of trust and faith at the centre, where it belongs, but the grids surrounding the centre reflect the 'vectors' of disturbance that fall out and away from the king's rash deed. A daughter discarded, a future son-in-law alienated, a court thrown into turmoil, an inner doubt and anxiety in the old king adumbrated by the presence of the Fool, impending collapse and disintegration – all these complexities are reflected in the spatial relationships of the actors in the *mise-en-scène*. It is Shakespeare without words, indeed without montage, but it is also eloquent testimony as well to the power of the art of mime.

Where film most differs from stage, however, is in the capacity to handle the kinds of vast outdoor spectacles suggested in so many of Shakespeare's plays and embodied in *King Lear* in the struggle between the armies of France and England. Warde's *King Lear* did not offer anything quite so spectacular as, for example, the celebrated 1927 Abel Gance *Napoleon* with its triple screens and thunderous musical accompaniment, but freed, as it were, from the 'unworthy scaffold' and 'wooden O', the film revels in the great battle scene, which was shot in and around the environs of a 'castle' located in New Rochelle, New York. For that time, when heavy equipment made cameras immobile, the results are impressive. A series of reaction shots depict a gloating Goneril and Regan ecstatic over the carnage spread out before them; dozens of extras outfitted in costume armour carry out a rousing cavalry charge while foot soldiers hack away with menacing-looking long swords or hurl boulders on the helpless wounded. Intercut are reaction shots of an angelic and anguished Cordelia. And even as the film attempts to sever the ancient bond with the theatre, the veteran actor, Warde, as did the more celebrated Forbes-Robertson in his *Hamlet*, offers a documentary of how a nineteenth-century actor approached a major Shakespearian role.

At the very end, when for no apparent reason the film abruptly terminates – after Cordelia has been strangled in prison by brutes, after Regan has been poisoned in close-up, and after Goneril has stabbed herself – Lear carries his daughter out of prison and the card title informs the audience that he is saying, 'She's gone forever.' Then the old king, in anticipation of the 1970 Michael Birkett/Peter Brook ending of *King Lear*, literally falls out of the frame. Whether advertent or inadvertent, this camerawork perfectly captures a cosmic truth in Lear's story. He too, like Cordelia, is 'gone forever'. He too has experienced the 'nothingness' with which the play begins and ends. It is a nothingness that is always on the edge of curving back into somethingness, like the theoretical physicist's nothing that is inherently ready to turn back into something. And that hint of grace also comes through in the stately, dignified, thoroughly old-fashioned performance of Mr Warde.

II

As others have pointed out,[12] Peter Brook's 1970 film of *King Lear* did not spring forth from the head of its creator without gestation.[13] Not only had Brook directed the 1962 RSC stage version starring Paul Scofield, but prior to that he had acted as artistic adviser for a 1953 US television performance with Orson Welles in the title role. This expertise should have shielded him against the obloquy that descended on Sam Taylor for a reputed credit to the 1929 Douglas Fairbanks-Mary Pickford *The Taming of the Shrew*: 'with additional dialogue by Sam Taylor'. That light-hearted jest was solemnly misread as *prima facie* evidence of Taylor's innate vulgarity.[14] Despite his establishment credentials, Brook proved to be a lightning-rod for hostile criticism. If the Thanhouser-Warde *Lear* belongs to the Bardolatry school of forelock-tugging, then the Brook film has been identified with another species of body language – nose-thumbing. The reviewers developed a litany of complaints about his *King Lear*: it is 'depoeticized';[15] inept 'in handling of film medium . . . a travesty';[16] 'an image, not of regeneration, but of moribundity and sad decay'.[17] Pauline Kael didn't just 'dislike' it; she 'hated it'.[18] The complaint that Brook had made a Shakespeare movie that could not be understood by people who had not read the play surfaced again,[19] as though a Shakespeare film's only function is to serve as a glorified comic book.

Others saw matters differently: Guy Allombert wrote that 'Brook va plus loin; il connaît ses spectateurs. Il traite d'égal à égal. Son film est celui d'une certaine élite. Il la fascine. Il la séduit. Il n'émeut jamais';[20] Frank Kermode thought (though with some qualifications) that Peter Brook had made 'the best of all Shakespeare movies';[21] and the late Lillian Wilds went even further than that in a thoughtful essay that viewed the movie's alleged flaws as artistic triumphs.[22] What Brook did was simply to declare independence from the constraints of page and stage and to make a genuine effort at converting the Shakespearian experience into a cinematic idiom. Ideology became confused with artistry, however, and in the chorus of disapproval over his 'gray and cold' vision (has anyone ever thought of *King Lear* as cheerful?) his pioneering efforts were overlooked.

Brook's film really does not set a 'nose-thumbing' attitude against Warde's 'forelock-tugging'. Brook took seriously the mandate to find visual signifiers for what Shakespeare's words signified. The epic scale of Shakespeare's apocalyptic tragedy demanded radical experimentation with filmic *Verfremdung* to represent the unrepresentable. That the film was not frivolously planned is evidenced in the interview with the producer of the film, Michael Birkett, in Roger Manvell's *Shakespeare and the Film*;[23] or in the 1968 draft shooting script, which painstakingly describes the blocking for each scene, though indeed many alterations from this version occurred by the time the film was actually made.[24]

Insofar as this film also is not just a representation of *King Lear* but a movie about making movies, it exploits meta-cinematic rhetoric. Unlike the Warde

16   A long shot of Lear's train showing the bleak landscape in the Peter Brook 1970 film version

Lear, it is not in the least defensive about being a film, but instead flaunts its identity. Filmed in North Jutland, Denmark, its black-and-white starkness shows a winter world of ironic despair in grainy shots and deliberate out-of-focus frames. It is perversely cinematic in its Godardian techniques of alienation and in its deliberate break with Hollywood slickness. Like a 'New Wave' director, Brook employs discontinuities: zoom-fades, accelerated motion, rapid editing, complex reverse angle and over-the-shoulder shots, montage, jump cuts, overhead shots, silent-screen titles, eyes-only close-ups, and hand-held cameras as well as stationary, immobile ones. The influence of Jan Kott's 'Grand Mechanism' and of Bertolt Brecht's epic theatre are present also.[25] But for Brook in the late sixties all the world was no longer a 'stage' but a movie screen. At the end, a gravelly voiced Paul Scofield as the dying king literally falls out of the frame (as in the ending of the Warde silent film) to be replaced by white nothingness.

The pervasive view of Brook's film as having been shaped by Brecht and Kott as much as by Shakespeare, however, somewhat obscures the influence on the film of the earlier 1953 television version that Brook helped to produce in North America. The technical realities of television as much as ideological considerations nudged Brook more towards the play's vision of 'death' over 'life'.[26] The tyranny of time demanded sacrifice of optimistic elements in the Gloucester subplot to compress the performance into seventy-three minutes. That shortened 'Omnibus' version of *King Lear*, starring the late Orson Welles, was nationally televised in the United States one Sunday afternoon in October 1953.[27] Framed between commercials for Greyhound buses, bath tissues and textiles, the commentator for the 'wraparound', a youthful Alistair Cooke, then just beginning his career as the master of making the art of introduction look easy, opined that while the Gloucester subplot had been thrown away (subplots, he said, were only in Elizabethan plays to rest the main actors anyway), 'everything that bears on the tragedy of *Lear* is in this version'.

Cooke exaggerated, though. The scrapping of the subplot with its redemptive thrust in the behaviour of Edgar, of Albany, and of Gloucester (despite his 'As flies to wanton boys are we to th' gods' (4.1.36))[28] almost guaranteed a victory of existentialism over essentialism. Cooke's introduction reductively, but nevertheless accurately, seems to have prefigured Kott's vision of the play: 'We give you *King Lear* in the hope that you may learn more from Shakespeare's pessimism than from the optimism of lesser men.'

Constraint can be and often is the mother of invention. So it was with this television version of *King Lear*. Like the 'wooden O' of the Globe, the small box of television requires ingenuity, a feel for the 'meta-cinematic', to overcome its limitations. The opening sequence of the production becomes a dumbshow for the style of representation that is to follow. A curtain with an enormous map of England painted on it is suddenly ripped apart and through the tear steps Orson Welles's King Lear to begin the division of the kingdom. The violation of the map foreshadows the violation of the text; that act of aggression signals an approach that privileges themes of power and assertiveness embodied in images of domination and subjugation.

This is a 'bondage' *King Lear*. As Marvin Rosenberg has also noticed,[29] the overtones from Alfred Hitchcock's spy thrillers are pervasive. A major influence, besides the intellectualization of despair by Brecht and Kott, is Hitchcock's obsession with human degradation. Iron gates, steel bars, hempen ropes, and other hints of sado-masochism fill the frames. A portcullis rises at Gloucester's castle, its iron bars reminiscent of the famous cage imprisoning Iago at the beginning of Orson Welles's 1952 filmed *Othello*. The prison-house motif persists as Regan and Cornwall are viewed peering through iron bars at a Kent caged and stocked. It continues as the Lear party takes refuge from the storm in a windmill. Ropes, grinding wheels, chains – all foreshadow 'the rack of this tough world' (5.3.315) upon which the old king will figuratively be stretched. Poor Tom, a relic of the jettisoned Gloucester plot, suddenly and inexplicably turns up. Whirling windmill blades and Virgil Thomson's film music of muted horns and muffled drums offer visual and sonic punctuation for Lear's inner confusion. In the windmill, now clearly an emblem for the old king's spiritual bondage to a foolish appraisal of reality, Gloucester is seized, bound, and has his eyes gouged out by the venomous Cornwall, who uses his thumbs, not his spurs. A wooden-faced Regan looks on without pity.

Wellesian camera angles and imaginative ballet-like blocking of the characters, as well as Welles's own flamboyant performance, make this production from the infancy of televised Shakespeare memorable. Only Jane Howell with her 1983 BBC productions of the minor tetralogy has achieved nearly so much in transferring Shakespeare to television.

Had Welles lived in the nineteenth century he would have been applauded for the robust talents that make him comparable to a Forbes-Robertson or a Frederick Warde. From the first sequence, as the Fool cowers under his master's dining table while Goneril dominates the old king in a low-angle shot, to his bellowed 'Who put my man in the stocks?', to the frightening moment when his daughters circle him like wolves until he cries out his heart-breaking 'I gave you all', to the memorable closing scene when he drags poor Cordelia in (after the manner of the Italian actor Salvini before him), as though she were a rag doll[30] – Welles's performance is pitched at the highest level of energy.

Indeed the latter scene wrings the most out of primitive studio lighting conditions by correlating darkness with chaos, light with harmony. The old king's howls originate and intensify in darkness and dwindle as he moves into the light. The audience's sudden perception that the *thing* he is dragging along the ground is actually Cordelia simultaneously arouses pity and fear. The loyal daughter has become a rag doll, a child's toy, in the hands of a man who has himself reverted to childlike innocence. The slow movement from dark to light, as Welles painfully crawls back up to the throne that he had so foolishly given away, visualizes the shift from isolation to community. Like Warde in the Thanhouser film and Scofield in the Brook version, the king moves into what Henry Vaughan spoke of as 'the world of light'. Albany is given the final lines; there is a slow fade; and the music comes up. Despite this performance, reviewers were harsh, even cruel. One went so far as to write that Welles resembled 'a man who had been hauled off a park bench and hastily pressed into service as Macy's Santa Claus'.[31]

III

Paradoxically what seems most remarkable about Grigori Kozintsev's 1970 Russian-language version of *King Lear* is that it is apparently unremarkable.[32] That is to say, there is no tie to a past of page or stage hidden away in the film's rhetoric ('forelock tugging'); nor is there on the other hand the baroque style of the Brook film, which might open it up to charges of 'nose-thumbing'. Kozintsev, perhaps because of his many years of experience as a film-maker and consequent ability to resist the temptation of over-using a camera, elegantly realized the impossible task of making *King Lear* possible on screen. With Kozintsev, the camera probes as much as records; it is an x-ray, not a mirror. He accomplishes his goals through patient contemplation of the problem at hand rather than through superficial tricks. He searches for a deeper structure in Shakespeare's play that needed to be brought to the surface for effective cinema. The solution seems to be the close scrutiny of faces, all kinds of faces – those of the king, his daughters, of Kent, of Cordelia, of the Fool, of Edmund – to allow the camera to reflect the inner passions expressed in the glitter of eyes, the curl of a lip, or the toss of a head.

Essentially the only thing remarkable about the film is that the dialogue is in Russian, using Pasternak's translation. Even there, a curious anomaly lies in the fact that the star of the film, Yuri Yarvet, an Estonian non-speaker of Russian, had to force himself to learn the language to avoid the infelicity of dubbed-in speech. Yarvet was actually the last actor cast after many had been auditioned for the leading role. The subjecting of each aspirant to three entire weeks of rehearsals simply for the auditions[33] was entirely typical of the relentless pains that Kozintsev took in the pre-shooting phase.

17 In the Kozintsev 1970 *King Lear*, Lear (Yuri Yarvet) and Cordelia (V. Shendrikova) are led off to prison

From its famous opening shot, one that depicts hundreds of peasant feet clumping and toiling up a stony hillside that looks like some druidic boneyard, to its closing shot as Edgar silently moves forward against the backdrop of a fertile pasture, Kozintsev invests this legendary tale of shattered human trust with a serene dignity. The film's dominant motifs and images are not quickly forgotten: the sound of the Fool's bells ('a tongue stuck out against pomposity', as Kozintsev himself said)[34] before the old king enters, laughing, for the 'division of the kingdom' scene; the 'presence' (in a post-structuralist sense) of Yarvet as king, a scrawny little man who nevertheless can speak with the authority of thunder and who serves notice that his essence is not subject to usurpation; in the hearth of the great hall a fire through which the king is glimpsed as though he were himself in flames (as he will be) and the linking, as Kozintsev wrote, of that fire with the recurring images of flaming torches in the king's train of carts, the army campfires, the searing tar hurled at the fortress with catapults, and a gutted city that resembles Hiroshima; Lear's incendiary diatribe against Cordelia, his throwing of the map around this way and that, as he rumbles his awful wrath over her apparent ingratitude; the old king vigorously striding through the palace selecting household objects and animals for his journey – the hawks, greyhounds, setters, everything that a king with a hundred knights should have in his train; the scathing denunciation of and then spitting upon Kent, which even though uttered in Russian makes clear that Kent's sentence has gone beyond exile to the level of ritual excommunication or perhaps exorcism; and then in unexpected contrast the quiet, meditative speaking of the 'O reason not the need' speech in soliloquy at Gloucester's castle; the way that Regan in a white heat to possess Edmund rips off his clothing, only shortly thereafter to plant an erotic kiss full on the lips of Cornwall's corpse; the quick cut (Kozintsev prefers the cut to the dissolve) to 125 frames (five seconds) obscenely displaying the hanged Cordelia high above the castle walls; the funeral cortège bearing the bodies of the fallen while the Fool (now transformed into a Russian village idiot) sits amidst the rubble mourning the loss of his master and of his own identity; and an over-the-shoulder shot of the king looking down on a throng of peasants and crying out (he who has himself been dragged through the mud and a hovel with Kent and Mad Tom): 'O, [you] are men of stones!' (5.3.258).

In short, Kozintsev has approached the making of a film as a sculptor who would suggest rather than articulate the innermost character of his subjects. Wherein, however, is the film meta-cinematic? How does it show awareness of itself as a work of art and how does it work out the buried fear of subservience to page or stage? Is this film, too, still fettered to page and stage? The answer must be that Kozintsev moved very close to that ideal stage of film-making advocated by V. F. Perkins,[35] in which the medium informs the subject and the subject informs the medium. It is a balance that favours neither the accumulation of detail (*mise-en-scène*) nor the selection of detail (montage), but interweaves through skilful editing all elements into a coherent design. The commentary that Kozintsev makes about his film within his film is clandestine, implicit, expressed as much through what is not seen as through what is seen. If Brook is the Brecht of film-makers, then Kozintsev becomes the Pinter. Brook favours theatricality; Kozintsev, silence. This difference does not mean that Brook should be indicted as a director guilty of using 'bombast and rhetoric', but rather that two gifted filmmakers have discovered different ways of capturing the extraordinary complexity of Shakespeare's greatest tragedy. To be dangerously reductive, Brook favours montage and Kozintsev *mise-en-scène*.

A major reason for Kozintsev's understated, covert rhetoric may well be that much of what he thought about the movie had already been expressed in his diaries before he began filming. His astonishing book, *King Lear: The Space of Tragedy*, is unmatched as a record of a film director's artistic struggles. The book is the meta-cinematic side of his production because all the theorizing about the film, and about the problems of making a film, went into it before the film itself was made. It made a cinema without prefixes possible. Probably its genius, its status as one of the great works of this century, has never been properly acknowledged. J. W. Lambert came close, though at the end of his review essay he undercut his own estimation with a stock complaint of cinemaphobes: 'is the resulting experience [of film] any deeper, any stronger, any better, or even as good, as a good director with a good cast will arrive at in six weeks or so in the theatre?'[36] Studded with polished anecdotes and aphorisms, Kozintsev's book meditates on film-making as an art. It probes the configurations of the reality that shaped his awareness. The effect of a stone in a Kyoto garden, of the Hiroshima museum, of Noh drama, of the influence of Meyerhold, of Brecht, of Zen, of his own association in the early twenties with Sergei Yutkevich in FEKS ('The Factory of the Eccentric Actor'), and of the grotesqueries of Gogol and probings of Dostoevski – all in one way or another lie behind the conception of his *King Lear*. Little is said about Marxism, though there is a tendency for some Westerners to ferret out evidence that Russian film directors employ Marxist assumptions about power relationships.[37] Kozintsev circumvents political theory in favour of timeless themes of evil and injustice. Even so, his apparent indifference to hard-core socialist realism did not prevent acclaim from Soviet as well as Western critics,[38] and through his personal appearance in 1971 at the International World Shakespeare Congress in Vancouver, Canada, Kozintsev was one of the first film-makers to win a serious hearing from a wide range of Shakespeare scholars.

IV

Since the 1953 Brook-Welles *King Lear*, television has undergone a technological growth that makes it unreasonable to discuss recent and past productions as
though they were of the same genre. The three major televised *King Lears* of the
past two decades – those with James Earl Jones, Michael Hordern, and
Laurence Olivier in the title roles[39] – have been produced using studio
equipment that was unimaginable in the 1950s with its 'live' performances
fraught with potential disasters: an actor doing a swaggering Petruchio could
stumble on the stairs or a Lady Macbeth could muff a cue in front of millions.
And yet as television approaches the technical competence of film it gains an
'air-brushed' slickness at the expense of spontaneity, ironically the same
complaint that theatre advocates have always made about filmed
Shakespeare.[40]

Even television reduces itself into further subsets when one considers that the
1977 broadcast in the United States of the James Earl Jones *King Lear* was
actually a recording of an earlier Delacorte Theater production in New York
City's Central Park. Camera becomes merely a tool or service to the stage,
though even that assertion needs qualification because some recordings of stage
productions have obviously been done with greater expertise than others. The
Richard Burton/John Gielgud Electronovision *Hamlet*, for example, used no
less than fifteen cameras,[41] which did not guarantee its success but does suggest
the magnitude of the production's mechanical problems.

The chronicle of making a 'television movie' from *King Lear* will focus here
on Jonathan Miller's 1982 BBC TV/Time-Life version starring Michael
Hordern, and the 1983 Granada Studios *King Lear* starring Laurence Olivier.
Both these television plays appeared at almost the same time, just as the two
film versions of Brook and Kozintsev made their premières within a few
months of each other. Like the Brook and Kozintsev films, the Miller television
version also gestated on stage before being subjected to the permanent record
of the camera.

As well as in a 1975 television production, Miller had directed Hordern in a
1970 Nottingham Playhouse production of *King Lear*, which in London
appearances received mixed reviews: J. W. Lambert found Hordern's 'grizzled'
style and the 'grey sets' faithful to the Shakespearian intention,[42] but Eric
Shorter seems to have had an opposite impression, summed up in a laconic
conclusion: 'I still do not understand those costumes.'[43] The television
version[44] apparently adhered very closely to the style of the stage production in
its stress, as Miller put it, on an 'absence of regality' in the person of the old king.
Indeed, anyone calling for 'regality' is in peril of being dismissed by Miller as a

18 Penelope Wilton (centre), Gillian Barge (right) play the wicked sisters in the 1982 BBC production, with Brenda Blethyn (left foreground) as Cordelia

kind of lout with 'lower middle class' sensibilities.[45] There is not room here to do full justice to Hordern's thoroughly professional and competent performance in this startlingly original conception of the old king, nor to Frank Middlemass's Fool. The measure of how far it is removed from the cliché King Lear is to think of Albert Finney's Lear in *The Dresser*, which carries all the old

19 Michael Hordern as a grizzled King Lear with Frank Middlemass as the Fool in the 1982
    BBC production directed by Jonathan Miller

stereotypes to the point of a *reductio ad absurdum*. Then again, however, one recollects the wild old hirsute king of Frederick Warde's nineteenth-century America and grave doubts settle in. Has the loss of regality been bought at the expense of innate dignity? Has the Jove figure been reduced to Job?

Whatever the answers to these questions, in putting the play into a monochromatic, late Renaissance ambience and in attempting to turn the disadvantages of acting in a television studio into advantages, Miller used the medium to serve Shakespeare's words rather than Shakespeare's words to serve the medium. At the same time, there is no defensiveness about televison's being neither a play script, nor a stage play, nor a film. Quite the contrary. One senses an aggressive, even robust, relish for working with the medium. With such an attitude, the technicians on the set replace the live audience in the theatre, as Hordern once commented. There is a willingness to work with what is on hand rather than a restless search to recover the lost glories of either stage or film. As with Kozintsev, most of Miller's thoughts about making a television movie out of a Shakespearian tragedy apparently took place at the planning stage, not in production. This is not a *King Lear* that readily responds to a search for elements of either metatheatre or 'meta-television'; it both records and reaffirms the Shakespearian text. Its hidden agenda may be that the Nottingham theatre origins partially subverted remaking of the play for television. Along the way, however, Michael Hordern, in becoming less the king-man and more the man-king, displays a special brand of competence, summed up in John J. O'Connor's homespun comment: 'While he is not overwhelming, he is mightily convincing.'[46]

V

To complete the figure, however, of metatheatre to 'meta-cinema', the promise of my subtitle, the Olivier/Elliott *King Lear* offers a splendid coda. What could possibly be more self-referential, more 'meta-television', than the world's greatest actor playing himself as an aged monarch in the declining years of his career?[47] More than that, the veteran supporting cast is virtually a real-life counterpart to the old king's hundred knights. From all accounts they also brought a Kent-like loyalty on the set to the aged monarch,[48] which in a way is reflected in the 'division of the kingdom' scene when they lie prostrate in awe of the king's majesty. A retinue of stars in their own right, they include Diana Rigg as a surprisingly reptilian Regan and Colin Blakely, a memorable Antony in the BBC *Antony and Cleopatra*, as Kent. Dorothy Tutin's Goneril is quietly degenerate but no doubt Leo McKern as a throaty Gloucester offers the most memorable of the supporting performances.

The producers also constructed a studio replica of Stonehenge to endow the play with timelessness. Enormous hunks of cowhide make up the map of England in the first scene, and a Stonehenge setting at the beginning and ending of the play hints at dark druidic mysteries of sacrifice. Moreover Stonehenge, as Tucker Orbison once observed,[49] is set off against an oak tree to punctuate the nihilistic and regenerative side of the Lear tale.

20   Laurence Olivier as King Lear with Diana Rigg as Regan in the 1983 Granada Television
production

Olivier himself never loses his gift for canny stage business, particularly in the mad scenes when, to signify his pathetic vulnerability, he washes clothes, exposes the breasts of his withered body, slaughters a rabbit and consumes its raw flesh, makes a necklace of flowers, and plays with a mouse. Shorn of his beard at the end, not even grizzled like Hordern, Olivier is the very opposite of the Warde King Lear of the nineteenth century. This King Lear of the post-holocaust era, of the post-monarchial period, of the electronic age, cannot somehow achieve the sublimity of the past. He must be made, as with the Hordern King Lear, as much man as king. And yet neither the medium nor the director is actually decisive. It is the genius of the actor that makes audiences either sit up and take notice or switch to another channel. Olivier's remarkable voice, which can turn a vowel or a diphthong into discovery of a lost chord, does not desert him even in his advanced years and guarantees the enduring viability of his production.

Having said all that, however, one is still left uneasy about this representation of Shakespeare's greatest tragedy. In spite of the expenditure of huge sums of money by Granada Television, in spite of the star quality of the cast, and in spite of the brilliance of Olivier's performance, the result still illustrates the obstacles to literal representation of Shakespearian tragedy on screen. Something undergoes a sea change from stage to screen. What works perfectly at an RSC performance in the Barbican may turn leaden on screen. Only the star-quality performance of Olivier saves this production from sinking without a trace. As one reviewer said, the cast and Olivier were simply too large for the production.[50] It would seem that all attempts at literal representation only lead back to the conclusion that Shakespeare on film is most interesting when least representational.

As we have seen then, since the early twentieth century directors have undertaken to represent the unrepresentable by putting *King Lear* on the big screen of movies and then, subsequently, also on the small screen of television. Haunted by the stage traditions of the past, self-conscious about the film and television medium of the present, and anxiety-ridden by the burden of their responsibility to the world's greatest dramatist, they have inevitably allowed their perturbations to creep into their moving pictures. In turning our attention back to the inexhaustible problems of reading, acting, producing, interpreting, and filming the canon, 'meta-cinema' offers yet another way to approach and understand the art of William Shakespeare.

Notes

The author expresses his thanks to Dr Thomas Berger of St Lawrence University, Candace Bothwell of the Folger Shakespeare Library, Patrick Sheehan of the Motion Picture Division of the Library of Congress, Roger Holman of the National Film Archive, and Gillian Hartnoll of the British Film Institute, without whom this work could not have been accomplished, as well as to the Graduate College, University of Vermont, for funding of travel.

1 Grigori Kozintsev, *King Lear, the Space of Tragedy*, trans. Mary Mackintosh (Berkeley, 1977). p. 55.

2 For interrelationships between film and theatre, see Roger Manvell, *Theater and Film* (London, 1979) and A. N. Vardac, *Stage to Screen* (Cambridge, Mass., 1949); relevant studies appearing after the preparation of this article include Anthony Davies, *Filming Shakespeare's Plays* (Cambridge, 1988), Lorne M. Buchman, *Still in Movement* (Oxford, 1991), and Samuel Crowl, *Shakespeare Observed* (Athens, Ohio, 1992). Anne Righter's *Shakespeare and the Idea of the Play* (London, 1962) discusses metatheatricality.

3 'Advertisement', *Bioscope* (2 March 1911), p. 21.

4 'Interview with C. Hepworth', *Bioscope* (24 July 1913), 275–9; p. 275.

5 '*Romeo and Juliet*', in *Figures of Light: Film Criticism and Commentary* (New York, 1971), pp. 112–14; p. 113.

6 'Shakespeare on the Screen', *Shakespeare Survey 18* (Cambridge, 1965), pp. 70–4; p. 70. For other general views, see Roger Manvell, Alan Dent, Philip Hope-Wallace, 'Can Shakespeare Be Filmed? A Discussion . . .', a BBC Radio programme, 1948 (typescript in British Film Institute Library); Marvin Felheim, 'Criticism and the Films of Shakespeare's Plays', *Comparative Drama*, 9 (1975), 147–55; N. McDonald, 'The Relationship Between Shakespeare's Stagecraft and Modern Film Technique', *Australian Journal of Screen Theory*, 7 (1980), 18–33; and most recently S. Giantvalley, 'Shakespeare on the Screen: A Symposium', *Quarterly Review of Film Studies*, 7, (1982), 102–3.

7 *King Lear*, USA, 1916, pro. Edwin Thanhouser; dir. Ernest Warde; with Frederick B. Warde (King Lear), Lorraine Huling (Cordelia), Ernest Warde (Fool), Ina Hammer (Goneril), Wayne Arey (Albany), Edith Diestal (Regan), Charles Brookes (Cornwall), b/w, 43 min.

8 Alan Woods, 'Frederick B. Warde: America's Greatest Forgotten Tragedian', *Educational Theatre Journal*, 29 (Oct. 1977), 333–44; p. 335.

9 In much the same way, Harry Baur in *Shylock* (France, 1913), dir. Clement Maurice, appears first as himself and then dissolves to the character of Shylock.

10 Robert Hamilton Ball's *Shakespeare on Silent Film* (London and New York, 1968) pioneered in dispelling this perception.

11 'Shakespeare in Film, Radio and Television', in *Shakespeare: A Celebration, 1564–1616*, ed. T. J. B. Spencer (Harmondsworth and Baltimore, 1964), pp. 97–113; p. 113.

12 Robert A. Hetherington, 'The *Lears* of Peter Brook', *Shakespeare on Film Newsletter*, 6, no. 1 (1982), p. 7.

13 *King Lear* GB, 1970, pro. Michael Birkett; dir. Peter Brook; camera Henning Kristiansen, with Paul Scofield (King Lear), Irene Worth (Goneril), Jack MacGowran (Fool), Alan Webb (Gloucester), Cyril Cusack (Albany), Patrick Magee (Cornwall), Robert Lloyd (Edgar), Tom Fleming (Kent), Susan Engel (Regan), Annelise Gabold (Cordelia), Ian Hogg (Edmund), Barry Stanton (Oswald), Soren Elung-Jensen (Burgundy). b/w. 137 min.

14 Talbot Rothwell, scriptwriter for *Carry on Cleo*, GB 1965, a travesty vaguely under the influence of Shakespeare's Roman history plays, carried the Taylor joke one step further with his credit line, 'From an original idea by William Shakespeare'.

15 Normand Berlin, 'Peter Brook's Interpretation of *King Lear*: "Nothing Will Come of Nothing" ', *Literature/Film Quarterly*, 5 (1977), 299–303; p. 303.

16 William Johnson, '*King Lear* and *Macbeth*', *Film Quarterly*, 25 (1972), 41–8; p. 43.

17 Sylvia Millar, '*King Lear*', *Monthly Film Bulletin*, 38 (1971), 182–3; p. 183.

18 'Peter Brook's "Night of the Living Dead" ', *The New Yorker*, 11 December 1971, 135–7; p. 136.

19 Millar, '*King Lear*', p. 183.

20 '*Le roi Lear*', *Image et Son*, 282 (March 1974), p. 103.

21 'Shakespeare in the Movies', *New York Review of Books*, 18 (4 May 1972), 18–21; p. 19.

22 'One *King Lear* for Our Time: A Bleak Film Vision by Peter Brook', *Literature/Film Quarterly*, 4 (1976), 159–64.

23 London, 1971; rev. edn (Cranbury, NJ, 1979), pp. 136–43.

24 Microfilm copy deposited in Folger Shakespeare Library, Washington, DC.

25 Kozintsev thought the influence of Brecht somewhat overrated: 'their [i.e. directors who thought that they had been influenced by Brecht] first teacher, whether they know it or not, was [Vsevolod] Meyerhold, and the fantastic realism of Gogol and Dostoyevsky' (*Space of Tragedy*, p. 93). Meyerhold was director of Moscow's Theatre of the Revolution in the post-revolutionary era.

26 Jack J. Jorgens, *Shakespeare on Film* (Bloomington, 1977), p. 236, makes a nice distinction between the optimistic and pessimistic sides of the play that co-exist within the same text.

27 *King Lear*, USA, 1953, pro. Fred Rickey. Staged by Peter Brook, dir. Andrew McCullough; music, Virgil Thomson; with Orson Welles (King Lear), Natasha Parry (Cordelia), Arnold Moss (Albany), Bramwell Fletcher (Kent), Margaret Phillips (Regan), Beatrice Straight (Goneril), Alan Badel (Fool), Frederic Worlock (Gloucester), Scott Forbes (Cornwall) b/w, 73 min.

28 Shakespeare quotations from the *Riverside Shakespeare*, ed. G. Blakemore Evans *et al.* (Boston, 1974).

29 'Shakespeare on TV: An Optimistic Survey', *Quarterly Film, Radio and TV*, 9 (1954–5), 166–74; p. 171.

30 Marvin Rosenberg, *The Masks of King Lear* (Berkeley, 1972), p. 312. ' "Drag it" Salvini did, with failing energy; Welles would do the same . . .'

31 Quoted in Hetherington, 'The *Lears* of Peter Brook', p. 7.

32 *King Lear*, USSR 1970, dir. Grigori Kozintsev; music, Dmitri Shostakovich; trans. Boris Pasternak, c. Jonas Gricius; with Yuri Yarvet (King Lear), E. Radzins (Goneril), G. Volchek (Regan), V. Shendrikova (Cordelia), O. Dal (Fool), K. Sebris (Gloster (*sic*)), L. Merzin (Edgar), R. Adomaitis (Edmund), V. Emelyanov (Kent), A. Vokach (Cornwall), D. Banionis (Albany), A. Petrenko (Oswald), b/w, English sub-titles, 139 min.

33 *Space of Tragedy*, p. 75.

34 *Ibid.*, p. 119.

35 *Film as Film: Understanding and Judging the Movies* (London, 1972), p. 24.

36 'Shakespeare and the Russian Soul', *Drama*, 126 (1977), 12–19; p. 19.

37 E.g. Morris Carnovsky in *Literary Review*, 22 (1979), 408–32, p. 423. He speaks of 'what we might expect from a Soviet artist' in the 'heavy contrast between the rulers and the ruled'.

38 See Barbara Hodgdon, 'Kozintsev's *King Lear*: Filming a Tragic Poem', *Literature/Film Quarterly*, 5 (1977), 291–8; Nigel Andrews, '*King Lear*', *Sight and Sound*, 41 (1972), 171–2; and Alexander Anikst, 'Grigori Kozintsev's *King Lear*', *Soviet Literature*, (1971), 176–82. All express enthusiasm for the film, Hodgdon's essay perhaps most effectively. For mention of Kozintsev's appearance at Vancouver, see J. M. Welsh, 'To See it Feelingly: *King Lear* Through Russian Eyes', *Literature/Film Quarterly*, 4 (1976), 153–8; p. 154.

39 Neither the Joseph Papp production starring James Earl Jones nor the Jonathan Miller 1975 television version, which preceded the BBC production, starring Michael Hordern will be discussed here because of their current unavailability.

40 For a thoughtful analysis of Shakespeare on television, see Sheldon P. Zitner, 'Wooden O's in Plastic Boxes: Shakespeare and Television', *University of Toronto Quarterly*, 51 (1981), 1–12.

41 Brenda Davies, '*Hamlet*', *Monthly Film Bulletin*, 39 (1972), p. 163.

42 'Plays in Performance,' *Drama* (Summer 1970), 15–28; p. 24.

43 'Plays in Performance,' *Drama* (Spring 1970), 27–31; p. 30.

44 *King Lear*, GB, 1982. BBC TV/Time-Life Inc. pro. Shaun Sutton; dir. Jonathan Miller; with Michael Hordern (King Lear), Gillian Barge (Goneril), Penelope Wilton (Regan), Brenda Blethyn (Cordelia), Frank Middlemass (Fool), col. ½" VHS, 180 min.

45 Henry Fenwick, 'The Production [of *King Lear*]', in *King Lear, The BBC TV Shakespeare*, ed. Peter Alexander *et al.* (London, 1983), p. 22.

46 'TV: A No-Nonsense *King Lear*', *The New York Times* (18 Oct. 1982), p. 16.

47 *King Lear*. GB, 1983. Granada Television, prod. David Plowright; dir. Michael Elliott; with Laurence Olivier (King Lear), Colin Blakely (Kent), Anna Calder-Marshall (Cordelia), John Hurt (Fool), Leo McKern (Gloucester), Diana Rigg (Regan), Dorothy Tutin (Goneril), col. ½" VHS, or Beta, 158 min.

48 Peter Cowie, 'Olivier at 75 Returns to *Lear*', *The New York Times* (1 May 1983), Entertainment sec., 1–2.

49 'The Stone and the Oak: Olivier's TV Film of *King Lear*', *CEA Critic*, 47 (1984), 67–77. See also Frank Occhiogrosso, ' "Give Me Thy Hand": Manual Gesture in the Elliott-Olivier *King Lear*', *Shakespeare Bulletin*, 2.9 (1984), 16–19.

50 Lloyd Rose, 'Television: A Winter's Tale', *Atlantic* (Feb. 1983), 90–2; p. 92. The production combines 'genius and schlock'.

13

KUROSAWA'S SHAKESPEARE FILMS: *THRONE OF BLOOD, THE BAD SLEEP WELL*, AND *RAN*

ROBERT HAPGOOD

Throne of Blood, Akira Kurosawa's 1957 film based on *Macbeth*, is among the few transpositions of Shakespeare's dramas into other performing arts that have been widely regarded as masterpieces in their own right. Verdi's operas *Otello* and *Falstaff*, Prokofiev's *Romeo and Juliet* ballet, Tchaikovsky's *Romeo and Juliet* fantasy overture, and Mendelssohn's overture and incidental music for *A Midsummer Night's Dream* are others among that select number. Although there have been many successful film versions of Shakespeare, thus far only *Throne of Blood* has been often spoken of as a 'great film'; it has been particularly admired by other directors of Shakespeare films – Grigori Kozintsev, Peter Brook, and Peter Hall.[1] What sets these masterworks apart from other treatments of Shakespeare? To a large extent it is their sheer, intrinsic artistry. Yet their success also has to do with their relation to the Shakespearian original. On the one hand, they have their own integrity and can be enjoyed on their own terms without reference to Shakespeare: it apparently helps if their creators are of a different nationality and make no direct use of Shakespeare's own language. On the other hand, although they may take considerable liberties with the original, they are faithful in their own ways to some essence in it. This fidelity includes form as well as content. With their aid we see that there is much that is operatic about *Othello*, balletic about *Romeo and Juliet*, musical about *A Midsummer Night's Dream*. By common consent, Kurosawa in *Throne of Blood* has located something compellingly cinematic about *Macbeth*. Some of the secrets of its success can be revealed by comparison with his other films based on Shakespeare: *The Bad Sleep Well* (1960) and *Ran* (1985), themselves extraordinary motion pictures. Considering all of them together will highlight certain features of Kurosawa's general way with Shakespeare and provide a context for defining the distinctive qualities of the three films, especially the unique excellence of *Throne of Blood*.[2]

I

To begin with differences: in every way *Throne of Blood* is closer to *Macbeth* than *The Bad Sleep Well* is to *Hamlet* or *Ran* is to *King Lear*. In plot, for example, apart from the chanting chorus that provides a frame at the very beginning and end, *Throne of Blood* adds very little to its original. The chief omission, the MacDuff family subplot, makes even tighter a progression that is already tight; and very little else is left out. One of the film's strengths is that it so closely follows *Macbeth*'s compulsive progression from the initial prophecies to the final movement of the Wood. In *The Bad Sleep Well*, the film is half over before the connections to *Hamlet* begin to present themselves. They become unmistakable when the hero Nishi is at the point of taking revenge for his father's forced 'suicide'. In retrospect, one can then see earlier resemblances, and as the plot unfolds further parallels ramify.[3] But these are always surrounded by developments that have no direct Shakespearian counterparts. In contrast, it is toward the end of *Ran* that the parallels to *King Lear* become less important than they were at first. *Ran* is in general closer to its original than is *The Bad Sleep Well*, and from its opening scene of a ruler dividing his realm among his three children the Shakespearian analogies are manifest, even though the children in the film are not daughters but sons. Analogous features continue throughout, yet in the latter part they are subsumed under the overarching revenge plot of Lady Kaede, plus subplot excursions into the sufferings of Lady Sué and Tsurumaru and the manoeuvres of the rival chieftains.

The three films also differ in genre. The Japanese distinguish broadly between *jidai-geki* (period pictures) and *gendai-mono* (modern-story films). *The Bad Sleep Well* clearly belongs to the latter type. It was designed as a topical exposé of the corrupt interlocking of business and government in post-war Japan. *Throne of Blood* and *Ran* are both *jidai-geki*, but with a difference. Unlike most films of this genre, they are far from being mere 'costume dramas'. Kurosawa prides himself on his knowledge of Japanese history and culture and goes to great trouble and expense to achieve authenticity. Both films reflect that concern and hence reward the survey of their parallel cultural contexts that I am about to undertake. Yet this survey will reveal differences that add up to two distinct kinds of film.

Both films are set in the *Sengoku Jidai* or 'Age of the Country at War' (1392–1568).[4] Within that era *Ran* seems the later of the two, both in weaponry (it takes place after muskets had been introduced; only arrows are used in *Throne of Blood*) and decadence (in *Throne of Blood* violations of the samurai code of loyalty are whispered about in private; in *Ran* the degenerate times are openly acknowledged). To a lesser degree, both films also echo the other main period of civil war in Japan, the great twelfth-century struggle between the Heike and Genji clans recorded in *The Tale of the Heike*.[5] Both are influenced by medieval battle scrolls. Kurosawa studied these scrolls before shooting *Throne of Blood*. The twelfth-century 'Burning of San-Jo Palace' scroll may well have influenced the burning of the castles in *Ran*, and elsewhere in the film – just as in the scrolls – scenes of nature punctuate episodes.[6]

Both Lady Asaji in *Throne of Blood* and Lady Kaede in *Ran* have precedents from these periods, in which politically powerful women were uncommon but historically important. Asaji's unexpected pregnancy – announced just when her husband is about to name the son of his ally to be his successor – is one of the most striking of Kurosawa's departures from Shakespeare. The situation may well have been suggested by the unexpected pregnancy of Tomiko Hino (1440–96), wife of the shogun Yoshimasa. A year after Yoshimasa had given up hope of a male heir and named his younger brother to be his successor, Tomiko bore him a son, whose claim to the succession she fiercely and triumphantly maintained, thus sparking the Onin War (1467–77). Unlike Asaji and Kaede, who exercised power through their manipulation of men in power, Tomiko appears to have worked more independently, although in collaboration with her older brother, amassing a fortune through her rice speculations and usury.[7] Closer to Kurosawa's two women in this respect is Ike no Zenni (mid-twelfth century), stepmother of the priest-warrior Kiyomori Taira, who disastrously persuaded him to exile rather than execute young Yoritomo, who would later topple the house of Taira. Closest of all is Yoritomo's wife Masako Hōjō (1157–1225). After his death, with the aid of her father she took the position of shogun away from her older son and gave it to his younger brother, whose rule she then defended against various plots and insurrections. One of these was led by her father, whom she exiled with the aid of her brother. She is aptly known as the 'nun shogun'.[8]

On the whole *Ran* has many more *sengoku* associations than does *Throne of Blood*. Kurosawa has explained that its initial inspiration came not from *King Lear* but the Japanese warlord Motonari Mōri (1497–1571) and his three sons.[9] In Japan Motonari is legendary as the source of the parable that Great Lord Hidetora tells his three sons of the three arrows that may be broken when they are separated but not when they are together. Like Motonari, Hidetora rose to power by defeating two rival clans and won a famous victory against the Sué family (from which the name of Lady Sué in the film appears to derive).[10] The devastating use of firearms by Saburō's forces may well have been suggested by the Battle of Nagashino (1575), celebrated in Kurosawa's film *Kagemusha*.

In every way *Ran* is very much of its historical moment. Only in the rejection of the two defectors, who are paid off and dismissed, does the film run contrary to historical trends. For in this period turncoats were common and were usually welcomed by the opposing side.[11] Otherwise the film validly reflects those times. Even the twist Kurosawa places on the Mōri family is in keeping with the period. In an interview Kurosawa remarked on how Motonari's three sons are admired as 'paragons of virtue': 'What might their story be like, I wondered, if the sons had not been so good?'[12] One need not look far in this time to find precedent for sons who turned against their fathers. Takeda Shingen in 1541 expelled his father from the position of military governor and replaced him as head of the family; in 1566 Saito Dōsan was killed by his son. And brothers fighting brothers abound, as family after family was split by disputes over succession. Vassals deposed their lords so commonly that Japanese historians characterize this topsy-turvy period with the term *gekokujō*, 'the overturning of those on top by those below'.

Ran also has more echoes of *The Tale of the Heike* than does *Throne of Blood*. It's true that the ominous flock of birds that descend on the doomed Washizu's council chamber in *Throne of Blood* may well have flown in from *The Tale*, where a flight of waterfowl terrified and scattered the Heike forces (p. 331); so may the arrow through the neck that provides Washizu's coup de grace: *The Tale* tells of a warrior shot through the Adam's apple (p. 495). But there are a good many more such echoes in *Ran*, including references to the fox consort of the Chinese King-Yu (pp. 115–16), the rotting of heads in hot weather (p. 707), a warrior whose eye is pierced by an arrow (p. 549), a fleeing prince (p. 242) who leaves behind his treasured flute (his servant is, like Kurosawa's prince, named Tsurumaru). *The Tale* makes frequent mention of what a 'degenerate age' this is (p. 695) and occasional references to how men resemble demons (p. 552) and experience 'the first tortures of hell in this world' (p. 473), an infernal perspective that is suggested in *Throne of Blood* and insisted upon in *Ran*.

In their inner landscapes both films anticipate in this world the same region of the Buddhist hell to come, the realm of the fighting spirits, presided over by the demon Ashura, where warriors continue their destructive ways. The priest Genshin described this region in *Ōjō Yōshū* ('Essentials of Salvation') in 985:

the creatures of this realm fight and groan and cry. Their cries sound like a hundred or a thousand thunderclaps. They slash one another and their lacerated bodies are hurled down so that their crushed bones and streaming blood flow down like one huge red wave . . .[13]

Visually such sufferings were horrifyingly depicted in twelfth and thirteenth-century Scrolls of Hell.[14] Verbally there is no better evocation of this realm than the 'warrior plays' that constitute the second category of Noh drama. They take us inside the psyches of the damned and the persisting passion for battle that confines them to an afterlife of unending rage.[15]

In the published screenplay of *Ran* Kurosawa is explicit about evoking this realm.[16] He describes the sequence of battle scenes at Second Castle as a 'scroll of hell' (its 'river' of blood may have been suggested by Genshin's 'red wave') and often refers to the warriors' demonic expressions. In the film itself Hidetora tells Lady Sué that '[The Buddha] is gone from this evil world. His guardians are in exile . . . routed by the fury of Ashur'; later he flatly declares, 'This is hell, the lowest level of hell.' *Throne of Blood* is subtler. At the very moment the opening chorus chants that the hero's 'spirit walks still', the mists clear to show sulphur springs, with their association with hell. Where *Ran* sees the present moment as hell on earth, *Throne of Blood* emphasizes its persistence through the ages.

Ran and *The Bad Sleep Well* both partake deeply of the times they depict. The latter takes the documentary approach of an investigative reporter; the hardboiled journalists at the beginning keynote a prevailing point-of-view. The former is a 'chronicle history' in the Shakespearian sense, epic in scope.[17] In contrast, there is something 'out of time' about *Throne of Blood*, or, more precisely, the film creates its own time and space. Where in *Ran* the various cultural contexts are readily identifiable and separable, in *Throne of Blood* they have been transmuted into a single whole. The ingredients of this creation are historical yet their historicity is not at all so localized as *Ran*'s. As the film's designer Yoshirō Muraki has said, 'We created something which never came from any single historical period. To emphasize the psychology of the hero, driven by compulsion, we made the interiors wide with low ceilings and squat pillars to create the effect of oppression.'[18] The location of the film is more a state of mind than a place, a nightmare Shangri-la or Brigadoon. Verging on expressionism, *Throne of Blood* is more than anything else a mood piece.

The distinctive character of the three films may thus be defined in terms of the particular balances they strike in their treatment of Shakespeare and of Japanese culture. *Throne of Blood* may be further differentiated from the other two by the daring of its form and style, amounting to a redefinition of what is cinematic; as Kozintsev observes, Kurosawa 'has not been afraid to refute everything that was considered to be the basis of cinematographic art'.[19] In this redefinition the Noh drama was central; Kurosawa has explained that he was attracted to Noh in part because 'its form of expression is so far removed from that of film'.[20] The various Noh features in the film (the forest hag, the chanting chorus, drums, and shrill flute, the masklike faces, Asaji's choreography, the general who starts a dance and an all too pertinent chant at the banquet), have been thoroughly charted by commentators.[21] The connections go still deeper. The whole energy system of the film derives from the pattern of extreme containment followed by explosive release that characterizes the rhythm of Noh. Kurosawa's way of describing Noh's pervasive *jo/ha/kyū* structure as 'introduction/destruction/haste' is full of suggestion when applied to *Throne of Blood*.[22] Perhaps the deepest connection is one of perspective. Kurosawa has explained that he aspires in his directing to 'watch with a detached gaze', as Zeami the Noh playwright and theorist put it. In practical terms, he explains: 'While the cameras are rolling I rarely look directly at the actors but focus my gaze somewhere else. By doing this I sense instantly when something isn't right.'[23]

In many ways Kurosawa invites the viewer of *Throne of Blood* to 'watch with a detached gaze'. Commentators have pointed out the film's obsessive concern with a few motifs (rain, mist, strong winds, forest, castles, night), the rigorous geometry of verticals, horizontals, diagonals, and circles,[24] the renunciation of close-ups. Far from the colourful panoramic sweep of *Ran*, Kurosawa's canvas here is small, his palette ascetically restrained, his technique bold and sure. Control is all. With frank artifice, wipes indicate a lapse of time, hurrying the action forward; other situations (such as the funeral procession) are protracted. The four 'acts' are indicated by fades followed by comments by Washizu's retainers, marking in turn his accession to North Castle, his possession of Forest Castle, and finally his declining fortunes.

The resulting tone is not only detached but sardonic. In contrast to *Ran*, no tears are shed by the men in *Throne of Blood* and few by its women (we hear only the ritual mourning by the ladies-in-waiting for the deaths of the Great Lord and his Lady, the sobs of the old woman who announces that Asaji is near death, and her own mad weeping). Instead the film resounds with scornful laughter: of the forest spirits; of Washizu and Miki at how the forest labyrinth will confuse the enemy and at their own, prophesied, good fortune; of Washizu at Asaji's suspicions and of Asaji (pretendedly) at his 'drunkenness' at the banquet, of Washizu and his men at the idea that the forest might move against them. Asaji's one smile (when she tells Washizu of the dark desires she knows he harbours in his heart) is more like a rictus, as is the still more malevolent smile of the Spirit before she makes her prophecy about the forest moving. Kurosawa himself seems to mock Washizu's boast, 'Let even your thousands attack my castle!' In the very next shot he shows thousands of Washizu's adversaries on the march against him.

In style as in genre *Throne of Blood* is one of a kind.

II

Although the three films are thus quite different from one another, they share a number of common features. At this stage in his career Kurosawa had despaired of heroic solutions to his country's problems and looked abroad to Dostoevsky and Gorky as well as Shakespeare for ways to express his despair.[25] Indeed, he goes Shakespeare one better. In moral dynamics, Kurosawa consistently changes Shakespeare to emphasize the guilt of his authority figures. Unlike Duncan, the Great Lord in *Throne of Blood* came to power by murdering his master. King Hamlet was not without sin, but the hero's father in *The Bad Sleep Well* was plainly guilty of the very corporate corruption at high levels that his son is fighting against. Unlike King Lear, Hidetora's rise to power was bloody and ruthless. Nor in the course of the films is there a cleansing of the body politic or a clearcut restoration of order. Instead of the new 'spring of time' Malcolm promises, *Throne of Blood* does not make it clear how Ashizu will be replaced.[26] Indeed, Kurosawa's decision to show among the attacking forces the equivalent not only of Malcolm but of Fleance may hint at grounds for strife between the two in the future. Or will Inui, the off-camera rival chieftain, himself seize control? In *Ran* it seems certain that with Hidetora and all his sons dead, their rule will give way to a struggle between the two rival clans they had earlier kept in check. At the end of *The Bad Sleep Well* the hero has clearly died in vain. Although the executive under attack is removed from office (he bows to the telephone which transmits his removal), the higher-up from whom he takes orders remains untouched. In these corrupt worlds good impulses are ineffectual or counter-productive. Washizu's appeals to codes of trust and loyalty are demolished by Asaji's cool analyses of power politics. In *The Bad Sleep Well* well-meaning disclosures by the hero's wife and step-mother contribute to his downfall. In *Ran* Saburō's highminded attempts to rescue his father and avoid war fail completely and lead to their deaths.

In addition to these darkenings, Kurosawa plainly sees Shakespeare as a source of themes on which he can play variations. *Throne of Blood* is relatively restrained in this respect (here as elsewhere the film is closer to its original than are the other two), but it does show several patterns of *elaboration*. The forest motif is not confined as it is in Shakespeare to the final movement of Birnam Wood but figures throughout, from the opening titles, which are seen through a web of branches (the Japanese title, *The Castle of the Spider's Web* is much apter than is *Throne of Blood*). Shakespeare mentions horses that break their stalls (*Macbeth* 2.4.16); Kurosawa gives horses major significance, especially Miki's horse, which ominously is all but ungovernable before its master is murdered and whose return riderless wordlessly conveys his fate. Lady

21 Kurosawa's *Throne of Blood*. Washizu, right (Toshirō Mifune) and Miki (Minoru Chiaki) struggle to find their way to the Castle of the Spider's Web through the labyrinth-like woods

Macbeth mentions the scream of an owl at the time of the murder (2.2.15); Kurosawa makes repeated use of birds that we can see or hear. *Throne of Blood* also has an instance of *substitution*. Having cut the slaughter of the Macduff family, Kurosawa gets the effect of Washizu's bloody-mindedness by having a spirit warrior in the forest advise, 'If you would shed blood, then let it run as a river'; Washizu responds, 'I will! I will paint the entire forest!'

In *Ran* the most common variation is one of *displacement*. In it Kurosawa picks up Shakespeare's vein of polite cruelty (much fine feeling is displayed by Cornwall, Edmond, Goneril and Regan concerning the shutting of the gates on Lear and Edmond's betrayal of his father – *The Tragedy of King Lear* 2.2.470–81; 3.7.5–7) and shows it in other situations. Lady Kaede is all graciousness in inviting Hidetora to take a seat that is demeaningly below herself and her husband; she thinks it 'too cruel' to allow the beautiful head of Lady Sué (whose decapitation she has ordered) to rot in the summer heat without being preserved in salt. Often a Shakespearian feature is displaced from one character to another. Jirō, the legitimate second son, feels Edmond the bastard's envy for his older brother's primacy (1.2.15–21). Lear's crown of weeds (4.3.3–6) becomes the straw hat that Kyōami, the jester, presents to mad Hidetora, with lilies for plumes. It is Hidetora who gouges out the eyes of an enemy. Where Gloucester leapt from an imaginary cliff (4.5.42–7), Hidetora actually jumps from a high wall and lies as if dead at the bottom.

In *The Bad Sleep Well* a character named Wada can be seen as a tissue of *Hamlet* displacements. A would-be suicide, he observes his own maimed funeral rites (watching the public piety of his treacherous colleagues while listening to a tape-recording of them crowing over his downfall); later he impersonates his own ghost. The film also develops a range of themes involving elaborate deception and concealment, spying and checking-up, betrayal. These are no doubt to be expected in any revenge tragedy, yet they are notably like the particular complex to be found in *Hamlet*.

The most distinctive hallmark of Kurosawa's general approach to Shakespeare is his constant pull toward the graphic, the immediate, the concrete, the simple, the extreme. These tendencies are true of Kurosawa's whole approach to cinema. In *Something Like an Autobiography* he recounts a formative experience he had while preparing his first filmscript. Following closely the story he was adapting, he had its hero see an edict on a signboard and report it to his comrades. When Kurosawa's mentor, the director Kajirō Yamamoto, revised the script, he commented that this scene was 'fine for a novel' but 'too weak' for a film; he had the hero 'uproot the signboard and arrive carrying it on his shoulders. He plants it in front of his comrades and says, "Look at this!"' Kurosawa concludes: 'I was awed.' (102–3) In turn Kurosawa has passed on Yamamoto's doctrine to his own associates. Shinobu Hashimoto, who with others collaborated with Kurosawa on the scripts for *Throne of Blood* and *The Bad Sleep Well*, has recalled: 'Everything he says is clear and particular and concrete. Everything that is meaningful and strong – that is Kurosawa. How much have I not learned from him about real and strong expression?'[27]

Again and again in his Shakespeare films, Kurosawa himself applies this lesson. There is an especially striking case in point in *Ran*. In the screen play Kurosawa had a messenger *inform* Hidetora that his sons' forces are attacking him (scene 59). In the film Kurosawa has Hidetora hear sounds that wake him from sleep, rush up to a lookout, and *see* the attacking forces. Only then does a messenger confirm who they are. In *Throne of Blood*, Washizu's heroic exploits are not reported after the battle is over as are Macbeth's (1.2) but while the battle is taking place; his promotion is not reported by emissaries (1.3) but conferred directly by the Great Lord. Lady Asaji does not, like Lady Macbeth, simply talk of braining a child (1.7.54–8); she bears a child who is still-born. Macbeth speaks of scorpions in his mind (3.2.37); Washizu wears a centipede as his insignia. In *The Bad Sleep Well* Nishi, Kurosawa's Hamlet, marries his Ophelia, as part of his revenge-plot against his Claudius, her father. In *Ran* Hidetora's youngest child is not merely reticent like Cordelia but deliberately insulting, and his rebellious children not only shut their father out but join in attacking the castle he is occupying and burn it down.

Repeatedly, Kurosawa pushes Shakespeare to extremes, reflecting his general feeling that 'extreme manifestations contain all that is most true to life'.[28] Where Hamlet dies from the poisoned foil, Nishi is left in a car to be demolished by a train. Where Lear threatens to strike the Fool with his whip (1.4.109), Hidetora actually does strike Kyōami; where Kent trips up Goneril's man (1.4.85), Hidetora himself kills his first son's retainer; where Goneril and Regan are drawn to Edmund by simple lust, Lady Kaede's seduction of Jirō is sado-masochistic, made worse by her traditional white mourning robes.[29] In *Throne of Blood* the contrast Shakespeare draws between the coldly calculating, obdurate wife and her more sensitive, wavering husband is pushed to choreographic ultimates. Physically, Asaji is virtually immobile while, mentally, she never stops forging ahead toward her goals; in contrast, Washizu's mental turmoil is reflected in the constant movement of his body and face, as though he is about to burst with pent-up energy. Kurosawa pays a high price for this formulation of their relationship. Washizu lacks Macbeth's imaginative sensitivity and moral ambiguity (Asaji bears most of the guilt).[30] But it does release the extraordinary energy, as played by Toshirō Mifune, that is the film's most compelling feature.

At times these tendencies can make for an excess of explicitness concerning the hero's moments of moral recognition and conversion. In *The Bad Sleep Well* Kurosawa plucks out the heart of Hamlet's mystery. Instead of the strange inertia that possesses Shakespeare's hero and mystifies even himself, Nishi faces a clearcut dilemma between his love for his wife and his hatred for her father. Instead of Shakespeare's gradual widening of the implications of Hamlet's quest, Nishi is given a single scene where he realizes the destructiveness of his hatred and where his motives of personal revenge are explicitly converted to a desire for social justice. In *Ran*, too, Kurosawa is less willing than Shakespeare to give a central and decisive place to what is finally inexplicable in human conduct. Puzzled by the virulence of Goneril and Regan toward their father,[31] Kurosawa makes Hidetora a bloody tyrant, thus exaggerating his faults beyond the subtler manifestations of self-centredness that underlie King Lear's pride and folly. Instead of Lear's zig-zagging progress from self-pity to self-condemnation, Hidetora's realization of his wrong-doing and of his son's love comes abruptly and all at once after he totters, mad, out of his burning castle.[32] In *Throne of Blood*, on the other hand, Washizu's moment of recognition is confined to a single exclamation 'Fool!' followed once again by scornful laughter – or is it for once mixed with grief? – after he learns that his wife is near death and their child was still-born. If he repents of his previous murders he shows no sign of it. Uniquely combining Zeami's reserve with Yamamoto's immediacy, Kurosawa leaves much undisclosed about this pair. What sensitivities lie behind Asaji's cool rationalism? Something causes her, at first, to turn her head away from the direction of the murder, to start at seeing Miki's assassin as if she were seeing Miki's ghost, finally to go mad. But Kurosawa chooses to do no more than hint at her hidden vulnerabilities. What dark motives lie unspoken behind Washizu's inarticulateness? The forest spirit, Asaji, and Miki all seem confident that they are there, but he never confides them to us. It is as though the couple wear inner masks.

III

To understand the power of such maskings there is no better guide than Junichirō Tanizaki's profound essay 'In Praise of Shadows' (1933).[33] In it he laments the passing of a time when the magic and mystery of shadows was appreciated in Japan as opposed to the encroachments of the antiseptically 'clean, well-lighted' look of the west. Traditionally, he observes, the Orient has valued the religious, aesthetic, and erotic stimulus of obscurity – the patinas of age, the lustre of lacquer against a background of darkness, the variation of heavy and light shadows in a traditional room, the way darkness wrapped around a beautiful woman in 'the sleeves of her kimono, the folds of her skirt, wherever a hollow invited' (p. 35). All these appeals derive from the readiness of Orientals 'to immerse ourselves in the darkness and there discover its own particular beauty' (p. 31). Literature and the arts offer the last hope:

> I would call back at least for literature this world of shadows we are losing. In the mansion called literature I would have the eaves deep and the walls dark, I would push back into the shadows the things that come forward too clearly. (p. 42)[34]

Kurosawa in *Throne of Blood* shares with Tanizaki this readiness to immerse himself in darkness. But to Tanizaki the shadows are a source of tranquillity whereas to Kurosawa they have an edge of danger and are a prime source of the film's dynamism. Again and again its characters are confronted by a dense fog, a huge closed gate, a tangled wood. Tapers in hand, Washizu's retainers must open the sliding door of the forbidden chamber where the traitor died and enter its darkness. The film's thematic action is to penetrate what is concealed or obscure.[35]

A degree of progress can be made in this effort, yet the resulting clarifications are usually partial and never secure. Lost in the wood, Washizu and Miki feel that they must be enchanted; they charge ahead as if into battle, Miki with his spear couched, Washizu shooting arrows. They seem to break through the spell since they find the spirit in her hut. At first her voice is no more than a hum, but it becomes intelligible, Washizu opens the latticed door, and the prophecies are delivered. When the spirit vanishes, the two warriors move through the hut, which in turn vanishes, to discover the pile of helmeted skulls and bones. Their efforts have brought them a series of revelations. And yet far from being immediately released from the labyrinth, they remain lost in the fog, seemingly interminably.

Eventually they find the castle. But soon Washizu confronts a still more threatening obscurity concerning the motives and intentions of the Great Lord and Miki. Washizu, who thought he knew the trails through the wood, feels confident in his trust in the two men. It is Asaji who takes the lead in trying to penetrate what may be concealed. Her fears that Miki will betray the prophecies to the Great Lord and may already have done so appear to be confirmed when reports come to them of the Great Lord's forces approaching. To Washizu's relief, this then appears to have been a false alarm, as the Great Lord is reported to be on a hunting trip. Yet the apparent clarification begins to fade when the Lord reveals that he is not really engaged in a hunting trip but a foray against his enemy. And it fades further when the Lord names Washizu to head the attack while Miki protects the Forest Castle. Washizu at first takes this as evidence of the Lord's regard until Asaji warns him that by putting Washizu at risk the Lord might be ridding himself of a potential rival while rewarding Miki's treachery.

After the assassination, Miki's intentions at first seem as impenetrable as the gate to Forest Castle. They are gradually disclosed. First his rejection of the Great Lord's son is shown by the gate's being left shut, followed by one arrow shot at him and his companion, then a shower of them. When Washizu arrives, the gate again remains threateningly closed until, at Asaji's instigation, the Great Lord's casket arrives and the long slow funeral procession enters the castle. They are met by Miki who silently turns his horse to ride side-by-side with Washizu. Only after they have gone some distance does Miki offer his support to Washizu for the succession. Yet the apparent clarity is then again undercut by Asaji's assured pronouncement that Miki has not acted – as Washizu liked to think – out of friendship.

That this pattern is not confined to the principals may be seen when, much later, another apparent threat is apparently explained away yet lingers. The lookout from Washizu's castle is at first alarmed by the sound of chopping wood but then reassured by another guard who thinks they are making stakes. In retrospect we may realize that these were the sounds of preparations to make the forest move.

Washizu's efforts to reach Asaji at the end are repeatedly obstructed. His attempted incursion into the women's quarters is blocked by a kneeling old woman. When he finally does go to Asaji she is at first screened from his (and our) sight by her robes hanging on a rack. When at last their encounter does occur, he cries her name and grabs her hand, which she resists; yet he still is not able to reach her since she has withdrawn utterly into madness.

At times both Washizu and Asaji find themselves on the border of hallucination and paranoia. We like Washizu can at first see Miki's ghost; yet when we can see that it is no longer there, Washizu continues to slash his sword at emptiness. Similarly Asaji keeps washing her hands in a 'bowl' even after Washizu in frustration has knocked the real bowl away.

The audience too is very much involved in trying to penetrate obscurities. We repeatedly find ourselves peering through tangled branches, straining to make out dim figures through a mist, staring into the darkness of a corridor, pondering what lies behind a masklike face (the staring eyes of Washizu and Asaji scarcely blink). We never know whether Asaji's suspicious fears are true or false. The Chorus's chant at the beginning and end would seem to provide thematic clarification. Yet its condemnation of pride and ambition doesn't fit Washizu so much as his wife; his problems come chiefly from weakness and fear. And the Chorus's moral world of retributive justice is contradicted by the Spirit's nihilistic song of futility, which seems no less authoritative, though itself cryptically elliptical.

In places we are obliged to question the reliability of our own senses: Washizu and Miki talk of having been in the wood when all we have seen is mist, no trees. They say that they can see the castle, but again all we can see at that moment is mist. Can that dark stain that Asaji sees on the floor after the assassination be blood? At the beginning it is disconcerting that the site marker for the castle is some distance through the mist from where we see the castle itself. The end is even more disorienting. We see the castle while the Chorus declares the scene 'desolate', and the marker appears to be much closer to the castle than before – and on the reverse side from where it was in the beginning.

Hell is indeed murky. Of course there are shadows in *Macbeth* as well. Questions linger about Macbeth's motivations, the degree to which human free will and supernatural influences control events, what finally happens to Fleance. The hero dies off-stage. Darkness dominates. In *Throne of Blood* this atmosphere is further elaborated. It is of the essence that the film begins and ends in mist. A degree of clarification is achieved. Washizu's 'fame is known' at the end, as it was not at the beginning. Like Asaji the film disappears into utter darkness, to emerge with a wine that will prove fatal. We come to see how the two of them have been doomed to doom themselves – the film's deepest thematic resemblance to *Macbeth*. Yet finally there is no release: 'still his spirit walks' amid mist and shadows.

Notes

1 Grigori Kozintsev, *Shakespeare: Time and Conscience* (New York, 1966), p. 29; Geoffrey Reeves, 'Shakespeare on Three Screens: Peter Brook Interviewed by Geoffrey Reeves', *Sight and Sound*, 34 (1965), 66–70; Peter Hall, *Sunday Times* (26 January 1969). Among critics, J. Blumenthal, '*Macbeth* into Throne of Blood', *Sight and Sound*, 34 (1965), 190–5 declares that 'the film is a masterpiece in its own right' (p. 190). Noel Burch, *To the Distant Observer: Form and Meaning in the Japanese Cinema* (Berkeley and Los Angeles, 1979) particularly admires the film's 'geometry' (pp. 310–17). A contrary view is taken by David Desser, *The Samurai Films of Akira Kurosawa* (Ann Arbor, 1983); he feels that the film stands 'outside of Japan's main stream' in its 'lack of humanity' (pp. 70–5).

2 In interviews Kurosawa has made it clear that he regards only *Throne of Blood* as an 'adaptation' of Shakespeare; however, his restriction of the term to a version that is very close to its original is narrower than that in general usage. Michael Healy, 'Kurosawa's long answer said a lot', *Denver Post* (Sunday, 6 Oct. 1985), p. 11; Peter Grilli, 'Kurosawa Directs a Cinematic *Lear*', *New York Times* (Sunday, 15 Dec. 1985), p. H1, 17.

3 In 'Kurosawa's *Hamlet*: Samurai in Business Dress', *Shakespeare on Film Newsletter* (Dec. 1990) p. 6, Marion D. Perret surveys many of these parallels.

4 George Sansom, *A History of Japan 1334–1615* (Stanford, 1961) and the relevant items in the *Kodansha Encyclopedia of Japan*, 9 vols. (Tokyo, 1983).

5 *The Tale of the Heike*, trans. Hiroshi Kitagawa and Bruce T. Tsuchida (Tokyo, 1975).

6 Ana Laura Zambrano, '*Throne of Blood*: Kurosawa's *Macbeth*', *Literature/Film Quarterly*, 2 (1974), 262–74, considers cultural backgrounds that may be extended to *Ran* as well. Unaccountably, this article misspells Kamakura as Kakamura, an error perpetuated by other scholars who have drawn on it. In *Emakimono: The Art of the Japanese Painted Hand-Scroll*, trans. J. Maxwell Brownjohn (London, 1959), Dietrich Seckel analyses the style of the scrolls; his discussions of 'narrative method' (pp. 43–6) and 'space-time continuity' (pp. 58–66) are especially relevant to Kurosawa's film-making.

7 Sansom, *A History*, pp. 190, 220, 229–30. Similarly, Yodogimi (1567?–1615) unexpectedly bore a son to Hideyoshi Toyotomi shortly after he had named his nephew as successor.

8 A revenge motive such as Lady Kaede's may have been suggested by Junichirō Tanizaki's novella set in the 1550s, *The Secret History of Lord Musashi* (1931–2). Its heroine, whose servant is named Kaede, has much in common with Lady Kaede. She too was forced to marry into the clan that destroyed her father; she too takes revenge by conniving against her husband in such a way as to disgrace him and destroy his clan.

9 Grilli, 'Kurosawa Directs', p. 17.

10 Sansom, *A History*, pp. 234–5.

11 Sansom, *A History*, p. 91.

12 Grilli, 'Kurosawa Directs', p. 17.

13 A. K. Reischauer, 'Genshin's Ōjō Yōshū: Collected Essays on Birth into Paradise', *Transactions of the Asiatic Society of Japan*, Second Series, vii (1930), p. 50.

14 In the Kadokawa Shoten *Japanese Scroll Paintings* series, volume 7, edited by Saburo Ienaga, is devoted to 'Scrolls of Hells, Scrolls of Hungry Ghosts and Scrolls of Diseases' (Tokyo, 1976). Volume 9, 'Kitano Tenjin Engi Emaki' (Tokyo, 1977), edited by Toyomune Minamoto, includes a plate (34) vividly depicting 'The World of Fighting Spirits, one of the Six Worlds of Reincarnation'.

15 Thomas Hare, *Zeami's Style* (Stanford, 1986), Chapter 5, discusses 'The Martial Mode' in general.

16 Akira Kurosawa, *Ran* (Boston, 1986).

17 Brian Parker, '*Ran* and the Tragedy of History', *University of Toronto Quarterly*, 55, 4 (1986), 412–23, p. 416.

18 Donald Richie, *The Films of Akira Kurosawa*, rev. edn with additional material by Joan Miller (Berkeley, 1984), p. 213.

19 Grigori Kozintsev, *King Lear: The Space of Tragedy*, trans. Mary Mackintosh (London, 1977), p. 11.

20 Akira Kurosawa, *Something Like an Autobiography* (New York, 1982), p. 147.

21 The best insight comes from an interview with Kurosawa himself, quoted in Roger Manvell, *Shakespeare and the Film* (New York, 1979), pp. 103–4. The hostile appositeness of the courtier's banquet chant is no accident. Identifiable by his grey, handlebar moustache, he later sees the incursion of birds as a bad omen and demands of Washizu as his men turn against him, 'Who killed his lordship?' Stylistically, the Noh elements in *Ran* are relatively superficial and parodic, as when Kyōami puts mad Hidetora's vision into words, intoning and dancing his version of a passage from the Noh play *Funa Benkei* (*The Noh Drama*, Rutland and Tokyo, 1955, p. 180) that reads:

> The Heike clan
> Defying gods and buddhas
> Committed untold sins and crimes
> And were by Heaven chastised
> And drowned beneath the waves, –
> I see now the erstwhile emperor and his lords
> Rising in swarms out of the sea.

In Kyōami's version this becomes:

> The wonder of it!
> I see on this withered plain
> All those I destroyed –
> A phantom army,
> One by one they come floating,
> Rising before me.

22 Kurosawa, *Autobiography*, p. 193.

23 Kurosawa, *Autobiography*, p. 195.

24 E. A. Davies, *Filming Shakespeare's Plays* (Cambridge, 1988), pp. 156–63.

25 Stephen Prince, *The Warrior's Camera*, (Princeton, 1991), p. xix.

26 E. Pearlman, '*Macbeth* on Film: Politics', *Shakespeare Survey 39* (1987), pp. 67–74, p. 72.

27 Richie, *Films*, p. 214. For a translation into English of a film script of *Throne of Blood* see Hisae Niki, *Shakespeare in Translation in Japanese Culture* (Tokyo, 1984).

28 Kozintsev, *King Lear*, p. 13.

29 As extreme as the film of *Ran* can be, Kurosawa's screenplay for it was in many respects even more so; see my note '*Ran* from Screenplay to Film', *Shakespeare Bulletin*, 10, 3 (1992), pp. 37–8.

30 John Gerlach, 'Shakespeare, Kurosawa, and *Macbeth*: A Response to J. Blumenthal', *Literature/Film Quarterly*, 1, 4 (1973), 352–8, pp. 357–8.

31 Grilli, 'Kurosawa Directs', p. 1.

32 Healy, 'Kurosawa's Long Answer', p. 10 quotes Kurosawa's eloquent explication of this realization.

33 Junichirō Tanizaki, *In Praise of Shadows*, trans. Thomas J. Harper and Edward G. Seidensticker (New Haven, 1977).

34 Kurosawa's *Dodesukaden* (1972) contains a character who, like Tanizaki, dreams of an imaginary ideal house; he remarks: 'The Japanese prefer soft light to bright sunshine. We like the shade more than the sun.'

35 Peter Donaldson, *Shakespearean Films/Shakespearean Directors* (Boston, 1991) observes how often 'we see the action through a screen or curtain', including balustrades and railings, barred windows, a rack of arrows (pp. 74–5). Treating the film as 'an allegory of cinematic practice' (p. 89), he finds that such 'screens' serve as a self-reflexive 'double for the movie screen and a reminder of its interposition between the spectators and the action' (p. 76). This seems to me far-fetched. The 'screens' do distance the observer at first, I would agree; but the film's characteristic dynamic is to move our vision past such barriers.

14

MACBETH ON FILM: POLITICS

E. PEARLMAN

Each of the three important directors – Welles, Polanski, and Kurosawa – who attempted to recreate *Macbeth* on the screen has had to come to terms with the play's reverence for monarchy. Despite idolatrous claims that Shakespeare was not of an age but for all time, the royal play of *Macbeth* unabashedly celebrates a semi-divine monarch in terms specific to the first years of Stuart absolutism. King Duncan is thoroughly paternal, compassionate, and regal. Of him even devilish Macbeth testifies that he 'hath borne his faculties so meek, hath been / So clear in his great office, that his virtues / Will plead like angels, trumpet-tongu'd, against / The deep damnation of his taking-off' (1.7.17–20).[1] *Macbeth*'s politics are cyclical, and the play cannot conclude until the pure and untainted Malcolm, Duncan's son and the usurper's successor, invites home 'our exil'd friends abroad / That fled the snares of watchful tyranny' (5.9.32–3), and, invoking the 'grace of Grace', sets out to be invested at Scone. The play's satisfaction with the traditional order, though severely tested by the reign of the tyrant, is confirmed when a second exemplary monarch succeeds his father.

Shakespeare expands on the contentment with divine or semi-divine monarchy in two interpolated episodes. Both appear in the difficult but elegant scene in which the play temporarily escapes the witch-dominated claustrophobia of Scotland for redemptive England. In the initial passage, Malcolm first confesses to a variety of monstrous sins, then immediately reverses himself to assert his purity. He claims that he has pretended villainy only to test Macduff's devotion to virtuous rule. The scene is designed so that Malcolm may extol, in a parade of abstractions which sacrifices poetry to panegyric,

> The king-becoming graces,
> As Justice, Verity, Temp'rance, Stableness,
> Bounty, Perseverance, Mercy, Lowliness,
> Devotion, Patience, Courage, Fortitude.
> (4.3.11–14)

Shakespeare has digressed from the principal action of the play in order to evoke a monarchic ideal which has been lost or beclouded during the reign of the tyrant. A second episode in the same scene celebrates (some suppose for a specific command performance) the thaumaturgic King Edward, who touches for the evil. Malcolm reports on a miracle he has seen with his very own eyes:

> How he solicits Heaven,
> Himself best knows; but strangely-visited people,
> All swoln and ulcerous, pitiful to the eye,
> The mere despair of surgery, he cures;
> Hanging a golden stamp about their necks
> Put on with holy prayers; and 'tis spoken,
> To the succeeding royalty he leaves
> The healing benediction.   (4.3.149–56)

The 'succeeding royalty', as a Jacobean audience would well know, includes King James himself, a putative descendant of Banquo and a healer of scrofula. These two excrescent episodes are included only to clarify the play's royal bias.

Macbeth assumes that misgovernment enters the community not because of defects in the system of monarchy, but at the behest of agents of darkness. The kingdom has prospered under Duncan and will again see good days under Malcolm. The reign of Macbeth is foul but aberrant. In the end Scotland regains its good health and the play ends on an optimistic note. Even though there is always the danger that kingship may degenerate into tyranny, in the world of *Macbeth* monarchy remains the only conceivable form of government.

Although monarchy is a relic of the past, the acquisition and disposition of power is of eternal concern. Indifferent to the politics of absolutism, modern interpreters of *Macbeth* inevitably represent political ideas which are more germane to our century than to Shakespeare's. Orson Welles unsuccessfully labours to strip *Macbeth* of its political content. He eliminates the episodes crucial to a theory of monarchy and reduces both Duncan and Malcolm to ciphers. To fill the gap, he substitutes an allegorized conflict (as his own sonorous voice pronounces in a didactic voice-over prologue) between 'agents of chaos, priests of hell and magic . . . [and] christian law and order'. The film's principal iconic device opposes the spindly forked twigs of the witches – a symbol of their demonism – to the crucifixes of the newly converted Scots. The overthrow of Macbeth is achieved not so much by the march of Birnam Wood as by a moving forest of Celtic crosses. Morality-play elements are clearly embodied in Welles's pedestrian 'Holy Father' – a personage conjured up of shards stolen from four of Shakespeare's minor characters. Welles even goes so far as to invent a primitive but obtrusive ceremony in which the Father leads the multitude in abjuring 'Satan and all his works'. The priest – unfortunately a trifle malevolent and greasy for the moral weight he is asked to bear – is killed when Macbeth's pagan spear pierces his heart. In spite of such murky or inexplicable moments, Welles strives valiantly to minimize politics and emphasize religion.

In defiance of this intent, the film inadvertently generates a rudimentary political vision of its own. By concentrating so exclusively on Macbeth (a devotion which shadows Welles's own achievement as producer, director, scriptwriter, costumer and principal player), the film ruthlessly subordinates all other interests to his, and turns the play into an exploration of both dictatorship and the cult of personality. Huge Macbeth dominates the foreground of innumerable frames of this egocentric production. Other characters, petty men in comparison to Welles's colossus, are pushed into corners or confined to the margins of the frame. When Macbeth encounters the witches for the second time, the camera locates him as a speck in the middle of a distant heath (or soundstage), then tracks him with single-minded intensity until the entire frame is filled with his distorted shape. Except for the dominating presence of Macbeth, the film allows little but the anarchy of faceless masses, from whom (it is presumed) no alternative government could possibly arise.

Attempting to exclude politics, Welles engendered a film in which Shakespeare's poles of monarchy and tyranny have been replaced by a right-wing world view which can admit nothing other than dictatorship or disorder. It is no surprise that he should see the world in these terms. Welles had already demonstrated his simultaneous attraction and repulsion from the Übermensch in a number of films, the most familiar of which is Citizen Kane. He again wrestles with proto-fascism in this 1948 Macbeth. In it, he is both (as Macbeth) the embodiment of the wicked dictator and (as director) the creator of the civilization that bulwarks us against that horror. In his hands, Macbeth becomes a parable of fascism narrowly averted. Yet no more than Shakespeare can Welles imagine an alternative to absolute power, and when, at the end of the film, the camera grants us one last look at its papier-mâché castle, it leaves a Scotland in which the regime of Macbeth has been overthrown, but the threat of dictatorship still looms.

At the end of the original Macbeth, Shakespeare's confidence in monarchy remained steadfast. Orson Welles is indifferent to monarchy and fascinated by an inchoate but primitive Christianity. He is repelled by the fascism he has figured forth, but cannot find his way to a convincing moral or political alternative.[2]

Welles's version of Macbeth was influenced by the bleak events of the 1930s and forties. Roman Polanski's contact with repressive regimes has been more intimate. Displaced by the Nazis as a child, he has been in voluntary exile from Polish communism for most of his adult life. He has said that, in his *Macbeth* (1971), the superfluous brutality of the hired killers who invade Macduff's castle at Fife recalls an SS intrusion into his own home during the Second World War. If Welles creates a film in which religion is central and politics inadvertent, Polanski, whose vision is even more despairing, offers a *Macbeth* in which both Christianity and monarchy are deliberately and systematically replaced by satanism.

Shakespeare depicted a world in which dark-age mythology was overlain and perhaps even superseded by Christian morality. Polanski attempts to purge *Macbeth* of its Christianity and at the same time to amplify elements of the supernatural or uncanny. The only specific Christian reference is fleeting and irrelevant – when Fife is ravaged a huge wooden structure in the shape of a cross momentarily appears in flames. The film is otherwise without Christian content. In order to salvage a dark-age setting, Polanski even falls into the anachronism of juxtaposing late medieval fortifications and armaments to neolithic religion. While Welles imagines a ceremony in which the multitude forsake pagan religion, Polanski invents a rite of coronation in which, within a ring of cardboard menhirs, Macbeth himself is lifted aloft on an improbably weightless circular stone. Such legitimate claim to kingship as Macbeth possesses seems to derive from this pseudo-druidic ceremonial. Polanski's Scots are on the whole depicted as a spiritually primitive population ripe for invasion by demons.

Stripped of Christian comfort, Scottish civilization is primarily composed of two antithetical secular elements. On the surface, the Scottish populace is depicted as healthy and prosperous. Macbeth and his wife are picture-book handsome, while Duncan looks like nothing so much as the King of Hearts. Macduff is strong and virile; Lady Macduff, in her one brief scene at Fife, a model of maternal solicitude. Seyton is a reliable soldier, the physician a responsible tradesman. Even members of the subordinate classes are healthy and attractive. When Duncan visits Macbeth's castle, Polanski lavishes a great deal of attention on preparations for the feast. Well-fed servants bustle about sweeping up and arranging the sleeping quarters. The household is apparently democratic – Lady Macbeth herself helps shake out the mattresses and strew the rushes. At the feast itself, the frame is filled with bright colours, cheerful servants, and the generous participation of musicians and singers. Unlike Welles's world, which is menacing and brooding, or Kurosawa's spare and joyless universe, Polanski's world is characterized by song, dance, and even a degree of joy. Yet there is a sinister underside to this apparently prospering community. It is permeated by the gratuitous violence for which Polanski has become notorious. The film takes as its text Macbeth's 'I am in blood / Stepped in so far, that should I wade no more, / Returning were as tedious as go o'er'; its catalogue of bloody horrors does not require rehearsal here. Polanski's Scotland, whether under the rule of Duncan or the usurper, is as brutal as it is beautiful.

To the opposition of natural prosperity and natural cruelty, the film adds a third and dominant note – the ugliness and power of the demonic. The two aged witches in the opening scene are hideous, the younger one pocked and verrucose. Their collection of enchanted objects is even fouler to the eye than Shakespeare's list of ingredients to the ear. The massed ugliness of the naked witches in their cave is an imaginative expansion of the misogyny of the original play. The world of *Macbeth* is almost perfectly Manichean. Polanski has devised a population which is natively attractive (though violent and irreligious) but prey to a powerful and supernaturally sanctioned cult.

The only gods who matter in this *Macbeth* are the demons. They control (or seem to control) the actions of men. In the strong opening moments of the film, the witches bury a number of objects on a sandy beach, most prominently a severed arm and hand with a knife in its grasp. A few moments later a bloody battle takes place on the spot – at the command of the witches, it would seem. These witches are not fantastical; they are exactly what they seem. They do not disappear 'into the air', as do Shakespeare's fiends, but into an underground cavern. Their power overwhelms both religion and monarchy. While government and other human institutions are fragile, witchcraft is perpetual. In Polanski's film, the demonic has penetrated to the core of Scottish society and displaced all other forms of power. As a result, even Macbeth's acceptance of the prophecy, a subject of troubled soliloquy in Shakespeare's play, offers only the slightest moral qualms to Polanski. Macbeth commits himself to the witches at their first meeting when he lies to Banquo and announces that the witches have simply disappeared. While Shakespeare acknowledges the witches' power, he never forgets that goodness and truth are also native to mankind. In Polanski's version of *Macbeth*, human political institutions are regularly subordinated to demonic power.

The penetration of evil into this world is revealed by one of Polanski's principal alterations of Shakespeare's text – the change in the character of Rosse. Rosse figures in the revised plot in a number of places (he is the shadowy Third Murderer, for example), and is one of the agents by which the politics of the film is defined. When he is not granted Macduff's title after aiding in the destruction of Fife, he deserts Macbeth to join the fugitives. In the film's concluding moments, it is Rosse who picks up Macbeth's fallen crown and presents it to Malcolm. This is of the greatest political significance, for when the corrupt and venal Rosse handles so important a symbolic object he contaminates it. In Shakespeare's play, the crown is divine. In Polanski's film, it is a gift to the new king by a murderer and a machiavel. Malcolm had originally been conceived of as an 'innocent lamb'; in this film, he is just another politician, tainted by both his hench-men and his own ambition.

The climax of the film is the prolonged and undignified tussle between Macbeth and Macduff. Where tradition demands a heroic duel between superb warriors, Polanski offers a brawl which borders on farce. In Polanski's version, Macbeth does not lose because he had been betrayed by the equivocation of the fiends, nor Macduff win because the prophecy is fulfilled. Macduff's victory is not inevitable, but accidental. At the point of exhaustion, he strikes a lucky blow and happens to impale his opponent. Shakespeare's confidence in the triumph of justice has been transformed into our favourite contemporary cliché – that all events are merely accidents of an indifferent universe.

The supersession of the demonic over the divine is a reiterated theme, but for those members of the audience who might possibly have missed it, Polanski provides an unequivocal and unsubtle epilogue. Donalbain, Malcolm's brother, distinguished by his jealous glare and awkward limp, heads for the lair of the witches. He will commit himself to them and attempt to displace the reigning monarch. Just as the film began with the witches, so does it end. While Shakespeare's cycle is from one legitimate king to the next, Polanski's is from demon to demon.

In Welles's *Macbeth*, the alternative to monarchy is anarchy; in Polanski's version, the alternative is diabolism. Welles's characters are prey to their basest characteristics. Polanski's version is even bleaker, and offers even less hope for a successful polity. In his world there is no reason to build political institutions, since they are all subordinated to a powerful and uncontrollable evil. It is a remarkably pessimistic view of the world, antithetical in almost all respects to Shakespeare's.[3]

Neither Welles nor Polanski places a great deal of confidence in man's political capacity. Kurosawa's *Throne of Blood* (1957) represents politics in a far different light. At the end of his film, the question of royal succession is deliberately left unresolved, and the throne of the fallen usurper remains unclaimed. While Shakespeare offers us a pure Malcolm and Polanski a compromised one, Kurosawa breaks with tradition and precedent and brings his film to a conclusion without even bothering to install a new monarch. Instead, he distracts our attention from the problem of succession by focusing on the fall of Washizu (Macbeth).

No viewer can forget one of the most remarkable sequences in film – that in which Washizu is assassinated by his own soldiers. Isolated on the balcony from

Mifune?.

which he has been haranguing his troops, he becomes the target of innumerable arrows. A final arrow pierces his larynx and the soundtrack becomes preternaturally silent. Washizu tumbles down a flight of wooden steps, and, still attempting to draw his sword, gapes at the camera for a long moment before collapsing. The scene is very powerful and creates a great impression of finality. But contrary to the memory of most audiences, the death of Washizu is not the last event in the film. *Throne of Blood* can be thought of as ending three times, and Washizu's death as only the first of these. The third and final conclusion is, of course, the reprise of the chant with which the film began – the lament for the ambition that leads only to death. The chorus distances the events of *Throne of Blood* by placing them somewhere in an unspecified past, and turns the inset story into a parable in which Washizu becomes the type of the ambitious man. Yet between Washizu's grotesque death and the moment the chorus begins to sing, still another 'ending' takes place on the screen. For not more than two or three seconds, the audience is returned to the perimeter of Forest Castle to catch a brief glimpse of the attacking forces who have found their way through the natural labyrinth of the forest. They have covered themselves and their battle wagons with boughs and branches and are poised for an assault. But Kurosawa withholds the satisfaction of a climactic and conclusive battle and cuts directly and precipitously to the distancing chorus. The event which resolved the earlier films, and which all versions of *Macbeth* have traditionally offered – the battle and the crowning of a new monarch – is simply omitted. Kurosawa has frustrated our natural desire for closure. A battle at this moment would be out of place, for Kurosawa has rearranged the order of events, and Washizu has already been slain. By abandoning the story just at the moment of the assault, Kurosawa does not have to decide who should succeed to the lordship of Forest Castle, and therefore sidesteps the conventional political problems raised by *Macbeth*. When he leaves Forest Castle without a master, Kurosawa forces us to think about its social and political problems in a new way. Unlike Shakespeare's *Macbeth*, which invests monarchy with the potential for justice and morality, *Throne of Blood* does not contain the seeds of a healthy polity within its ruling élite. On the contrary, Kurosawa portrays a community so defective that it must be transformed root and branch before a legitimate government can be installed.

The distinguishing marks of the society of *Throne of Blood* are inequity, corruption, and frigidity of personal relationship. The gap between the feudal lords and the common people is so great that it often seems as though we are dealing as much with two species as with two classes. The members of the ruling élite rarely acknowledge the existence of the subordinate classes. In the occasional instance when circumstances require communication, intercourse is stylized, formal, and stilted. When messengers bring news, as they do in the opening sequence, they prostrate themselves fearfully before the generals. At one point the Lord of Forest Castle makes a surprise visit to Washizu. There is a long shot from an elevated point of view of peasants working in a field. (This may be the sole evidence of an economic base to a society totally preoccupied by war, feuds, and dynastic squabbles.) The peasants are not seen as individuals and the camera treats them rather as objects than as people. After a few seconds, a line of horses makes its way down a path while peasants on both sides of the row humbly bow their heads. The visual statement of the distance between warriors and peasants is forcefully made. On the whole, power is the monopoly of a very few, and it is used only for the benefit of those who possess it. The society of *Throne of Blood* is also deeply corrupt. Unlike *Macbeth*, where the witches invade a basically healthy universe, Kurosawa's universe is devoid of political virtue. The present master of Forest Castle, Kunihara, has become its lord not by inheritance or election but by murdering the last occupant of the office. In one emblematic scene a group of soldiers discusses the decay of Washizu's castle. The castle is shaking, they assert, because 'the foundations have long been rotting. Even the rats have begun to leave.' The allegory tells us that not only the castle but feudalism itself is rotten. In addition to being inequitable and corrupt, the community is also without warmth. Love (or even affection), loyalty, generosity, confidence, or pleasure are rarely if ever expressed. The society is characterized instead by narrow self-interest, distrust, constant fear, and the easy recourse to violence. Relationships between individuals are remarkably sterile. In one memorable scene, when Washizu and his wife Asaji converse, they sit far apart in a conventionally bare room. Propped up on the wall behind them and separating them is an unsheathed sword – a perfect metaphor for a marriage of understated but unrelieved hostility, and an expressive symbol of the distrust which seems to characterize all human relationships. There are in fact only a handful of moments in the film in which the characters make physical contact with each other; for the most part they do not touch, and when they do, it is at such moments as Asaji's wrenching Washizu's lance from his hands. Kurosawa even contrives it so that when more than one member of the feudal élite is in the frame, the images of the persons do not overlap. On the other hand, when soldiers and servants gather, as they do for periodic choral discourse, they are disposed in more informal and intimate patterns.

It is only when this film turns away from human social and political institutions that it discovers a new world of beauty and mystery. Things made by man pale in comparison to animate nature. The rigid and futile geometry of manufactured structures is continually contrasted to the fertility, magic, and

riot of the forest. The most memorable scenes juxtapose frail human institutions to the greater power of the natural world. When Washizu is in the forest
he is regularly photographed through a thick tangle of vines and branches. It is
clear that he is merely an intruder in an enduring world. Washizu antagonizes
nature and its spirits by shooting arrows into the trees, but the forest ultimately
claims its revenge. The great scene of the two horsemen lost in the fog, the
miraculous invasion of Forest Castle by the crows, and the slow-motion march
of this film's Birnam Wood all stress the power of nature. It is as though the
attempt of Japanese feudalism to impose its rigidities on this world is both
doomed and hubristic. In *Throne of Blood*, tyrants come and go, but the earth
abides. If the film has an occidental moral, it is not Shakespeare's but Shelley's:
the forest is as permanent as the lone and level sands stretching away from the
shattered statue. Even Washizu's death can be understood as a symbolic act by
which the forest asserts its dominance over the tyrant. This has always been
implicit in Shakespeare's fable. No event in literature so clearly sets forth the
triumph of the natural world over the human than Birnam Forest picking itself
up in order to expel the wicked king. Kurosawa expands the metaphor by
making Washizu the victim not only of the forest itself but of arrows which
combine the wood of the trees with the feathers of its birds. This is an entirely
appropriate way for offended nature to regain control over an evil usurper.

It is in this context that Washizu's ghastly end acquires its fine political
importance. The common people, the nameless soldiers of Washizu's army,
mobilize themselves to commit not a mindless act of violence but an
assassination – an act of specific political rebellion. These are the people whom
the film treats as the exploited and nameless victims of Japanese feudalism.
They lack authority and autonomy; they have no leaders and no individuality.
In fact, when Washizu is felled, Kurosawa arranges it so that an audience is
conscious not of the archers but only of their arrows. It is as though the arrows
appear from nowhere, and are not launched by any specific person. Yet the
arrows stand for the collective mind of the masses, who, the film seems to say,
have had enough of tyranny. Washizu is not killed by one arrow, or ten, or a
hundred, but by thousands. The moral is obvious: the tyrant and the rotten
feudalism for which he stands cannot be brought to its knees by one individual
or a hundred, but can be overcome by the people acting in concert. It is
nevertheless an equivocal ending. Insofar as the assassination of Washizu can be
regarded as a political act, it offers some cause for optimism; to the extent that
the assassination simply expresses the opportunism of the soldiers, it is
dreadfully pessimistic. The death of Washizu can therefore be conceived of as
mildly exhilarating and cautiously optimistic. The film can offer no improve-
ment over tyranny, nor can it provide a successor for Washizu, but it does

suggest how the first step might be taken towards a different kind of government.[4]

Of the three films, *Throne of Blood* is the most akin to Shakespeare in the grandeur and spaciousness of its vision. While the two English-language versions of the play vie with each other in fashionable and even facile pessimism, Kurosawa grants his characters the power to challenge and refashion imprisoning social systems. *Throne of Blood* is uplifting not only for its remarkable craft, but for its confidence in human capabilities. While Kurosawa offers no easy answers, neither does he permit his film to succumb to authoritarian or demonic presences.

Notes

1 Citations to *Macbeth* are to Kenneth Muir's Arden edition (London, 1951; Cambridge, Mass., 1953).

2 For general information on Welles's *Macbeth* see Jack J. Jorgens, *Shakespeare on Film* (Bloomington, 1977). The best essay on Welles's Shakespeare is James Naremore's 'The Walking Shadow: Welles' Expressionist *Macbeth*', *Literature/Film Quarterly*, 1 (1973), from which I have borrowed a number of ideas. Other useful information is contained in Charles Higham's *The Films of Orson Welles* (Berkeley, 1970), the collection of essays on *Macbeth* in the *University of Dayton Review*, 14 (1979–80), as well as the bibliographies and notes included in the valuable *Shakespeare on Film Newsletter*.

3 Other films by Polanski come to the same conclusion. *Rosemary's Baby* offers a remarkable parallel to *Macbeth*. An isolate, Rosemary Woodhouse is intrigued against by a group of elderly witches. In the last and climactic scene, Rosemary accepts the responsibility for mothering the demonic child to whom she has given birth. Evil is invested with the same continuity as is implied by the Donalbain episode. In Polanski's lone attempt at comedy, the execrable *Famous Vampire Killers*, a young woman (played by Sharon Tate), apparently rescued from vampires, reveals her newly elongated teeth and bites Alfred (Polanski himself) on the neck. A voice tells us that evil is now loosed on the world. A more subtle version of the same idea appears in the entirely secular *film noir* masterpiece *Chinatown*. Noah Cross, who is guilty of murder, incest, and the systematic perversion of the laws, and who has the semi-demonic ability to survive a bullet unscathed, is in total control of events at the picture's conclusion. The last moments of the film, according to Barbara Leaming (*Polanski, A Biography* (New York, 1981), p. 147), were altered by Polanski to emphasize Cross's power (in the original film script Evelyn Mulwray had escaped with her daughter-sister).

4 Many of Kurosawa's films deal with feudalism, which by some reckonings survived in Japan until 1945. The critique of feudalism in film may be understood as a similitude of recent Japanese history. *Kanjincho* for example, made in 1945, and 'one of the strongest indictments of feudalism ever filmed' according to Donald Richie (*The Japanese Film*, rev. edn (Tokyo and New York, 1982), p. 76), was suppressed until 1953. In Kurosawa's most remarkable film, the *Seven Samurai* (1954), a group of farmers employ masterless samurai,

then neglect them. The film pays homage to feudal and military achievement but also regards it as slightly archaic compared to the continuing and more fundamental dramas of harvest and love. Just as Washizu is overthrown by his followers, so the samurai are superseded by the peasantry. In *Hidden Fortress* (1958), which immediately followed *Throne of Blood*, the emphasis is on the point of view of the peasants. In the end, the defection of General Hyoe dissolves feudal loyalty.

INDEX

Titles and names in the filmography (pages 18–49) have not been indexed

INDEX

INDEX